Transient Criminality

Transient Criminality

A Model of
Stress-Induced Crime

ANTHONY R. MAWSON

PRAEGER

New York
Westport, Connecticut
London

In Chapter 2, the letter of December 22, 1986 was taken from the "Dear Abby" column by Abigail Van Buren. Reprinted with permission of Universal Press Syndicate. All rights reserved.

Library of Congress Cataloging-in-Publication Data

Mawson, Anthony R.

    Transient criminality.

    Bibliography: p.
    Includes index.
    1. Occasional criminals. 2. Criminal psychology.
3. Stress (Psychology) 4. Aggressiveness (Psychology)
I. Title
HV6051.M39 1987   364.2'4   87-11741
ISBN 0-275-92552-8 (alk. paper)

Library of Congress Catalog Card Number: 87-11741
ISBN: 0-275-92552-8

First published in 1987

Praeger Publishers, One Madison Avenue, New York, NY 10010
A division of Greenwood Press, Inc.

Printed in the United States of America

The paper used in this book complies with the
Permanent Paper Standard issued by the National
Information Standards Organization (Z39.48-1984).

10 9 8 7 6 5 4 3 2 1

CONTENTS

LIST OF FIGURES AND TABLES

FIGURES

TABLES

ACKNOWLEDGMENTS

The central theme of this book is that much criminality is associated with a stress-induced increase in physiological arousal, alterations in cognitive and perceptual functioning, and increased stimulation-seeking behavior. This proposal was first aired at a postgraduate criminology seminar at Keele University, U.K., in 1971. Despite a moderately encouraging reception to the talk, it was not until 1978, after having moved to the United States and taught sociology and criminology for several years at Loyola University in New Orleans, that I began writing this book. A draft of the first eight chapters was completed in 1981, but the remaining (and most difficult) chapters were not written until November 1984. Another 18 months elapsed while a publisher was sought.

Apart from the many commitments which prevented me from completing the work much earlier (including study for master's and doctoral degrees in epidemiology at the School of Public Health and Tropical Medicine, Tulane University, from 1979 to 1986), the ideas themselves took years to elaborate — particularly the application of the general model to specific types of crime (Chapters 9–14).

Developing the ideas expressed in this book, and searching the social and life sciences literature for relevant data, has been a satisfying and rewarding personal adventure, lasting many years.

I am very grateful to the many people who have helped to make this book a reality, although none bears any responsibility for the book's errors or deficiencies. First, I would like to acknowledge the stimulus and encouragement I have received from my teachers, especially Mr. Donald Parren and Mr. David Robertson at Aldenham School, Professors Maurice Pinard and Wallace Lambert at McGill, Professors Alasdair MacIntyre, Ioan Davies, and Roland Robertson at Essex University, Professors David Downes and Terence Morris at the London School of Economics and Political Science, and more recently Professors Dorothy

Clemmer, Virginia Ktsanes, and Janet Rice, at the School of Public Health and Tropical Medicine, Tulane University.

Next I would like to thank the many friends and colleagues who have offered useful criticism, suggestions, and advice over the years, regarding my theories particularly (in rough chronological order) Paul Cornes, John Whittaker, Eileen Sullivan, Jim Good, Frank Coffield, John Grundy, Ronald Frankenberg, Donald MacKay, Greg di Marchi, Peter Venables, Margaret Christie, John Clarke, "Jake" Jacobs, Terry Christensen, and Beth Mueller. I owe a special debt of gratitude to Carol Deinhardt. I would also like to thank the many fine students I have taught, and learned from, since 1967 — unfortunately too many to name individually.

"Jake" Jacobs, Terry Christensen, and Mannie Bowerman kindly read and commented upon early versions of several chapters. Colleen Collier and Jill Alleman prepared the index.

I would also like to thank Gladys Washington, Yvette Winchester, Bronwyn Williams, Debbie Brown, and Stephanie Scholl for expert clerical assistance.

Finally, I would like to thank Dr. George Zimmar of Praeger Publishers for his valuable editorial advice.

Transient Criminality

1

INTRODUCTION

ANALYSIS AND SYNTHESIS IN CRIMINOLOGY

In every branch of science, research ideally involves a constant interplay between analytical types of studies and attempts to synthesize the known facts into summary propositions of ever-increasing generality (Kaplan, 1964). Yet, at different times in the history of a science, one mode of inquiry — either analysis or synthesis — tends to be given special emphasis (Berlin, 1973). In criminology, the 1950s and 1960s were periods of synthesis, i.e., theory-building. One thinks, for instance, of the important theoretical works of Merton (1949), Cohen (1955), and Cloward and Ohlin (1960), in the "anomie" tradition; the originality of Matza's (1964) "naturalistic" essays on crime; the emergence of "labeling theory" (Lemert, 1972; Becker, 1963; Wilkins, 1965); psychological theories in the "learning" tradition (e.g., Sutherland & Cressey, 1974; Trasler, 1962, Eysenck, 1978), and the re-emergence of Marxism (Turk, 1969; Taylor et al., 1973). However, by the mid-1970s fashions had changed and the analytic approach came to dominate the field. There were several reasons for this.

First, the general theories of crime proposed in the 1950s and 1960s failed to specify in detail how the many different types of activity subsumed under the rubric of "crime" were brought about. While both Marxist approaches and those emphasizing thwarted aspirations for success could explain property crime, neither could explain crimes against the person.

Second, the period was marked by a gradual disillusionment with criminological theory as a whole. Enormous injections of federal funds into the criminal justice system in the late 1960s and early 1970s failed to influence either the volume or rate of crime. Despite legislative efforts to improve the system, crime rates were either unaffected or continued to rise.[1] Prisons were filled beyond capacity and living conditions in many of them were, and still remain, deplorable. By January 1, 1977, the United States had an imprisonment rate of 244 per 100,000 population, the highest in the free world, and only 2 percent of offenders served terms of less than one year (Doleschal, 1979).

Although valuable research of the "analytic" type was published throughout the period,[2] administrative disappointment was further fueled by a much publicized review of some 231 "methodologically sound" rehabilitation programs, which claimed to show that not a single form of rehabilitation actually "worked" (Martinson, 1974). Soon thereafter, federal subsidies for criminal justice projects were curtailed, and in 1981 the Law Enforcement Educational Program was abolished.

Within the criminological profession itself there was a gradual disillusionment with theory. Hitherto, it was widely assumed that advances in understanding crime and rehabilitation depended on discovering an adequate theory of human behavior (e.g., Michael & Adler, 1933; President's Commission, 1967, p. 8). However, several authors proposed a return to the eighteenth-century classical view that crime — indeed all human action — results from the exercise of "free will" (e.g., Matza, 1964; Morris, 1974; Wilson, 1975; van den Haag, 1975; Fogel, 1975; von Hirsch, 1976). At the same time the societal response to crime became increasingly punitive, and the death penalty was reintroduced into states which, not many years before, had abolished it. Illogical though it may be to imagine that punishment will succeed because previous methods of treatment have failed, considering that "*the most proven failure* in the history of corrections and penology is punishment" (Jeffery, 1977, p. 27), the classical doctrine continues to enjoy a vigorous renaissance.

A third reason for the switch to analysis — or, more precisely, a general argument against synthesis — is the obvious heterogeneity of crime, and the belief that different types of crime require a separate explanation. To quote D. J. West (1967, p. 289):

> Delinquency, like ill-health, consists of a vast conglomeration of different phenomena, and no simple explanation or cure will be found to fit more than a small segment of the whole. The problems are so many-sided, so changeable, and so complex in all their social and psychological ramifications that we have hardly got to the stage of stating the issues coherently, let alone resolving them.

This view of crime is analogous to the view that diseases are similarly heterogeneous and not amenable to general explanations. The comparison between crime and disease is instructive. Just as medical science was successful only when it turned to the elucidation of specific diseases (so the argument runs), criminologists are likewise exhorted to search for specific causes of specific types of crime. A dominant view is that "more and better data" are needed, and research should be restricted to limited aspects of crime.

While it is surely true that a single theory cannot explain every aspect and type of crime, it does not follow that each form of crime requires a separate explanation; or, in other words, that single explanations of more than one kind of crime are impossible.[3]

The purpose of this book is to propose a general theory of *transient criminality*. The term transient criminality refers to criminal acts — major as well as minor — committed on an occasional or once-only basis by individuals who normally obey the law. What the theory attempts to do is to explain how ordinarily noncriminal individuals become temporarily involved in a wide range of criminal behaviors; that is, it attempts to explain distinctly aberrant behavior on the part of the perpetrator.

Consider the main objection to general theories, outlined immediately above. Is it true that, like disease, each form of crime requires a separate explanation? This notion led to many dramatic successes in the "bacteriological era" (Rosen, 1958) of public health. But even in the case of infectious and deficiency diseases, where the idea of one-cause/one-disease[4] seems most applicable, it has serious shortcomings (Dixon, 1978). The specificity model has also been criticized with respect to cardiovascular and degenerative diseases, mental disorders and cancer (Moss, 1973; Cassel, 1976; Dixon, 1978), chronic diseases that are now of primary importance in westernized societies (Kramer, 1980).

First, there is considerable overlap in the symptoms of different diseases, suggesting that the boundary lines between diseases are drawn somewhat arbitrarily. Certainly there are many symptoms common to diseases with ostensibly different causes.[5] Second, there is much nonspecificity both regarding the *causes* of particular diseases and the *effects* of particular disease agents; that is, many (if not all) of the chronic diseases are multifactorial in origin, and particular factors are often linked to numerous pathological states or outcomes. Marital separation, for instance, is associated with an increased risk of diverse mental and physical disorders (Syme, 1974; Cassel, 1976; Bloom et al., 1978), and the same is true of cigarette smoking. "Cigarette smokers have higher mortality rates than non-smokers for a wide variety of diseases, including all forms of cardiovascular disease, malignancies of all sites in the body, cirrhosis, ulcers, accidents, murder, and suicide" (Syme, 1974, p. 1,044). Furthermore, host resistance (and/or susceptibility) is not confined to a particular disease factor and subsequent illness but to a wide range of factors and diseases. Thus, considerable *nonspecificity* exists in terms of disease susceptibility as well as causation and symptomatology. This has led to the suggestion that concepts of disease based on the "specificity model" should be replaced by a broader, integrative approach to disease in general (Syme, 1974; Cassel, 1976; Dixon, 1978).

Returning to the subject of crime, very similar criticisms can be leveled at the "specificity model" as it applies here also. The classification of crime is still in a rudimentary stage compared to that of diseases,[6] the usual approach being to classify crimes and criminals legalistically, that is, in terms of particular offenses such as burglary, larceny, or robbery (Clinard & Quinney, 1973). However, the difficulty with this mode of classification is that offense-specialization is the exception rather than the rule.

Both young and adult offenders tend to become involved in a wide range of criminal as well as other forms of deviant behavior (Farrington, 1979a; Klein, 1984). For instance, in a prospective study of delinquency in 411 boys carried out in Cambridge, England (West & Farrington, 1973), 11 of the 13 boys found guilty of violent offenses also had convictions for theft. Later, when the boys were 18 to 20 years old (West and Farrington, 1977, pp. 11–15), there was again little evidence of criminal specialization. Of 20 individuals convicted of violent crimes, 14 had adult convictions for property crimes. In a study of men convicted of robbery in London (McClintock, 1963), 89 percent of the group with two previous convictions for violence had been convicted of a nonviolent offense. Similarly, very few drug offenders (Mott, 1973), arsonists (Soothill & Pope, 1973), rapists (Soothill, et al., 1976), or other types of serious sex offenders (Soothill & Gibbens, 1978) have previous convictions for the same type of criminal activity in the past. Most previous convictions in all such cases are for property offenses. A cohort study of 9,945 boys born in Philadelphia in 1945 and followed until the age of 18 (Wolfgang et al., 1972) indicated that the probability of committing the same type of crime twice in a row was unaffected by the number of previous offenses of the same type. The probability of committing a particular type of crime was also unrelated to the type of crime committed on the last occasion.

Studies of delinquent behavior using anonymous questionnaires, like those based on official records, also indicate a high degree of versatility in offending (Hindelang, 1971; Farrington, 1973). Other evidence indicates that delinquent gangs or groups, instead of specializing in certain types of antisocial behavior (cf. Cloward & Ohlin, 1960). tend to engage in several kinds of deviant activity (Short & Strodtbeck, 1965; Miller, 1965; for reviews, see Hood & Sparks, 1970, and Gibbons, 1977, pp. 294–98). In sum, most offenders cannot be assigned to particular, mutually exclusive legal categories such as "robber," or "burglar," or subtypes thereof.

To put the matter more concretely, take the case of burglary. From the "analytic" point of view, what is needed are more detailed studies of burglars and patterns of burglary, and specific explanations of burglary. Proponents of "synthesis," on the other hand, while agreeing that detailed studies of burglary are needed for a variety of reasons (e.g., law enforcement and crime prevention), argue that the assumption of a specific type of criminal ("the burglar") and criminal activity ("burglary") is not supported by the evidence. Individuals who break into houses appear to be generalists in crime, not limited to this specialty. Hence, any explanation of burglary must account for associated patterns of criminality.[7]

In addition to a high degree of nonspecialization in crime, offenders also tend to engage in other types of antisocial or deviant behavior such as excessive alcohol consumption and gambling, illicit drug use, dangerous driving, and self-injury (Hirschi, 1969; Eysenck, 1978; West & Farrington, 1977; Jessor & Jessor, 1977; Robins, 1978). For instance, in her 30-year follow-up study of children referred to a child guidance clinic in St. Louis, Robins (1978) found that children who stole also ran away from home, were aggressive, enuretic, disciplinary problems in school, and pathological liars. As adults, they had problems with the police, were divorced, placed in mental hospitals, prone to alcoholism and vagrancy, sexually promiscuous, in debt, and had difficulty holding jobs. Similarly, the Cambridge study of West and Farrington (1977) revealed that individuals convicted up to age 18 tended to exhibit numerous forms of deviance, including sexual promiscuity, alcoholism, heavy smoking, drug dependence, heavy gambling, high aggressiveness, driving convictions, and unstable, low-status job histories (Farrington, 1979a; p. 306). Thus, the same types of individuals are susceptible not just to criminality but to multiple forms of social deviance. Furthermore, without embarking on a detailed review of the relevant findings, while many different sorts of causal factors have been implicated in criminality, most of these same factors have been implicated in other types of deviant behavior (see, e.g., Rutter & Madge, 1976).

These examples of "nonspecificity" in the criminological field are analogous to those that have been found in relation to chronic disease; just as in the latter case, they point to the value of developing broad, synthesizing models of criminality (or "deviance"), rather than attempting to account for supposedly elemental forms of criminal behavior one at a time, as is the usual practice today.

LEVELS OF INVOLVEMENT IN CRIMINALITY

Assuming that the "nonspecific" approach to crime is justified, the next problem is to decide on a provisional method of classification. As an alternative to classifying crimes and criminals in terms of discrete types of offenses, it may be useful to look at the phenomenon in terms of degrees of involvement in criminality; that is, as a continuous behavioral trait (cf. Eysenck, 1978), varying from one individual to another in terms of frequency, seriousness, and duration. The suggestion is that if a representative sample of offenders were evaluated in terms of degrees of involvement in crime, three relatively distinct patterns would emerge. These patterns are here referred to as: transient, age-specific, and chronic criminality. Although it remains for future research to define their precise characteristics, there is already much evidence for their existence.

Level 1: Transient Criminality

The term transient criminality refers to a pattern or characteristic way of offending; the category includes individuals for whom criminal deviance represents an occasional and usually not very serious aberration from an otherwise law-abiding existence. In cases where the persons involved are very young, the "transient criminality" pattern would be expected to reveal itself only after a number of years. For instance, a juvenile arrested for shoplifting may lack a previous history of antisocial acts or delinquent tendencies. However, this one act may signal the beginning of a lengthy career of subsequent offending. Even an adult arrested, say, for shoplifting, with a previously unblemished record, should not be immediately categorized in terms of criminality levels on the basis of this one offense, since further inquiries may reveal numerous offenses in the past that never came to the attention of the police. The labels "transient," "age-specific," and "chronic" criminality can therefore be reliably applied to specific individuals only in retrospect, after a lengthy period of observation.

The phrase "occasional and usually not very serious . . . " describes the first of the postulated levels of criminality. "Occasional" implies that a criminal act has been committed one, twice, three, or perhaps four times in the course of a lifetime. The greater the frequency of criminal acts, the less serious and persistent they have to be in order to qualify for the label of transient criminality. The acts may be spaced many years apart, in which case they would still represent aberrant episodes of antisocial behavior. Alternatively, they may occur within a matter of days or weeks of each other. "Usually not very serious . . . " refers to the gravity of the offense and implies that the act is typically a misdemeanor rather than a more serious felony. The qualifier "usually," allows for the possibility that one or more of the acts in question may be extremely serious, for example, murder.

The data in Figure 1.1 represent the criminal life charts of three hypothetical individuals whose pattern of offending could be described as transient.

As a topic for investigation, transient criminality has received scant attention compared to that devoted to persistent offenders. Nonetheless, its existence has long been recognized. In the nineteenth century, Henry Mayhew (co-author of *Criminal Prisons,* 1862) distinguished between "professional criminals, who earn their living through criminal activity, and accidental offenders, who commit criminal acts as a result of unanticipated circumstances" (cited in Clinard & Quinney, 1973, p. 7). Years later, Alexander and Staub (1931), in addition to postulating three

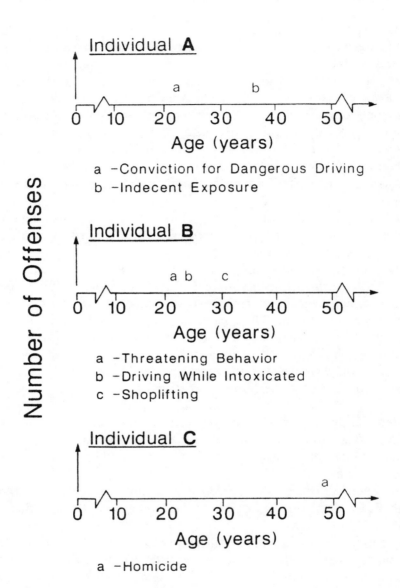

Figure 1.1
Criminal life charts of three hypothetical transient offenders.

Source: Compiled by author.

types of "permanent" criminals (the neurotic, normal, and biological), described the "acute criminal" as one who commits criminal acts under the stress of present circumstances. Lindesmith and Dunham (1941) postulated the "situational or accidental" type of criminal, and cited the example of a murderer who, prior to the crime, was a law-abiding person (Clinard & Quinney, 1973, p. 7). More recently, on the basis of a self-report study of delinquent behavior among 15- to 17-year-old white males in Utah, Erickson and Empey (1963) suggested that the clearest way of distinguishing between offenders was in terms of criminal "persistency"; that is to say, one-time offenders were found to be easily distinguishable from persistent offenders, the latter of whom also committed more serious offenses. Gibbons (1977, pp. 229–33, 270–71, 316–19) is one of very few contemporary authors to emphasize "situational criminality," as exemplified by the "one-time property offender."

The most extensive recent treatment of the topic is to be found in Clinard and Quinney's (1973) *Criminal Behavior Systems,* in the chapter on "Occasional Property Criminal Behavior." Criminal behaviors other than property offenses, however, are excluded by these authors. The most extensively studied occasional property offenses are check forgery, adult shoplifting, vandalism, and auto theft. Occasional property criminals, Clinard and Quinney point out, are the opposite of career criminals: they commit the same types of offenses as those committed by the career criminal, but they do so infrequently, irregularly, and often crudely, and small, relatively inexpensive articles tend to be stolen. Lemert (1953), in his study of "naive check forgery" (see Chapters 2 and 3 of this volume for further discussion), found that about 75 percent of all check forgers did not view themselves as criminals and had no previous history of such behavior.

In her study of shoplifting in a Chicago department store, Cameron (1964) found that most pilferers lacked any kind of wider involvement in crime. Chicago police statistics indicated that over 90 percent of women officially charged with shoplifting had never before been convicted of an offense. Department store records also showed that, at most, 2 percent of the women and 12 percent of the men caught shoplifting had a criminal record. The homes of store pilferers were widely distributed throughout the city and corresponded to those of the lost-and-found claimants of the store. The value of merchandise taken was "small" and chiefly involved luxury items, notably dress accessories and jewelry. When first apprehended and interrogated, pilferers seemed genuinely ignorant of criminal folkways and arrest procedures and seemed to have given no thought to the possibility and consequences of being arrested and searched. Many gave false names, offered to pay for the stolen goods, and signed what amounted to complete confessions and waivers against filing suit. Many also confessed to previous acts of shoplifting, acts which in some cases "had been memorable events arousing and continuing to arouse strong feelings of guilt" (Cameron, 1964, p. 148). Pilferers tended to differ in one outstanding respect from regular thieves: they did not think of themselves as thieves. Even when arrested, they strongly resisted the idea that they had actually engaged in theft.

Studies of juveniles arrested for stealing automobiles and joyriding similarly show that most arrestees either have no criminal record or none other than for auto theft, and tend to come from conventional middle-class families (Wattenberg & Balistrieri, 1952). Studies of the records of adults on probation indicate that many offenders have been involved in "isolated, nonrecurrent acts of illegality" (Gibbons, 1977, p. 318). For instance, a study of the records of 500 federal probationers (England, 1955) revealed that most were older, white, married males who had been sentenced for a wide variety of offenses, although nearly 50 percent had been convicted of liquor law violations. Most of these individuals "had been law-abiding prior to the offense, and about 80 percent had remained free of recidivism for five years after being released from probation" (Gibbons, 1977, p. 318).

Although little is known about transient criminality, its incidence in the general population may be very high compared to the crimes committed by persistent offenders, for, as West (1967, p. 46) observes, ". . . the majority of dishonest acts, and presumably also the majority of delinquent acts, are the work of more or less normal individuals who break the rules now and then when opportunity arises or occasion demands." Self-report studies of the general population, using anonymous questionnaires, strongly suggest that criminal behavior is not confined to a small group of persistent offenders but is widely prevalent in all age groups and in both sexes. There is a tremendous amount of "hidden" criminality, most of it relatively minor, which is neither detected nor reported to the police. Empey (1978) reviewed a number of studies indicating that about 90 percent of all illegal acts come into this category.

Furthermore, there is evidence to suggest that nearly everyone breaks the law at least once in the course of a lifetime. A classic study by Wallerstein and Wyle (1947) found that 99 percent of a sample of upper-income adults admitted committing one or more acts for which they could have been arrested and charged by the police. In a self-report study of young adults in the United States (Sheley, 1975), 28 percent of the respondents reported having stolen articles or causing damage to property valued at $10.00 or less. Williams and Gold (1972) found that 88 percent of a national sample of U.S. adolescents reported having committed at least one chargeable offense. Belson (1975) carried out a self-report survey of delinquency among 1,425 boys in London (U.K.) and found that *all* admitted to at least some stealing. Stealing was widely distributed throughout occupational strata, but somewhat more prevalent among the sons of unskilled workers (34 percent) than among those in the professions (22 percent). Longitudinal surveys indicate that a substantial minority of males are eventually arrested or convicted of offenses (Farrington, 1979a, pp. 295–98). Wolfgang (1974) found that 35 percent of a cohort of over 9,000 males were arrested before their eighteenth birthday, and 43 percent before their twenty-seventh birthday. The British National Survey of Health and Development found that 18 percent of males and 2.5 percent of females were convicted or officially cautioned before their twenty-first birthday (Wadsworth, 1979). Most youths, however, do not progress to serious or persistent delinquency (Wolfgang et al., 1972, pp. 244–55; Hood & Sparks, 1970, pp. 46–63, for a review). Most first offenders, especially older ones with strong family ties and stable work records, do not become recidivists after their first arrest or after prison sentence (Glaser, 1979, p. 213). Thus, the profile of the typical "transient offender" emerging from these studies is that of an adolescent male. This would certainly be expected, given that males between the ages of 12 and 20 are heavily overrepresented in criminal statistics. However, a large percentage of individuals in the population as a whole also appears to engage in transient criminality at some time in their lives.

Level 2: Age-specific Criminality

Age-specific criminality refers to relatively frequent and often serious delinquency which persists throughout a particular age group. The one age group in which delinquent activity tends to be heavily concentrated is, of course, adolescence, which is defined as approximately ages 12 to 20 for boys, and 10 to 18 for girls (Valadian and Porter, 1977). In describing age-specific criminality as Level 2, the implication is that this is, overall, a higher level of involvement in crime than Level 1, even though an individual who commits a single very serious offense, but only one in the course of his or her lifetime, may be treated more harshly by the courts than one committing a series of lesser offenses. Relatively frequent offending implies approximately four or more criminal offenses in the course of a lifetime, and relatively serious implies that some of these acts are felonies. Persistent and age-specific implies that the offenses are heavily concentrated within a limited span of years.

The data in Figure 1.2 represent the criminal life charts of two hypothetical individuals whose pattern of offending would be described as age-specific.

There is considerable evidence for age-specific criminality as a well-defined level of offending. The age distribution of criminal convictions both in the United States and Great Britain indicates a marked increase in the early teenage years (U.S. Department of Justice, 1982; Home Office, 1981), a peak which varies according to offense type in the middle teens — violent crime tending to peak two or three years later than property crime (McKissack, 1973; Farrington, 1979a) — and a fairly rapid decline thereafter to the mid-thirties (Strasburg, 1978).[8] At that time the incidence of convictions is approximately the same as for children aged ten. It then declines gradually with advancing age (Roth, 1968; see Figures 1.3 and 1.4). Conventional crime is heavily concentrated in the 15- to 25-year-old age group. In 1974 in the United States, persons under 25 years of age accounted for 58 percent of all arrests, 77 percent of all robberies, 85 percent of all burglaries, and 85 percent of all reported auto thefts (Gibbons, 1977, p. 111). These figures change little from year to year.

Although many, but not all forms of criminal activity are concentrated in the adolescent years, further research on the natural history of delinquency is needed to clarify more precisely the developmental or "career" aspects of juvenile offending (Farrington, 1979a). The available

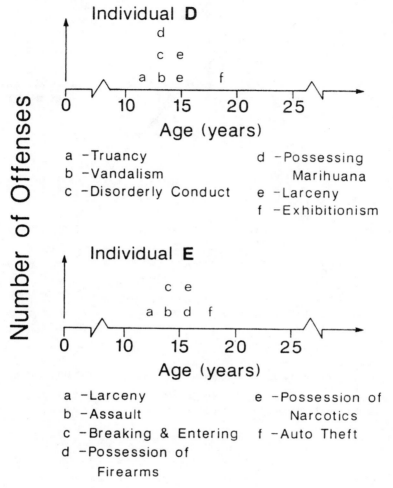

Figure 1.2
Criminal life charts of two hypothetical age-specific offenders.

Source: Compiled by author.

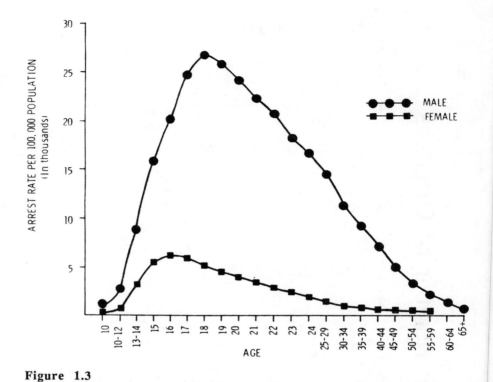

Figure 1.3
Age-specific arrest rate, United States, 1981, per 100,000 population.

Sources: Federal Bureau of Investigation, *Uniform Crime Reports,* 1981; U.S. Department of Commerce, *Statistical Abstract of the United States,* 1982–1983. Reprinted with permission.

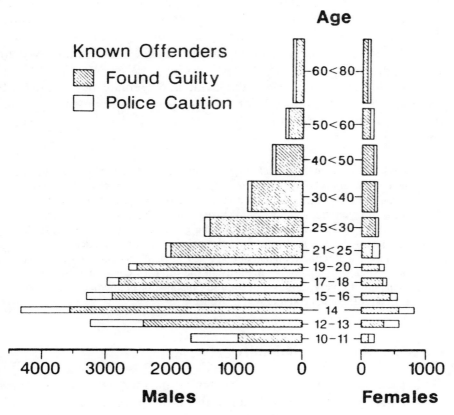

Figure 1.4
The proportion of male and female known offenders per 100,000 population in each age group (indictable offenses only), based on the criminal statistics for England and Wales, 1965.

Source: McClintock and Avison, 1968, p. 158. Reprinted with permission.

data nevertheless lend support to the concept of age-specific criminality as a relatively distinct "level" of offending. Various studies have indicated that more individuals begin criminal careers during adolescence than at any other age, and most of these individuals cease offending by their early twenties (Wolfgang et al., 1972; Robins, 1978). West's (1967, p. 271) conclusion to his review of the literature on delinquency in 1967 still provides an accurate summary of what is known developmentally about the typical juvenile delinquent (or what we have labeled age-specific criminality):

> Regardless of age, most first offenders are not reconvicted, and the minority of young offenders who are convicted repeatedly nevertheless have a strong tendency to cease being convicted in their early twenties. Hence, as far as records of convictions go, it would appear that delinquent habits are for the most part only very sporadic and that the great majority of young people grow out of them. The long term criminal career is a statistical freak in comparison with commonplace delinquency of an occasional and not very serious kind. . . . (T)he great majority of the offenses committed by young persons are not very serious, not carefully planned or premeditated, and not part of a professional commitment to crime.

Level 3: Chronic Criminality

For individuals in the chronic level of criminality, delinquency begins early in life, typically in association with various physical and psychiatric problems, and remains both frequent and serious well into adulthood. Figure 1.5 depicts the criminal life chart of one hypothetical case of chronic criminality.

Several studies (e.g., Sellin, 1958; Wolf, 1965; West & Farrington, 1977) have shown that the younger the individual when first convicted, the more persistent and serious his or her subsequent criminality is likely to be. For instance, in their prospective study, West and Farrington (1977) found that the small minority of offenders first convicted between age 10 and 12 had six convictions on average by age 21, and half were reconvicted by age 19 or 20. Retrospective studies also indicate that recidivists tend to begin their criminal careers earlier than nonrecidivists and commit a greater number of previous offenses (Payne et al., 1974; McGurk et al., 1978). Wolfgang et al. (1972) identified a group of

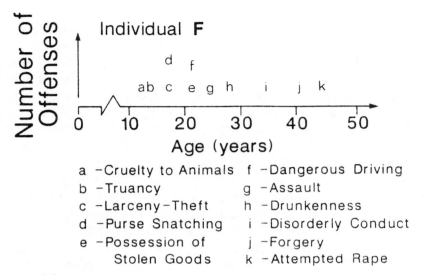

Figure 1.5
Criminal life chart of one hypothetical chronic offender.

Sources: Compiled by author.

"chronic offenders" in the Philadelphia cohort study, defining them as boys who had been involved in more than four violations. These boys made up 18 percent of the total group of offenders in the group, yet they were responsible for over 50 percent of all known offenses. Since 35 percent of the total sample of boys had at least one police contact, 6.3 percent (i.e., 18 percent of 35) of the sample was responsible for about half the total number of offenses committed by the cohort. Not only were they more frequently involved in serious offenses but they tended to begin their delinquent activities by committing relatively serious offenses.

A subsidiary pattern of "chronic criminality" appears to begin in adulthood. Retrospective studies of persistent adult offenders suggest that a large proportion have convictions neither as juveniles nor as young adults (Hammond & Chayen, 1963; West, 1963). In the Cambridge study, 46 percent of convicted young adults had not been convicted as juveniles (Farrington & West, 1977); in the Philadelphia study (Wolfgang, 1974), the comparable figure was 34 percent.

CRIMINOGENIC FACTORS

In the literature on crime and criminals, long-term and/or predispositional sorts of causal factors have been emphasized almost exclusively. Most theories assume a more or less constant "readiness" to engage in crime as a result of relatively enduring influences, for example, blocked opportunities for success (Cloward & Ohlin, 1960), status frustration (Cohen, 1955), exaggerated working-class values (Miller, 1958; Wolfgang & Ferracuti, 1967), acquiring a delinquent identity as a result of being "labeled" a delinquent (Lemert, 1972), weak self-concepts (Reckless, 1967), weak social attachments (Hirschi, 1969), and inadequate social conditioning combined with poor innate conditionability (Trasler, 1962; Eysenck, 1978; Wilson & Herrnstein, 1984).[9]

By contrast, little is known about the role of situational factors and other types of short-term influences, including biological ones, on criminal behavior (Cohen & Short, 1971, pp. 115–16; Short, 1974, p. 406; Gibbons, 1977). R. V. G. Clarke (1977, 1980a) has similarly pointed out that psychological theories of crime have been largely concerned with the personality traits of criminals or, more generally, with what Tizard (1976) described as "fixed psychological characteristics." Possibly more influential in the causation of crime, however, may be recent life events or crises such as becoming unemployed, running out of money, losing a girlfriend, or being beaten-up (Clarke, 1977). It is noteworthy that in other fields of social science, and in medicine, there has been a tremendous interest in stressful life events within the past two decades. There is now a vast literature indicating that "stressful" events play a role in mental and physical disorders, accidents and illicit drug use (see e.g., Dohrenwend & Dohrenwend 1974, 1978, 1980; Rabkin & Struening, 1976; Brown & Harris, 1978; Andrews et al., 1978; Rahe, 1979; Sarason & Spielberger, 1979; Johnson & Sarason, 1979a; Schofield, 1980; McFarlane et al., 1980; Susser, 1981; Sterling & Eyer, 1981; Berger, 1981, pp. 11–13). However, the correlations between stressful events and illness are generally small, accounting for about 10 percent of the variance, indicating that stressful events, by themselves, are weak predictors of illness (Rabkin & Struening, 1976; Rahe, 1979).

Greater predictive power can be achieved by utilizing more complex models (Jenkins, 1979) which take into account such factors as distinctive coping styles and personality traits (Glass, 1977), and, in particular, the extent and availability of pre-existing social supports. Thus Caplan (1974, p. 4) states that the most important factor affecting the outcome of a psychosocial crisis is "the quality of the emotional support and task-oriented assistance provided by the social network within which the individual grapples with the crisis event." A large number of studies, in many different contexts, have shown that individuals who have recently experienced a number of stressful life events, yet who have frequent and intimate contacts with relatives or other persons, are much less prone to become mentally or physically ill than those experiencing comparable amounts of stress, but with minimal supports (see Cobb, 1976; Cassel, 1976; Dean & Lin, 1977; Henderson, 1977, 1984; Kaplan et al., 1977; Pilisuk & Froland, 1978; Mueller, 1980; Gottlieb, 1981; Lindheim & Syme, 1983; Berkman, 1984). Thus strong social bonds play a key role in "protecting" individuals from the harmful effects of simultaneous environmental stress.

While even massive psychosocial stress — such as internment in Nazi concentration camps — can be successfully coped with if the exposed individuals enjoy strong social supports (Davidson, 1979), severe stress in a context of diminished supports appears to lead to illness in virtually anyone who is exposed to it for an extended period of time, regardless of premorbid characteristics. After the Second World War, a study was carried out on a representative sample of about 1,000 U.S. Army and Navy veterans who developed neurotic symptoms while in the services (Brill & Beebe, cited in Hocking, 1965). All had been screened for personality defects before enlistment, yet all developed their symptoms during wartime. Apart from low educational level, no other pre-enlistment characteristic was associated with psychological breakdown, including broken home, previous personality and family history. The rate of psychiatric casualty was, however, directly related to the experienced degree of battle stress. It was higher in infantry regiments with exposure to combat than in regiments serving in quieter zones, and higher still in men with the most stressful jobs compared to men with less stressful jobs. Yet not everyone succumbed to neurosis. Breakdown did become universal, however, when individuals had been subjected to prolonged bombardment and when 65 to 75 percent of their comrades — their social supports — had either been killed or wounded (Swank, 1949).

It might be argued that the experiences of combat or internment in concentration camps are of such rarity and magnitude as to bear little relation to the types of stresses encountered in everyday life, and hence to the sorts of effects that could be expected of such stresses. However, the single most important factor determining the willingness of troops to enter combat, and to continue fighting, has been found to be the existence of close personal relationships between the men (e.g., Shils & Janowitz, 1948; Janis, 1963). The ability to maintain small, familylike groups in the concentration camps has likewise been credited with the successful postwar adaptation of former internees who were members of such groups (Davidson, 1979). Indeed, there is reason to believe that neuropsychiatric breakdown in combat and "passive surrender" in the concentration camps were both due largely to the destruction or absence of close personal bonds between the affected individuals rather than to the experience of combat itself or the day-to-day quality of life in the camps.

The destruction or absence of close personal relationships is, of course, an experience which can happen to anyone. Hence, when such occurrences are temporally linked with other stresses such as being "fired" from a job, or having severe financial problems, the experience is probably not unlike that of combat troops who are about to become psychological casualties, or concentration camp internees who are on the point of "giving up."

OUTLINE OF THE PRESENT WORK

Psychosocial stress combined with the destruction of close personal relationships is associated with an increased risk of mental and physical illness, and of premature death from a variety of causes (e.g., Berkman & Syme, 1979; Sterling & Eyer, 1981); moreover, stressful life events and the loss of supports increase the individual's vulnerability to disease in general, not susceptibility to specific diseases (Cassel, 1976; Bloom, 1979).

The aim of this book is to suggest that this vulnerability extends to deviant behavior in addition to mental and physical disorders; its thesis is that transient criminality is largely the result of stressful events combined with the simultaneous absence or destruction of social bonds. The suggestion is that transient criminality is due more to environmental influences than to enduring characteristics of the person committing the act. As Milgram (1968, p. 274) expresses the idea, but in a different context, "in certain circumstances it is not so much the kind of person a man is, as the kind of situation in which he is placed, that determines his actions."

Situational factors are also likely to play a role in age-specific and chronic criminality. This is suggested by the observation that criminal activity is relatively infrequent even among persistent offenders (Wolfgang et al., 1972; Petersilia et al., 1977) and tends to occur at certain times of the day and on certain days of the week. In the case of age-specific and chronic criminality, host factors (i.e., personal attributes) are probably more important from the point of view of causation than they are in transient criminality, just as stress generally leads to illness only in persons with some form of predisposition to illness (Hinkle, 1974; Bieliauskas, 1980). Host factors will undoubtedly be given due emphasis when actual investigations of transient criminality are mounted, and it is hoped that the present work will provide a stimulus for such studies.

In brief, the plan of the book is as follows. First, examples of situational and stress-induced crime, drawn from both the scientific and popular literature, are presented (Chapter 2). Second, contemporary theories of situational deviance are reviewed (Chapter 3). Third, in the remainder of the book, an alternative model of transient criminality is presented, based on a synthesis of previously known facts and prior conceptualization (Chapters 4–15).

NOTES

1. The U.S. National Crime Survey (NCS) victimization data indicate that, for the period 1973 to 1980, the overall rate of juvenile offending (ages 12–17) in personal crimes showed a steady decline, whereas the rate for young adults (ages 18–20) showed a steady or increasing pattern (Laub, 1983). The national survey of self-reported delinquency similarly indicated that the level of delinquent behavior remained about the same during the decade of 1967–77 (Office of Juvenile Justice and Delinquency Prevention, 1980). Recent trends in crime in Britain are discussed by Rutter and Giller (1983).

2. For instance, several nutritional, biochemical, and biophysical factors were suggested as possible determinants of criminality (Hippchen, 1978), and a considerable

amount of descriptive information appeared, most notably cohort studies on delinquent and criminal "careers" (e.g., Wolfgang et al., 1972; West, 1969; West & Farrington, 1973, 1977; Mednick & Christiansen, 1977).

3.   On the basis of his 20-year longitudinal study of delinquency, West (1982, p. 27) concluded that the "versatility of most young delinquents' misbehavior makes it reasonable to study an entity of 'generalized' offending, but even so it is unlikely that all categories of law-breaking, including such minority offenses as domestic violence or deviant sex, and including all degrees of seriousness or persistence, can be accounted for by a single causal model, however comprehensive." With this statement we are in complete agreement.

4.   Mason (1974) refers to it as the "specificity model" of disease.

5.   This "nonspecific" element in disease symptomatology had an important place in Brown's "integrative" theory of disease, which enjoyed widespread popularity in the nineteenth century (Trotter, 1978). Similar observations have been made more recently by Selye (1956, 1973). "In 1926, as a second-year medical student," Selye (1973, p. 696) writes, "I first came across this problem of a stereotyped response . . . I began wondering why patients suffering from the most diverse diseases have so many symptoms in common. Whether a man suffers from severe loss of blood, an infectious disease, or advanced cancer, he loses his appetite, his muscular strength, and his ambition to accomplish anything; usually the patient also loses weight, and even his facial expression betrays that he is ill." Selye's observations on common manifestations of disease — what he describes as the "syndrome of just being sick" — provided the starting point for his classic concept, the General Adaptation Syndrome [but see Mason's (1975) critique, and Selye's (1975) reply].

6.   The following typologies are a sample: (1) offense-based, sociological, psychiatric, psychoanalytic, and psychological (Megargee, 1971); (2) prior probability, reference-group, behavior, psychiatric, social perception, and interactional (Warren, 1978); (3) violent personal, occasional property, public order, conventional, political, occupational, corporate, organized, and professional (types of criminal behavior) (Clinard & Quinney, 1973; see Glaser, 1974, for reviews).

7.   The fact that there is considerable "nonspecificity" in criminal behavior should not be taken to mean that criminality is totally nonspecific — in other words, that anyone committing a specific offense is equally likely to commit any other type of offense. One would suspect, however, that those who have committed a serious offense would be likely to have committed a range of lesser offenses, whereas individuals who have committed a relatively minor offense would tend to restrict their criminality to other types of minor offenses. Recent evidence suggests that, over age 21, there is a slight tendency toward increasing specialization (Farrington, 1982). However, this may not necessarily reflect an increase in conscious planning; it could, for instance, reflect a general decline in aggressive behavior which occurs with advancing age.

8.   Of course, far more crime is actually committed than leads to convictions or is reported to the police. Shapland (1978) found that the level of self-reported crime is even greater among 11- to 14-year-old boys than that admitted by 16-year-olds in the

Cambridge study (West & Farrington, 1973). For a discussion of the relationship between age and criminality, see Hirschi and Gottfredson (1983).

    9.   Rutter and Madge (1976), Johnson (1979), Hippchen (1978), and Rutter and Giller (1983) may be consulted for a wider selection of other hypothesized causal factors.

2

SITUATIONAL FACTORS IN CRIME

Many observations in the scientific literature and popular press suggest an association between stressful life events and crime. However, life events and crime do not seem to be linked to one another in any specific way. There appears to be a considerable amount of nonspecificity regarding both the supposed causes of particular types of crime and the criminogenic effects of particular factors; that is, a given form of crime can have multiple causes, and a given causal factor is linked to many different types of crime.

OPPORTUNITIES VERSUS INDUCEMENTS

The types of situational factors to be discussed in this chapter represent a different category from that of situational opportunities for committing crime.[1] Although "opportunity" appears to be important in some crimes, there are fewer robberies, for instance, than would be expected if "opportunity" was the main explanatory factor; most people desist from crime even when opportunities are available. While situational opportunity represents a kind of "passive determinant" of crime, the emphasis in this chapter is on events that can be regarded as actively inducing or provoking such behavior.[2] These events will be discussed under the following headings: crowd situations; stressful life events; multiple, overlapping stresses; and transient physiological disturbances.

REVIEW OF THE LITERATURE[3]

Crowd Situations

A classic account of criminality arising in crowd situations is that of the French physician and social commentator, Gustave LeBon (b. 1841, d. 1931). LeBon (1895/1977, p. 27) noted that:

> The most striking peculiarity presented by a psychological crowd is the following: whoever be the individuals that compose it . . . the fact that they have been transformed into a crowd puts them in possession of a sort of collective mind which makes them feel, think, and act in a manner quite different from that in which each individual of them would feel, think, and act were he in a state of isolation.

According to LeBon, individuals take on the following characteristics when immersed in a crowd.

1. *Impulsiveness.* An isolated person knows that by himself he "cannot set fire to a palace or loot a shop, and should he be tempted to do so, he will easily resist the temptation. . . . Making part of a crowd, he is conscious of the power given him by the number, and it is sufficient to suggest to him ideas of murder and pillage for him to yield immediately to temptation. An unexpected obstacle will be destroyed with frenzied rage" (p. 38).

2. *Excessive Suggestibility.* A crowd is usually in a "state of expectant attention, which renders suggestion easy" (p. 39).

3. *Simple and Exaggerated Sentiments.* Suspicions are immediately transformed into incontrovertible evidence. "A commencement of antipathy or disapprobation . . . becomes at once furious hatred . . ." (p. 50), while at other times crowds are capable of "heroism and devotion and of evincing the loftiest virtues" (p. 51). Allied to the tendency toward simplicity and exaggeration is a lowering of intellectual and reasoning abilities (see his chapter 3).[4]

4. *Intolerance and Conservatism.* Although people as individuals may be prepared to accept contradiction and discussion, crowds are far less apt to do so. The slightest contradiction on the part of a speaker at a public meeting is greeted with "howls of fury and violent invective, soon followed by blows and expulsion should the orator stick to his point" (p. 53).

5. *Variable Morality*. The morality of crowds can range from "murder, incendiarism and every kind of crime" (p. 57) on some occasions, to "very lofty acts of devotion, sacrifice, and disinterestedness" (p. 57) on others. In his chapter on "Criminal Crowds," LeBon focused on crimes committed during riots and revolutions. "The usual motive of the crimes of crowds is a powerful suggestion, and the individuals who take part in such crimes are afterwards convinced that they have acted in obedience to duty . . ." (p. 160).

> The murder of M. de Launay, the governor of the Bastile, may be cited as a typical example. After the taking of the fortress the governor, surrounded by a very excited crowd, was dealt blows in every direction. It was proposed to hang him, to cut off his head, to tie him to a horse's tail. While struggling, he accidentally kicked one of those present. Someone proposed, and his suggestion was at once received with acclamation by the crowd, that the individual who had been kicked should cut the governor's throat.
>
> The individual in question, a cook out of work, whose chief reason for being in the Bastile was idle curiosity as to what was going on, esteems, that since such is the general opinion, the action is patriotic and even believes he deserves a medal for having destroyed a monster. With a sword that is lent him he strikes the bared neck, but the weapon being somewhat blunt and not cutting, he takes from his pocket a small black handled knife and (in his capacity of cook he would be experienced in cutting up meat) successfully effects the operation (pp. 160–61).

LeBon's work has been criticized for attributing group violence solely to immediate psychological influences, thereby neglecting the sociopolitical context in which crowds develop, for example, sudden rises in the price of bread and the fear of starvation (Rude, 1964). Other criticisms have centered on his tendency to reify crowds, his elitist prejudices, his supposedly exaggerated descriptions of crowd behavior (Nye, 1975), and his failure to consider different types of crowd leaders (Freud, 1922). Summarizing LeBon's achievements, Merton (1960) will allow only that these lay in his ability to identify important problems in social psychology, not in having solved them. Nevertheless, according to Mannheim (1965, p. 647), ". . . except for LeBon's now universally rejected concept of the group mind, most of the differences between the LeBon School and their modern opponents are of degree only. There is hardly any quarrel with the view that human beings in a crowd are likely to behave differently from the way they would behave in isolation."

LeBon's observations and ideas have often been reiterated by subsequent investigators. In a seminal article dealing with military psychology and wartime atrocities, Janis (1963) notes that individuals in groups may carry out deviant actions that would be unthinkable to the individual acting on his own. Janis also concurs with other writers on group delinquency (e.g., Matza, 1964; Wade, 1970) in suggesting that many individuals experience severe guilt, remorse, and loss of self-esteem after committing antisocial acts in groups. Thus, there seems to be wide acceptance of the view that there is something about being in a crowd that can lead people to act in ways that contradict their usual beliefs and values.

Experimental work on the "polarization phenomenon" (Lamm & Meyers, 1978, for a review) supports the notion that individuals in crowds are prone to oscillate behaviorally from one extreme to another. The term "polarization phenomenon" refers to the tendency of people in loosely structured groups to make decisions that are either more risky or more cautious than the average of the individual decisions prior to group membership. When rediscovered in the early 1960s, the phenomenon was one-sidedly labeled the "risky shift." Later, it was recognized that groups may also adopt positions that are more *cautious* than the average position of the individuals comprising them; hence the generic term "polarization phenomenon" (Stoner, 1968).[5]

There are numerous contemporary accounts of criminal acts occurring in crowd situations such as parades, parties, festivals, sporting events, and other social gatherings. The following report (see Figure 2.1), published in the New Orleans's *Times-Picayune* is typical.

Harrington (1972) investigated "soccer hooliganism"[6] in England and found that most such acts were committed by males of low socioeconomic status between the ages of 15 and 19. Although many had previous criminal convictions, it was often observed that "young schoolboys with no previous criminal record would get carried away by the excitement of the game and run on the field, and youths of good background and character [would also] become involved in rowdyism particularly where large numbers of rival fans [were] collectively engaged in fighting" (Harrington, 1972a, p. 53).

1,000 Young Gangsters Vandalize British Town

SCARBOROUGH, England (AP) — More than 1,000 youths, mostly members or supporters of the "Mods" youth gang, vandalized part of this south Yorkshire seaside town overnight Saturday, smashing shop windows, setting fire to beach chairs and injuring three policemen.

Authorities arrested 106 youths and sent police patrols — some teams bolstered by dogs — into the town Sunday.

"They just wanted a confrontation with the police," Superintendent John Carlton, chief of Scarborough police, said of the youths.

In recent years, at least one of Britain's youth gangs — who include the Mods, Teds, Punks, Skinheads, or Rude Boys — massed at a seaside resort during Easter for drinking and brawling. The Mods tend to see themselves as smartened-up leather-outfitted punks.

Police said the trouble started after Scarborough's pubs closed at 11:30 P.M. Scuffles broke out in the town center as the youths ran riot, smashing the windows in at least four shops, and using broken beer bottles and torn-apart deck chairs to fight the police.

Carlton said the biggest cause of the trouble was not the Mods themselves but their supporters. Police were able to herd the gangs towards the beach — where they could not smash shops — and arrested 106 on charges of assault.

Figure 2.1

Source: Times Picayune, April 7, 1980, Sn. 1, p. 3. Reprinted with permission.

A more recent study (Trivizas, 1980) was based on 652 offenses committed during soccer matches between the years 1974–76. These offenses were compared with a sample of offenses recorded by the London Metropolitan Police during the same period and classified under the same official labels (N = 410), but which were committed independently of football events. Contrary to the stereotype of soccer hooliganism as vandalism, the most frequent football-related offense was threatening behavior or insulting words (67 percent), followed by assault on a constable (7.7 percent) and willful obstruction of the highway (7.1 percent). Criminal damage only accounted for 3.7 percent of the cases. Other findings of note were that 99.2 percent of the offenses were committed by males; the mean age of arrested persons was 19 years; 58.6 percent of all offenses were committed by persons between the ages of 17 and 20; and 68.1 percent of those charged with football-related offenses were manual workers. Of special interest in view of LeBon's thesis that persons in crowds are prone to act differently from the way they would when not in a crowd, was the observation that people arrested in crowd situations were more likely to be first offenders than those arrested in noncrowd situations.

In his valuable review of group delinquency, Gibbens (1970) concurs with other authors in suggesting that, when arrested, individuals involved in hooliganism are "often at a loss to account for their behavior" (p. 123). Most such behavior is minor and consists of "small groups of youths using insulting language and behavior." (p. 123). Yet, actions which begin as hooliganism may culminate in vandalism. While Gibbens recognized that "crowd psychology" may play a role in vandalism, he agrees with Stanley Cohen (1971) that most so-called vandalism is not pointless or senseless — as implied by its definition as "wanton damage," and as suggested in earlier literature (e.g., Shalloo, 1954) — but is carried out for a variety of reasons, for example, to acquire something, to make a protest, for publicity, for revenge, or fun. On the other hand, some authors contend that involvement in group vandalism occurs in a rapidly escalating process over which the participants themselves have limited personal control. Wade (1970) has suggested that destruction results more from collective interaction at the moment than from predetermined motives and that participants, looking back at what they have done, sometimes reevaluate their behavior from having a positive, "fun" connotation, to a negative connotation. Feelings are usually mixed, and guilt is often present; many admit feeling relieved and even pleased that they were apprehended. However, the prevalence or degree of subsequent guilt should not be overstated, especially when "hooliganism" is virtually an institutionalized form of protest, as it is today in many parts of the world. Where the victim is known to the participants and is defined in negative terms, the feeling expressed may be one of delight rather than guilt at having been a party to the act. Nevertheless, even in such cases (Wade is referring to school-related types of incidents, not to paramilitaristic vandalism and assaults on the police), sentiments are often verbalized that the acts "went further" than the participants had intended. It is this "gap" between motives prior to the act, and the extent of actual damages inflicted, so often reported in the literature, which suggests that more is involved in crowd criminality than two or more individuals having a goal, forming an intention, and then acting upon it. As in many other areas of human social life, intentions and motives do not always coincide with actual behavior.[7]

Rape is another type of crime that is frequently carried out in groups. Several studies from different parts of the world indicate that 6 to 26 percent of all reported rapes take place in groups of three or more individuals (Dietz, 1978). Compared to rapes by solitary offenders, multiple-offender rapes tend to cluster at times of maximum recreational interaction, for example, summers, weekends, and evenings; to involve younger offenders; lower status ethnic groups; alcohol to a greater extent; offenders with a lower probability of a previous arrest for a violent or sex-related offense; and offenders who live nearer the scene of the crime and the victim's residence. Multiple-offender rapes also begin more frequently in the street and are committed more frequently in automobiles and less frequently in the residence of one of the participants; they involve offenders who are more frequently neighbors of their victims and less frequently intimate acquaintances; and they involve a greater degree of physical force (Dietz, 1978).

Stressful Life Events[8]

There is evidence to suggest that a wide variety of criminal and delinquent acts can be precipitated by stressful life events. One of the most frequently mentioned factors is some form of separation experience involving attachment figures and/or familiar surroundings. The category of separation includes death, abandonment (or the threat of abandonment), and forced or voluntary separation resulting from occupational activity, migration, etc.

Gibbens and Prince (1962), in a British study of shoplifting, found that about twice the expected number of shoplifters lived alone; the incidence of separation, divorce, and widowhood was much higher than in the general population, and 29 percent of the shoplifters were immigrants. In another investigation of a group of 50 thieves, as many as 14, all of them female, had recently been bereaved and were depressed (Medlicott, 1968). In a study of murder, almost a third of 63 male murderers had been separated from their wives just prior to the crime (Mowat, 1966). A study of persons who had made homicidal threats revealed that many husbands who had threatened to kill their wives had themselves been threatened with abandonment (Macdonald, 1968). The threat of abandonment or separation has also been implicated in cases of matricide (O'Connell, 1963) and filicide (Meyerson, 1966).

Case Study 1. A "Dear Abby ..." letter (*Times-Picayune/States-Item,* New Orleans, February 13, 1981, Sn. 3, p. 7) provides a classic illustration of transient criminality following the loss of a spouse.

DEAR ABBY: Please help me. I don't have anybody else to ask about this and it's tearing me apart. I have recently been through a very emotional time. I lost my husband a year ago and did some stupid things. I seemed to have lost control.

I was recently picked up for shoplifting a $2.50 article I didn't need or want, so now I have a record. I am so ashamed and embarrassed, I can't stand myself. I have lost all self respect.

Now I want to go back to work — selling — but I am worried about this shoplifting offense being on my record. Do companies check into a person's background thoroughly to find out something like this? Can this keep me from getting employment? I need to work not only to support myself, but to help me keep my sanity. I am 50. NO NAME, NO TOWN.

DEAR NO NAME: The chance that this single offense will prevent you from getting employment is very, very small. Put it out of your mind, apply for work and forget it. Should you be questioned about the incident, explain that it occurred while you were under stress.

Case Study 2. A bizarre case of separation-induced homicide was described by Galvin and Macdonald (1959). A 23-year-old married man was intensely but ambivalently attached to his mother. After living apart for a few years, the mother came to live with him and his family. One day she decided to visit her daughter in a distant part of the country. This came as a great shock, as the son had finally begun to feel that his mother really cared for him. Despite his vehement wish that she not go, she left, but without giving him a "satisfactory" explanation. She was to travel by airplane. He responded by placing a time bomb in her suitcase. The bomb exploded shortly after takeoff, killing all of the 44 people on board.

Case Study 3. A well-publicized case of "amok murder" occurred some years ago in New Orleans, apparently related to a separation experience. As reported in the *Times-Picayune* (November 8, 1977, Sn. 1, p. 1. Reprinted with permission):

Nine men and women were gunned down by a man who police said went on a rampage Monday from the Carrollton area to the French Quarter and into the Central Business District ... Carlos R. Poree, 35 ... was arrested about 11:45 A.M. immediately after five men were shot in and around the offices of Merrill Lynch. ... Poree is accused of starting his wild shooting spree by wounding his estranged wife ... and her father ... about 9:30 A.M.

Poree had been employed as an auditor with the Internal Revenue Service and was a Vietnam War veteran. A friend (cited in the same newspaper report) described him as a "very level and strong individual." However, it later emerged that he had shown signs of personality disintegration prior to his wife's leaving him, and his subsequent violent rampage.

Case Study 4. There are suggestions that the notorious murder-suicide of over 900 members of the People's Temple cult in Jonestown, Guyana, in November 1978, may have been due in part to a threatened separation (Kilduff & Javers, 1978, p. 197). The group's leader, the Reverend Jim Jones, had had an illegitimate child by one of his followers and raised the child, named John-John, himself. For two years prior to the massacre, the child's mother and her husband had been trying to obtain legal custody. According to Charles Garry, Jones's lawyer, Jones was extremely attached to John-John and feared losing custody of the boy (Kilduff & Javers, 1978, p. 197). Jones first threatened mass suicide in September 1977, when the Guyanese courts were about the hear the case (Krause, 1978, p. 115). According to Krause (1978, p. 57),

> Grace Stoen, by whom Jones claimed to have fathered the son, John-John, was the first to become disenchanted at the virtual brutalities and financial practices of Jones. She broke away in July, 1976, and began a custody action to regain possession of her son. . . . Jones kept the Stoen child in his own household at the colony. So visibly attached to the boy was Jones that some followers believed the possible loss of John may have been central to the preacher's decision to go ahead with the flight to Guyana, and later, the suicides. It is doubtful, however, that any competent witness on that point survived the holocaust.

Criminal acts can be precipitated by a wide variety of other stressful events in addition to separation experiences and crowding. Interpersonal conflicts, occupational, and financial crises have been implicated in robbery (Camp, 1967), embezzlement (Cressey, 1953), "naive" check forgery (Lemert, 1953), shoplifting (Gibbens et al., 1971), and many other crimes.

Occasional or "naive" check forgery refers to the writing and passing of "bad" checks. As Don Gibbons (1977, p. 305) has pointed out, "many instances of behavior that qualify technically as forgery probably go unreported because they are suspected of being accidental. Persons do fairly commonly write checks that 'bounce' unintentionally. . . . As a result, the demarcation point between mistakes and willful misconduct is hazy." Lemert (1953) examined the case records of over 1,000 naive check forgers in California and personally interviewed a number of them. Most were white males, older on average than other probationers. Before the forgery the majority of offenders had either been laid off work, experienced gambling losses, gone on alcoholic sprees, had difficulties in military service, been estranged from their families, or suffered other kinds of emotional setbacks. Marital difficulties were especially prevalent among the group, and about 40 percent were divorced.

Approximately 20 percent of a group of individuals arrested for shoplifting were suffering from "acute stress." One woman went shoplifting the day before she was to take her son, who had a sarcoma of the elbow, to see a surgeon. "Rather younger women may have had a recent miscarriage, fear sterility, or mourn the death of children" (Gibbens et al., 1971, p. 615). According to the authors, most such individuals tend to be convicted only once.

Turning to violent crime, Macdonald (1968) found that 40 percent of a group of individuals who had threatened to kill their wives had recently lost their jobs or suffered business failure. Public humiliation (Westermeyer, 1972; Frazier, 1974) and gambling losses (Westermeyer, 1972) have been reported as precipitating factors in homicide. Loss of employment and recent social isolation have also been implicated in child abuse (Steele & Pollock, 1974).

Case Study 5. An unusual case was reported in which a man, fearing he had cancer, kidnapped a physician and held him hostage for several hours before releasing him unharmed (*Times-Picayune,* New Orleans, July 21, 1977, Sn. 1, p. 20. Reprinted with permission):

Leroy Menendez, 43, . . . was booked with aggravated kidnapping of Dr. Richard Street Wednesday after Menendez' release from Veterans Hospital. Menendez had been in the hospital since the June 24 incident in which he held Dr. Street, 60, at gun-point for four hours in the physician's office. . . . Menendez was treated prior to the incident by the VA and elsewhere for a stomach ulcer. The VA had ruled he had a 20 percent disability. Believing he had cancer and no one would tell him, Menendez demanded a 100 percent disability. Police theorized he chose Street as his prisoner because the

physician had treated him previously at no charge and suggested he seek help
at the VA hospital.

Another factor which has been implicated in group vandalism and
other forms of delinquency is peer pressure. Short and Strodtbeck
(1965), in their study of Chicago youth gangs, reported that delinquent
behavior often occurred in response to real or imagined threats to a boy's
social status in the group, brought on by teasing, cajoling, or "dares" to
carry out hazardous acts. More extreme forms of "pressure," including
harassment, nagging, ridicule, and open aggressiveness, have led to
criminal violence (Lester & Lester, 1975; Newman, 1979). Nagging or
ridicule has been known to provoke a child into murdering a parent
(Malmquist, 1971). "Victim-precipitated" homicide (in which the victim
is the first to use physical force in the fatal incident) accounted for 26
percent of the 158 criminal homicides recorded in Philadelphia between
1948 and 1952 (Wolfgang, 1958). In the typical victim-precipitated
homicide, a black male assaulted his wife and was then killed by her.

A considerable variety of apparently minor provocations have incited
individuals to violence and murder. A list of incidents of this sort
appeared in a syndicated article in the Chicago *Daily News* by Barry
Felcher (reprinted in the *Times-Picayune* of September 11, 1976, Sn. 1,
p. 17), entitled "I Told You — Don't Eat My Corn Flakes." The article
described how one man shot his brother after the brother failed to wish
him a happy birthday; how a stabbing occurred over the naming of a
goldfish; and how murders were committed after one victim was warned
not to eat a bowl of corn flakes and another was warned not to slice the
turkey so thickly. One man, on seeing that the guppies in his fish tank
had eaten the goldfish, went into a rage, pulled out his shotgun and blew
up the tank, inadvertently shooting and killing his friend at the same time.

Multiple, Overlapping Stresses

To the extent that situational stress leads to crime, the expected pattern
is more likely to be one in which a particular "minor" event, such as those
referred to above, serves to "trigger" antisocial behavior after a *series of
stressful experiences*. As Justice and Justice (1976, p. 30) noted in their
study of child abuse:

The reason that a broken washing machine — or some other seemingly minor problem — may assume the proportions of a crisis in the eyes of the potentially abusive parent is that he has been bombarded for a long time with a series of stressful changes. Thus his ability to cope with even minor problems is at a low point and he is unable to exercise his usual control over lashing out at others.

Severe situational stress, involving a series of stressors, has been suggested as a determining factor in a proportion of rapes and as a basis for identifying a certain type of rapist. Rada (1978b) observes that such individuals have a history of severe stress in their lives immediately before the crime. A typical case would be that of a 20-year-old man who "flunks out of college, begins drinking heavily, and shortly prior to the rape, loses his wife" (p. 123). At the time of committing rape, many individuals are undergoing a moderate to severe agitated depression. Some carry out their crime impulsively, in a mood of anger and defiance, although excessive force is rarely used. Afterwards, they are unable to account for their behavior, and feelings of guilt, shame, and depression are common. Hartman and Nicolay (1966) have also reported that the various stresses associated with being an expectant father may precipitate sex offenses in vulnerable males.

Case Study 6. The following case study illustrates the notion of multiple stressors in the causation of rape (Rada, 1978b, pp. 124–25). This was a 26-year-old, married truck driver, with an apparently normal, uneventful childhood and early adulthood. One year before the rape his father died, and he became depressed. He responded by working harder at his job and spending longer periods away from home. Six months before the rape his pay was unavoidably reduced at a time when his wife was four to five months pregnant and he had recently moved to a new home. He began drinking on the road and had several extramarital sexual encounters, all of which left him with a feeling of extreme guilt. The relationship with his wife deteriorated and sexual relations between the two became practically nonexistent. Shortly after the child was born, a member of his wife's family died, causing the wife to become depressed and to increase her emotional demands on the subject. One week before the rape he was forced to choose between making cross-country runs or leaving the firm. He chose to quit his job rather than be away from home during this time, but was unable to find alternative employment. Several days before the rape he and his wife had a serious quarrel in which she threatened to leave him. On the day of the rape he filed for unemployment compensation. Afterwards, feeling ashamed and despondent, he began wandering around the downtown area. A young woman crossed the street in front of him. He followed, pulled her into the open doorway of a building, forced her to the floor, and attempted to rape her. The woman screamed several times and the subject was quickly apprehended. At the time of the psychiatric examination he was very depressed and felt exceedingly guilty about the rape, which he now found "totally inexplicable."

Turning to the few existing studies on the association between stressful life events and crime, Justice and Justice (1976) compared a group of 35 child-abusing parents on the Holmes and Rahe stress scale[9] with an equal number of nonabusers, matched for age, education, and income (see Table 2.1). The mean life change score of the abusing parents ($\overline{X}$ = 233.63) was nearly twice that of the nonabusing parents ($\overline{X}$ = 123.62). Holmes and Rahe (1967a) classify any score above 150 as a "mild crisis," and anything above 300 as a "major crisis." The mean score of the abusing parents thus represents more than a mild life crisis but less than a major one, and so would be classified as moderate. Some abusers, however, scored almost 650. Justice and Justice suggest that life *change* is the critical factor leading to child abuse, abusing parents having experienced too many and too many sudden changes (see also Friedrich & Einbender, 1983).

Masuda et al. (1978) used the Schedule of Recent Experience (Holmes and Rahe, 1967b) — based on the Social Readjustment Rating Scale — to study the relationship between life events and the onset of incarceration among 176 male prisoner volunteers. The mean annual life change score during the year before incarceration was significantly higher than the mean scores of the preceding four years ($p < .0005$). Younger prisoners experienced more life changes than older prisoners, and whites had higher scores than blacks (see Figure 2.2). The pattern and magnitude of life changes among prisoners were similar to those observed at the time of onset of a wide variety of diseases, suggesting that "the commission of, apprehension, and incarceration for crime parallels the signs and symptoms of an illness" (Masuda et al., 1978, p. 203).

TABLE 2.1
Social Readjustment Rating Scale

Rank	Life Event	Mean Value
1	Death of spouse	100
2	Divorce	73
3	Marital separation	65
4	Jail term	63
5	Death of close family member	63
6	Personal injury or illness	53
7	Marriage	50
8	Fired at work	47
9	Marital reconciliation	45
10	Retirement	45
11	Change in health of family member	44
12	Pregnancy	40
13	Sex difficulties	39
14	Gain of new family member	39
15	Business readjustment	39
16	Change in financial state	38
17	Death of close friend	37
18	Change to different line of work	36
19	Change in number of arguments with spouse	35
20	Mortgage over $10,000	31
21	Foreclosure of mortgage or loan	30
22	Change in responsibilities at work	29
23	Son or daughter leaving home	29
24	Trouble with in-laws	29
25	Outstanding personal achievement	28
26	Wife begin or stop work	26
27	Begin or end school	26
28	Change in living conditions	25
29	Revision of personal habits	24
30	Trouble with boss	23
31	Change in work hours or conditions	20
32	Change in residence	20
33	Change in schools	20
34	Change in recreation	19
35	Change in church activities	19
36	Change in social activities	18
37	Mortgage or loan less than $10,000	17
38	Change in sleeping habits	16
39	Change in number of family get-togethers	15
40	Change in eating habits	15
41	Vacation	13
42	Christmas	12
43	Minor violations of the law	11

Source: Holmes and Rahe (1967a). Reprinted with permission.

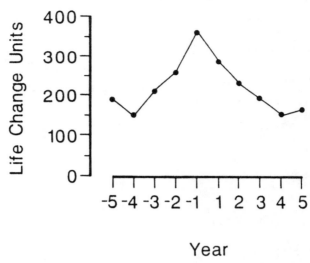

Figure 2.2
Annual life change units before and during imprisonment.
Source: Masuda et al., 1978, p. 200. Reprinted with permission.

Based on over a decade of research on family violence, Murray Straus and his associates (e.g., Straus, 1980; Straus et al., 1980) have concluded that the family, in spite of being a haven of love, support, and gentleness, is at the same time "the most violent institution, group or setting that a typical citizen is likely to encounter" (Straus, 1980, p. 229). A major cause of violence within the family is the "high level of stress and conflict characteristic of families" (p. 230). Stress is believed to result in familial aggression only if:

> (a) the individual has learned an "aggressive" response to stress; (b) if such a response is a culturally recognized script for behavior under stress; and (c) if the situation seems to be one that will produce rewards for aggression (p. 233).

The data used to test this hypothesis were based on interviews conducted on a national area-probability sample of 2,143 American adults. Persons aged 18 to 70 years of age who were living with a member of the opposite sex as a "couple" were eligible for inclusion in the study. Life stress during the previous year was evaluated using a modified version of the Holmes and Rahe (1967a) scale, and family violence during the same time period was assessed by means of a checklist of items ranging from nonviolent approaches to resolving conflict at one end of the spectrum, to physical acts of aggression at the other end. The most frequently occurring stressor (reported by 40 percent of the sample) was the death of someone close to the respondent. About 2 percent of the males and 1 percent of the females were "arrested or convicted of something serious." Violent attacks by men which were classified as "wife-beating" occurred in almost 4 percent of the couples, while attacks by women which were classified as "husband-beating" occurred in 4.6 percent of the couples.

In general it was found that the higher the stress score, the higher the rate of assault between husband and wife. "For the wives, the curve approximately fits a power function. For the husbands the relationship shows a general upward trend but is irregular" (p. 239; see Figure 2.3).

Both verbal and physical aggression were positively related to the stress score. Husbands with high stress scores and whose father (but not mother) had hit them severely as children, assaulted their wives more frequently than husbands with similar stress scores but whose father did not hit them severely. The assault rate of husbands whose father had hit their mother was more than twice that of men whose father never hit their mother. The assault rate of husbands was even higher in cases where their *mother* had hit the father, rather than vice versa. Men who did not belong to social or professional organizations assaulted their wives more frequently than men who belonged to many organizations. As noted by Straus, this finding is consistent with the hypothesis that "social support" moderates the effect of stress, thereby reducing the risk of violence and/or criminality. However, seemingly contrary to the social support hypothesis, couples with many relatives living within an hour's travel time had a *higher* assault rate (husbands on wives) than couples with few relatives living nearby. This was interpreted as indicating that such networks are of the traditional, working-class variety, in which wives are often encouraged by their mothers to put up with beatings "for the sake of the children," and to try to become better wives.[10]

Although not dealing explicitly with crime, Stanley Milgram's (1963, 1968, 1974) work on "obedience to authority" offers virtually an experimental model of transient criminality. Adult male volunteers (carefully selected to provide a cross-section of ages and occupations)

Transient Criminality

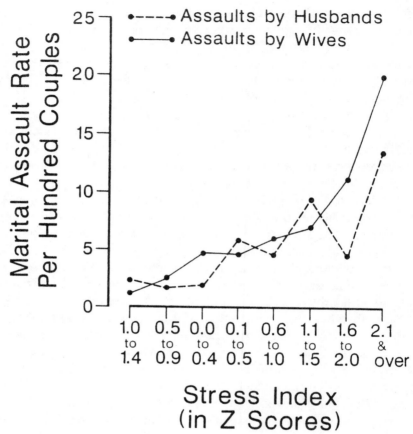

Figure 2.3
Marital assault rate by stress index score.

Source: Straus, 1980, p. 240. Reprinted with permission.

were recruited from the New Haven, Connecticut, area to take part in an experiment ostensibly dealing with the effects of punishment on learning ability. The real purpose of the experiment, however, was to determine the extent to which normal adults were prepared to inflict pain on their fellow humans merely because they were told to do so by a psychologist-experimenter. The experiment required volunteer subjects to administer graded intensities of electric shock to a "learner" whenever he failed to remember a list of paired-associated words. The learner, who was an accomplice of the experimenter, was seated out of sight in an adjoining room. The shocks began at 15 volts, with 15-volt increases each time the learner "failed" to remember the words. *No shocks were actually delivered,* but the learner was instructed to shout and groan appropriately and realistically according to the level of shock. Subjects were given a real 40-volt shock before the experiment began to familiarize them with shocks of this intensity. All believed they were taking part in a genuine experiment. Subjects stood in front of a shock generator that was clearly marked at the 350-volt level: Danger, Severe Shock.

Before the experiment, several psychiatrists were asked to estimate the proportion of subjects they thought would deliver the maximum shock of 450 volts. The average prediction was 0.1 percent. In fact, however, in spite of increasingly anguished shouts and other forms of simulated protest from the learner, and very real distress on the part of most subjects, 65 percent of the subjects delivered the maximum shock level. As the experiment progressed the learner would "fail" to remember the words, a shock would be delivered, and the learner would bang his fist on the adjoining wall and cry out as if in pain. The learner would "fail" again, and the volunteer would turn anxiously to the experimenter for instructions. The learner was surely hurt . . . in great pain . . . shouldn't they stop now? The experimenter would calmly tell the volunteer that he had agreed to take part in the experiment and that he must continue. Even silence on the part of the learner was interpreted as a "failure," to be followed by shock. Yet despite their obvious reluctance, most subjects continued to inflict still higher levels of shock. "With numbing regularity," Milgram (1968, p. 275) writes, "good people were seen to knuckle under to authority and perform actions that were callous and severe." Afterwards, when the real purpose of the experiment was explained to them, most subjects admitted with shame that they were unable to say how or why they could have acted as they did.[11]

Internal-Physiological Factors

These include temporary physiological states induced (1) exogenously, via the use of drugs, or (2) endogenously, as a result of internal physiologic changes. (We are not concerned here with chronic dysfunctions, including addictions, and their role in crime.)

Exogenous Factors. There is considerable evidence that the ingestion of certain drugs is associated with crimes of violence. Alcohol is by far the most commonly cited drug in this connection.[12] A high incidence of alcohol intoxication has been reported among murderers (Goodwin, 1973) and murder victims (Virkkunen, 1974), and among other individuals convicted of criminal violence. Murderers tend not to be chronic alcoholics, however; most, according to Goodwin (1973), are moderate-to-heavy drinkers who happen to be intoxicated at the moment of their crime. Mayfield (1976) studied over 300 males who had been imprisoned for committing assaultive crimes (80 percent had been convicted of homicide). The subjects were mainly young adults; most of the assaults had occurred in the home of either the subject or the victim, and firearms were the most commonly used weapon (74 percent). Fifty-eight percent of the subjects and 40 percent of the victims had been drinking at the time of the assault. The attacks themselves were typically unpremeditated; that is, sudden, impulsive acts, "too frivolous of motivation to be convincingly labeled 'crimes of passion'" (Mayfield 1976, p. 290). As in many other studies, Mayfield found "the triad of familiarity, guns and alcohol to be common ingredients in serious assaultive acts" (p. 290). In another investigation (Tinklenberg and Woodrow, 1974), incarcerated male adolescents were divided into three subgroups: assaultive, sexual, and nonassaultive offenders. Although alcohol was the drug most frequently associated with serious assaultive and sexual offenses, secobarbital was overrepresented in violent crimes compared to other drugs. In fact, secobarbital was overwhelmingly selected by experienced drug-using delinquents as the substance most likely to increase aggression. Marihuana was relatively underrepresented in serious assaultive and sexual crimes and was considered a drug which decreased aggressive tendencies (see also Elliott, 1978, p. 182). Hashish, psychedelics, and the opioids were also in general felt to decrease aggressiveness. The "assaultive" offender group did not necessarily prefer drugs which they felt decreased aggressiveness. However, the "nonassaultive" and "sexual" offender groups preferred drugs that they expected would decrease aggressiveness.

Endogenous Factors. There is evidence to implicate cyclic hormonal changes in the causation of criminal deviance among females. Much research has been carried out on the behavioral, psychological, and physiological correlates of the menstrual cycle, and it is generally accepted that most women experience dysphoric symptoms during the few days before menstruation or during menstruation itself (Dalton, 1964; Steiner & Carroll, 1977).[13] Among the many symptoms of the premenstrual tension syndrome are tension, irritability, anxiety, depression, insomnia, fatigue, nausea, headaches, dizziness, thirst, increased appetite, and altered sexual interest. Dalton (1961, cited in Steiner & Carroll, 1977, p. 323) describes the phase as follows:

> In premenstrual depression the mood changes are short-lived, the depression lasting only a few days at a time, with improvement, often abrupt, occurring during menstruation. But the depth of depression may be extreme, reaching suicide level, or a temporary psychosis may develop. The depression is accompanied by tension, irritability with aggression which may result in a battered baby or bruised husband, and lethargy, both mental and physical.

Although earlier work has been criticized on methodological grounds (Parlee, 1973; Ruble et al., 1980), there are indications that many kinds of deviant behavior are more likely to occur among women in the premenstruum than in other phases of the cycle. Morton et al. (1953) studied 24 female prisoner volunteers and found that 51 percent experienced dysphoric premenstrual symptoms. The criminal histories of 58 women who had committed violent crimes were studied. Sixty-two percent of this group were found to have committed their crimes in the premenstruum, and another 17 percent committed their crimes during menstruation. Thus, as Shah and Roth (1974, p. 124) observe, 79 percent of these crimes occurred during the premenstrual and menstrual periods. Dalton (1964) reported that nearly half of a sample of female prisoners had committed their crimes during the premenstrual or menstrual phase, with violent and nonviolent crimes following the same pattern. Accidents (Dalton, 1960; Liskey, 1972), suicide, and suicidal thoughts (Ribeiro, 1962; Wetzel et al., 1971) also tend to occur disproportionately in the premenstruum.

The extent to which dysphoric emotional changes during the premenstruum account for the behavioral reactions has been questioned by d'Orban and J. Dalton (1980). Their subjects consisted of a consecutive series of 50 women charged with violence against persons and/or property. To be included in the study, subjects had to have admitted committing the act for which they had been charged; the date of their offense could be accurately determined; they had a regular menstrual cycle; and none suffered from any diagnosed physical illness. Unlike many previous studies, special precautions were taken to increase the reliability of the subjects' self-assessments regarding their menstrual phase, and K. Dalton's (1964) method of dividing up the menstrual cycle was adopted for purposes of comparability, that is, days 1–4 (menstruation) and days 25–28 (premenstruum) were collectively termed the paramenstruum. The results indicated that a statistically significant 44 percent of the women committed their offenses during the paramenstruum, compared to the expected figure of 29 percent. More offenses than expected were committed during the premenstruum, but only menstruation itself was significantly associated with offenses. Conversely, there was a significant absence of offenses during the ovulatory and postovulatory phases (from day 13 to 24). However, with regard to premenstrual symptoms, only 23 percent of the 22 women who committed their offenses during the paramenstruum reported experiencing such symptoms, and only two women thought that their menstrual periods had influenced the offense for which they had been charged (see Figure 2.4). Thus the commission of violent crimes during the paramenstruum does not appear to be related to dysphoric symptoms. Instead, endocrinological factors may be responsible for the association between violent offenses and the paramenstruum. D'Orban and Dalton (1980, p. 358) conclude:

> Perhaps too much emphasis has been placed on premenstrual tension symptoms as an aetiological factor in female crime; it is cyclically recurrent, observed behavioral changes (of which the woman herself may be unaware) rather than subjective symptoms which should be looked for, as some may benefit from progesterone or other form of specific therapy.

Hypoglycemia (low blood glucose) has often been cited as a contributor to crime (e.g., Hill & Sargent, 1943; Wilder, 1947; Bovill, 1973; Yaryura-Tobias, 1978; Bonnett & Pfeiffer, 1978; Schauss, 1980) but the evidence is scanty and mainly anecdotal. Hypoglycemia may be due to hyperinsulinism, excessive sugar intake, endogenous secretions that are insufficient to counter a normal insulin level (as found in Addison's disease, hypothyroidism, and a number of pituitary dysfunctions), allergies, and starvation (Bell, 1978; Schauss, 1980).

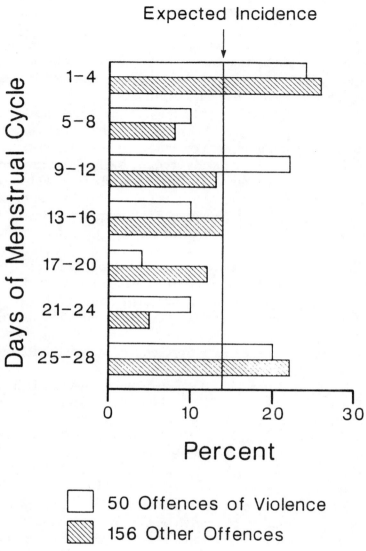

Figure 2.4
Distribution of 50 offenses of violence and 156 other offenses (Dalton, 1961) during 4-day periods of the menstrual cycle

Source: d'Orban and Dalton, 1980, p. 357. Reprinted with permission.

Sorokin (1975) provides a fascinating account of hunger and its effect on crime in pre-Bolshevik Russia, based partly on his own experience. The classic paper by Wilder (1947), however, is still the most comprehensive discussion of hypoglycemia in relation to crime.

The normal fasting blood-sugar level in man lies between 90 and 119 mgm. percent.[14] If this level falls below 60–70 mgm. percent, symptoms such as hunger, perspiration, tremor, bradycardia, hypotension, and a staring facial expression are typically seen. Below 50–60 mgm. percent, symptoms become more marked, leading ultimately to convulsions and paralysis. These symptoms can be speedily reversed by intravenous injection or oral consumption of glucose. Apart from diseases resulting in spontaneous hypoglycemia (e.g., hyperinsulinism), the condition may be brought on by "starvation, especially lack of carbohydrates; muscular overexertion; diarrhea and vomiting; lactation; and sometimes menstruation" (Wilder, 1947, p. 103). It has been claimed that an extremely high proportion of incarcerated adult offenders have hypoglycemic symptoms (averaging 80–85 percent) and that many inmates are sugar addicts (D'Asaro et al., 1975; Schauss, 1980, pp. 24–26; but see *Nutrition Reviews,* Supplement, May 1986, for critical reviews of this literature).

Hypoglycemia has been linked to a very wide range of criminal acts (Hill & Sargant, 1943; Wilder, 1947). However, very few systematic investigations — either clinical or epidemiological — have been undertaken to determine the association between hypoglycemia and criminality. Bolton (1973) studied the relationship between hypoglycemia and aggression among the Qolla tribe of Southern Peru and Bolivia. He calculated the homicide rate of Incawatana — a small Qolla village — as 55 per 100,000 population, one of the highest homicide rates recorded worldwide. Eighty homicides occurred on average every year, about one in every three households. A four-hour glucose tolerance test was given to a sample of 54 adult males in the village. It was found that 42.6 percent were moderately hypoglycemic (10–25 mgm. percent below the fasting glucose level), 13 percent were severely hypoglycemic (a drop of more than 25 mgm. percent), and only 44.4 percent appeared normo-glycemic (a drop of less than 10 mgm. percent). Moderately hypoglycemic subjects tended to be ranked higher in aggressiveness by key informants in the village than were the other groups of subjects. Bolton attributed the high prevalence of hypoglycemia among the Qolla to: lower basal glucose levels and faster rates of glucose uptake, such as are known to occur in natives living at high altitudes (Monge & Monge, 1966; Picon-Reategui, 1966); low per capita income; low agricultural productivity; dietary deficiencies in protein and other essential nutrients; long intervals between meals; the high rate of premature births; the high rate of disease; extremes of temperature; high levels of personal anxiety; hypoxia associated with an altitude of 3,800 meters above sea level; high levels of consumption of ethyl alcohol; coca chewing; and a high population density (Bolton, 1973, pp. 261–62).

Several other relatively "short-term" factors have also been implicated in transient criminality, but cannot be discussed here because of space limitations. These are: brain tumors, infections involving the central nervous system, cerebrovascular disease, other miscellaneous neurological diseases (Elliott, 1978; Monroe, 1978), hormonal changes involving the menopause (Medlicott, 1968), allergic reactions to certain foods (Moyer, 1976; Wunderlich, 1978; Schauss, 1980, pp. 75–84), and various other ecologic-biochemical factors (Hippchen, 1978).

NOTES

1. Alterations in crime rates partly reflect changing opportunities for engaging in crime (Clarke, 1977, 1980a, 1983; Trasler, 1979a). For instance, auto thefts and bank robberies have increased in recent years partly as a function of greater numbers of vehicles available to steal and banks available to rob (Gould, 1969), and the easy availability of handguns may explain the high rate of violent crime in the United States (Rushforth et al., 1977; Ray et al., 1978). Significant decreases in crime have also occurred as a result of reducing opportunities for crime (Brody, 1976). Thefts from English telephone booths were virtually eliminated when steel coin boxes were installed; car theft in West Germany was reduced more than 60 percent when steering-wheel locks were made compulsory on all old and new vehicles in 1963 (Clarke, 1977, 1980a, 1983); and motorcycle theft in England and Wales was reduced unintentionally as a result of a new law requiring motor cyclists to wear crash helmets (Mayhew et al., 1976). Observations such as these suggest that much criminal behavior "is committed by people who would not ordinarily be thought of as 'criminal' . . ." (Clarke, 1977, p. 283).

2. A distinction between "opportunities" and "inducements" to commit crime may not always be easy to make. A valuable item placed for sale in a very exposed position in a store may have the same effect on a potential thief in terms of "arousing" him or her to steal, as the "situational" factors to be discussed below.

3. For another discussion of situational factors and crime, see Monahan and Klassen (1982).

4. "The characteristics of the reasoning of crowds are the association of dissimilar things possessing a merely apparent connection between each other, and the immediate generalization of particular cases" (LeBon, 1895/1977, p. 66). Examples of this mode or reasoning would be that of "the savage who imagines that by eating the heart of a courageous foe he acquires his bravery; or of the workman who, having been exploited by one employer, immediately concludes that all employers exploit their men" (LeBon, 1895/1977, p. 66).

5. The suggestion of a possible connection between crowd behavior and the polarization phenomenon is of fairly recent origin (see, e.g., Johnson & Feinberg, 1977; Johnson et al., 1977; Johnson & Glover, 1978). Few experimental studies dealing with the sociopsychological mechanisms of group violence or with other forms of criminality have been conducted (Gurr, 1974). However, several earlier experiments have considerable relevance for understanding the relationship between crowds and criminality, for example, Sherif's (1936, 1947) classic work on the emergence of group norms, and that of Asch (1956), indicating that individuals in groups of three or more tend to acquiesce to group perceptual judgments that are clearly and visibly incorrect.

6. Hooliganism has been defined as "rowdy behavior by groups, large and small, who cause a breach of the peace sometimes leading to actual violence to people" (Gibbens, 1970, p. 112). For an interesting account of the history of sports-related crowd disorders in Britain from 1870 to 1914, see Vamplew (1980).

7. Crowd behavior often does appear to be senseless and irrational; the participants' intentions are not always clearly worked out and are often confused. Thus, crowd behavior does not always make sense at the level of individual motives and intentions. However, the fact that it may at times seem inexplicable to observers, or even to the actors themselves, does not necessarily mean that the behavior cannot be explained according to certain "rational" principles about which no one presently has any knowledge (see Marsh et al., 1978; Pearson, 1983; and Ingham, 1985, for alternative views of "football hooliganism").

8. Recently, the concept of post-traumatic stress disorder has been widely discussed and, in a few cases, linked to criminal violence (see, e.g., Kinzie et al., 1984). The reason for not including this topic in the review of situational factors is that the adverse effects of severe and prolonged trauma, such as that experienced in prisoner-of-war or concentration camp, appear to be extremely persistent, even permanent. Insofar as criminality is produced by such experiences, the expected pattern would be chronic criminality rather than transient criminality. Long-term follow-up studies of Vietnam War veterans should serve to clarify this point (see MacPherson, 1984, pp. 207–66).

9. The Holmes and Rahe (1967a) technique involves a self-administered, 43-item checklist of the most common types of stressful experiences. Each item is assigned a numerical weighting according to its relative severity, and subjects are required to endorse an item if it occurred within the previous year. The weightings are summed

arithmetically to give a subject's cumulative stress score. Each item on the scale is assigned a weighted value based on extensive testing in the general population. In constructing the scale, "death of a spouse" was first rated the most stressful type of life event and was assigned the arbitrary value of 100. Other events were then given weights between 0 and 100. "Marital separation," for instance, was given the value of 65, and "son or daughter leaving home," the value of 29. Mean "Life Change Units" (LCUs), that is, the total weighted score divided by the number of life events, can then be calculated. Holmes and Rahe have suggested, however, that it is the *number* of life events experienced by individuals within a given time period rather than LCUs which may be the single most important measure for comparing different groups (Dohrenwend & Dohrenwend, 1978). This checklist, referred to as the Social Readjustment Rating Scale, has proved useful as a weak predictor of episodes of illness in large samples of subjects (Rahe, 1979). While having the advantage of being quick and easy to administer, the scale has been criticized for failing to distinguish between stressful events that represent *causes* of, say, disease (or accidents, etc.), and those that are in fact *symptoms* or *consequences* of the disease (Dohrenwend & Dohrenwend, 1978). Another difficulty is that the scale is considered "insensitive to the biographical context in which life events occur and so overlooks important information regarding the meaning of life events to individuals" (Totman & Kiff, 1979, p. 142; Susser, 1981).

10. The assault rate of blue-collar husbands was 70 percent higher than that of white-collar husbands. It may be that a situation of having many relatives living nearby is more closely associated with a blue-collar than with a white-collar life-style. The appropriate comparison here should perhaps be between high-stress husbands with high and low social supports *within* occupational strata.

11. Some subjects, however, obeyed the instructions of the experimenter with little, if any, expression of emotion or reluctance. While genuinely believing that they were inflicting severe electric shocks on a fellow "volunteer," they appeared to be indifferent to the victim's suffering.

12. Abuse of phencyclidine ("angel dust") has recently become a cause for concern in view of its capacity to induce violence, even among individuals with no previous history of violence (Fauman & Fauman, 1979).

13. These cyclical changes are either not seen or are seen to a statistically insignificant extent in hysterectomized women (Beaumont et al., 1975). Menstruation occurs, on average every 28–30 days in mature women. The entire menstrual cycle is divided into four phases: (1) follicular, lasting 10–14 days; (2) luteal (during which ovulation occurs), lasting 8–10 days; (3) premenstrual, 4–6 days; and (4) menstrual, 3–7 days (which overlaps somewhat with the follicular phase) (Segal, 1974).

14. That is, mgm. (or mg.) per 100 ml. (or mg/dl) of blood. The range of the "normal" fasting blood-glucose level varies greatly between laboratories; normal fasting levels can range from 65–100+ mg/dl.

3

MECHANISMS

REVIEW OF PREVIOUS THEORIES

Current explanations of crime tend to emphasize causal factors of a fixed or long-standing nature. In addition, they tend to invoke relatively slow-acting mechanisms to account for criminal behavior. Witness the much discussed criminogenic mechanisms of "reaction formation" (Cohen, 1955), "differential association" (Sutherland & Cressey, 1974, pp. 75–77), "conditioned avoidance" (Trasler, 1962; Eysenck, 1978), becoming a member of a "violent subculture" (Wolfgang & Ferracuti, 1967), the workings of "capitalist economics" (Taylor et al., 1973), and the viscissitudes of "social power struggles" (Turk, 1969; Chambliss, 1976). Each theory postulates what might be described as a gradual molding of criminal tendencies in the individuals concerned.

Just as little is known about situational factors in crime, so too there have been few attempts to study short-term or rapidly acting mechanisms of crime. As Albert Cohen (1965) put it several years ago, we know little about "the social psychology of the deviant act." In reviewing the literature, certain common themes can be identified. They can be classified under three general headings: (a) situational crisis; (b) group psychology; and (c) cognitive disorganization.

Situational Crisis

Lemert (1953), Cressey (1953), and Camp (1967), in their studies of naive check forgery, embezzlement, and bank robbery, respectively, all found a variety of stresses to be present in the lives of individuals shortly before their involvement in crime. Camp (1967) suggested that bank robberies tend to be carried out by desperate men as a final attempt to resolve a major crisis. For Lemert (1953), naive check forgery resulted from stress-induced social isolation and an increasing sense of "psychological closure". Check forgery came to be seen by the individual as the only way of resolving his problem. Based on a study of 133 individuals charged with embezzlement, Cressey (1953) concluded that embezzlement was not due solely to financial difficulties since some offenders had experienced severe financial stress earlier in their lives without resorting to theft. Cressey's view was that embezzlement occurs when a financial problem is, first of all, unshareable, that is, cannot be communicated to others without shame or loss of face; second, when it can be resolved secretly, by embezzlement; and third, when violators can rationalize their conduct in such a way as to maintain their self-image as trusted persons, for example, by telling themselves that they will return the money later on.

Group Psychology

Most early and mid-adolescent delinquency is carried out in loosely structured groups consisting of between two and three members (Hood & Sparks, 1970), and appears to be common at temporary social gatherings such as sporting events, parades, and celebrations (e.g., Mann & Pearce, 1979; Vamplew, 1980). Most theories of antisocial behavior in crowds deal with specific types of crowds such as soccer game spectators.

According to LeBon (1895/1977, pp. 30–31), antisocial outbursts in crowds have three basic causes. First, "the individual forming part of a crowd acquires, solely from numerical considerations, a *sentiment of invincible power* which allows him to yield to instincts which, had he been alone, he would perforce have kept under restraint" (p. 30, emphasis added). Second, thoughts and actions in a crowd are quickly communicated and emulated as a result of *contagion,* a process said to be akin to hypnosis. "In a crowd every sentiment and act is contagious, and contagious to such a degree that an individual readily sacrifices his personal interest to the collective interest" (p. 30). The third, and "by far the most important" cause, is *suggestibility,* which refers to the heightened readiness of individuals in crowds to believe what they are told and to obey orders and instructions.

There are a number of difficulties with LeBon's account. First, the determinants he mentions are not independent of each other, for he notes

(p. 31) that contagion is an *effect* of suggestibility. Second, observation and hypothesis are confused in that LeBon lists suggestibility as a characteristic of crowd behavior yet at the same time proposes suggestibility as the main cause of crowd behavior. Third, even if suggestibility is a cause of crowd behavior, the question still remains as to what it is about being in a crowd that induces the state of heightened suggestibility.

Other theories on the mechanisms of group criminality are those of Matza (1964), Janis (1963), Wade (1970), and Short and Strodtbeck (1965). Both Matza and Janis, and to a lesser extent Wade, believe that individuals participate in delinquent acts without fully intending to do so; they become involved as a result of processes which they do not understand and over which they have little control. At the time of the act they rationalize their behavior in various ways, yet afterwards experience feelings of guilt, shame, and perplexity. Matza (1964) contends that most delinquents are not committed to delinquency in the sense of holding antisocial values; they are only marginally more committed to delinquency than nondelinquents and tend to "drift" into it rather than being propelled into it or actively searching for delinquent opportunities. Delinquency arises, he suggests, in a "situation of company," (i.e., a gathering of peers). During the course of conversation, or while exchanging banter, someone may jokingly propose doing something delinquent. As the discussion continues, a situation of "pluralistic ignorance" develops in which each person believes that the others are more committed to carrying out the act than they really are. Rationalizing their behavior in various ways, they perform the deed in a state of "shared misunderstanding." Five types of rationalizations or "techniques of neutralization" are described in the well-known paper by Sykes and Matza (1957). Individuals may deny responsibility for their actions, saying it was not their fault ("denial of responsibility"); they may deny causing harm to anyone ("denial of injury"); they may claim that the victim(s) deserved to be victimized ("denial of victim"); they may argue that the police and other officials are more corrupt than they are ("condemnation of the condemners"); finally, they may claim that the deed was done not out of a desire for personal gain or satisfaction, but out of loyalty to the group ("appeal to higher loyalties"). One difficulty with the theory is the problem of distinguishing in practice between true beliefs and rationalizations; that is, distinguishing between an individual who has accepted conventional norms yet uses "neutralizing" excuses from time to time after violating them, and one who has rejected conventional norms altogether (Ball, 1983). However, the evidence does seem to support Matza's view that criminality is not necessarily related to the possession of values condoning or prescribing crime (Bolton, 1973; Ball-Rokeach, 1973; Erlanger, 1974; Curtis, 1978).

Janis (1963) touches on the subject of group delinquency in a valuable paper on combat motivation. Recalling earlier work by Redl and Wineman (1960), Janis observes that many of the criminal acts carried out by individuals in groups are made possible by a variety of rationalizations which may or may not diminish a simultaneous sense of guilt. Certain cultural norms may also be operative in facilitating deviant acts, both in adolescent groups and combat troops. These norms include: a tough-minded attitude, involving a taboo on emotionality; the creation of an illusory belief in the ethical validity of the act, that is, "it must be okay if everyone's doing it"; and an illusory sense of power, that is, "we're all in this together, so they can't punish us."

Wade (1970) argues that acts of collective vandalism mostly result from situational pressures and opportunities and are seldom planned in advance. By participating in the acts, membership in the group is assured and social status is enhanced. Wade identifies five stages in the typical act of vandalism.

Stage 1. Waiting for Something to Turn Up. Often, vandalism begins as a form of play or competition.

Stage 2. Removal of Uncertainty. Exploratory "gestures" are made in the form of overt acts.

Stage 3. Mutual Conversion. Challenges are offered (i.e., "dares"), reinforced by derogatory epithets (e.g., "chicken") which threaten the individual's self-image, and mass participation ensues.

Stage 4. Joint Elaboration of the Act. One act of vandalism may lead to other acts. Three factors contribute to this stage of the process: a state of mutual excitation, a temporary loss of personal identity, and a feeling of security in the mass.

Stage 5. Aftermath and Retrospect. Destructive acts are retrospectively evaluated by participants in terms of the motive(s) which led them to participate.

Wade's scheme may be useful as a description of the situational development of group vandalism, but it does not provide a causal explanation of such acts.[1]

Cognitive Disorganization

The association between life stress and antisocial behavior has also been explained in terms of alterations in cognitive functioning. Some interesting work has been done by R. D. Laing (1961) on the phenomenology of violence. Particularly insightful is his analysis of the murder of the old pawnbroker by Raskolnikov in Dostoyevsky's novel *Crime and Punishment*. Laing's essay on it can be considered an attempt to develop a model of transient criminality. It is, at the very least, an interesting discussion of the mental mechanisms underlying an admittedly fictional crime of murder by a previously noncriminal individual. Before the crime, there had been an accumulation of stressful life events: separation from home and family; a new life, with few friends, in a strange city; extreme financial hardship, which forces Raskolnikov to leave the university; and then, the receipt of a letter from his mother, alternately communicating intense love and intense reproachfulness, which informs him that his sister is about to marry — for his own and the family's sake — a rich but unscrupulous man whom she does not love. As Laing (1961, p. 169) describes the hidden message of the letter, "while being given implicit grounds for hatred, resentment, bitterness, or simply unhappiness, at the same time he is being told that it is inconceivable that he could be anything but happy. . . ." Raskolnikov lay down for a time, lost in thought, his "heart beating fast and his thoughts . . . in a whirl. At last he felt stifled and cramped in that yellow cubby-hole of his. . . . He grabbed his hat and went out, [and walked] as though he were in a hurry . . . but, as usual, he walked without noticing where he was going, muttering and even talking aloud to himself, to the astonishment of the passers-by, many of whom thought he was drunk" (Dostoyevsky, 1951, pp. 38 et seq., cited in Laing, 1961, pp. 167–68). Raskolnikov dearly loved his mother and sister, but at the same time he hated them intensely for their unwanted sacrifices. Something drastic had to be done to prevent the marriage. Raskolnikov lay down in a city park and had a vivid and terrible dream in which he is a young boy with his father, forced to witness the brutal beating and killing of a mare on a country road. Awakening in a cold sweat, Raskolnikov asks himself if he really is going to murder the pawnbroker, as he had tentatively planned. Laing suggests that Raskolnikov awoke in terror as though it were he who had been flogged to death, and then immediately recalls his intention to kill the old lady in a similar fashion — by hitting her on the head. Laing (1961, p. 55) writes:

> From these data ... it seems that Raskolnikov's experience of his "own" body is in terms of a physical identification with both the old nag and the old woman. ... He does not "imagine" himself to be an old woman. On the contrary, "in his imagination" he is as far as possible from the situation in which he participates in his dream or in his phantasy. While in his dream he is a little boy empathizing with an old nag, while in his phantasy his own body participates in the death of an old nag and old woman, he — as we learn later — is imagining himself to be "Napoleon." He has almost completely lost his own true possibilities, "lost" between (i) his imagination, where he thinks of himself as Napoleon, and (ii) his dream, where he is a little boy, and (iii) his phantasy, where he is a beaten mare or old woman about to die.

Knowing that he will kill the old woman the next day, he suddenly feels himself like a man sentenced to death; thus, on a fantasy level *he* is the victim, whereas in his imagination and in reality, he is to be the executioner. Laing is suggesting that shortly before and at the moment of the crime, the normal interrelations between fantasy, imagination, and reality became confused.

> Raskolnikov may have murdered the old woman "to be Napoleon", "for money", or just "for spite" as he later speculates, but we have before us, I think, the disclosure of a phantasy, a modality of action and experience, a *physical dream,* in which he is submerged and contained. Thus in bondage, he is quite estranged (with, however, transitory moments of emergence) from participating in the "real" world as a young man in his own person. While he is in this state, the genuine recognition of who the other is remains unavailable to him (Laing 1961, p. 56).

A somewhat similar argument is put forward by Milgram (1963, 1968) to explain the main result of his experiments on "obedience to authority"; namely, the fact that many subjects continued to administer progressively higher levels of electric shock in spite of their evident reluctance to do so. Milgram suggests that the subjects were placed under considerable strain because, while they wanted to comply with the experimenter's demands, they were reluctant to hurt their "fellow subject" in the adjoining room. As a result of the intense conflict, Milgram suggests that the subjects entered an altered state of consciousness which allowed them to cope with the situation. This was an altered state of thinking characterized, first, by a tendency to concentrate on the narrow technical performance of the task, thereby permitting the subjects to ignore the real meaning of the words they were uttering and the switches they were pulling. Second, it involved the belief that the experimenter, rather than the subject himself, was responsible for what was happening. Third, it involved a counter-anthropomorphic feeling of impersonality, inexorability, twilight, and unreality. In effect, a mental "bind" occurred between their politeness and desire to uphold their initial promise to participate in the experiment, and their dread of interpersonal confrontation with the experimenter.

To summarize, the mechanisms proposed to account for the relationship between precipitating factors and transient criminality include social isolation and psychological closure (where crime seems to be the only possible solution to the individual's problem), in the cases of embezzlement and naive check forgery (Cressey, Lemert). In the case of group and/or crowd criminality, feelings of invincible power, emotional contagion and suggestibility (LeBon); and various processes of rationalization (Janis) or techniques of neutralization (Sykes and Matza). And possibly in a wide variety of crimes, altered states of consciousness such as a fusion of fantasy, imagination, and reality (Laing), or feelings of impersonality and unreality (Milgram).

OVERVIEW OF THE MODEL

The model presented in this work builds on the theoretical views described above. It incorporates the ideas of increased emotional arousal, suggestibility, and altered states of consciousness, as well as the suggestion that rationalizations of various kinds are used by offenders. In addition, the model represents a synthesis of assumptions, concepts, and observations drawn from several disciplines, social as well as biological. The justification for these assumptions and concepts will be provided at different points in the ensuing discussion. The main points of the model are outlined below.

From the moment of conception, human beings have a basic biological tendency to seek sensory stimulation. This tendency is expressed in any type of movement, but especially those that entail contact with external objects or surfaces (including the subject's own body), since such movements provide greater amounts of stimulation. After birth, these movements are oriented toward "stimulating" sources such as lights, sounds, smell, and moving objects. Also from the very beginning, the organism's search for stimulation is constrained by innate and learned standards which guide it toward familiar types and familiar quantities of stimulation, and away from unfamiliar stimuli. These internal standards orient the organism's stimulation-seeking behavior toward the familiar and are at the same time reinforced and preserved by the subsequent reception (or "feedback") of familiar stimuli. Thus there is a basic tendency to approach familiar stimuli and contact with such stimuli serves to preserve the internal standards of familiarity (see Figure 3.1).

As the developing infant becomes increasingly motile it acquires a cognitive map of the key individuals, objects, and places in its environment, as well as abstract concepts such as beliefs, values, and normative standards. It is assumed that the cognitive representations of

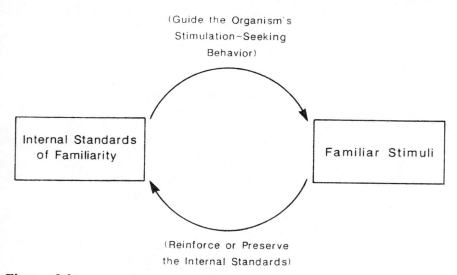

Figure 3.1
Internal standards of familiarity guide the organism's search for stimulation, while contact with familiar stimuli at the same time reinforces or preserves the internal standards.

Source: Compiled by author.

animate and inanimate objects consist of elemental stimulus units (viz., light, sound, touch, smell, taste), which have been combined into unique and complex patterns. ("Mother," for instance, represents a unique combination of elemental stimulus units for her child.) These acquired patterns of stimulation are stored in the brain and added to the core of basic internal standards, and together they constitute the individual's cognitive map. Just as a fundamental tendency exists to seek familiar *kinds*[2] and *amounts*[3] of stimuli, so the maturing organism continues to seek familiar *patterns* of stimulation and to avoid unfamiliar ones. The successful search for such patterns at once reinforces and gradually expands the organism's cognitive map of its environment, thereby widening the range of stimulus familiarity.

A more formal statement of the model now follows.

1. Individuals build cognitive maps of their interpersonal and physical environment.[4] A cognitive map is defined as an internalized representation of the sensorial environment.[5] Starting with a core of familiar kinds and quantities of stimuli, a cognitive map of people, objects, places, and abstractions is constructed, using elemental stimulus units as building blocks. Stored in the cognitive map are the person's own sense of self or identity, the sensory properties of people, places, and inanimate objects, as well as internalized expectancies about the conceptual environment in general.

2. Cognitive maps are ranked in terms of psychological salience. Human reactions to object-loss indicate that some aspects of the environment are psychologically more meaningful and important than other parts (Harvey & Schroeder, 1963; Stokols, 1978, pp. 39–42). These highly valued items typically consist of a few "significant others" (Mead, 1934) or "attachment objects" (Bowlby, 1969, 1973), as well as specific places (e.g., home, neighborhood, country), attitudes, and beliefs (e.g., "it is wrong to steal"; "it is dangerous to walk alone in the city at night"; "the Democratic Party cares about the working man," etc.).

3. Individuals attempt to maintain their cognitive maps. While human beings display a limited amount of curiosity and capacity for change, for the most part they resist change, being highly conservative in thought, word, and action. This "conservative impulse" (Marris, 1974) is expressed in a multitude of different ways; for instance, in the tendency of individuals to retain over many years, sometimes for their entire adult lives, the same living quarters or residential area, the same social contacts, the same possessions, and the same attitudes, beliefs, and

habits. Cognitive maps, then, tend to be maintained "in equilibrium," so to speak, just as physiological functions such as heart rate and blood pressure are maintained within narrow limits.

4. Individuals maintain their cognitive maps by seeking congruent feedback. This means that individuals seek out and remain close to the environmental objects (i.e., people, places, sources of ideological support) whose characteristics have been internalized in their cognitive maps. Being in, or with, "the familiar," serves to reinforce the cognitive map. This tendency is manifested particularly strongly in situations of alarm or danger — or, in general, "incongruity" — where individuals will hold on and cling ever more determinedly to the familiar world. For ample demonstration of this principle, consider, for instance, the tendency of individuals to remain close to home and loved ones when threatened by natural or manmade disasters (Baker & Chapman, 1962); the tendency to "search" for and even to emulate the missing object when bereaved (Bowlby, 1973; Marris, 1974); and the tendency to adhere ever more vigorously to one's beliefs when they are threatened by contradictory information.

Corollary. In the absence of congruent feedback, the cognitive map begins to disintegrate. This can occur as a result of prolonged separation from the objects that have been internalized in the cognitive map, and in the face of severe incongruity when coupled with unavailable or inaccessible "social supports" (i.e., attachment objects).

5. Environmental events perceived as incongruous with the cognitive map initiate a process designed to maintain or restore congruity. Events perceived by the individual, at some level of awareness, as unfamiliar or threatening (as "incongruous"), evoke a congruity-seeking response. This takes the form of a graded increase in the intensity of stimulation-seeking behavior, depending on the degree of incongruity, aimed at familiar kinds and patterns of stimulation. The response is at once general (or nonspecific), in the sense of being aimed at a multitude of available and familiar stimulus objects, and at the same time capable of being highly localized or specific, depending on the source of the incongruity. If the source of incongruity is an unfamiliar or threatening event in the environment, congruity-seeking behavior is directed at key attachment figures, places and objects; that is, movements are directed away from the unfamiliar and toward the familiar (cf., Bowlby, 1973; Salzen, 1978). If, on the other hand, the source of incongruity is an event in the individual's immediate and intimate social environment (e.g., a rebuff from one's

lover), congruity-seeking behavior takes the form of movement *toward* the attachment object — movement that may be of such intensity as to cause injury or even death (Mawson, 1980; Chapter 12, this volume).

We turn now to an overview of the mechanisms believed to be responsible for maintaining and restoring congruity.

6. According to the model, congruity is maintained by two groups of neurotransmitter systems in the brain. These systems, labeled S and P (standing for sympatheticlike and parasympatheticlike, respectively — Chapter 4), have a mutually inhibitory, balance-type relationship with each other, such that when one is active the other tends to be inhibited, and vice versa (cf., Domino & Davis, 1975). The S-system is responsible for progressive increases in the intensity of all movements, the P-system for progressive decreases in movement, eventuating in sleep. As noted earlier, a state of congruity exists when events in the environment are perceived by the individual as consistent with his or her cognitive map. This state is recognized in theory as one in which the S- and P-systems are in perfect balance, a situation that presumably occurs infrequently; more commonly, varying degrees of incongruity are encountered from moment to moment, reflected in proportional departures from S- and P-system balance. Furthermore, these environmentally determined fluctuations in neurotransmitter equilibrium take place against a background of endogenous rhythmic oscillations in the relative dominance of the two systems (cf., Luce, 1971; Levi, 1972).

7. Inhibition by sensory feedback: the proposed mechanism for restoring congruity. Mild to moderately severe degrees of incongruity lead to a proportional increase in S-system arousal. This in turn leads to a proportional increase in stimulation-seeking behavior, aimed at familiar stimuli. It is postulated that the sensory input so obtained is fed back into the central nervous system where it is compared with the cognitive map. If the stimulation is evaluated as congruous, the P-system is activated, and this system in turn inhibits the S-system, leading to a physiological status quo ante and a state of behavioral quiescence (Mawson, 1978a; Chapter 7, this volume).

TRANSIENT CRIMINALITY

The implications of the model for crime prevention are outlined first, followed by implications regarding the causation of crime.

The model proposes that legal and moral rules represent one aspect of the familiar psychosocial environment. These rules are internalized in the cognitive map just as other aspects of the familiar environment are internalized. It has been postulated that individuals attempt to preserve their cognitive maps by "seeking the familiar." Hence, conformity to social and legal norms is viewed as one expression of the tendency to seek the familiar and to remain within the territorial boundaries defined by the cognitive map (see Chapters 8 and 9, this volume).

With regard to crime causation, the model proposes that an individual is "at risk" of committing criminal or antisocial acts under the following conditions:

1. One or more life events occur (as described in Chapter 2) that are perceived as "incongruous" with the individual's cognitive map, leading to increased S-system arousal. Alternatively, often in conjunction with environmental stress, internal–physiological disturbances occur, also leading to an increase in S-system arousal.
2. Increased S-system arousal leads to a proportional increase in the intensity of stimulation-seeking behavior aimed at familiar kinds and patterns of stimulation (i.e., congruity).
3. Key attachment figures and other familiar objects and social supports, however, are inaccessible or unavailable.
4. As a result of the failure to obtain congruent sensory feedback, the individual's level of S-system arousal (which would otherwise be dampened by the congruity-induced increase in P-system arousal) increases further. This is postulated to have three interrelated effects:

    (a) Increasingly intense stimulation-seeking behavior, that is, all movements and directional activities increase in vigor.

    (b) A temporary, partial disintegration of the individual's cognitive map. This means that the more abstract, differentiated or "patterned" aspects of the cognitive map undergo a progressive dissolution. Internalized "boundaries" separating the class of familiar people, places, and objects, including the "self," from that of unfamiliar people, places, and objects, partially disappear.

    (c) An increase in susceptibility to social influence.
5. These changes increase the probability of transient criminality occurring in at least three ways (see Chapter 9):

    (a) Stimulation-seeking behavior may exceed socially acceptable levels of intensity and be publicly defined as antisocial or criminal.

(b) Intense stimulation-seeking behavior increases the speed and impulsivity of actions, thereby increasing the likelihood of performing actions with injurious and/or criminal consequences (e.g., negligent homicide).

(c) The combination of a disintegrating cognitive map, heightened suggestibility, and increased stimulation-seeking behavior serves to increase the probability that the individual will say or do things that are considered criminal — actions that under normal circumstances would be alien to the individual and completely inconsistent with his or her customary habits and life-style. Because of the loss of internalized moral and legal standards and territorial boundaries due to the disintegration of the cognitive map, and the continuing high level of S-system arousal, the individual's stimulation-seeking behavior is no longer guided by internalized norms. Under these conditions a considerable variety of criminal actions are possible, depending on the sources of stimulation immediately available (see Chapters 10–13). The key concepts and causal chains of the theory are shown in the flow chart below (see Figure 3.2).

The next four chapters describe the available evidence supporting the major links in the model. The remaining chapters focus on the explanation of transient criminality and review the evidence linking suggestibility, cognitive disturbances, and stimulation-seeking behavior with particular types of crime.

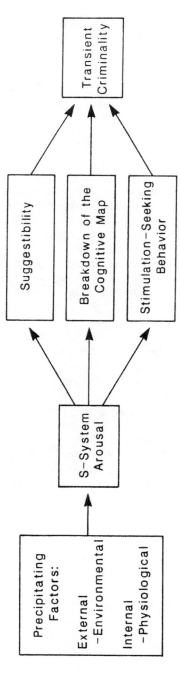

Figure 3.2
Flow chart of the model of transient criminality.

Source: Compiled by author.

63

NOTES

1. A very different hypothesis has been put forward by Short and Strodtbeck (1965) to explain the motivation of delinquent gang members to expose themselves to the risks of serious injuries resulting from gang fights. They propose that gang fights represent "a game played for small reward with little risk of loss, save that when the loss does occur it involves great costs" (p. 248). They suggest that the behavior is rational, not impulsive, and involves a careful balancing of potential risks; in particular, a rational balancing of the definite loss of status in the group (for not participating in a fight), against the more remote possibility of punishment by the larger society for the incident. Whether or not such behavior is properly viewed as transient criminality, however, is moot. Presumably, if the behavior is persistent and serious, it would not qualify as transient criminality.

2. That is, auditory, tactile, olfactory, etc.

3. That is, stimulation within a restricted range of intensity.

4. It should be noted that the teleological aspects of the model (e.g., "individuals build cognitive maps . . .") are not necessarily recognizable at the level of intentions, reasons, and motives (D. M. MacKay, personal communication, 1973). The hypothetical processes referred to are biological and/or psychological, not conscious ones, although of course individuals can become conscious of them — assuming they exist — and intervene to attempt to alter them in various ways.

5. Although the concept of cognitive map was popularized by Tolman (1948) and recently elaborated by O'Keefe and Nadel (1978, 1979), it has appeared in the literature at different times under a variety of labels, e.g., "models" in the brain (Craik, 1943; MacKay, 1956, 1966; J. Z. Young, 1964; Bowlby, 1973), "perceptual schemata" (Piaget, 1952), "conceptual schemata" (Harvey & Schroeder, 1963), "neuronal model" (Sokolov, 1960), and "assumptive worlds" (Parkes, 1971). All of these concepts refer basically to the same idea of a memory store in the brain, coupled with a "comparator" device (MacKay, 1966; O'Keefe & Nadel, 1978; Rossler, 1981) for evaluating incoming stimuli as either consistent or inconsistent with the store.

4
STRESS AND S-SYSTEM AROUSAL

PSYCHOSOCIAL STRESS

It is suggested that environmental and physiological factors precipitate transient criminality by inducing a state of increased S-system arousal (see below). These environmental conditions, collectively termed *stressors,* are assumed to cause an increase in S-system arousal because they are appraised by the individual, at some level of awareness (Lazarus, 1966), as novel, extreme, unpredictable, threatening, noxious, or, more generally, as *incongruous* with his or her cognitive map, that is, with stored memories and expectancies.[1] The perception of incongruity does not necessarily imply a pleasant or unpleasant emotional state. The stimulus could evoke amusement, joy, grief, anger, fear, or any one of a number of states. Incongruity is associated more with the *intensity* of emotion than with the type or *quality* of emotion. However, negatively appraised events appear to have more deleterious consequences for health and social behavior than positively evaluated events (Johnson & Sarason, 1979a; Lloyd, 1980). Although incongruity is difficult to measure independently of its presumed effect on arousal level, the concept is consistent with a number of other theoretical formulations based on the idea of a mismatch between stimulus inputs and previous experience (e.g., MacKay, 1956, 1966; Berlyne, 1960; Hunt, 1963; Pribram, 1967; Stokols, 1979). Taken in conjunction with the testable features of the model, it offers a heuristic framework for organizing the data and suggesting avenues for research.

With regard to endogenous physiological factors, it is suggested that they also increase the level of S-system arousal — not because they are appraised as incongruous, but because they initiate processes that bypass cognitive mechanisms and activate physiological systems directly.

Before discussing the evidence linking environmental and physiological factors and S-system arousal, it is necessary to say more about the concepts of S- and P-system. These concepts refer to a coordinated pattern of biochemical and physiological activities throughout the body. Increased S-system arousal is associated with a general increase in behavioral activation, increased P-system arousal with a general inhibition or arrest of behavior. The labels S and P refer to the two divisions of the autonomic nervous system (A.N.S.). Although the systems are generally sympatheticlike and parasympatheticlike in terms of autonomic functioning, they are not coterminous with the A.N.S. and are conceived as having a broader overall function: that is, the S-system serves to increase sensory stimulation via behavioral activation, while the P-system serves to reduce it via behavioral inhibition.[2]

The term *S-system* refers to activity in certain areas of the brain, brain stem, and adrenal medulla, leading to the synthesis and release of the catecholamines (CAs), dopamine (DA), noradrenaline (NA), and adrenaline (A); and to an integrated pattern of sympatheticlike physiological and peripheral changes including heart rate and blood pressure increases, palmar sweating, pupillary dilatation, and a redistribution of blood from the skin and viscera to the skeletal musculature (Ganong, 1979, chap. 13). The term *P-system* refers to activity leading to the release of the brain neurotransmitters acetylcholine (ACh) and 5-hydroxytryptamine (5-HT, or serotonin); and parasympatheticlike changes such as heart rate and blood pressure decreases, pupillary constriction, and increased gastric activity, associated with increased blood flow to both skin and viscera (e.g., Kiely, 1974; Ellison, 1975).[3]

Few research findings are available as yet for evaluating the hypothesized relationship between environmental factors, S-system arousal, and criminality. One reason for the paucity of research on stressors and plasma catecholamines (CAs) has been the absence, until recently, of methods for measuring extremely small amounts of CAs in the peripheral circulation (Barchas, 1976); another is the fact that plasma levels of NA and A vary rapidly over a wide range in response to minor disturbances, including the procedures for collecting blood samples themselves (Lake et al., 1976).[4]

Several lines of evidence suggest an association between acute environmental stress and S-system arousal. Walter B. Cannon (1929) showed that the adrenal medulla responded immediately to various emergency situations (the well-known "fight or flight" reaction). More recent work indicates that increases in S-system arousal — as measured by CAs in plasma and urine — occur in response to a wide variety of environmental changes (Frankenhaeuser, 1976, 1979; Barchas & Barchas, 1977; Lynch, 1977, pp. 96–100; Cox, 1979, pp. 61–65; Eliasson, 1984). The types of situations that have been studied in relation to CA activation include: preparing to enter a boxing match; riding in a centrifuge; acrobatic, supersonic, and space flights; participation in medical and scholastic examinations; dental treatment, and admission to a hospital. Using urinary measures of adrenaline and noradrenaline, Frankenhaeuser (1976) has found that the level of adrenaline is low during the night, doubles during the day, and increases three or four times above the resting level under conditions ranging from mild to moderately stressful (see Figure 4.1). Conditions of both understimulation and overstimulation lead to increases in CA secretion; generally, the more familiar the situation the lower the output of CAs. A wide range of emotional states and environmental conditions are associated with an increased secretion of CAs. Intense emotions, whatever their particular quality (joy, anger, fear, etc.), are accompanied by increased secretions of both A and NA.

Apart from CAs and their metabolites in urine and plasma, there is evidence that a wide variety of environmental changes are associated with increases in S-system arousal in man and other species, as measured by autonomic indicators such as heart rate, blood pressure, and skin conductance (e.g., Lader & Marks, 1971; Venables & Christie, 1975). With regard to the environmental factors mentioned in Chapter 2 in relation to criminality (i.e., separation from attachment figures, and crowding), there is evidence that both separation and crowding are associated with brief increases in S-system arousal. Experiences related to separation or perceived abandonment are highly distressing to individuals of many species (Rutter, 1972). Observations on infant monkeys shortly after separation from the mother reveal marked increases in heart rate and body temperature in conjunction with intense behavioral agitation (Reite et al., 1978; Mineka & Suomi, 1978). Lynch (1977) reviewed several studies of humans indicating that pronounced increases in heart rate and blood pressure occur when individuals are asked to recall traumatic experiences, especially those involving the loss of a significant person. Lynch also notes that coronary care patients often feel lonely, depressed, and abandoned after being transferred to a new ward, since it

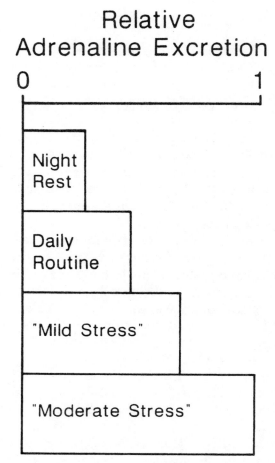

Figure 4.1
Levels of adrenaline excretion during "the stress of everyday life"

Note: The level is low during night rest, doubles during daily routine activities, and rises 3–5 times above the resting level under conditions of "mild" to "moderate" stress.

Source: Frankenhaeuser (1976, p. 175). Reprinted with permission.

entails losing a close personal tie with a particular physician or nurse, and that such losses may result in severe cardiovascular abnormalities and complications.

With regard to the topic of separation from the familiar, short periods of social isolation or sensory deprivation are associated with increases in S-system arousal. The arousal effect depends on the subject's age, his or her interpretation of the situation, the length of time in isolation, and the nature of the isolation procedure itself (Walters & Parke, 1964). Zuckerman and associates (1964) found that at least three hours of social isolation were needed before any arousal effect was observed in normal subjects, and that deprivation of two sensory modalities (e.g., silence and darkness) was more arousing than restriction in only one modality (e.g., darkness with sound, or silence with light), as indicated by electrodermal measures. In some studies of sensory deprivation, subjects have experienced severe panic and refused to participate further, giving unbearable anxiety, tension, or panic attacks as their reason for leaving (e.g., Smith & Lewty, 1959).

Regarding the factor of crowding,[5] it has been found that prison inmates living in crowded dormitory conditions tend to have higher levels of palmar sweating (Paulus et al., 1975) and blood pressure (D'Atri & Ostfeld, 1975; Paulus et al., 1978) than prisoners living in one- or two-man units. Using undergraduate volunteers as subjects in an experiment on crowding, Evans (1979) found that crowded subjects had significantly higher pulse rates and blood pressures, exhibited more stereotyped behavior and defensive postures, and expressed greater discomfort and hostility than the controls. Elaborating on earlier studies (e.g., Aiello et al., 1975) indicating that crowding increases electrodermal activity, Aiello and associates (1979) studied the effects of short-term crowding on skin conductance in fourth-, eighth-, and eleventh-grade children. Their results showed that brief periods of close physical proximity were associated with significant increases in skin conductance levels in every age group, with males in particular displaying greater increases in skin conductance level than females. Children in the high spatial-density conditions also reported feeling more tense, annoyed, uncomfortable, and frustrated than those in the low density conditions.

These results support the view that crowding can lead to increases in S-system arousal. According to the model, increases in S-system arousal are directly proportional to the degree of incongruity generated by particular situations of crowding. A given crowd situation can be more or less incongruous in a number of different ways, for example, by the mere presence of strangers, the location and circumstances of the crowding situation, and the physical distances between individuals in the group. In view of implicit social norms governing interpersonal distance (Hall, 1959), one would expect perceived incongruity to vary as a function of distance. Most of the crowd situations relating to criminality discussed in Chapter 2 involved groups of comparative strangers, as did the experimental studies on crowding referred to above.

In summary, many of the environmental factors associated with criminality, such as separation, loss, and crowding, are associated with increases in S-system arousal.

PHYSIOLOGICAL FACTORS

Alcohol. Despite considerable research, little is known about either the causes or the physiological effects of alcohol consumption. To quote Myers (1978, p. 126), the "act of drinking, intoxication, tolerance, and physical dependence on alcohol are all due to unknown mechanisms in the central nervous system." A commonly held view is that psychosocial stress increases both the level of arousal and the likelihood of alcohol consumption, and that alcohol serves to reduce the level of arousal and associated feelings such as anxiety (Cappell, 1975). Supporting the view that alcohol intake is associated with increased S-system arousal, followed by a temporary calming effect, (a) anger-hostility is the mood state most closely associated with the craving for alcohol (Matthew, 1979); (b) hypomania is a frequent manifestation in chronic alcoholics in the two-week period following detoxification; (c) hypomania is associated with increased excretion of a major metabolite of noradrenaline; and (d) lithium, which activates the serotonergic (P-) system, is effective in preventing recurrences of alcoholism (Lubman et al., 1983).

Although there is evidence that alcohol reduces anxiety and emotional reactivity to stress (see Pohorecky, 1981, for a comprehensive review), alcohol can also increase arousal and anxiety under certain conditions (Allman et al., 1972). Small-to-moderate amounts of alcohol tend to increase brain noradrenaline turnover in rodents (e.g., Carlsson &

Lindquist, 1973; Myers, 1978), suggesting an increase in S-system arousal. Similarly, the increased *behavioral* excitation (Carlsson et al., 1972) and euphoria (Ahlenius et al., 1973) seen in man after moderate doses of alcohol may be mediated by the release of catecholamines.

Alcohol ingestion leads initially (and characterically) to increases in peripheral vasodilation ("flushing"), muscle tension, rapid eye movement, finger pulse volume, and increased heart rate (Doctor et al., 1966). Whether alcohol increases or decreases physiological and behavioral arousal may depend on several factors including, first, the *pre-existing level of arousal*. If arousal is initially high, alcohol may have a calming effect; conversely, if arousal is initially low, alcohol may have an arousing effect. Wayner (1973) has shown that the basal activity of single neurons in the hypothalamus affects their subsequent response to alcohol. If neuronal activity was high, alcohol led to a decrease in activity; if activity was low, the same dose of alcohol produced an increase in firing rate. A second factor may be the *social context* in which drinking occurs. Schachter and Singer (1962) have shown that the quality of emotion produced by a state of arousal is critically dependent on the cues available in the social setting.[6] In a classic series of experiments, they showed that individuals tend to label their emotional state according to their appraisal of the immediate social environment; thus, if other people are behaving angrily, they too tend to become angry, whereas if others appear to be happy or euphoric, the same emotion tends to be experienced by the subjects. A third determining factor is the *duration of drinking*. Studies of alcoholics have shown that alcohol consumption initially produces a decrease in anxiety and a general feeling of well-being, while prolonged drinking leads to a steady increase in depression, anxiety, and irritability (e.g., Tamerin & Mendelson, 1969; Kissin, 1974; Pohorecky, 1981, for review). A fourth factor is the *amount of alcohol consumed*. Taylor and Gammon (1975) found that high doses of alcohol increased aggressiveness whereas low doses tended to reduce it. Finally, *expectancy* or "set" is another determining factor. For instance, Lang and his associates (1975) reported that male social drinkers who were led to believe they had consumed alcohol were significantly more aggressive than those who thought they had consumed a nonalcoholic drink, regardless of the actual alcohol content of the beverages.

A review of the effect of alcohol on aggression (Graham, 1980) mentioned at least 14 different "theories of intoxicated aggression."

However, none included CA (i.e., S-system) arousal, and physiological mechanisms received only a brief comment. Taken together, the above findings suggest that the association between alcohol consumption and aggression may be mediated more by extraneous factors than by any intrinsic property (or properties) of alcohol itself. In his review of the subject of drug dependence as a whole, Falk (1983) similarly concluded that the circumstances of drinking or consuming other drugs produce greater changes in behavior than do the chemical properties of alcohol or drugs themselves.

The Premenstrual Tension Syndrome. There are indications that the premenstrual phase of the cycle is also associated with increased S-system arousal; however, few consistent findings have emerged to date. Classically, the mental disorders of the premenstruum were referred to as "sympathetic-like" (Henley, 1928), and many studies have shown that acute anxiety is associated with increased S.N.S. arousal (Lader & Wing, 1966; Lader, 1975a). A review of autonomic functioning during the premenstruum concluded that the findings, on balance, point to "an increase in overall level of autonomic arousal" (Asso, 1978, p. 51), together with sudden intense swings in arousal (Asso, 1978, p. 53). With regard to psychological arousal, emotional *fluctuations* rather than enduring mood states have been suggested as characterizing the premenstruum.

Most studies have focused on hormonal changes during the menstrual cycle, but there is little consensus on the nature of these changes (Steiner & Carroll, 1977). The ovarian hormone progesterone rises following ovulation and falls immediately before the onset of menstruation; that is, during the premenstruum (Johansson, 1969), and progesterone seems to be inversely related to certain measures of autonomic arousal (Mackinnon & Harrison, 1961; Little et al., 1974). Several authors have suggested that premenstrual symptoms are associated with the decline in progesterone level (Hamburg et al., 1968; Lloyd & Weiss, 1972; Backstrom & Carstenen, 1974), since administration of progesterone relieves premenstrual tension and irritability (Dalton, 1964). The brain neurotransmitters DA and/or NA are believed to regulate the secretion of pituitary hormones, including luteinizing hormone and follicle-stimulating hormone, and these in turn regulate the ovarian hormones estrogen and progesterone (Zacur et al., 1978). Alterations in plasma catecholamines (CAs) and their metabolic enzymes would therefore be expected to coincide with endocrine changes during the menstrual cycle. While some investigators have observed a *midcycle* increase in plasma NA concentrations and dopamine-ß-hydroxylase activity, the enzyme that converts DA to NA, others have failed to observe a consistent association between these variables (Zacur et al., 1978).

Monoamine oxidase (MAO) is a major enzyme responsible for converting CAs into their metabolic products, and it is thought that increased MAO activity reflects decreased CA activity, and vice versa. Several studies have examined the relationship between MAO activity and phases of the menstrual cycle. Belmaker and associates (1974) found that the lowest level of MAO activity in blood platelets occurred premenstrually. There was, however, no significant relationship between MAO activity and mood.[7] Decreased MAO activity during the premenstruum was reported in two other studies (Gilmore et al., 1971; Redmond et al., 1975), again supporting the hypothesis that the premenstruum is associated with increased S-system arousal. However, a study of women suffering from premenstrual symptoms failed to find an association between reduced platelet MAO levels and the premenstruum (Feine et al., 1977).

A major difficulty in studying the physiological correlates of the premenstruum is that its features are protean, ill-defined, and often contradictory. This has prompted the suggestion that there are several distinct emotional syndromes within the premenstruum; namely, depression, elation, and hostile irritability (Steiner & Carroll, 1977). Hence, particular emotions may be associated with specific hormonal profiles. If this is the case, more detailed studies should be undertaken of emotions and hormones within the premenstruum rather than continuing the attempt to link the premenstruum with a distinct pattern of physiological changes. One difficulty with the idea of distinct subtypes within the overall syndrome is that most women experience a combination of emotional symptoms (Steiner & Carroll, 1977). Second, as noted earlier, there is no evidence that specific emotions are associated with specific hormonal patterns (Frankenhaeuser, 1975a). Third, as noted in Chapter 2, there is no association between criminal behavior during the premenstruum and dysphoric emotions (d'Orban & Dalton, 1980). To conclude, it is perhaps not the quality of emotion but the intensity of emotion that is associated with increased S-system arousal and criminality during the premenstruum.

Hypoglycemia. It is well established that hypoglycemia is a potent stimulus to sympathetic discharge and increased secretion of catecholamines, particularly adrenaline; sympathetic overactivity probably explains the tremors, palpitations, and nervousness of hypoglycemia (Ganong, 1979, p. 267).

The way in which hypoglycemia leads to increases in S-system arousal is summarized by Bonnet and Pfeiffer (1978, p. 196):

> Shortly after a meal, glucose absorbed in the small intestine enters the bloodstream. Cells in the hypothalamus of the brain detect the raised blood sugar and signal the pancreas to release insulin. The hormone insulin promotes rapid absorption of glucose from the blood by the body cells and facilitates the transport of glucose into the liver cells; the liver converts glucose into glycogen for storage. *When the blood sugar drops enough, the hypothalamus signals the pituitary to stimulate the adrenal gland to release adrenaline and the glucocorticoid hormones which antagonize insulin activity.* These hormones also stimulate the pancreas to secrete glucagon, which converts glycogen to glucose in the liver. The glucose is then released into the bloodstream (emphasis added).

The mechanisms proposed to explain hypoglycemia-induced crime (especially violent crime) have centered on neurophysiological rather than neurochemical processes. It has been suggested that hypoglycemia results in abnormal (often epileptiform) electroencephalographic (EEG) rhythms, and these in turn result in disturbances of consciousness (Wilder, 1947; Bovill, 1973). Others have related these abnormal EEG rhythms to a possible malfunction of the "limbic system" of the brain, that is, the septum-hippocampus-amygdala complex (Elliot, 1978; Monroe, 1978).[8]

The increase in adrenal catecholamines following hypoglycemia was first reported by Cannon and his associates (1924), and the response is now believed to be triggered by adrenoreceptors in the brain. Since increased CA arousal is associated with eating behavior (Gugten & Slangen, 1977) and aggression (Reis, 1972; Goldman, 1977; Yaryura-Tobias, 1978), both of which have been linked to hypoglycemia, increased CA arousal may act as a biochemical mediator between hypoglycemia and criminality. On the other hand, severe hypoglycemia is marked by sweating, facial flushing, and muscular weakness rather than by agitation and violence, and no correlation has been found between glucose levels and the intensity of aggression in violent offenders

(Yaryura-Tobias & Neziroglu, 1975, p. 186). Moreover, according to Elliott (1978, p. 178), "rage does not appear during the hypoglycemia induced by a five-hour glucose tolerance test, even in people who suffer from hypoglycemic anger outside the laboratory." This may indicate the importance of social setting as a key factor related to outbursts of violence in hypoglycemic individuals, as noted by Elliott. Possibly, to, in a hypoglycemic state, individuals may be prone to oscillate rapidly from fatigue to states of high sympathetic and behavioral arousal, and this could explain the almost simultaneous presence of contradictory symptoms. Clearly, the association between hypoglycemia and criminality remains enigmatic (see *Nutrition Reviews,* Supplement, May 1986, for critiques of the diet-crime literature).

Arousal and the Criminal

Research on the association between physiological states and criminality has so far dealt almost exclusively with persistent criminals, especially those diagnosed as psychopathic (see e.g., Hare, 1970; Trasler, 1973; Mawson, 1977; Mawson & Mawson, 1977; Mednick & Christiansen, 1977; Hare & Schalling, 1978; Elliott, 1978; Monroe, 1978; Siddle & Trasler, 1981; Mednick et al., 1982; McCord, 1983). One of many difficulties in this area of research has been continuing confusion about the definition of, and hence criteria for diagnosing, psychopathy, although there is at least partial agreement that psychopathy is defined by persistent tendencies toward aggressiveness, impulsivity, egocentricity, irresponsibility, shallow affect, and guiltlessness (Hare, 1970; McCord, 1983). Despite the use of varying measures, many studies have reported evidence suggesting that psychopathy is associated with low levels of autonomic and cortical arousal compared to nonpsychopaths, and lower degrees of arousability. These measures have included skin conductance, cardiovascular and electroencephalographic responses (Hare, 1970; Mednick & Christiansen, 1977; Mednick et al., 1982; Wadsworth, 1976), and, more recently, catecholamines (Lidberg et al., 1978; Schalling et al., 1983) and indoleamines (Brown et al., 1982).

This low level of arousal is thought to lead to criminal behavior (and related forms of sensation-seeking activity), as a means of raising the level of arousal (Hare, 1970; Eysenck, 1978). According to another popular theory, the characteristics of low arousal and arousability, while not leading directly to crime, are associated with crime insofar as they signal an inability to inhibit aggressive or other antisocial behaviors following punishment (Mednick, 1977, pp. 3–4).

Evidence for the hypothesis of low arousal and arousability is, however, far from compelling. First, the data are inconsistent, some studies suggesting lower arousal levels in psychopaths (as already noted), some higher levels of arousal, and some no differences between psychopaths and controls (Mawson & Mawson, 1977; Syndulko, 1978; Blackburn, 1978; Zuckerman, 1978a; Siddle & Trasler, 1981; McCord, 1983). Related findings, indicating an association between aggressive criminality and low plasma levels of 5-hydroxytryptamine, a metabolite of serotonin (Brown et al., 1982), suggest that criminality is associated with a high rather than a low level of S-system arousal.[9]

In attempting to make sense of these findings it is important to recognize that the existing literature fails to establish either that the psychopath's arousal level is chronically or characteristically lower than that of the nonpsychopath or, more crucially, that a low level of arousal leads to or accompanies actual criminal behavior. Most studies reporting lower levels of arousal and arousability in psychopaths have been carried out in situations that required the subject to sit or lie quietly in a darkened room for periods of up to an hour or more. Measures of peripheral autonomic activity obtained under such conditions are not necessarily representative of the subject's overall level of arousal; they could reflect merely the subject's response to the testing situation. The reaction of most people in such situations is, in fact, to become drowsy or fall asleep; and what the psychopath appears to do is to fall asleep faster than the nonpsychopath. However, this does not mean that the psychopath is generally more drowsy than the nonpsychopath or prone to fall asleep in *all* situations. Clinical experience (and indeed the very meaning of the diagnosis of psychopathy) suggests that in other situations the psychopath is more impulsive, reckless, and aggressive — or, in general, more readily aroused to action than the nonpsychopath.

Such considerations led us, several years ago, to propose the hypothesis that what distinguishes the psychopath from the nonpsychopath, physiologically, is not a higher or lower mean level of arousal but a greater degree of variability in arousal level and arousability (Mawson & Mawson, 1977). It was proposed that, compared to controls, psychopaths oscillate between very high and very low levels of arousal (i.e., show a higher amplitude of both S- and P-system arousal), and tend to oscillate more rapidly, depending on prevailing environmental conditions. Thus, in situations perceived by the psychopath as stressful, he would be expected to become more aroused, and more quickly aroused physiologically and behaviorally, than controls; conversely, in restful or calming situations, he would be expected to enter a deeper level of sleep and fall asleep faster than his nonpsychopathic counterpart.

Psychopaths are often described as manifesting brain abnormalities in that many studies indicate a high proportion of delta (1–3 Hz) or theta (4–7 Hz) waves in the electroencephalogram (EEG). However, these patterns are characteristic of normal sleep, and EEG studies rarely report on or control for behavioral state. Therefore, rather than pointing to any abnormality of the brain, the presence of delta and theta waves may indicate merely that the psychopath has fallen asleep during the testing situation (Mawson & Mawson, 1977; Syndulko, 1978, also alludes to this possibility).

To resolve the debate about the psychophysiology of psychopaths and other persistent criminals, one or more aspects of arousal should be studied over a much longer time period, for example, 24 hours. This could be accomplished by telemetry or the use of 24-hour heart rate recorders (which can be attached to the subject and worn inconspicuously). Only in this way can a valid assessment be made of an individual's characteristic or mean level of arousal and the extent of autonomic variability.

Arousal and Crime

It has been suggested that the psychopath is characterized by larger and more rapid oscillations in S- and P-system arousal rather than by a chronically low level of arousal. Here it is also suggested that aggressive and other forms of criminal behavior occur during phases of high S-system arousal, or during the switch from P-system to S-system arousal. However, in view of the obvious difficulty of determining physiological activity while individuals are actually engaging in crime, little is known about the physiological correlates of criminal behavior itself. Studies on the physiology of aggression and motor behavior suggest that aggressive crimes, at least, are associated with a high overall level of S-system arousal. Also, there is evidence that a high level of S-system arousal accompanies the impulsive shoplifting that certain patients with anorexia nervosa are prone to engage in during episodes of overeating (see Chapter 10). In his book on *Burglary and Theft*, Macdonald (1980, pp. 113–18) notes that a high level of excitement is commonly associated with crimes against property. One burglar stated that, while opening a safe, he would sweat so much that his clothes would be wringing wet. A few burglars also, according to Macdonald, "report a sexual thrill at the time of the burglary or restoration of sexual potency following the crime" (p. 115). Some burglars masturbate at the scene of the crime. Heirens, a former university student who committed over 500 burglaries and 3 murders "had an erection at the sight of the window through which he was to enter [and] ejaculated as he went in" (p. 115).[10]

With regard to the question of whether the occasional crimes of normally law-abiding persons are committed in a state of high S-system arousal, the evidence is sparse indeed. Sources of indirect evidence include laboratory experiments on cheating and research on the correlates of low monoamine oxidase levels. In his review of experiments on "dishonesty," Farrington (1979b) points out that while several studies suggest that cheating is more likely to occur as perceived benefits outweigh perceived costs, additional factors are clearly involved. Just as "arousal" is associated with aggressive behavior (e.g., Zillman et al., 1972), so arousal may facilitate dishonesty. For instance, in an experiment by Dienstbier (1972), one group of students was given a placebo and told to expect a pounding heart (the "arousal" condition); a second group was also given a placebo and told that they would start yawning (the "control" condition). Students who had been told to expect a pounding heart cheated more than those in the "yawning" condition.

Berkowitz (1974) reviewed several studies indicating that the presence of a weapon is more likely to lead to aggression if those exposed to it are emotionally aroused. In states of high arousal, Berkowitz suggests, aggression tends to be impulsive or involuntary; when the individual is less aroused, aggression tends to be more planned and directed. In apparent contradiction of the arousal hypothesis, however, a study by Schachter (1971) showed that students who had been given the antipsychotic drug chlorpromazine (which reduces arousal), were *more* likely to cheat than those who had been given a placebo.

Other studies bearing on the S-system arousal hypothesis of transient criminality concern monoamine oxidase (MAO). Since MAO-inhibitory drugs lead to an accumulation of brain noradrenaline (Ganong, 1979, p. 162), low MAO levels are thought to be associated with increased S-system arousal. Platelet MAO (i.e., that located in the platelet mitochondria in blood cells) appears to reflect brain MAO activity, and the former is used — for ethical and practical reasons — as an index of brain MAO activity in experiments on human subjects.

In one such study, Buchsbaum and associates (1976) screened 375 college student volunteers for low platelet MAO activity. From this group, two smaller groups were selected representing the upper and lower 10 percent of the distribution of platelet MAO levels. Low-MAO males were found to have a significantly higher frequency of criminal convictions for nontraffic offenses. Official records also indicated that first-degree relatives of the low-MAO males had committed or attempted suicide eight times more frequently than first-degree relatives of the high-MAO sample of males. In related studies, low-MAO men reported significantly more difficulties with the police, more drug use, and more psychiatric contacts than high-MAO men (Schooler et al., 1978), and scored higher on three scales of the Minnesota Multiphasic Personality Inventory (MMPI): hypochondriasis, hysteria, and psychopathic deviate (Coursey et al., 1979).

Since MAO activity appears to be mainly under genetic control and is relatively stable within individuals (Murphy, 1973; Murphy et al., 1977), it has more of the characteristics of a *trait* than it does a temporary physiological *state* (cf., Redmond et al., 1979). Insofar, then, as MAO activity contributes to criminality (by way of the postulated increase in S-system arousal), it would be considered a predisposing rather than a precipitating factor. Possibly, decreased MAO activity is associated with a lowered threshold for criminal behavior in response, say, to environmental stress.

With regard to the question of whether S-system arousal contributes to transient criminality, the evidence suggests that within a "normal" (i.e., presumably noncriminal) population of males, those with reduced MAO activity are at greater risk of involvement in crime than men with high-MAO activity. As to the question of whether transient criminals have higher arousal levels than noncriminals, the appropriate studies have not yet been carried out. However, since both "self-report" data and official statistics indicate that criminality is largely the work of adolescent males (e.g., Gibbons, 1977), the hypothesis would predict that adolescents in general have higher arousal levels than all other ages groups, and that males have higher levels than females.

In support of this expectation, Karki (1956) studied urinary CA excretion in males and females ranging in age from one and a half to six years, 7–16, 17–29, 30–59, and 60–96 years. After controlling for body weight, significant differences between the age groups were found for noradrenaline (NA) but not for adrenaline (A). The highest output of NA occurred in the 7-to-16 year age group, after which NA values decreased progressively with age. No significant differences were observed in the study between males and females with regard to NA or A. However, a more recent investigation of 12-year-old boys and girls indicated that A and NA levels in boys increased more than those of the girls while watching an emotionally "neutral" movie or taking an arithmetic test, and resting levels of both A and NA were also generally higher in boys than in girls (Johansson, 1972). Another pertinent finding (Frankenhaeuser & Johansson, 1975, p. 121) is that 12-year-old males have higher excretion rates of A than adult males. Similar findings were reported by Young and his associates (1980) in a study of platelet MAO in 108 mentally disturbed adolescents and children ranging in age from 4–21 years, and 67 normal controls (age range, 2–52 years). Platelet MAO activity was greater in females than males in every group comprising the total population, as would be expected on the hypothesis that MAO activity is inversely related to S-system arousal; furthermore, a decrease in platelet MAO activity occurred in both sexes during puberty. Parallel developmental changes in MAO activity are also known to occur in brain tissue (Robinson et al., 1977). As Young and his colleagues (1980, p. 238) note: "The contribution of this trend to the expectable emotional upsets of adolescence or the onset of severe disorders, such as schizophrenia, remains to be explored."

Based on such findings, it is tempting to speculate that there is an underlying physiological basis for two of the best-documented epidemiological facts about criminal behavior: namely, the disproportionate involvement of young people, and especially young males, in crime. As predicted, adolescent males appear to have higher levels of S-system arousal (as measured by platelet MAO and urinary CA activity) than any other age or sex group.

However, the S-system arousal and crime hypothesis is contradicted by data on the association between adrenaline and measures of emotionality, which suggest an exactly opposite relationship to criminality than the one predicted. Thus, high levels of urinary adrenaline are associated with low scores on questionnaire-based measures of aggressiveness and anxiety (Frankenhaeuser et al., 1968). Another study (Johansson et al., 1973) of adrenaline excretion and teachers' ratings of emotional behavior in 12-year-old children indicated that higher excreters were less aggressive, less restless, more emotionally stable, and better able to concentrate. A similar but statistically nonsignificant trend in the same direction was found for girls. Frankenhaeuser and Johansson (1975, p. 123) conclude, "the overall picture derived from a number of studies suggests that, among normal healthy individuals, those who secrete relatively more adrenaline tend to be socially and emotionally better adjusted than those who secrete less adrenaline." Whether the same association holds between age-sex differences in emotionality and *noradrenaline,* however, is uncertain. Simultaneous assays of MAO activity and urinary (or plasma) adrenaline and noradrenaline in criminal populations, preferably taking a random series of measurements at different times of the day and night so as to determine the true extent of variability, may help to resolve these discrepancies.

NOTES

1. As used here, the term stressor differs from its customary meanings; namely, as an "aversive" stimulus, or as one that causes pain or distress. It is not an aversive or avoidance-producing stimulus since it can, in fact, lead to approach behavior. Nor is a stressor an experience that exclusively causes distress, since it can lead to either positive or negative emotions.

2. The S- and P-system may be anatomically and biochemically identical to the concepts of ergotropic and trophotropic systems described by Hess (1957) and Gellhorn (1967), but are not identical to them in function: the latter systems are defined in terms of the release and conservation of *energy,* respectively, whereas the S- and P-systems are conceived as functioning, respectively, to increase and decrease *sensory stimulation.*

3. The concepts of S- and P-system represent provisional, heuristic devices for integrating psychological, biochemical, physiological, and behavioral data. Although there is considerable evidence to indicate that the two systems interact in a reciprocal

inhibitory fashion, and the concept of neurotransmitter imbalance is useful in understanding many mental and physical disorders (Davis & Janowsky, 1974; Kiely, 1974; Pradhan, 1974; Anisman, 1975; Ellison, 1975; Roth & Bunney, 1976; Davis & Berger, 1978), more fine-grained analysis points to difficulties in the model. Many questions remain about the supposed continuity between brain and periphery in the internal and behavioral functions of the different neurotransmitters, their neuroanatomical substrates, and whether they are indeed separately identifiable systems (Bannister, 1971). There have also been suggestions that brain NA and DA function in opposite directions (Antelman & Caggiula, 1977) rather than in the same direction. With respect to the question of the specificity of hormonal responses to environmental stimuli, there are indications that some degree of stimulus specificity exists for plasma CAs. Thus, Dimsdale and Moss (1980) reported that physical exercise is associated with a threefold increase in plasma NA and a 50 percent increase in A, whereas the stress of public speaking leads to the virtually opposite reaction of a 50 percent increase in NA and a twofold increase in A. Also, there are several other brain neurotransmitters in addition to the four comprising the S- and P-systems. The recently discovered brain opiates (endorphins and enkephalins) are already known to have profound effects on emotion and behavior (Adler, 1980; Berger et al., 1982).

4. Sensitive and specific radio-enzymatic methods are now available for measuring minute amounts of circulating NA and A (e.g., Weise & Kopin, 1976).

5. Stokols (1972) distinguishes between *density* — an objective term defined on the basis of the number of people per unit area — and *crowding*, which refers to the subjective response to varying density levels. Stokols's concept of density has been criticized, however, for failing to distinguish between the number of individuals per unit area and *interpersonal proximity* (Worschel & Teddlie, 1976), the latter of which can vary greatly without any corresponding change in the former. Here, the term crowding refers to groups of three or more strangers or relatively unacquainted individuals interacting together or congregated within close physical proximity of each other.

6. Schachter and Singer's (1962) research findings are more relevant to the question of how alcohol leads to anger, given that it has already produced a high level of physiological arousal.

7. This would be consistent with d'Orban and Dalton's (1980) study, in which no association was found between premenstrual criminality and mood state.

8. For a brief description of the limbic system, see Shah and Roth (1974, pp. 111–15).

9. Serotonergic activity is inversely related to catecholamine activation (Ellison, 1975), that is, low 5-hydroxytryptamine levels imply high catecholamine levels.

10. There are, however, a number of reports (cited at various points in this book) suggesting that violent behavior may occur under conditions of extreme fatigue and/or lack of sleep. Whether behavioral fatigue can be equated with a low S-system arousal is uncertain. Extreme fatigue is sometimes associated, paradoxically, with mental alertness and an inability to sleep.

5

STRESS, AROUSAL, AND COGNITION

The literature reviewed in the preceding chapter suggests that the various factors associated with transient criminality appear to have the common effect of eliciting an increase in S-system arousal. Here it is further suggested that increased S-system arousal leads to three more or less simultaneous changes in cognition and behavior: (a) an increase in susceptibility to social influence; (b) a temporary, partial breakdown of the individual's cognitive map; and, (c) an increase in stimulation-seeking behavior, which will be discussed in Chapter 6 (see Figure 5.1).

SUSCEPTIBILITY TO SOCIAL INFLUENCE

Several studies have demonstrated a relationship between arousal and various measures of increased susceptibility to influence (Walters & Parke, 1964; Flanders, 1968). For instance, in Schachter and Singer's (1962) well-known study, several groups of subjects were given an injection of adrenaline, the effect of which is to produce an increase in heart rate and blood pressure. Some subjects were told to expect these reactions, others were told nothing. Each subject was then introduced to a confederate who pretended to be either jovial or angry, and the subject's behavior was observed. Subjects who received the injection of adrenaline but had not been told what reactions to expect were more likely to imitate the confederate's behavior than those who had been correctly informed of the drug's effects. Although the results were interpreted by the authors as supporting the view that specific emotional states are a joint product of increased arousal and cognitive cues available in the immediate situation, Walters and Parke (1964) have suggested an alternative interpretation: namely, that arousal increases a person's susceptibility to influence. Walters and Parke also cite evidence indicating that a state of physiological arousal intervenes between a wide range of stressful conditions (such as isolation, separation, and punishment) and indices of susceptibility to influence; furthermore, a state of increased arousal is common to many different emotions such as fear, anxiety, pain, hunger, and thirst. Thus Kimbrell and Blake (1958) found that subjects who had been made *thirsty* tended to imitate someone who broke a rule against drinking more readily than nonthirsty subjects, and Berkowitz and Geen (1966) found that *angry* subjects tended to imitate an aggressive model more readily than less angry subjects. Anxiety is also associated with increased arousal (Lader & Wing, 1966) and conformity to group pressure (Sherif & Harvey, 1952; Flanders, 1968).

Since social isolation and sensory restriction are associated with increases in S-system arousal (Berlyne, 1960; Zuckerman, 1979), these conditions would also be expected to produce a high degree of suggestibility. Several studies have shown this to be the case, although few controlled explicitly for arousal level (Suedfeld, 1969a, 1969b). Subjects in isolation tend, more than controls, to choose materials to listen to that they would ordinarily find tedious (Bexton et al., 1954); change their opinions on such matters as the existence of psychical

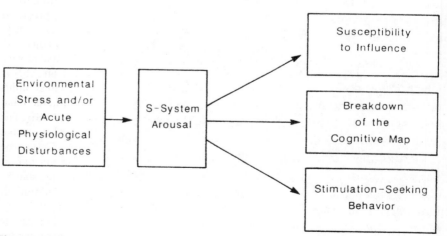

Figure 5.1
Diagram of the hypothesis that stress-induced changes in cognition and behavior are mediated by an increase in S-system arousal.

Source: Compiled by author.

phenomena (Scott et al., 1959); and accept the validity of propagandalike statements (Suedfeld, cited in Vernon, 1963).

Many observers, going back at least to LeBon (1895/1977), have noted that individuals become highly suggestible in crowds, and when anxious or afraid. The military writer Munson (1921, p. 175) observed that "the man who coughs at a lecture, drinks from his canteen, sings, criticizes, starts to eat his lunch, goes over the top, or runs to the rear induces others to follow his example unconsciously." Phillips (1943, p. 295) noted that a distinct set of features characterize individuals entering or preparing to enter battle, including "sensitiveness to the habits and customs of the group . . . subjection to the opinions of the herd . . . (and) . . . susceptibility to leadership." Marshall (1947, p. 145) observed that troops "will always let down at every opportunity . . . they will always bunch unless they are insistently told by voice to stop bunching. They will always run if they see others running and do not understand why."

William Sargant has noted the similarities between reactions to combat and those observed under a variety of noncombat conditions involving extreme arousal or excitement. Using a Pavlovian model to explain these observations, Sargant (1957, 1973) provides many examples of the increase in suggestibility that occurs when individuals are aroused. Under such conditions, the central nervous system becomes "transmarginally" stimulated, resulting in what Pavlov called a "rupture in higher nervous activity" (Sargant, 1973, p. 23). Three phases of *transmarginal inhibition* succeed each other: first, an equivalent phase, in which "all stimuli of whatever contrasting strength produce the same sort of final result" (p. 23); second, a *paradoxical* phase, where "weak and formerly ineffective stimuli can produce more marked responses than stronger stimuli" (p. 23); and third, an *ultraparadoxical* phase, in which "positive conditioned behavior and responses suddenly start to switch to negative ones, and negative ones to positive. The dog may then, for instance, be fond of the laboratory attendant he had previously hated, or attack the master he had previously loved" (pp. 23–24). According to Sargant, the mental state of human hysteria is similar to that of dogs in a state of transmarginal inhibition. He writes (p. 24):

This can cause greatly increased suggestibility (or sometimes equally great counter-suggestibility). The individual suddenly starts to take notice of happenings and influences around him, to which he would normally have paid little or no attention. In this "hypnoid" phase of brain activity, human beings become open to the uncritical adoption of thoughts and behavior patterns present in the environment, which would normally not have influenced them emotionally or intellectually.

In his earlier book, *Battle for the Mind,* Sargant (1957) wrote that the critical factor leading to heightened suggestibility and subsequent mental alterations is a nonspecific increase in physiological arousal. Discussing the relationship between the effects of John Wesley's evangelist preaching on his listeners and Pavlov's experiments on conditioning in dogs, Sargant (1957, pp. 86–87) writes:

(T)he effect of getting too emotionally involved either positively or negatively, with Wesley's preaching, was to increase the likelihood of being converted. It often happened, quite unexpectedly for the person concerned, that when he had been roused to the greatest pitch of indignation and anger by the proceedings, he suddenly broke down and accepted every belief demanded of him. . . . (A)nger as well as fear . . . can induce disturbances of brain function which make a person highly suggestible and reverse his conditioned behavior patterns or even wipe the "cortical slate" clean.

Sargant (1973) described similar reactions in hypnotized individuals and in certain drug-induced mental states, sexual rituals, "spirit possession," "mystical possession," and religion revivals. "A state of heightened suggestibility, intense sensitivity to one's surroundings and a readiness to obey commands — even when they go against the grain — is one of the most striking characteristics of hypnotized behavior. . . ."

The environmental conditions listed by Sargant as likely to produce heightened suggestibility include those cited earlier as precipitating factors in transient criminality, that is, various kinds of stress situations most obviously connected with states of high S-system arousal, as well as supposedly "calming" types of conditions such as fasting, meditation, social isolation, and sensory deprivation — factors which, at least under certain conditions or at certain times in the course of their duration (Mawson, 1979), lead to increases in S-system arousal.

COGNITIVE MAPS, S-SYSTEM AROUSAL, AND SOCIAL SUPPORTS

The term *cognitive map* refers to an internalized representation of an individual's physical and psychosocial environment. It is a memory store of perceptual experiences, hierarchically organized in terms of psychological salience, that is, emotional significance. For instance, at the top of the salience hierarchy are internalized representations of the attributes of significant others (e.g., mother, father, spouse, children, and other immediate relatives) as well as internalized representations of the self, including one's social roles and statuses. Beyond the "primary group" (Cooley, 1909, p. 23) and extended family, other important aspects of a person's psychosocial environment include: close friends; home — the "territorial core" (Porteus, 1976);[1] neighborhood, extending to a somewhat wider yet still familiar geographical area (Gould & White, 1974); and citizenship. Intimately connected with the above are certain beliefs and values, that is, concepts of normative behavior, moral and ethical standards, and subtle, taken for granted rules of behavior (Garfinkel, 1967) that are shared with key associates and family members, and which (in part) contribute to the individual's definition of self and locate him or her in social and geographical space. Closely allied with these beliefs about social norms, ranging all the way from folkways to laws (Sumner, 1906/1940), are subtle perceptual standards that are also in part culturally specific (McBurney & Collings, 1977, pp. 266–69). Finally, there are internalized expectancies regarding sensorial aspects of the environment, that is, expected quantities and types of physical sensation. This last group of expectancies is presumably acquired in early pre- and postnatal life, and provides a structural basis on which all subsequent qualitative patterns of stimuli are constructed, evaluated, and stored (see Figure 5.2).

A great deal of an individual's cognitive map, then, is shared in common with other members of his immediate neighborhood, wider society, culture, and perhaps species. Presumably, it is this large element of shared information which makes it possible for individuals of the same and even very divergent societies to communicate with each other. Yet there are other parts of an individual's cognitive map, possibly the most important ones from a psychological point of view, that are unique to him or her alone. But the types of objects that are internalized and endowed

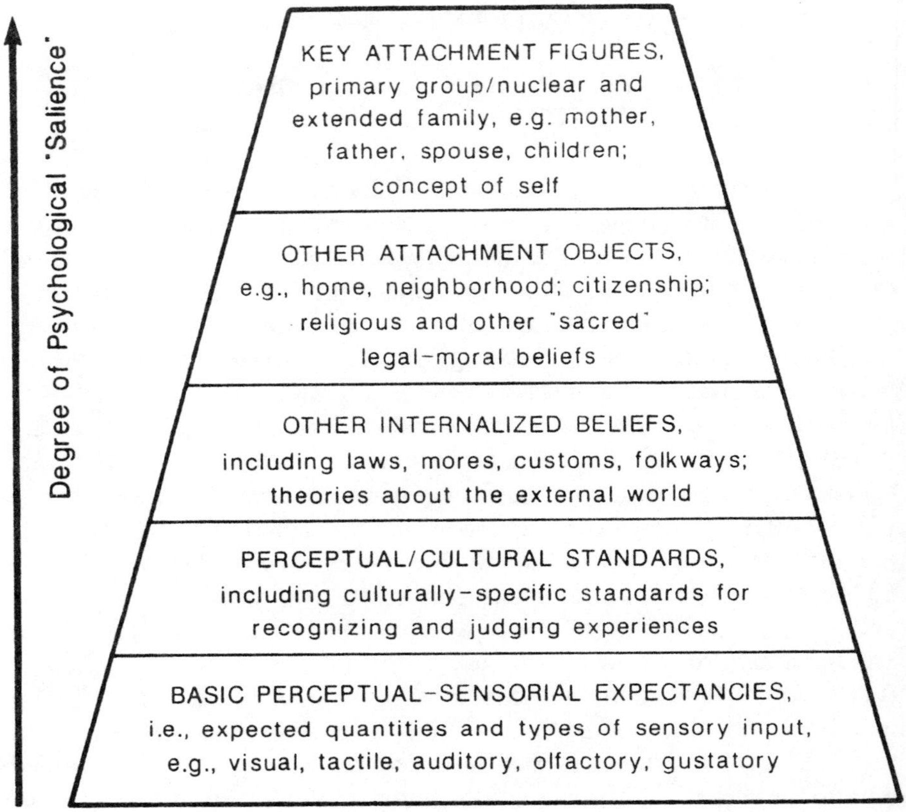

Figure 5.2
Schematic representation of an individual's cognitive map. Increasingly complex, abstract, and psychologically important types of internalized representations are assumed to be derived from combinations of "basic" sensorial experiences, as indicated by the wide base of the structure in relation to its apex.

Source: Compiled by author.

with special significance — notably attachment figures such as father, mother, spouse, and children — tend to be the same for almost all members of the species.

One of the assumptions of the model outlined in Chapter 3 was that *individuals try to maintain their cognitive maps*; in other words, they try to maintain the internalized representation of their environment. It is hypothesized that this is accomplished by seeking out and remaining close to the objects and persons whose sensory properties have been internalized. A child maintains an internalized map of his mother, for instance, by "keeping in touch" with her (both literally and figuratively). Preserving a cognitive map of a specific person is, of course, another way of talking about preserving a *social bond*. Although such bonds are psychologically of great importance, the individual is, in a sense, "bonded" to all aspects of his familiar environment to a greater or lesser degree. Fried (1963) has pointed out that persons who have "lost" their homes and been forced to relocate often show all signs and symptoms of grief. Thus, the idea of "preserving a cognitive map" means that there is a tendency to try to preserve "the familiar", in general, whether this be persons, places, inanimate objects, ideas, values or beliefs. To the extent that the individual tries to preserve the familiar by seeking it out, remaining in its presence, defending it, and grieving for its loss, he can be described as exhibiting an "attachment" for it.

In the course of remaining close to a specific "attachment figure" (a term popularized by Bowlby, 1969, 1973), the properties of the object are compared with those already stored in the cognitive map. If the former continue to "match" (or be congruous with) the latter, the cognitive map is successfully preserved.

It was also suggested in Chapter 3 that both psychological and physiological homeostasis are intimately connected with the preservation of cognitive maps. Thus perceived incongruity in the environment is hypothesized to activate the S-system, leading to congruity-seeking behavior. A state of "congruity," in which environmental conditions match the expectancies stored in the cognitive map, is hypothesized to activate the P-system (cholinergic and/or serotonergic pathways in the brain), leading to a generalized state of calm.

Assuming that some parts of the environment are psychologically more salient than other parts, and that congruity elicits a calming, P-system response, it follows that if the individual can maintain proximity with key attachment figures during times of environmental stress, his S-system arousal reaction to the incongruity will be considerably smaller in amplitude than if he is obliged to experience the incongruity in a state of social isolation, or with strangers. Thus, the congruous sensory feedback from familiar persons activates the P-system to such an extent that it effectively dampens or counterbalances the simultaneous S-system response to environmental incongruity. Presumably, this same mechanism is operative in relation to short-term as well as long-term environmental conditions.

A major inference to draw from the above is that possessing and maintaining familiar social relationships serves a vital protective function with regard to health and social behavior. According to the model, congruity-induced P-system activation has a generalized calming effect, and also serves to dampen the S-system response to environmental stress. Although the physiological aspects of the hypothesis await experimental evaluation, there is considerable evidence to support it with regard to behavioral and health implications (e.g., Lindheim & Syme, 1983, for review). First, it has long been known that married persons have lower mortality rates (e.g., Ortmeyer, 1974) and are at greatly reduced risk of a wide range of physical and psychosomatic disorders compared to single, widowed, or divorced persons of the same age (Lynch, 1977). Evidence in support of the protective function of intimate social bonds was obtained in a nine-year follow-up of a random sample of nearly 7,000 adults in Alameda County, California. By measuring the extent and quality of "social ties" directly, and controlling for a large number of possible confounding factors, Berkman and Syme (1979) showed that for every age group and for both sexes, people with many social contacts had the lowest mortality rates, while those with the fewest contacts had the highest mortality rates. The relative risks between these groups ranged from just under 2 to over 4.5. Of special interest was the finding that people who had many friends and relatives, but who were not married, had mortality rates equal to those who were married but who had fewer contacts with friends and relatives. It did not appear to be important whether a person's social contacts consisted of friends or relatives; it was in the absence of either that a significant increase in the risk of death occurred during the nine-year period of follow-up. Thus, social bonds with friends or relatives may be equivalent in terms of their protective effect.

Many studies have shown that the possession of intimate social and community ties promotes resistance to disease and moderates the harmful mental and physical effects of psychosocial stress (e.g., Cobb, 1976; Cobb & Jones, 1984; Cassel, 1976; Brown & Harris, 1978; Johnson & Sarason, 1979a; Henderson, 1980; Cohen & Syme, 1985).[2] Closely related to these types of studies on the long-term health consequences of social bonds (or their absence), are studies indicating that individuals tend to remain calm in dangerous or stressful situations if they are with familiar persons or in familiar surroundings. Conversely, distress and adverse physiological consequences are more likely to occur if the individual is alone, in the presence of strangers, or in unfamiliar surroundings (Rutter, 1972; Bowlby, 1973). This effect has been demonstrated in a number of different species (Bovard, 1959; Epley, 1974). To mention a few examples from the literature, it has been noted that civilian populations tend to remain calm and seldom "panic" during wartime bombing attacks and natural disasters (Janis, 1951; Baker & Chapman, 1962); the fighting effectiveness and morale of troops is high during combat when close proximity with buddies and familiar officers can be maintained (Marshall, 1947); and children are generally much less frightened on admission to a nursery or hospital if they are accompanied by a sibling or parent than if they are admitted alone (Bowlby, 1973).

The physiological effects of different social environments have been explored in a number of experiments on animals and humans (Kiritz & Moos, 1974).[3] In one well-known study, a small group of strangers undergoing the stress of having blood samples drawn showed a higher resultant plasma level of free fatty acids (an indicator of S-system arousal) than did comparable groups of friends undergoing the same experience (Back & Bogdonoff, 1964). Thus, returning to an earlier point, there is reason to believe that "crowd" conditions are more likely to be associated with increased S-system arousal if the individuals comprising the group are strangers. Such findings appear to be directly relevant to the problem of explaining the excitability of crowds and the link between crowd membership and transient criminality.

The possible role of social support or strong social ties in reducing the risk of criminal behavior is a largely unexplored field of research. Several studies have shown that the families involved in child and/or spouse abuse are socially isolated (Gelles, 1982). Fathers who neither belong to nor attend organized groups are also more likely to be violent toward their children than fathers who do belong to such groups (Straus et al., 1980). Other studies suggest that parolees with strong social ties are less likely to be reconvicted than those with weak ties (Monahan & Klassen, 1982, pp. 302–3).

BREAKDOWN OF THE COGNITIVE MAP

We have seen that a person's ability to remain calm under stress is crucially dependent on the strength and immediacy of his social ties; or, in terms of the model, on the extent to which his cognitive map is reaffirmed by "congruous input" in the form of close proximity and contact with key attachment figures, whether these be friends or relatives. It was suggested that congruity activates the P-system of the brain, which in turn dampens the individual's S-system response to psychosocial stress. By the same token, if the individual is alone, in the presence of strangers, or in other ways cut-off from the familiar (i.e., his "social supports"), he will obviously be less likely to achieve congruity in the event of experiencing additional psychosocial stress.[4] His S-system arousal response to incongruity will thus remain unchecked by the P-system, and be amplified accordingly.

Here it is suggested that one of the consequences of an intense amplification of S-system arousal is that the cognitive map itself begins to break down or disintegrate. This can occur either from extreme incongruity (e.g., from a combination of general adversity and the absence of social supports) or from internal-physiological disturbances. Very little research has been carried out on the association between life stress and alterations in cognitive functioning. Persons experiencing considerable stress would, however, be expected to display, "problems of attention, memory and performance, as well as perhaps other difficulties in the processing of information" (Johnson & Sarason, 1979b, p. 229). The relationship between (S-system) arousal and cognitive functioning is believed to take the form of an inverted U-shaped curve: very low *or* very high levels of arousal lead to a decline in intellectual functioning, while moderate levels improve it (Hebb, 1955; Cox, 1979, pp. 42–45).[5] The decline, deterioration, or breakdown in the cognitive map (and in cognitive functioning in general) at high levels of arousal, is postulated to include the following types of changes: a partial loss of identity (or weakening of "ego boundaries"), and a sense of being depersonalized; a decline in self-esteem; alterations in memory and perception; a partial loss of other abstract standards including cultural, ethical, moral, and legal rules; and a general decline in intellectual functioning, for example, loss of concentration, decline in problem-solving ability, etc.

Several lines of evidence suggest that increases in S-system arousal are associated with the above types of changes; that the types of criminogenic factors discussed in Chapter 2 result in a deterioration in cognitive functioning; and that the association is mediated by increases in S-system arousal. This evidence is reviewed under the headings of combat and natural disasters; isolation and sensory restriction; schizophrenia and the response to drugs; and physiological factors.

Combat and Natural Disasters

Such conditions are known to result in increased S-system arousal and numerous forms of cognitive disturbance. Extremely high levels of arousal produce a hypervigilant state, a marked lowering of efficiency in cognitive functioning, a narrowing of the field of attention (Easterbrook, 1959), and an increase in errors of judgment (Janis & Mann, 1977a, 1977b, for reviews). The state of acute fear is characterized by "temporary impairments in perception, cognition and motor control" (Janis & Leventhal, 1968, p. 1059), feelings of bewilderment, puzzlement, confusion (Diethelm, 1932), a temporary disorganization of thinking (Ranson, 1949), and the loss of a sense of personal identity (L'Etang, 1966). Under the constant influence of shell explosions, "a person develops a tension which gradually diminishes his self-confidence. . . . Increasing acuity of hearing and sensitiveness to noises, a bitter taste in the mouth and stomach, a feeling of pressure in the stomach and diarrhea characterize the further increase in tension. . . . Visual or auditory hallucinations may [appear] . . . in such a fear state" (Diethelm, 1934, pp. 1300–1). A study of individual reactions to community disasters disclosed that only about 12 to 25 percent of people responded appropriately (i.e., by fleeing) when informed that their apartment house was on fire or that a flash flood was imminent. An equal number exhibited confusion and paralyzing anxiety, and more than 75 percent made apparently aimless or irrelevant movements (Tyhurst, 1951).

Isolation and Sensory Restriction

These conditions are associated with increases in S-system arousal and with cognitive disturbances of many different kinds. The following changes are frequently mentioned by subjects undergoing experimental sensory restriction: feelings of confusion, apprehension, disorganization, dizziness; disturbances of body image, including depersonalization; perceptual disturbances, including reduced visual-motor coordination, an increase in apparent movement phenomena, a loss of figural after effects, difficulties in focusing, and fluctuations in the curvature of lines and surfaces (Kubzansky, 1961; Brownfield, 1965; Grassian, 1983, for a review). These effects have been described as reflecting a breakdown of internal norms (Kubzansky, 1961); or, in other words, a weakening of standards against which to evaluate perceptual experience. These phrases describe very concisely what is meant by a deterioration of the cognitive map.

Similar phenomena are known to occur in aviators (Bennett, 1961), prisoners in solitary confinement (Burney, 1952), skin divers, and lone voyageurs (Brownfield, 1965; Byrd, 1938). A French geologist, Michael Siffre (1975), spent 177 days alone in an underground cave. He did this voluntarily, in order to provide data for determining man's ability to endure long periods of spaceflight. After 100 days of total silence and darkness he felt his mind had "temporarily collapsed" (p. 426). Thoughts and events, not written down, were immediately forgotten. Overcome with despair and self-pity, he toyed briefly with the idea of suicide. Minor physical symptoms led to hypochondrias and occasional panic. Movements of hands and fingers became slow and clumsy. Siffre (p. 435) summed up his experience in these words:

> I am convinced that final results of this experiment will reveal serious problems confronting future long-range space travelers. Whether because of confinement, solitude, or both, my mental processes and manual dexterity deteriorated gravely and inexorably toward the end of my stay in Mountain Cave.
>
> Now, long after my (experience), I still suffer severe lapses of memory. My eyesight has weakened, and I am a victim of a chronic squint. I suffer psychological wounds that I do not understand.

Eskimo fishermen reportedly avoid going out in their kayaks alone because they are well aware of the dangerous effects of total isolation in the vast, unchanging polar landscape. "Those who have gone out alone have been known either to hallucinate, or, because of the stultifying sameness of the snowscape combined with the rhythmic movement of paddling the boat, to lapse into a hypnotic trance-like state and keep paddling until they are far out to sea without hope of getting back" (Brownfield, 1965, p. 15). Hallucinatory phenomena have frequently been reported in sensory deprivation experiments, social isolation, and solitary confinement (Brownfield, 1965, pp. 101–2, 120–22). The more drastic the degree of sensory and perceptual restriction, the more rapidly the hallucinations and other aspects of cognitive disorganization tend to occur.

Schizophrenia and Response to Drugs

A third line of evidence on S-system arousal and cognitive dysfunction comes from research on the biochemistry of mental disorders; notably, that concerning the "dopamine hypothesis" of schizophrenia, and the wider "catecholamine hypothesis" of affective disorders (i.e., mania and depression). According to these hypotheses, excessive brain CA activity, especially dopaminergic activity, is associated with an exacerbation of schizophrenic and manic symptoms, whereas decreased CA activity is associated with the remission of schizophrenic symptoms and an increase in depressive affect (e.g., Schildkraut, 1974). The clinical picture of schizophrenia covers virtually the entire spectrum of mental disturbances listed earlier as reflecting a breakdown of the cognitive map (see, e.g., Hamilton, 1979). Paraphrasing Goodwin and Guze (1979, pp. 28–34), the hallmarks of serious mental disorder are hallucinations and delusions. The most common delusions in schizophrenia are those of being persecuted or controlled by outside forces or persons. Feelings of depersonalization and bizarre sensations of bodily change are also common. Hallucinations are typically auditory, although visual, tactile, and olfactory hallucinations are not uncommon. The patient hears voices criticizing, ridiculing, or threatening him, and sometimes urging him to do things that he knows are wrong. Affective disturbances also occur, ranging from the typically "flat" affect, in which the patient is withdrawn and unresponsive, to depression, and sometimes euphoria, at various times during the course of the illness. In milder cases, perplexity, confusion, and apparent disorientation may be seen; in severe cases, "catatonic" motor disturbances occur, including "waxy flexibility," in which the limbs, after being placed in odd poses, remain fixed, as if made of wax. Bizarre posturing and grimacing are also recognized as symptoms. As their name suggests, the major symptoms of "affective disorders" are in the area of emotion. The emotion most commonly encountered is depression, which can be either "unipolar" (meaning depression alone), or "bipolar" (meaning an oscillation between mania and depression). Cognitive disturbances, apart from slowing of thought and inability to concentrate, are less marked in the affective disorders, although mania may be accompanied by depersonalization and other alterations of self-image (Goodwin & Guze, 1979, p. 21).

Many pieces of evidence relating to the catecholamines seem to explain part of the puzzle of schizophrenia and affective disorders. The most persuasive evidence concerns the effects of drugs (Carlsson, 1978; cf. Frederickson & Richelson, 1979). Drugs which increase CA arousal, such as amphetamine, methylphenidate, and levodopa, either exacerbate or induce schizophrenic and manic symptoms such as agitation, stereotypies, and thought disorders. The electroencephalographic pattern shows low-voltage fast activity in schizophrenics during the height of their hallucinatory episodes (Stevens, 1973); such activity is considered an indicator of cortical arousal and hence increased S-system arousal. Conversely, drugs that reduce CAs by various means, such as phenothiazines and butyrophenones, have an opposite, antipsychotic effect, yet can also induce depression.

Physiological Factors

Regarding the "direct" effects of alcohol consumption, the premenstruum, and hypoglycemia, on cognitive functioning, it is widely accepted that the ingestion of even small quantities of alcohol results in an "impairment of time-limited intellected functions" (Kalant, 1973, p. 6). The precise nature of the cognitive changes resulting from increasing doses of alcohol, especially, in nonalcoholics, are only just starting to be elucidated (Hore, 1977). Moderate doses of alcohol produce adverse effects on "discriminative functions" such as the ability to distinguish between different types of sounds or intensities of light (Ludwig et al., 1977). Small doses of alcohol can diminish sensitivity to taste, smell, pain, two-point discrimination and signal detection (Keller, 1971, chap. 3). Alcohol also has acute toxic effects on recent memory (Goodwin et al., 1970). This can result in periods of amnesia lasting hours or days for events occurring during a drinking spree (Kissin, 1974).

Little is known about the cognitive changes (as distinct from affective and behavioral changes) during the premenstruum and other phases of the menstrual cycle. Such changes, if they occur at all, appear to be slight, or less noticeable and distressing than the affective changes. Wickham (1958) administered a large battery of intelligence and performance tests to women and found significant changes only in the menstrual phase, and only with respect to an "instructions" test. Sommer (1973), using the Watson-Gleser Critical Thinking Appraisal task, was unable to report any evidence of cyclical changes in intellect or performance, although she did find that women using the combination-type contraceptive pill had higher overall scores on the task, a finding consistent with other studies suggesting that women taking the combination-type pill have less trouble with mood swings than women not on the pill (Little & Zahn, 1974). In addition, "feelings of unreality" have been included in lists of reported premenstrual symptoms (Janowsky et al., 1966), and it has been suggested (Kopell et al., 1969) that the subjective changes occurring during the cycle may be part of a mild, transient, confusional state. Some excellent reviews are available on the methodological limitations of research on the premenstrual tension syndrome (Parlee, 1973; Seiden, 1976). According to Seiden (1976), at least one study (e.g., Rossi, 1974) has shown that women experience greater affective and behavioral fluctuations with the weekly cycle of work days and weekends than they do with the menstrual cycle itself.

Turning to the topic of hypoglycemia, the normal fasting blood sugar in man ranges from 90–110 mg. percent, with low and high margins of 80 and 120, respectively. According to Wilder (1947, p. 100), when blood sugar levels fall to 60 or 70 mg. percent the following types of mental changes are seen:

slight dullness; weakness of concentration; the thinking process requires some effort; there is difficulty in making decisions, even in things of minor importance; the mood might be depressed or a state of anxiety develops; there is a tendency to irritability or opposition.

Below 50–60 mg. percent, transitory neurological signs appear such as double vision, vertigo, ataxia, disturbances of sensibility, and speech disorders of aphasic or dysarthric character; vocal changes occur such as loss of voice, word repetition, or excessive loudness. Numerous cognitive changes are also seen, including: moments of thought arrest, extreme difficulty in concentration; impairment of abstract thinking; disorientation in time, space, and place; mental dullness to the point of seeming dazed or feeling unreal; irresistible sleepiness; lack of initiative to the point of loss of willpower ("abulia"), and inability to make decisions. "Amnesia usually follows not only severe but sometimes even very light hypoglycemic states" (p. 101). In an experimental study, adult volunteers were made hypoglycemic with injections of insulin. Subjects reported increased sweating, blurred vision, hallucinations, and feelings of unreality (Butterfield et al., 1966). There also appears to be an interaction between alcohol and hypoglycemia, in that alcohol ingestion can worsen the cognitive and other effects of hypoglycemia (Williams, 1970, pp. 841–42).[6]

Taken together, the findings reviewed in this chapter suggest that the various factors associated with transient criminality produce increased suggestibility and cognitive disorganization by way of increases in S-system arousal.

NOTES

1. This delightful article is recommended for its discussion of "home" as one of the central aspects of an individual's cognitive map (see also Porteus, 1977).

2. For discussions of the theoretical complexities and methodological problems in research on life stress and illness, see Miller and Ingham (1979), Thoits (1982), and Kessler et al. (1985).

3. Lynch's (1977) monograph on the physiological consequences of social isolation and loneliness provides a comprehensive and well-documented account of the points we have been discussing. Although the findings he describes are not interpreted in terms of the specific hypotheses stated here, the weight of evidence strongly

suggests that the presence of a companion who is either familiar or offers reassuring words or physical contact generally has a calming effect on the cardiovascular system under stressful conditions. Conversely, close proximity with unfamiliar individuals or even with familiar people who are acting in an unusual way has an excitatory effect on the cardiovascular system. For instance, in an earlier study of the cardiovascular responses of dogs to unsignaled electric shock (Lynch, 1977, pp. 169–70), it was found that if a person associated with the care of the animal entered the room and petted the dog during the shock, the dog's heart rate increase was reduced 50 percent compared to that observed when the dog was shocked alone. The study was then repeated, with the modification that a tone was presented 10 seconds before administering the shock. After a number of training sessions the dog's heart rate tended to accelerate 50–100 beats per minute at the sound of the tone. However, if "the person petted the dog during both the tone and the shock, the usual marked increase in heart rate to the tone and the shock was either eliminated or changed to a decrease in heart rate. When petted, some of these dogs did not even give the usual (foreleg) flexion response to the shock" (p. 170).

4. Merely *thinking* intensely about attachment figures may be sufficient to prevent the individual from being overwhelmed by disaster. This has been found to be one of the major characteristics of individuals who have successfully coped with and survived major disasters (Henderson, 1980).

5. It is uncertain whether the nature of the decline in cognitive functioning which occurs with very *low* levels of arousal is equivalent to that which occurs at very high levels.

6. A recent study (Pramming et al., 1986), on cognitive function in 16 insulin-dependent (type 1) diabetic men during hypoglycemia, indicated that a significant deterioration in cognitive function can occur during mild, asymptomatic hypoglycemia. None of the 16 patients reported symptoms when blood glucose concentrations were ≤ 52.3 mg/100 ml, despite significant alterations in cognition.

6

STRESS, AROUSAL, AND BEHAVIOR

THE CONCEPT OF
STIMULATION-SEEKING BEHAVIOR

In addition to increasing suggestibility and threatening the cognitive map with disintegration, S-system arousal also increases the intensity of stimulation-seeking behavior. Stimulation-seeking behavior (SSB) is defined here as any activity that enhances or facilitates contact between an organism's sensory receptors and external objects or surfaces (Mawson, 1978a). This is a broad response category encompassing behaviors conventionally classified as "motivational" (such as eating, drinking, and sexual activity) and "emotional" (e.g., aggression and flight), as well as voluntary and involuntary movement. To describe all of these activities in terms of a "search for stimulation" may seem counter-intuitive. Justification is therefore required.

The concept that organisms "seek stimulation" was originally postulated on the basis of observations indicating that (1) humans and a variety of other species would "work" (that is, press levers or bars and cross electrified cage grids) to receive visual, tactile, auditory and direct brain (intracranial) stimulation; (2) peripheral and intracranial stimulation were often selected in preference to so-called conventional reinforcers such as food, water, and opportunities for sexual activity (Kish, 1966); (3) prolonged sensory restriction produced neurophysiological deficits in the form of cellular damage, retarded growth, and altered electro-physiological activity (Zubek, 1969; Montagu, 1972); and (4) certain forms of stimulation could offset or correct these deficits, and even enhance development (Riesen, 1975).

These results showed that organisms have a physiological need for stimulation in addition to needs such as food and water. However, to this day the question remains unresolved of the relationship between stimulation-seeking behavior and other types of need-related behavior.

The key issue amounts to this: Is SSB a distinct type or system of behavior, in addition to feeding, drinking, and sexual activity? Or is it, instead, an inherent part of *all* motivational behavior?

For most authors, SSB (or the closely allied concept of sensation seeking, e.g., Zuckerman, 1978b, 1979), is a distinct "form" of behavior, manifested in thrill-and-adventure-seeking activities such as parachute jumping, motorcycle riding, and mountain climbing (Zuckerman, 1979, p. 101). However, Zuckerman (1979) for one has expanded his concept of sensation seeking, suggesting that stimulation can be obtained in a variety of different ways, for example, by drugs, cigarette smoking, sex, and spicy foods. He views sensation seeking as "a trait defined by the need for varied, novel, and complex sensations and experiences and the willingness to take physical and social risks for the sake of such experience" (p. 10). He proposes that sexual activity and drug taking are "secondary to a broader and perhaps earlier developing need for varied sensations" (p. 9).

Despite Zuckerman's expansion of the concept of sensation seeking, it is still unclear where sensation seeking ends and other kinds of motivational behavior begin. The alternative view suggested here is that the underlying biological motive in *all* motor-motivational activity is for sensory stimulation; that is, stimulation seeking is inherent in all active behaviors or movement, not simply as an adjunct to other motives that may be satisfied contemporaneously, but as the primary biological motive. Traditionally, feeding, drinking, sex, and aggression have been considered *distinct* motivational systems, motivated by separate needs or drives — for food, water, orgasm, and injury, respectively. Here it is argued that they are in fact, overlapping bands of intensity on a single continuum of stimulation-seeking behavior. This is not to imply that food and water are not needed and that stimulation alone is needed. Rather, the proposal is that the underlying motive in feeding, drinking, sex, and aggression is for sensory input, and that the needs for various nutritive substances are satisfied indirectly as a result of obtaining stimulation.

Before elaborating on this hypothesis, it should be noted, first, that while Zuckerman focuses on *novelty* as a key aspect of sensation seeking, the suggestion here is that organisms seek stimuli that are congruent with, or match, their cognitive maps. This view emphasizes the essential conservatism of organisms — the tendency to seek expected and familiar types, quantities, and patterns of stimulation. Insofar as stimuli are sought which are considered "novel," they are novel only within the subset of prior expectancies; that is, they are actually familiar in relation to the broad parameters of environmental experience laid down in the individual's cognitive map.

Second, the concept of seeking stimulation is not meant to imply that organisms attempt to "arouse" themselves. The idea is that organisms seek *sensory input* (or *sensations,* to use Zuckerman's term); the term stimulation-seeking behavior does not imply "arousal-seeking."[1] In fact, it is argued below that the sensory input obtained via SSB has a *calming* rather than an arousing (or "stimulating") effect on behavior, due to the activation of the P-system.

Third, with reference to the concept of stimulation *seeking,* this is not meant to imply a conscious search for increased sensory input, but a goal-directed activity in the biological sense of responding to certain conditions so as to maintain specific functions within predefined limits.

Let us return, then, to the proposal that all motor-motivational activity represents varying intensities of SSB. According to traditional views of motivation, specific behaviors serve specific biological or evolutionary-adaptive functions. When a given need arises, specific mechanisms elicit the specific behavior which in turn satisfies the need. Feeding, for instance, is said to satisfy the need for calories, and the behavior is supposedly elicited and terminated by mechanisms related to caloric depletion and repletion, respectively. In the case of evolutionary-adaptive needs such as protection from predators and reproduction, it is assumed that these needs are satisfied indirectly, as a result of a causal sequence involving the following steps: (1) the occurrence of specific environmental conditions (e.g., threat); (2) the activation of specific biological mechanisms (e.g., catecholamines, pathways in the limbic system of the brain); and (3) the appearance of specific behavior (e.g., aggression). However, regardless of the nature of each need, the basic assumptions are the same; namely, that each type of motivational behavior is a relatively distinct system in that the behavior is elicited and terminated by specific environmental conditions and/or internal mechanisms, and the behavior itself can be *identified independently* of other behaviors.[2]

Although this model of behavior has been extremely fruitful as a stimulus for research (Richter, 1943; Grossman, 1967; Mogenson, 1977), there are numerous difficulties. Here it must suffice to outline these difficulties and to offer an equally brief justification for the global concept of SSB. Concentrating mainly on feeding and aggression (see chapters 11 and 12), the critique focuses on (1) the connection between biological needs and behavior; (2) the notion of specific mechanisms underlying different behaviors; (3) the problem of identifying behaviors independently of each other; and (4) the importance of sensory factors in behavior.

1. Feeding is thought to result from caloric deficit, and satiety from caloric repletion. However, caloric deficit is neither necessary nor sufficient for feeding. Food deprivation is not necessary for feeding since animals and humans often eat when they are not in a state of caloric deficit; nor is it sufficient, since hungry animals and humans tend to refuse unpalatable or unfamiliar foods. One would expect the "urge to eat" to increase with the duration of food deprivation. However, this "urge" tends to decline, or occurs cyclically, after extended periods of food deprivation. Thus feeding can occur in the absence of caloric depletion (Wyrwicka, 1976).[3] Food ingestion is also neither necessary nor sufficient for satiety. It is not necessary because many different kinds of activity can temporarily assuage hunger and reduce the amount of food consumed when opportunities to eat are provided, for example, physical exercise, water consumption, and cigarette smoking; nor is it sufficient, since animals and humans tend to overeat and become obese when highly palatable foods are readily available (Wyrwicka, 1976). These observations suggest that feeding and satiety may be motivated by something other than, or in addition to, simple caloric deficit or repletion respectively.

2. Regarding the question of specific mechanisms, a notion which can be traced to the phrenologists of the nineteenth century is that specific behaviors are controlled by specific brain *centers*. Only recently has this view given way to the notion of specific brain *pathways* (Mogenson, 1977). Although even this concept has been challenged (Valenstein et al., 1970), there is still no corresponding challenge to traditional concepts of *behavior*. One of the main objections to the concept of motivationally specific neural mechanisms (i.e., centers, pathways, neurochemicals) is that a particular stimulus, such as electric shock (Hinde, 1966; Antelman & Szechtman, 1975), or direct electrical stimulation of the lateral hypothalamus of the brain, is capable of eliciting many different types of behavior, depending on what is available for the animal to do in the

testing situation (Valenstein et al., 1970). These observations suggest that the various elicited behaviors may in some way be functionally similar. Moreover, increasing intensities of electrical stimulation at certain brain loci elicit a progression of behaviors that includes "alerting," "grooming," and "feeding" at relatively low intensities, to "aggression" at relatively higher levels (Hess, 1957; Reis et al., 1973). The question is, do observations such as these indicate that specific behaviors are elicited at specific thresholds of intensity, or that the supposedly specific behaviors are part of a single continuum? The fact that many different behaviors can be elicited at the same level of intensity of brain stimulation, and at the same locus (Valenstein et al., 1970), appears to support the latter position.

The search for motivationally specific physiological mechanisms has proven exceedingly elusive. Although dozens of factors have been implicated in feeding and satiety, none is specific to feeding or satiety. Recent work, for instance, suggests that the peptide cholecystokinin serves as a "satiety signal." However, this substance also elicits sleep (Mansbach & Lorenz, 1983). With regard to aggression, a recent review concludes: "To date, efforts to establish the existence of a unitary neuroendocrine mechanism for aggression have not been successful" (Whalen & Simon, 1984, p. 265). To the contrary, much evidence indicates that a given factor can influence multiple behaviors and that a given behavior has multiple physiological influences.

3. Supposedly different "types" of behavior not only are elicited by identical stimuli but appear together more or less at the same time (Hinde, 1966). In addition, they are often *indistinguishable* from one another; that is, it is often difficult to decide what behavior (or behaviors) is actually being engaged in by an animal or human (see, e.g., Bindra, 1974; Fentress, 1978). Investigators are usually interested in elucidating the factors responsible for a single "form" of behavior at a given time, and define their measures of the dependent variable in advance of doing the experiments. As a result, they ignore any other behaviors which may be occurring while testing their chosen independent variable(s) under different conditions. Because of this "objective" procedure, problems of behavioral classification tend to be set aside or ignored. Investigators rarely just observe a subject under nonexperimental conditions and ask themselves what the individual is doing.

In theory, observed behaviors are classified either (a) by inferring motives or drives, or (b) by specific acts (e.g., chewing or swallowing = feeding; punching or scratching = aggression; and copulatory movements = sex). The problem of classifying behaviors by inferring motives is simply that: it is an inference. At times, the motive may be far from clear. For instance, when someone kills another in an apparently deliberate fashion, it is assumed that the killing was intentional. Yet injurious intent is absent in most homicides (Wolfgang & Ferracuti, 1967). With regard to the ambiguity of motives, there is uncertainty, for instance, as to whether nail biting reflects hunger (and hence is a manifestation of eating behavior), or anger (and hence is a manifestation of self-directed aggression). It is similarly uncertain whether rape has a sexual or an aggressive motivation; whether the so-called love bite is a form of feeding behavior, a form of aggression or a sexual response; and whether prey killing is to be classified as feeding or aggression.

In the case of classifying behavior on the basis of specific acts, the difficulty is that many of the same acts are common to supposedly different "forms" of behavior (Fentress, 1978). Subjecting these acts to factor analysis has failed to identify clusters of acts that uniquely distinguish one form of motivated behavior from another (e.g., Wiepkema, 1961, cited in Hinde, 1966).

A related difficulty is that certain behaviors cannot be accommodated into any of the usual functional or need-related categories. In such cases, new "needs" are often invented arbitrarily (e.g., a need for curiosity, play, exploration, movement, and stimulation).

4. With regard to the importance of sensory factors in behavior, there is evidence that such factors are of paramount importance, not only in feeding behavior (Mattes, 1987) but in many other behaviors. Several authors (e.g., Yudkin, 1963, 1978; Wyrwicka, 1976) have suggested that animals and humans eat for taste or palatability rather than for calories or specific nutrients. In addition to the points raised in (1), above, that are consistent with this interpretation, it may be noted that food-deprived rats, when offered a choice between solutions of glucose and saccharin (a nonnutritive substance), choose the latter, and die as a result of their preference for saccharin (Valenstein, 1967). In general, the stronger the degree of food deprivation, the greater the extent to which feeding is dominated by oro-sensory factors (Jacobs & Sharma, 1969). Foods that are high in calories also tend to be highly palatable (Yudkin,

1963); hence, carbohydrates (and fats) may be ingested because they happen to be very tasty.[4] However, when substances are available that are highly stimulating, for example, tasty, but contain little or no calories, they tend to be selected in preference to substances that are highly nutritious but unpalatable. Lesions of the brain which enhance or diminish feeding can also be interpreted as enhancing or diminishing stimulation-seeking behavior in general (cf. Wolgin et al., 1976).

Sensory factors are also of great importance in other behaviors. Taste, for instance, is very important in drinking (Wyrwicka, 1979). Holding, touching, and cuddling figure importantly in sexual activity (Montagu, 1972; Komisaruk, 1978); and visual, tactile, and kinesthetic forms of stimulation are of great importance in aggression (Johnson, 1972, pp. 36–37).

Our proposal, then, is that all forms of motor-motivational activity represent overlapping bands of intensity on a continuous spectrum of stimulation-seeking behavior. Mild forms of SSB include activities such as licking, sucking, looking around, and touching; moderate forms include walking, chewing, smoking, scratching, and rubbing; and stronger forms include self-mutilation (possibly leading to "suicide"), intense movements directed at other people ("sex," "aggression"), or vigorous running ("flight"). The proposal is that behaviors that are presently viewed as separate motivational systems are arbitrary points or bands on a continuum of stimulation-seeking behavior. Thus so-called "feeding" and "sexual activity" shade into "aggression" as the intensity of biting, chewing, copulatory, and other movements increase: and "aggression" shades into "flight" as leg and arm movements increase in intensity and frequency.[5]

This formulation provides a means of classifying acts that have been difficult to classify in terms of traditional categories, viz., rape, prey killing, play, exploratory activity, locomotor activity, nail biting, self-mutilatory activity, and addictive behavior. All of these activities may be reinterpreted in terms of varying intensities of SSB. Moreover, it is suggested that the underlying motive in "feeding" behavior is not for calories but for sensory input involving the taste, smell, texture, and appearance of substances.[6] Similarly, sexual activity is a general sensorial activity or experience which includes, but is not restricted to, orgasm or genital stimulation; nor is injury of the victim the biological motive of "aggression," nor escape the motive of "'flight" or agitated running. It is suggested that feeding, sexual activity, aggression, and flight represent progressively more intense levels of stimulation-seeking activity.

S-SYSTEM AROUSAL AND SSB

It is proposed that increases in S-system arousal elicit proportional increases in the intensity of stimulation-seeking behavior. This hypothesis is the reverse of conventional views of sensation-seeking behavior. According to these views (for reviews, see Mawson & Mawson, 1977; Zuckerman, 1979), organisms try to maintain an optimal level of arousal; this they do either by avoiding stimulation when arousal is too high, or by seeking stimulation when arousal is too low (see Figure 6.1).

Optimal-arousal theory[7] is diagrammed as follows (the downward-pointing arrows indicate decreases, the upward ones indicate increases, and the horizontal arrows indicate "leads to"):

$$\text{(Cortical) Arousal} \downarrow \longrightarrow \text{SSB}\uparrow \longrightarrow \text{Arousal}\uparrow$$

There is evidence to support an alternative view (Mawson, 1978a). Starting with the assumption that oscillations in S- and P-system activity are closely regulated, mild or moderate incongruity results in a temporary state of S-system dominance. The greater the degree of S-system arousal, the greater the intensity of SSB. The increased sensory input thus obtained (provided it is evaluated as "congruous" at some level of awareness, see Chapter 7) activates the P-system. The P-system in turn inhibits and thereby reduces S-system arousal, thus restoring neurotransmitter equilibrium. In summary, it is proposed that increased SSB results from, and in turn serves to reduce, S-system arousal, that is,

$$\text{S-system arousal} \uparrow \longrightarrow \text{SSB} \uparrow \longrightarrow \text{S-system arousal} \downarrow \\ \text{(via P-system arousal} \uparrow)$$

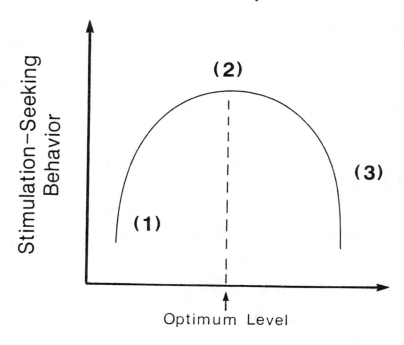

Figure 6.1
The "optimum-level-of-arousal" theory: when arousal is below the
optimum (1), stimulation-seeking behavior (SSB) increases and
serves to raise the level of arousal to the optimum level (2). If the
level of arousal is higher than the optimum (3), SSB decreases.

Source: Compiled by author.

Zuckerman (1979, chaps. 12, 13) has reviewed the available evidence and concludes, on balance, that it fails to support the optimum-
arousal hypothesis; as noted, Zuckerman now seems to favor the
notion that sensation-seeking behavior is a direct function of
noradrenergic and dopaminergic (S-system) arousal, a view consistent
with that suggested here, that is, S-system arousal↑ ⟶ SSB↑.
The evidence cited by Zuckerman involves experiments utilizing his
own sensation-seeking scale (SSS).[8] Although the SSS was developed
within the framework of optimum-arousal theory, it provides an
approximate but incomplete measure of what is described here as
stimulation-seeking behavior (SSB). The SSS, for instance, is strongly

correlated with activities that would be expected to reflect SSB. High scores on the SSS are correlated with: volunteering for experiments and risky activities, gambling, frequent and varied sexual activity, alcohol consumption, experimentation with drugs, cigarette smoking, preferences for spicy, sour, or crunchy foods, and hypomania (Zuckerman, 1978b, 1979).

Turning to the evidence, is SSB an inverse function of S-system arousal, as suggested by low- or optimal-arousal theory, or a direct function, as suggested here, and by Zuckerman?

1. The low-arousal hypothesis predicts that high sensation seekers (as measured by Zuckerman's sensation-seeking scale), would be likely to experiment with "arousing" types of drugs. However, high sensation seekers "will try any drug regardless of its effect on central arousal levels. The choice of drugs seems to depend more on what is available . . ." (Zuckerman, 1979, p. 316).

2. The low-arousal theory predicts that sensation seeking varies with the diurnal cycle in such a way that an optimal level of arousal is maintained. When arousal starts to decline toward the end of the day, individuals would be expected to increase their sensation-seeking activity. Using body temperatures as an index of arousal, Hauty (1978) found that it was lowest in the early morning and late evening, and highest at midday and in the early evening. When measures of sensation seeking were taken throughout the day and compared with the body temperature readings it emerged that, instead of being inversely related, the two variables followed the same curve. As Zuckerman notes, "Sensation-seeking state appears to be high at midday and early evening, when greater task demands coincide with arousal peaks. Therefore, sensation-seeking may not be compensatory to arousal level but may be a direct function of it" (p. 319).

The alternative view that S-system arousal varies directly with SSB, in the form of locomotor activity, is supported by the observation that physically agitated depressed patients tend to have high arousal levels, whereas physically withdrawn depressives generally have low (electrodermal) arousal levels and reduced electrodermal reactivity to auditory stimuli (Lader, 1975b, cited in Zuckerman, 1979, p. 327). The loss of dopamine (DA) in the striatum is associated with a greatly reduced ability to initiate skeletal movements; conversely, drugs that increase arousal by increasing brain DA activity also enhance motor (i.e., behavioral) functioning (Calne, 1970).

3. Studies undertaken by Zuckerman's group indicate that sensation seeking is associated with *increased* rather than decreased S-system arousal. Gonadal hormones are known to increase cortical (S-system) arousal and have an activating effect on behavior, possibly by reducing monoamine oxidase activity (MAO) (Broverman et al., 1968), thus increasing noradrenergic (NA) activation (Zuckerman, 1979, p. 373). Daitzman and associates (1978) assayed total androgens in 76 male undergraduates and found that they correlated significantly with the disinhibition subscale of the SSS; neither the age of subjects nor the time since last orgasm affected the statistical significance of the correlations (Daitzman et al., 1978). Since MAO is thought to be inversely related to catecholaminergic (CA) arousal, optimal-arousal theory would predict *high*--MAO activity to be associated with *low* S-system arousal and with *increased* SSB. However, the opposite set of findings has been reported: high-MAO monkeys tend to be inactive and solitary, whereas low-MAO monkeys play vigorously and initiate many social contacts (Redmond & Murphy, 1975; Redmond et al., 1979). Among humans, two studies using male and female undergraduates (Murphy et al., 1977a; Schooler et al., 1978) indicate significant negative correlations between MAO and parts of the SSS (especially the general SS scale). Low-MAO activity is associated with ego strength, positive mood, and high activity levels, whereas individuals with high-MAO levels tend to sleep more and watch more television than low-MAO types (Schooler et al., 1978). Administration of MAO-inhibiting drugs for therapeutic purposes is associated with elevated mood, increased energy, increased social activity, and aggressiveness, which in some cases can progress to hyperactivity and psychosis (Murphy, 1977). In sum, *low*-MAO levels appear to be associated with *high* SSB, as predicted.

4. The suggestion that increased S-system arousal is associated with other types of activities subsumed under the heading of SSB is supported by considerable evidence. Thus studies on (a) the implantation of neurotransmitter substances in the brain, (b) the stimulation and/or ablation of brain regions containing high concentrations of CAs, and (c) the use of drugs that enhance or diminish CA function, indicate that increased CA arousal elicits increases in feeding and drinking (Stricker & Zigmond, 1976), alcohol consumption (Myers, 1978), sexual behavior (Meyerson & Malmnäs, 1978), aggression (Goldman, 1977, p. 52), and locomotor activity (Wayner, 1974; Antelman & Szechtman, 1975;

Valenstein, 1976). These findings suggest that "catecholamine-containing pathways in the brain ... constitute a common neural substrate underlying a variety of different activities ..." (Herberg & Stephens, 1977, p. 363). Furthermore, there is evidence that the level of NA arousal is directly related to the intensity of the elicited behavior (Reis & Fuxe, 1969).

ENVIRONMENTAL STRESS AND SSB

It has been suggested that environmental stressors produce stimulation-seeking behavior via increases in S-system arousal.

There is much evidence that environmental stress elicits increased SSB. Minor disturbances elicit increased "orienting and attending responses" (Walters & Parke, 1964). Animals and humans will sit or stand up, look around, and listen intently for sounds. Progressive increases in the novelty (or incongruity) of environmental conditions elicit progressive increases in the intensity of many different kinds of behavior, depending on the contingencies available in the situation. Responses become more vigorous and more frequent (Hokanson, 1969, pp. 121 ff.). Supposedly irrelevant "drives" appear, such as eating, drinking, sexual activity, sniffing, and grooming (Hinde, 1966, p. 298). Still higher degrees of incongruity elicit affiliative responses, which in turn shade into "aggression,"[9] and from thence into "flight." With regard to specific stressors, separation from attachment figures has multiple effects on behavior. During World War II it was observed that young children separated from their parents and placed in foster homes engaged in intense and persistent thumb sucking and head banging. They were highly aggressive, masturbated frequently, had an "insatiable greed" for food, and tended to form passionate temporary attachments to strangers and guest workers (Burlingham & Freud, 1944). In human adults, reactions to separation or the threat of interpersonal loss commonly take the form of intense agitation, restlessness, and irritability (Weiss, 1976). Increased and relatively indiscriminate sexual activity is also known to occur between "relinquishment of the lost object and orientation to a new one" (Bowlby, 1960, pp. 20–21; see also Lindemann, 1944; Eliot, 1955). The suggestion that such activity represents SSB rather than purely sexual or reproductive activity is supported by the fact that it is frequently accompanied by a desire to be touched and held (Hollender,

1970; Montagu, 1972). Sexual urges are also said to increase in intense fear situations such as combat and prior to execution (Meerloo, 1950, p. 80). Other reactions in fear situations included under the heading of SSB are: staring or looking widely about; dilatation of the pupils and nostrils; sweating; changes in the peripheral receptors leading to increased visual, auditory, tactile, and olfactory acuity; and agitation (Diethelm, 1932, p. 1163).

Anecdotal observations certainly indicate that SSB increases markedly at all types of social gatherings such as parties, sporting events, and other outdoor activities. Increased drinking, smoking, eating, talkativeness, boisterousness, sexual interest, and aggressiveness figure prominently among these reactions. Increased smoking, drinking, and eating commonly occur in stressful situations as a whole (Adesso, 1979).

The experimental paradigms providing the clearest illustration of the thesis that stress leads to SSB via increases in S-system arousal have used electric shock and tail pinch in rodents. Varying intensities of electric shock elicit many different "kinds" of behavior in rats, depending on the intensity of the shock, the objects available in the test situation, and other factors (Johnson, 1972). Gnawing, feeding, drinking, alcohol consumption (Mills et al., 1977), aggressiveness, and escape, for instance, have been elicited by foot shock (Johnson, 1972, pp. 37–40). Mildly painful tail pinch can also induce SSB in a wide variety of forms, including eating, gnawing, drinking milk or saccharin solutions, biting, and increased locomotor activity (Margules et al., 1979). Antelman and Szechtman (1975) have reported evidence suggesting that tail-pinched-induced eating, gnawing, and licking behavior in rats depends on the integrity of the brain nigrostriatal dopamine system (but not, apparently, the noradrenergic system). Blockade of brain DA receptors with haloperidol, but not NA receptors, significantly reduced tail pinch-induced behavior. Chemical lesions of the nigrostriatal (dopamine-containing) system had the same effect.

Several findings from tail pinch and tail shock experiments are consistent with the view that the underlying motive for the elicited behavior is sensory stimulation. First, ordinary tap water tends to be rejected by the stressed animals (Antelman et al., 1976), presumably because lukewarm tap water provides insufficient sensory input, given the induced level of S-system arousal. However, it is surmised that ice-cold water would be consumed by the animals. Mills et al. (1977) have shown that with increasing foot shock, rats show parallel shifts in their drinking preferences. Under baseline conditions the animals prefer saccharin solutions to water. However, with increasing exposure to shock the rats first switch to 5 percent solutions of ethanol, and then to 10 percent solutions. Again, it is hypothesized that these shifts in preference reflect progressive increases in SSB following increasing S-system arousal due to prolonged electric shock. In terms of the stimulation value of the various substances, water < saccharin < 5 percent ethanol solutions < 10 percent ethanol solutions. Beyond the ranges of S-system arousal and the types of SSB encountered in the above experiments, responses such as vigorous copulation, biting and running, would be expected to provide quantities of sensory input proportional to the increases in S-system arousal.[10]

PARALLEL OBSERVATIONS ON SUGGESTIBILITY, COGNITIVE DISTURBANCES, AND SSB

Increased suggestibility, cognitive disturbances, and increased SSB are postulated to occur together in response to incongruity and increased S-system arousal. Experimental sensory deprivation (S.D.) is one area of research in which the simultaneous occurrence of these phenomena has been extensively described. The "craving" for stimulation reported by subjects undergoing S.D. is well documented (Brownfield, 1965; Suedfeld, 1969a, 1969b); the more severe and prolonged the S.D., the greater the craving for familiar sensations. In man and many other species, prolonged S.D. may result in intense agitation, restlessness, and self-stimulation, sometimes to the point of gross self-mutilation and injury (Johnson, 1972, pp. 110–14).

Parallel changes in cognitive functioning and SSB also occur following prolonged deprivation of rapid eye movement (REM) sleep. Deprivation of REM sleep in humans results in complaints of psychological discomfort and a tendency to overeat (Dement, 1960). Tyler (1955) deprived 350 males of REM and non-REM sleep for periods of up to 112 hours and found that psychotic-like reactions occurred in almost all subjects; 70 percent reported audiovisual hallucinations, and seven subjects became aggressive and combative.

Some investigators believe that S.D. increases suggestibility by way of increases in stimulus needs (e.g., Schultz, 1965); others propose that S.D. leads to a decrease in the "stability" of beliefs, and it is this that makes individuals more suggestible (Suedfeld & Borrie, 1978). S.D. is, however, only one of many different types of conditions that can lead to increased suggestibility, cognitive disturbances, and SSB. The causal relationship between the three variables is undoubtedly complex; there may also be some degree of mutual influence if not conceptual overlap between them — especially regarding suggestibility and cognitive disturbance. Suggestibility, for instance, may simply be an aspect of altered cognition rather than an independent phenomenon. Here it is assumed that the causal chain begins with increased S-system arousal (which itself may be due to S.D., or to other forms of incongruity and/or physiological factors), and that the three variables are independent, or analytically separable effects, of increased S-system arousal (cf., Walters & Parke, 1964).

NOTES

1. Zuckerman (1979) has modified his earlier theoretical views in ways that make them consistent with those expressed here. In addition to broadening the concept of sensation seeking, Zuckerman considers that the available evidence supports the hypothesis that "Sensation-seeking . . . is in some part a function of the levels of the catecholamines norepinephrine and dopamine in the reward areas of the limbic system, as well as the neuroregulators that control their availability at the synapses within these neural areas" (p. 372, italics omitted).

2. Just as feeding is said to be motivated by caloric deficit, aggression is elicited by threat and activated by "aggression centers," drinking is motivated by fluid deficit, and sexual activity is elicited by specific sex mechanisms, including hormones. The widespread acceptance of these assumptions is evident in the references that are frequently made to "basic drives," and in the fact that the aforementioned "types" of behavior are treated in separate chapters in most textbooks of physiological psychology. What this means is that the concepts of behavior themselves (most of which have existed for generations) are seldom questioned; the object of research is rather to elucidate the specific conditions and mechanisms responsible for each "type" of behavior.

3. Yudkin (1978) also marshalls evidence against the widely accepted view that depletion of specific nutrients leads to specific ingestive behaviors.

4. Apparently in opposition to this view are the findings of experiments by Wurtman and his associates (e.g., Wurtman & Wurtman, 1982/83), suggesting that carbohydrate consumption is specifically regulated, independently of taste factors, by alterations in the brain neurotransmitter serotonin (but see Mook et al., 1983).

5. Similarities between aggression and fear are discussed by Archer (1976). Parallels between sex and aggression are reviewed and discussed by Zillmann (1984).

6. Eating is closely associated with other forms of SSB, for example, drinking, smoking, meeting and conversing with others, reading, listening, and looking around. Eating is a general sensorial activity or experience.

7. The theory is also known as the low-arousal hypothesis, since SSB is said to result when the level of arousal decreases, that is, drops below the optimum.

8. The sensation-seeking scale consists of four 10-item subscales: thrill-and-adventure seeking, experience seeking, disinhibition, and boredom susceptibility. Respondents are required to choose between two statements such as (a) "I like 'wild' uninhibited parties" or (b) "I prefer quiet parties with good conversation."

9. See Chapter 11, this volume.

10. The concept of stimulation-seeking behavior has origins that long antedate research on sensory deprivation in the 1950s. Jacques Loeb's (1917/1973) work on *tropisms* in animals is particularly relevant in this connection. Loeb conducted numerous experiments showing that organisms have a tendency to move toward sources of energy or stimuli, for example, gravitation, light, chemical substances, touch pressure, and electricity. According to Loeb's "mechanistic" theory, animals and humans do not have "free will" and are literally pulled toward these sources of stimulation. Loeb also recognized movements of the whole organism toward the stimulus source as a fundamental category of behavior. He noted that organisms approach stimuli in addition to those related to their "instinctual drives," and proposed that "instincts" were tropisms; that is, forced movements toward sources of energy. Loeb also suggested that humans could transfer their tropistic responses to objects in their immediate environment by developing "memory images" — an idea that is very similar to the concept of "cognitive map." Like Loeb's concept of a tropism, SSB is viewed as a generalized response of the organism as a whole, directed toward stimulus sources in general. The proposal is that behaviors involving increased interactional commerce with the environment represent overlapping bands of intensity of SSB. The idea that SSB is guided by a primitive cognitive map and "tuned" to make progressively finer discriminations of approach behavior (see Chapter 7), can be considered an extension of Loeb's views. The concept of SSB differs from that of tropism, however, in that SSB is *actively directed* at stimulus sources, and can be "turned off" and reversed, either by excessive intensities of environmental stimuli, or by prolonged stimulus exposure. In short, SSB is "polyphasic" (cf. Hirsch, 1973, pp. xii–xiv), that is, fluctuating in an on-off fashion rather than occurring continuously in response to an invariant stimulus. For Loeb, on the other hand, a tropism was a *forced* movement (like the movement of iron filings to a magnet — an analogy he himself used), and the force was considered unremitting and constant. A reconsideration of

current research on SSB, sensory deprivation, stimulation-induced growth, "enriched" environments, and motivation in general, in light of Loeb's work and that of more recent investigations in the same tradition by Hirsch and his students, might prove valuable.

7

THE DIRECTION AND FUNCTION OF STIMULATION-SEEKING BEHAVIOR

THE DIRECTION OF BEHAVIOR

To summarize Chapter 6, several distinct, drive-related behaviors are conventionally assumed to exist, including feeding, drinking, sexual activity, aggression, attachment behavior, maternal behavior, and flight. More complex behaviors are thought to develop by becoming associated with the satisfaction of so-called "primary" drives, notably hunger (Hull, 1943).[1] The alternative view proposed in Chapter 6 was that the above "types" of behavior represent arbitrary points on a continuum of stimulation-seeking behavior, and the 40 or more substances needed for survival are ingested coincidentally while seeking stimulation. This is analogous to the idea that supposedly different colors represent overlapping wavelengths of the electromagnetic spectrum (ranging from about 380–750 mμ). "Feeding" behavior, for instance, is viewed as SSB within a certain range of intensities, shading into "aggression" at higher intensities.

It is suggested that behavioral specificity and complexity emerge gradually, in a sort of "deductive" process, in which SSB is "tuned" to make progressively finer discriminations of smell, taste, touch, hearing, and vision. The ability to discriminate in the evaluation of and search for stimulation is associated with an increasingly differentiated cognitive map. Thus, cognitive maps of specific persons, places, and objects, develop gradually from combinations of relatively simple, though familiar, sensory experiences. Because the organized "patterns" of familiar stimulation within the cognitive map are built upon a foundation of more basic stimuli, the individual's stimulation-seeking responses are at once *nonspecific yet capable of a high degree of specificity*. SSB is directed at familiar "basic" stimuli (oral, tactile, visual, etc.), but particularly at familiar *patterns* of stimuli. Incongruity activates SSB aimed at the entire internalized hierarchy of familiar stimuli. This may

117

account for the observation that a particular incongruous stimulus is associated with *diverse* behavioral responses. Such a conception of behavioral organization, at once very general yet capable of a high level of specificity, seems to allow for a greater degree of complexity and flexibility in behavior than one based on a limited number of drives for needed substances.

It is postulated that there are both "general" and "localized" aspects of stimulation-seeking responses (cf., Selye's [1965] concepts of the General Adaptation Syndrome [G.A.S.] and Local Adaptation Syndrome [L.A.S.]). Selye found that although different conditions give rise to an identical pattern of physiological responses (the G.A.S.), certain stimuli can elicit localized reactions (the L.A.S.) in addition to the G.A.S. A cold stimulus, for instance, may produce vasoconstriction, whereas heat may produce vasodilatation. Yet if either or both stimuli are prolonged or applied with sufficient intensity, common physiological effects occur, known as the G.A.S.

To clarify the distinction between localized and general stimulation-seeking responses, suppose that a child is missing. This represents an incongruous stimulus for mother, leading to increased S-system arousal and SSB. Her response is at once general and localized. The local response consists of attempts to contact the child. For instance, she may go outside to search and call for him. The *general* response takes the form of a nonspecific increase in motor and motivational activity, a progressive increase in the intensity of all movements, a rise in vocal pitch and volume, and increases in self-holding, touching, and other forms of self-stimulation. In addition, mother seeks congruous sensory input by approaching familiar persons and objects in the environment (neighbors, relatives, and friends), or by approaching unfamiliar persons in the *familiar* environment. Younger children may be summoned from play outdoors and gathered close about her. Only in exceptional circumstances will she go outside the circle of familiarity.

The generalized response is aimed at familiar stimuli in general, while the localized response is aimed at the particular person or object whose actions are considered incongruous. Thus the incongruous stimulus of a missing child elicits SSB of a very specific kind as well as SSB aimed at the entire hierarchy of familiar stimuli.

Although there is much nonspecificity in SSB, this is not to imply that any response has an equal probability of being elicited. What, then, determines the form and direction of SSB, given an incongruous stimulus? Notice that this question is different from asking: What causes feeding, as distinct from drinking, or aggression? The latter question assumes the validity of the categories that have been criticized. For this reason, the initial question was phrased in terms of *stimulation*. Another caveat is that the specificity of behavior should not be assumed without first studying its occurrence under various conditions. Fentress (1973) has pointed out that extreme behavioral specificity — where a particular stimulus elicits only a particular response — is very rare; so also is *total nonspecificity,* in which all outputs affect all inputs to an equal degree. This last caveat is relevant to such questions as: What determines whether an individual becomes an alcoholic *or* a criminal *or* a narcotic addict? Even if the question is phrased in terms of stimulation, that is, what determines whether an individual seeks stimulation in the form of alcohol *or* vandalism *or* opiates, one is usually not dealing with single manifestations of social deviance but with multiple manifestations. The concept of the "polydrug" user implies that some drug addicts use more than one drug. However, all addicts are polydrug users if the term "drug" is liberally defined to include tea, coffee, tobacco, and sugar.

Asking for exact specifications of future SSB is tantamount to asking for predictions of every facet of individual behavior, something which is manifestly impossible with present and probably future models of behavior. Nevertheless, the factors that influence the form and direction of SSB include: (1) the source of incongruity; (2) the nature of the stimulus; (3) the degree of development of the cognitive map; (4) the degree of integrity of the cognitive map; (5) the degree of incongruity; (6) the availability of stimulus objects; and (7) the sensorial properties of available stimulus objects.

1. The Source of Incongruity. The direction of SSB in relation to the eliciting stimulus (i.e., approach or avoidance) is fundamentally determined by the source of incongruity, that is, SSB is directed toward congruous stimuli, whereas incongruous stimuli are avoided. For instance, if a nine-month-old infant is faced with the incongruous stimulus of an unfamiliar person or object, the infant will tend to look away from the object and toward "the familiar" (i.e., his mother). Schaffer (1966, p. 100) interprets this response as an attempt "to preserve the familiar and thereby avoid the unfamiliar object." If, however, a familiar person behaves incongruously, the organism's

response is to *approach* the source of incongruity. Thus, an incongruous stimulus *embedded in an otherwise congruous object* (or person) elicits movement toward the object. Returning to the example of the infant, suppose that mother comes up close to the child and starts making uncharacteristic grimaces and noises. The child may laugh or cry, but the same congruity-seeking principle would be expected to apply. Since mother represents a pattern of familiar stimuli, the infant directs his SSB toward her, despite the fact that her behavior is incongruous. This does not mean that the infant seeks incongruity; instead, the infant approaches his attachment objects, even when they behave incongruously, in order to maintain or restore congruity.

2. The Nature of the Stimulus. A basic tenet in stress research is that the response to a stimulus depends on how it is appraised (Lazarus, 1966), and this in turn depends on the individual's prior set of expectancies, or cognitive map. A mother who believes that her child is missing engages in generalized SSB aimed at the familiar, as well as in search behavior directed specifically at the missing child itself. Where the incongruous stimulus relates to an *abstraction,* something which cannot be physically approached, such as of a *belief* that has been threatened by incongruous information, the event would be expected to elicit SSB aimed at maintaining the threatened belief. An illustration of this point can be found in the study *When Prophesy Fails* (Festinger, Riecken, & Schachter, 1956). This was a report about a group of people who believed that, at an appointed time, their area of the country would disappear in a flood, but that they themselves would be rescued by friendly creatures from outer space. When the hour arrived and there was no flood, and no visitation from space creatures, the members of the group came together after a short period of disarray and rationalized the incongruous outcome by telling themselves that their "faith" had prevented the flood. They then sought new converts and spread their beliefs about the space creatures even more vigorously than before.

3. The Degree of Development of the Cognitive Map. SSB aimed at "the familiar" is obviously limited by what is familiar to the individual. For the fetus and newborn, incongruity consists largely of changes in expected amounts and kinds of sensory input (cf., Hutt et al., 1969). Such changes initially elicit a nonspecific increase in SSB aimed not at specific individuals or objects, but at stimulating types of objects, that is, those that are congruous in the sense of providing familiar kinds and

amounts of sensory input. This notion is illustrated by Schaffer and Emerson's (1964) longitudinal study of the growth of attachments in Scottish children. Three phases in attachment formation were identified: (a) an "asocial phase," in which the infant seeks stimulation from all aspects of its environment; (b) a period of "indiscriminate attachment," in which proximity with any human being is sought; and (c) a phase in which specific attachments are formed to adults who provide them with the greatest amounts of stimulation.

4. The Degree of Integrity of the Cognitive Map. For older individuals who already have a cognitive map of their environment, the response to incongruity depends on the extent to which the cognitive map is maintained intact. According to the theory, SSB aimed at specific objects in the environment is normally guided by the cognitive map. The individual has an internal representation of the many different kinds of objects and their boundaries in his environment. He has a clear conception of self, and thus not-self; of what is familiar and what is unfamiliar; of what belongs to him and what belongs to others; and of what is expected of him, normatively approved, and normatively disapproved. Hence, SSB is aimed at familiar, congruous objects — objects that have been internalized in the cognitive map.

The maintenance of a cognitive map is crucially dependent on the ability of the individual to obtain congruent sensory feedback (Chapter 5, this volume). In the face of incongruity and an inability to obtain congruous sensory feedback, the cognitive map begins to disintegrate. It is proposed that as the cognitive map disintegrates, its more "differentiated" and abstract aspects disappear first, leaving intact the basic substratum of familiar kinds and amounts of stimuli. As a result, SSB is increasingly indiscriminate and may be directed at people and objects that were previously considered unfamiliar. As the more differentiated layers of the cognitive map disappear, the individual enters a state somewhat analogous to that of the "asocial" or "indiscriminate attachment" phase of infancy described by Schaffer and Emerson (1964). Consistent with this hypothesis, children who were separated from their families during World War II and placed in foster houses, (and who presumably experienced a partial deterioration of their cognitive maps as a result of this experience), tended to form passionate temporary attachments to strangers and volunteer workers (Burlingham & Freud, 1944). For adults, the response to interpersonal loss or destruction of the home follows a somewhat similar pattern. Recalling earlier points, several authors have observed that a period of sexual promiscuity often intervenes between the loss of an attachment object and the establishment of a new one. In the case of reactions to disaster, a noteworthy feature is the tendency of adults to seek identical forms of help and reassurance from many different persons (Tyhurst, 1951).

5. The Degree of Incongruity. The intensity of SSB is directly related to the degree of incongruity and the resulting level of S-system arousal. At low levels of incongruity and arousal, responses such as eating, drinking, smoking, and general restlessness would be expected to occur; at higher levels, progressively more vigorous forms of SSB appear such as manic activity, "aggression," and self-injury.

6. The Availability of Stimulus Objects. Within a particular "band" of SSB, the form and/or direction of SSB depend on the range of objects that are immediately available. This was demonstrated in an experiment with rats, using brain stimulation (Valenstein et al., 1970). It was found that electrical stimulation of the hypothalamus, using the same stimulus parameters and electrode placements, could elicit eating, drinking, wood gnawing, shuffling of food with the forepaws, sand digging, and sexual activity, depending on whether opportunities for the different types of behavior were provided by the experimenters.

7. The Sensorial Properties of Available Stimulus Objects. Finally, given a particular degree of incongruity and S-system arousal, and the presence of several stimulus objects, those objects will be approached which provide maximal amounts of stimulation within the range of intensities appropriate to the level of S-system arousal. In general, "stimulating" objects (i.e., those which are shiny, colorful, moving, or tasty) tend to be approached more readily than less stimulating objects.

THE FUNCTION OF SSB: INHIBITION BY SENSORY FEEDBACK

It is hypothesized that the sensory input derived from SSB, contrary to the low-arousal hypothesis, *reduces* rather than increases the level of S-system arousal; moreover, the stimulation-induced decrease in S-system arousal is independent of the particular emotional state associated with SSB whether this be pain, fear, grief, joy, or anger. Stimulation-seeking behavior, then, is postulated to have a nonspecific "calming" function. As noted, this view of the effects of the sensory input generated by SSB differs from the usual assumption that stimulation "arouses" or "stimulates." Of course, sensory stimulation can, at times, have an excitatory effect on behavior — presumably when perceived as "incongruous," at some level of awareness, with the individual's cognitive map. But at other times sensory input can have a calming effect on behavior. For instance, it is reported that one of the best ways of reducing fear among troops before entering combat is to involve them in any type of physical activity; the more a soldier's movements are restricted, the more likely he is to become a psychological casualty during military operations (Moran, 1945, p. 42; Marshall, 1947, p. 71; Bourne, 1970, p. 482). Physical exercise is now known to reduce blood pressure, blood lipids, heart rate (Clausen, 1979), anxiety (Morgan, 1979), and the physiological and psychological correlates of the Type A coronary-prone behavior pattern (Blumenthal et al., 1980). Likewise, aggressive acting-out can reduce blood pressure (Hokanson & Shetler, 1961). Both cigarette smoking (Dunn, 1978) and alcohol consumption (Hodgson et al., 1979; Levenson et al., 1980) temporarily dampen the physiological and psychological response to stress. Rocking, stereotyped movements (Bowlby, 1969), and even self-injurious behaviors (Simpson, 1976) also have arousal-reducing effects. Pain can be relieved by rubbing, scratching, needling, and related forms of peripheral stimulation (Melzack, 1973, pp. 183–84). A general sense of calm also follows other types of motor activity (Gal & Lazarus, 1975) such as eating and sex.

Although some of these stimulation-induced calming effects have long been recognized, there has been a tendency to try to explain each one separately rather than trying to formulate a general hypothesis. The fear-reducing effect of physical activity, for instance, is attributed by some to "distraction," as is the pain-reducing effect of massage and needling. The state of calm occurring in the aftermath of aggression and sexual activity has been explained in terms of the "release" of aggressive and sexual "energy" (Lorenz, 1966). The pain-reducing effect of peripheral stimulation has been explained in terms of the celebrated "gate-control" theory of pain (Melzack, 1973), and post-prandial relaxation is attributed to metabolic processes related specifically to the ingestion of protein and carbohydrates. There is, however, a considerable degree of nonspecificity both with regard to the stimuli capable of "reducing" a given emotional state and the emotional states that can be reduced by particular stimuli. Alcohol, for instance, can reduce pain, fear, or hunger; and a particular emotional state such as pain can be alleviated by many different types of stimulation.

The question therefore arises as to whether there may be something common to each of these stimuli which induces the general state of calm. The suggestion here is that the common factor is an increase in peripheral stimulation; further, the sensory stimulation thus obtained is "fed back" into the central nervous system where it is compared with the fundamental core of sensorial expectancies in the cognitive map. If found to be "congruous", the stimulus activates the P-system, which in turn inhibits the S-system. This hypothesized mechanism of "inhibition by sensory feedback" (Mawson, 1978a) may be built into the functioning of living systems in such a way that organisms actively seek stimulation so as to activate the inhibitory P-system. However, individuals may not be consciously "aware" of seeking sensory input, nor that the sensory input so obtained has an inhibitory effect in the central nervous system. Inhibitory stimulation can also, of course, be applied by other individuals or applied artificially. The greater the degree of S-system arousal, the more intense the stimulation must be in order to activate the inhibitory P-system and restore neurotransmitter equilibrium; hence, the greater the intensity of SSB.[2]

In summary, the thesis is that peripheral stimulation reduces S-system arousal by the activation of inhibitory pathways in the brain. The mechanism appears to apply not just to pain, hunger, or fear, but to any given emotional state; furthermore, SSB varies in intensity according to the level of S-system arousal.

THE RELATION BETWEEN SSB AND THE COGNITIVE MAP

With regard to the relationship between congruity seeking and stimulation seeking, it is postulated that from the moment of birth SSB is guided toward stimuli that are consistent with the rudimentary cognitive map. What begins as an attempt to obtain familiar amounts and kinds of stimuli, gradually becomes an attempt to obtain familiar patterns of stimulation. Thus the concept of stimulation-seeking behavior entails the notion of seeking congruous stimulation.[3]

The cognitive map of the fetus and newborn infant is initially presumed to consist of expectancies regarding quantitative features of its environment; that is, *amounts* and *kinds* of tactile, vestibular, visual, auditory, and other types of stimulation. Thus, when the newborn experiences unaccustomed changes in sensory input, its stimulation-seeking response is relatively indiscriminate. With a burst of general activity the infant directs his SSB at himself and at other stimulus objects in the environment.

Since the infant has yet to differentiate between familiar and unfamiliar stimulus patterns, the objects approached and "imprinted" upon are simply those that provide large amounts of stimulation. Animal studies show that colorful, shiny, sound-producing and moving objects are more likely to be approached by newborns than objects with the reverse set of properties (Smith, 1969). Human infants also become attached to adults who are highly responsive to them, or provide the most *stimulation,* not necessarily those who supply food and perform basic caretaking functions (Schaffer & Emerson, 1964), although these individuals are usually the same.

While maintaining proximity to these objects (i.e., seeking stimulation from them), the newborn begins to internalize their sensory properties as differentiated patterns of stimulation. The internal "map" of his mother, for instance, is a patterned collection of stimulus characteristics, for example, her smell(s), taste(s), appearance(s), sound(s), and habitual ways of touching and holding. Thus, distinct patterns of stimulation are constructed from the initial substratum of familiar types and quantities of stimuli, forming the class of attachment objects. With the development of linguistic skills and the capacity for symbolic communication, the cognitive map of the maturing individual further differentiates into overlapping patterns of internalized "meanings" — meanings connected with the self-concept, various affiliations such as neighborhood and citizenship, and with the values and norms of particular societies and subcultures. The cognitive map also becomes increasingly ordered in terms of psychological salience, with particular persons, objects, and ideas (e.g., religious beliefs) having greater psychological importance than other aspects of the environment (Stokols, 1979, pp. 39–42).

NOTES

1. Bolles (1979, p. 291) contends that "most psychologists have abandoned the hope of explaining social motives in terms of acquired drives . . . [and that] we appear to be entering an era in which virtually no one believes in the concept of drive. [Nevertheless] the word 'drive' . . . will probably continue in use for some time, as it was originally, i.e., to describe the existence or operation of some motivational system with a physiological basis." While the deficit-repletion model of feeding and drinking has been much criticized, the assumption still prevails that it is useful to think of behavior in terms of distinct motivational systems, viz. feeding, drinking, sex, aggression, etc. (see e.g., the periodic reviews on "basic drives" in the *Annual Review of Psychology*.)

2. Bowlby (1969, p. 294) notes that when a human infant is only mildly distressed he can be calmed by being given something to suck. With increasing levels of distress, progressively more vigorous stimulation, for example, rocking, is needed to pacify the infant. Simpson (1976) has reviewed studies indicating that individuals with a tendency to cut or mutilate themselves report that they do so in moments of extreme psychological distress ("S-system arousal"), yet immediately experience an overwhelming sense of calm and relief.

3. At this level, the terms incongruity and congruity represent theoretical abstractions or assumptions. In practice, deciding whether a particular stimulus is "incongruous" (or whether a particular response provides "congruity") depends on a detailed knowledge of the individual's cognitive map.

8

TRANSIENT CRIMINALITY: PSYCHOLOGICAL ASPECTS

Our thesis is that transient criminality is initiated by stressful life events in a context of low "social supports," often combined with physiological changes due to drugs or alcohol. It is assumed that people build cognitive maps of their environment, and that active attempts to preserve the cognitive map are initiated by incongruous events and/or increased S-system arousal. The latter in turn increases the intensity of stimulation-seeking behavior (SSB). SSB is at once nonspecific (in the sense of being aimed at congruous stimuli in general) and at the same time capable of being highly specific, depending on the factors outlined in the previous chapter. When stimuli have been obtained that match the cognitive map, the P-system is activated; this inhibits the S-system, leading to a general state of calm.

If S-system arousal increases and the individual is unable to obtain congruous stimulation (thereby activating the inhibitory P-system), three changes occur: (a) an increase in susceptibility to social influence; (b) a temporary partial breakdown of the individual's cognitive map; and (c) a further increase in SSB, all of which place the individual at risk of criminality.

This chapter discusses the contribution to crime of susceptibility to influence and disturbances of the cognitive map.

SUSCEPTIBILITY TO SOCIAL INFLUENCE

When highly aroused, individuals may be led to do and say things that would be unthinkable to them under normal circumstances. Hence, the leaders of crowds are critical in determining whether criminal or noncriminal acts are committed.[1] In addition, aroused individuals tend to adopt uncritically and act upon new ideas or beliefs to which they are exposed, all of which may increase the risk of criminal deviance.

Waves of imitative crime often occur after bizarre or dramatic crimes are reported in the news media (Tarde, 1912). Examination of the *Uniform Crime Reports* for 1960–1966 revealed that substantial increases in aggravated assaults and robberies occurred after the assassination of President Kennedy in November 1963 and after the murder of eight Chicago nurses in July 1966. Neither rape nor crimes against property increased after these events (Berkowitz & Macaulay, 1971).

Phillips (1974, 1977, 1979, 1980) reported that stories published in newspapers dealing with suicides appear to trigger additional, imitative suicides, many of which are disguised as automobile accidents; moreover, newspaper stories concerning murder-suicides trigger additional, imitative murder-suicides. Data on U.S. commercial and noncommercial airplane accidents were collected and related to newspaper stories dealing with murder-suicides. The stories chosen had to involve deaths in the United States, two or more victims, one murderer acting alone, and both murderer and victims dying within 48 hours of each other. Each story also had to be carried on the front page of the *New York Times* or *Los Angeles Times,* or appear on national television. In all, 18 stories met the criteria. The results showed that almost twice as many noncommercial airplane fatalities occurred on the third day after publicized cases of murder-suicide as would have been expected by chance. *Single-fatality* noncommercial airplane crashes, however, which by definition cannot involve both murder and suicide, tended to remain constant. Figure 8.1 shows the daily fluctuation of U.S. *commercial* air crash fatalities before and after murder-suicide stories. Fatalities increase just after the 0 date, and persist for seven to nine days, the initial peak occurring after three to four days, a secondary one after seven to eight days.

Many of these imitative murder-suicides would appear to qualify as instances of transient criminality, since there is no reason to believe that the perpetrators were chronic criminals. If the model is correct, the perpetrators would be expected to have recently experienced one or more incongruous life events and to have been in a state of heightened S-system arousal. In future research it would be of interest to supplement the epidemiological studies undertaken by Phillips with "psychological autopsies" of the individuals involved in these murder-suicides.[2] (See Platt, 1987, for a discussion of recent literature on imitative suicidal behavior.)

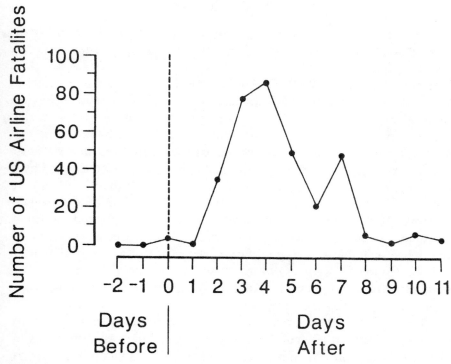

Figure 8.1
Daily fluctuation of U.S. air carrier fatalities for a two-week period, before, during (Day 0), and after newspaper stories about murder-suicides (U.S. 1950–73).

Source: Phillips (1980, p. 1012). Reprinted with permission.

BREAKDOWN OF THE COGNITIVE MAP

We turn now to the question of how criminality is associated with a breakdown of the cognitive map. The idea of the cognitive map "breaking down" and being associated with the commission of a crime appears similar to the notion of a *weakened conscience*. However, as discussed below, the concepts of conscience and cognitive map are entirely different.[3]

Cognitive Map Versus Conscience

The idea of a conscience has played a major role in theories of criminal behavior (Zilboorg, 1967) and continues to play a central role in psychoanalytic views of crime causation as well as in certain learning theories (e.g., Trasler, 1962; Eysenck, 1978; Mednick, 1977). Common to such theories is the notion that conforming (or noncriminal) behavior entails the *suppression of antisocial impulses*. Laymen refer to the mechanism of suppression as the "conscience," Freudians call it the "superego," and learning theorists speak of "conditioned anxiety." These theories also allow for the possibility that crimes may be committed as a result of immersion in a criminal subculture. According to Freudian theory, some individuals also have an overactive conscience, experience pathological guilt, and break the law in order to be caught and punished (Alexander & Staub, 1931). In sum, crime may result from (a) a *normal* conscience (where certain types of crime are expected as a part of a "way of life"), (b) from a *weak* or *absent* conscience (especially in the case of so-called psychopathic criminals), or (c) from an *overactive* conscience (in the case of so-called neurotic criminals).

The intent here is not to criticize each theory on its own, but to focus on the shared notion of a conscience — a notion which, in spite of many different labels, forms, and presumed origins, is still widely regarded as a necessary factor in psychological explanations of crime.[4] First, certain questionable assumptions in conscience theory are noted; second, an alternative model is outlined, utilizing the concept of cognitive map. Essentially, it is proposed that legal and moral norms are internalized as part of the cognitive map of one's environment; people attempt to maintain their cognitive maps by seeking "the familiar" and avoiding "the unfamiliar" and in so doing remain within the dictates of the law. The suggestion is that much criminality is associated with temporary or chronic disturbances in a person's cognitive map.

The term *conscience* refers to "the cognitive and affective processes which constitute an internalized moral governor over an individual's conduct" (Aronfreed, 1968, cited in Trasler, 1979b, p. 208). It includes: "an awareness of the nature and origin of social rules; the ability to evaluate morally one's own actions and intentions; the avoidance of forbidden behavior; the performance of socially approved behavior; and feelings of obligation, guilt, and remorse" (Trasler, 1979b). In view of these various meanings, it is important to be clear as to the specific meanings being criticized. There is no objection to the term conscience insofar as it means an awareness of right and wrong, or feelings of obligation, guilt, and remorse. What is being disputed is rather the theoretical framework in which the concept is embedded; namely, the assumptions that:

1. the conscience is a mental function or faculty separate from other aspects of cognition, and that
2. the conscience operates by suppressing behavior that would otherwise, in the absence of controls, be exhibited.

While the development of the conscience is believed to be tied to, and dependent upon, intellectual development as a whole (Kohlberg, 1969), it is considered a separate psychological realm — separate, that is, from the individual's sense of self or identity. Moral cognition, then, is thought to develop separately from other aspects of the cognitive structure. This is an ancient psychological distinction that can be traced historically from eighteenth-century German faculty psychology to Sigmund Freud. Freud's (1962) classification of mental faculties in terms of ego, id, and superego, is similar to that of German faculty psychology in terms of cognition, affection, and conation (Hilgard, 1980).

The second assumption is that the conscience plays a vital role in the suppression of antisocial urges, drives, or instincts. In Freudian theory, for instance, the superego is constantly battling to control antisocial, aggressive, and other self-centered urges of the id. Mednick (1977, p. 3) similarly contends that "there actually *are* some strong instincts and passions that society must channel and inhibit to maintain even the poor semblance of civilization we see around us." The assumption is that, without a conscience, basic drives would increase beyond the limit of self-control, leading to deviant or criminal actions. Moreover, according to these learning theories children acquire a conscience by means of avoidance conditioning; that is, by learning to associate desired but forbidden behavior with pain and punishment. The anxiety subsequently experienced at the thought of doing something wrong, and being punished for it, serves to override competing tendencies to perform antisocial acts (Mowrer, 1960; Eysenck, 1978, 1979).

While humans do behave "aggressively" at times, the assumption that aggressive and felonious tendencies constantly strive for expression (and *would* be expressed, if it were not for the conscience), is almost certainly incorrect. This model of human behavior also has ancient origins — traceable through Hobbes, the theological writings of St. Thomas Aquinas, and the Old Testament (Niebuhr, 1944) — and is commonly known as the "hydraulic" or energy model of motivation. One version of the theory is that human beings have sexual and aggressive "drives" which operate on principles similar to those of a steam engine. Just as steam energy builds up pressure and can blow the lid off a kettle or be harnessed to turn the wheels of an engine, so aggressive and sexual "energies" are believed to accumulate in the tissues, eventually to be "released" by certain stimuli in the environment (Lorenz, 1966). Despite the popularity of this model in the public mind — as shown by such common phrases as "blowing one's top," "bottling-up tension," and "letting off steam" — hydraulic concepts of energy, pressure, and release have no counterpart in physiological systems. The analogy between hydraulics and human motivation is therefore false and misleading (Hinde, 1960).

The assumptions concerning the cognitive map and its relationship to behavior are entirely different. Let us begin by restating the basic assumptions of the overall model:

- Individuals build cognitive maps of their interpersonal, physical, ideological, and normative environment.
- Cognitive maps are organized in terms of psychological salience.
- Individuals attempt to preserve their cognitive map.

What, then, is the relationship between moral concepts and other aspects of cognition? Our thesis is that legal and moral rules represent one aspect of the individual's familiar psychosocial environment and are internalized along with the self-concept, attachment figures, and other aspects of the individual's familiar environment as an integral part of the overall cognitive map. Thus, standards of right and wrong are as much a part of an individual's cognitive structure as are his internalizations of key attachment figures and his own sense of self. However, not all aspects of the environment (and of the cognitive map) are equally important from a psychological point of view. It is assumed that the cognitive map is organized in terms of psychological "salience" (Harvey & Schroeder, 1963; Stokols, 1979, pp. 39–62), meaning that threats to, or the loss of, certain aspects of the environment are much more disturbing than the loss of other parts. Mother, father, spouse, children, and the "territorial core" (Porteus, 1976) of the home, are generally the most important aspects of one's environment.

Just as objects and people vary in salience, so too do ideas, values, beliefs, and norms. Sumner (1908/1940), for instance, noted that there are certain rules one is merely *expected* to follow (folkways); other that one *ought* to follow (mores); and still others that one *must* obey (laws). The greater the degree of obligation implied by a rule, the greater the importance that is attached to it. Thus there are some moral, ethical, and legal norms which have virtually the character of *sacred* beliefs (e.g., laws against killing, stealing, and committing treason), while at the other end of the spectrum there are social practices or customs (e.g., throwing salt over one's shoulder) that have little if any psychological importance for most people.

Thus we are as "attached" to certain moral beliefs as we are to the significant persons, places, and objects in our lives; we are as distressed by the flouting of cherished beliefs as by attacks on attachment figures, and we defend our moral beliefs against criticism with as much vigor as we defend our families and our property.

Turning to the role of the cognitive map in "controlling" behavior, the assumption is recalled that individuals attempt to maintain their cognitive maps. Maintaining a cognitive map is accomplished by seeking out and remaining in the proximity of the objects, people, and places whose characteristics have been internalized, and by performing actions or adopting styles of behavior that reflect a commitment to internalized rules, values, and beliefs. Such actions are designed to match the expectancies in the cognitive map with actual events and stimuli, thereby reaffirming the cognitive map.

With regard to the relationship between the cognitive map and behavior, unlike the conscience, which serves to suppress antisocial drives and behaviors, the cognitive map is more like the flow chart of a computer program; or, as its name implies, like a map indicating spatial boundaries and frequented points and pathways in an animal's home range. Just as a flow chart *defines* rather than constrains the operation of the computer, and a map *portrays* the activities of an animal within its territory rather than suppressing it, so a person's internalized concept of self identifies that individual as the sort of person he or she is; it does not suppress an alternative ego struggling to assert itself. Similarly, internalized moral standards define or constitute a program of the person's moral actions; they do not force or oblige him to act contrary to his supposedly "natural tendencies" to be selfish or self-aggrandizing.[5]

This is not to imply that individuals passively follow the instructions of the cognitive map. Instead, they actively attempt to preserve their cognitive map by adopting certain behaviors as stipulated by internalized abstractions, for example, norms, values and beliefs, and by remaining physically close to the external objects whose sensory characteristics have been internalized. It is not that individuals are simply guided toward familiar objects and away from the unfamiliar. There is, as noted earlier, much evidence to indicate that individuals vigorously strive to maintain contact with familiar persons, places, and objects, and to maintain familiar habits or patterns of behavior, especially under stress ("incongruity") (Bowlby, 1973; Marris, 1974; Salzen, 1978; Rheingold, 1985).

To summarize, it is proposed that individuals build cognitive maps of their environment and that internalized rules represent one aspect of the overall cognitive map, not a separate mental faculty or function; moreover, just as certain persons are psychologically more important than others, so certain rules are valued more highly than others. Individuals attempt to preserve their cognitive maps by maintaining proximity to the objects whose characteristics have been internalized, and by adhering to internalized rules and habitual patterns of behavior. Conformity to rules is thus seen as one aspect of the process involved in maintaining a cognitive map.

Individuals are inherently motivated to follow the "instructions" of the cognitive map; the map "defines" how a person acts in his environment. Unlike the so-called conscience, which forces one to act morally despite powerful desires to act self-interestedly or antisocially, the idea of violating rules which have been internalized as a salient part of the cognitive map is as unthinkable to the individual as adopting a completely new and different persona. The suggestion is that it is precisely this conservative tendency to maintain one's cognitive map by seeking the "familiar" and avoiding the "unfamiliar" which ensures that individuals remain within their own territorial and proprietorial boundaries, and rarely violate social norms.

The ability to distinguish between familiar and unfamiliar indicates that clearly demarcated boundaries and criteria exist for so distinguishing them. Applying this notion to property crime, the individual recognizes certain objects as not belonging to him and therefore avoids them; or, if they have some "familiar" properties, he approaches them hesitantly and cautiously. In strange surroundings, or near strange dwellings, the individual experiences incongruity and S-system arousal and therefore moves away from them and toward familiar surroundings.

Consider the hypothetical example of someone browsing in a store. According to "conscience theory" the person's natural inclination is to take a desired item and leave without paying for it. He or she refrains from doing so, however, because the desire to steal is suppressed by conditioned anxiety. By contrast, the theory of cognitive maps says that the person acts within the law because he or she is aware, first, of being in territory that belongs to someone else, and second, that the items for sale must be brought to the cashier and purchased before being taken home and "possessed."

Consider next the case of residential burglary. Why are so few burglaries committed, in view of the high proportion of homes left unoccupied during the day? Conscience theory would attribute it to a strong superego, or successful avoidance conditioning. According to the theory of cognitive maps, burglary is rare because each person's home is "familiar territory" to that person and "unfamiliar territory" for almost everyone else; hence, individuals orient themselves toward their own homes and tend to avoid other people's homes — except when invited, or when there is a special and legitimate reason for going there. Even under these conditions, however, approaching other people's homes is fraught with potential sources of incongruity.[6]

The complicated rituals surrounding the entry of one individual into another's social space have been compared to the recognition ceremonies of nesting birds (Guhl, 1965; Porteus, 1976). Much like birds, people react strongly to the discovery that their home has been burgled or entered without their knowledge. The intrusion itself may be as disturbing as the loss of money and goods or the extent of damage to the house. Burglary victims often describe the experience in terms of a personal violation akin to "rape," and afterwards spend considerable time cleaning and washing their things, feeling that they have been spoiled and dirtied by the intruder (Waller & Okihiro, 1978, p. 30; Maguire, 1980; Walsh, 1980a, pp. 109–12).[7, 8]

In summary, the suggestion is that theft and burglary are normally prevented because the items available to be stolen and their location are perceived as "alien"; in addition, the majority of individuals have internalized as part of their cognitive map the complex set of rules involved in the exchange of goods.

With regard to the prevention of interpersonal crimes such as rape and assault, one's approaches toward and contact with other people are likewise highly ritualized in terms of numerous taken-for-granted rules of social interaction. Garfinkel (1967) has pioneered the study of such rules and conducted experiments showing that individuals become confused and distressed when they are made the victim of contrived encounters in which subtle interactional rules are deliberately broken. Familiar individuals are normally approached quite differently than strangers; there are also unwritten rules about interpersonal distance (Hall, 1959), the amount of eye contact and physical contact people are expected to maintain when interacting with others, all of which are strongly influenced by the degree of familiarity between the parties involved. The probability of someone engaging in a rape or assault will thus be reduced to the extent that interactional rules have been internalized in his cognitive map.

Cognitive Maps and Crime

With regard to the implications of the model for explaining crime, there are at least three ways in which cognitive maps may be involved:

1. Certain criminal acts may be internalized in the cognitive map as a normal or acceptable activity.
2. Crime can result from disturbances in the cognitive map.
3. Crime can be facilitated indirectly when the manmade environment fails to provide clearly demarcated boundaries between public and private space.

Crime as a Way of Life. For some, certain forms of criminal behavior can be a "way of life"; that is, activities that are considered criminal in society as a whole may be considered socially acceptable by the minority group or the individuals performing them. Examples include diverse sexual and matrimonial practices (e.g., bigamy in certain religious sects), stealing from public corporations or other business establishments, certain commercial practices, and some terrorist activities. Such practices and activities may reflect an intact cognitive map on the part of the individuals engaging in them. In other respects, the minority group may well share the attitudes and beliefs of the larger society. The average convict, for instance, has a special loathing for child molesters.

Disturbances of the Cognitive Map. Our thesis is that criminal behavior on the part of individuals who normally obey the law is associated with temporary disturbances in the offender's cognitive map.

Since the inception of the principle for determining criminal responsibility known as the M'Naghten Rule, in mid-nineteenth-century England, most courts have held that offenders are either "sane" (and therefore responsible for their crimes) or flagrantly "insane" (and therefore not responsible). However, between so-called sanity and severe psychosis lies a vast realm of subtle, subclinical mental disorder, involving perceptual and cognitive disturbances of many kinds. Such disturbances are believed to be widespread among incarcerated offenders, and there are suggestions that altered states of consciousness and cognition occur in normally law-abiding individuals before or during the commission of crimes (e.g., Cressey, Laing, Lemert, and Milgram — see Chapters 2 and 3, this volume). However, little in the way of systematic research has been carried out to determine their prevalence, nature, and practical significance.

There are formidable difficulties in conducting such research, not to mention using it for legal purposes. The mental aberrations may indeed be subtle and unremarkable in comparison to the gravity of the crime; there are few, if any, accepted neuropsychological tests available for measuring such deficits;[9] it may be very difficult to determine whether disturbances in cognitive functioning — if present at the time of examination — were present at the time of the crime, or arose *de novo* from the stress of criminal proceedings; lastly, while an offender may claim to have had a disturbed sensorium at the moment of the crime, this could be construed as a means of self-exoneration rather than a truthful statement about his mental condition. In this connection, Herjanic and Meyer (1977, p. 427) write:

> The common stereotype of friends and relatives drinking together on a weekend until a quarrel erupts and someone gets killed . . . was seen frequently enough among the cases we studied. . . . (T)he statement that he (the murderer) did not know what he was doing while under the influence of alcohol was encountered frequently, but even though it may be quite true, it is impossible to accept at face value because it was made to exonerate, and only possible to prove in exceptional circumstances.

The information presently available on cognitive impairments in persistent offenders, both juvenile and adult,[10] tends to involve impairments due to organic conditions, especially alcohol. The suggestion here is that similar types of cognitive impairment will be found in normally law-abiding individuals who have committed crimes while experiencing severe psychosocial stress.

If, as conscience theory predicts, crime is due to weakened inhibitory controls, then the cognitive impairments associated with this loss of control would be expected to be restricted to the sphere of legal and/or moral norms (i.e., a poorly developed "moral sense"). A different prediction can be made from cognitive map theory, which contends that legal-moral norms represent only one aspect of the total internalized environment. Hence disturbances of the cognitive map would be expected to take the form of diffuse cognitive impairments — disturbances in moral concepts, self-image, and cognitive perceptual functioning in general.

Although these hypotheses await empirical investigation, there are suggestions that one or more of the following types of disturbance may be experienced shortly before or during the commission of crime: a partial loss of identity; feelings of detachment or unreality; difficulty in concentration; language difficulties; and various kinds of perceptual and sensorimotor deficits. Following their crime, many offenders are reported as saying that they "did not know what they were doing"; that "something came over them"; that they felt an overwhelming sense of guilt and remorse, and even satisfaction at having been apprehended (see Chapter 2, this volume; Wade, 1970; Cameron, 1964; Rada, 1978a, 1978b; Bowerman, 1979).

Alcohol and Drugs. Although information is available on the disorganizing effects of particular agents and substances (e.g., alcohol) on cognition and perception, little information is available on such effects within a context of violence or other forms of crime. One study which does fulfill this requirement investigated the relationship between homicide and alcoholic amnesia (Wolf, 1980). The report dealt with five unmarried Alaskan men in their twenties and thirties who had no prior felony charge and who had committed first-degree murder while drinking, yet had no memory of the events in question. Amnesia was induced experimentally in these men by challenge doses of alcohol. After baseline measures were recorded, subjects were asked to drink four ounces of whiskey (or nine ounces of beer). Vital signs and blood alcohol concentration (BAC) were measured at 45-minute intervals for four hours and a 5-minute EEG was recorded, following the ingestion of another four ounces of whiskey. All subjects abruptly became angry and challenging one-and-a-half to two-and-a-half hours after drinking began, when the minimum BAC was 125 mg. per 100 ml. When the men were questioned the next day, gaps in their memory for events of the day before coincided with the observed change of mood. One subject actually became violent, while the others reported having violent feelings. Memory losses ranged from two to seven hours. Following the abrupt change in affect, subjects talked about events in their past that were intensely emotional and personal; yet, when questioned the next day, they had no recollection of these discussions. Wolf concluded that: (a) idiosyncratic blackouts can be reproduced in a controlled situation; (b) the memories of events occurring during the blackouts were not "state dependent" since they could not be recalled when the individual was again drinking; and (c) violent feelings tended to correlate temporally with EEG slowing[11] and with the subject's amnesia.

More recently, Senay and Wettstein (1983) described 24 cases in which homicide was committed in association with large amounts of psychoactive drugs. There was evidence of severe cognitive disturbance in close temporal association with the use of intoxicants. However, there was no evidence of premeditation, no avoidance of arrest, and no apparent motive. Consistent with the model proposed here, the offenders had experienced multiple losses or other severe stress in the months preceding the crimes, and the increase in stress was closely correlated with the increase in drug use. The authors theorize that excessive drug use increases the risk of violence by impairing the brain systems responsible for reality testing and judgment, that is, systems involved in distinguishing between inner and outer stimuli, perception, inner reality testing, awareness of the appropriateness and likely consequences of intended behavior, and the ability to integrate contradictory thoughts, feelings, and behaviors. The authors emphasize that such disturbances are not equivalent to a "toxic psychosis" since hallucinations and delirium are not always present, and the impairments primarily involve the ego functions of reality testing, judgment, and synthesis-integration.

Hypoglycemia. According to Wilder (1947), hypoglycemia can induce mental states similar to those produced by alcohol, and such states also tend to be followed by amnesia. The psychology of criminal acts committed during episodes of hypoglycemia is said to be based on impaired judgment, sensory perception and motor reactions, and on "the peculiar negativism of the hypoglycemic, reminiscent of catatonic negativism" (Wilder, 1947, p. 112). In striking contrast to the normal personality of the patient, authority figures are addressed negatively and defiantly. Irritability and aggression may also be manifested in domestic violence, homicidal ideas or threats, and suicidal behavior. Hypoglycemia may also be associated with disorderly conduct, exhibitionism, defecating in the living room, tactless sexual advances, masturbation in public, sadism, sodomy, embezzlement, and shoplifting. These acts may be followed by amnesia, or by deep shame and embarrassment. Speech is also affected; it may be exceptionally soft, or the person may have difficulty talking in a whisper. There may be a tendency to use foreign languages, to affect a sophisticated style, or to utter profanities " 'that would shock an Army Sergeant' " (p. 115). When crimes are committed during hypoglycemic episodes the patient is usually in an agitated state and the crimes are impulsive.

A case of hypoglycemia-related vehicular homicide described by Bovill (1973) is of interest because it provides a detailed account of the mental changes associated with hypoglycemia and with a homicide. A 42-year-old physician's wife drove her car through a nearby town late one night and a cyclist was found dead at the side of the road she had just passed. Damage to the woman's car and other evidence later connected her with the accident. After arriving at her destination (she was delivering a wedding present), she explained a cut finger by saying that a truck had backed into her car and smashed the near side window. Some of the broken glass had fallen on the front seat and cut her as she lifted the parcel. She spent two hours with her friends, appearing and acting normally. Returning home along the same road, she noticed that an accident had occurred and slowed down to offer help. Seeing that no help was needed, she continued on her way. On arriving home, her husband found her calm but detached. Later, she appeared to have no knowledge of the accident but did not deny having been in the area at the time it occurred. She appeared to have "an inaccurate impression of the time scale of the night's events" (p. 353). Breathalyzer tests were negative.

She was admitted to the hospital for observation. Several years earlier her husband had suffered coronary thromboses and from this time she had started moderate drinking. There were occasional episodes, about which she was subsequently amnesic, in which she was verbally belligerent and mildly paranoid. At times, sweating, tremor, and nausea suggested a hangover state. At other times she seemed detached, lacked a sense of time, and complained of exhaustion, anxiety, and depression. She denied lapses of memory, with the exception of the central one of the accident.

There had been "special stress" in the few days preceding the accident, and she had fasted for about 21 hours before the accident. Earlier in the evening the family noticed her by now familiar strangeness, lack of concentration, and unconcern for the passage of time, yet she did not seem incapable of driving.

While in the hospital she showed no cravings or withdrawal symptoms; her comportment suggested mild drunkenness on two occasions, but she had not been drinking. She showed normal grief and horror at what had occurred, exacerbated by the realization that she had committed a major crime without being aware of it. She had episodes of strangeness on two occasions, in which she was detached, offhand, and irritable, but fully coordinated. Subsequently, she was partially amnesic for these discussions.

The patient's history, her somewhat strange behavior, the low overall frequency of EEG rhythms, and a low resting blood sugar level, suggested hypoglycemia. This was confirmed by an extended glucose tolerance test (GTT), in which a profound hypoglycemia of 30 mgm. occurred at four hours. Later GTTs indicated a clear correlation between low blood sugar levels and abnormal cerebral function.

An attempt was made to duplicate the events which led up to the accident. After a 21-hour fast, the blood sugar level was measured, the patient was given 50 gm. of glucose, and EEG recording began. The blood sugar level began to drop from its peak of 176 mgm. after one hour and overbreathing produced bursts of (slow) EEG activity between two and six cycles per second (c.p.s.). Below 70 mgm. she had difficulty with simple calculations and answering quiz questions to which she knew the answers. Below 50 mgm. she was unable to cite nursery rhymes. At 44 mgm. and four c.p.s. on the EEG she became ataxic, uncoordinated and unable to perform automatic movements. At the end of the session she seemed unaware that over four and a half hours had passed. The results of the test suggested that nutritional conditions experienced by the patient, together with psychological stress and the small quantity of alcohol, both of which can enhance hypoglycemia (Williams, 1970), "would be highly likely to have brought her to the time of the accident in a severely hypoglycemic state, though not necessarily incapable of driving a car automatically" (p. 357).[12]

Impaired cognition and perceptual distortion are said to be ubiquitous in all types of psychiatric patients, as well as in prison inmates. Commonly encountered are impairments involving: worsening memory; problems in spatial orientation, including distance estimation; the comprehension of written information; borderline aphasia, for example, difficulty using nouns, even though on formal aphasic testing the objects presented to them can be named; borderline apraxias, where patients have difficulty carrying out familiar tasks; and other perceptual distortions, including strange-appearing lights, alterations in color perception, distortions in body image, and difficulty placing events in time sequence (Bowerman, 1979).

According to Bowerman, these defects are often unmasked by glucose tolerance testing. One patient twice became homicidal during the three days of high carbohydrate intake prior to glucose tolerance testing. Others became so ill during testing that they could not sit up. Patients admitted feeling hot one moment and cold the next, and many felt light-headed or faint on standing. Other symptoms included: ataxia, difficulty concentrating, blurred vision, motor restlessness, and anxiety alternating with depression. However, it was striking that "the patients themselves did not recognize a change in their level of adjustment during the course of the testing" (p. 229), and tended to rationalize any impairments or difficulties they experienced. Since many patients improved on a low carbohydrate diet much more than they did from chemotherapy and/or psychotherapy, Bowerman suggested the diagnosis of "carbohydrate intolerance."

Based on investigations on inmates in the Oregon State Prison, Bowerman (1979, p. 230) wrote:

> Immediately in doing psychotherapy in a prison the question about memory comes up among the individuals because they complain about it so much. The standard teaching about memory among inmates is that they have a memory deficit which they feign, to avoid the problems of guilt about their crime. After careful investigation it was quite evident that this concept is floridly false (Kramer, 1977). These men have a great many problems with all kinds of cognitive and perceptual disorders.

Bowerman also described a case which conforms exactly to our definition of a transient offender (p. 230):

> One inmate, who had been a former business executive with no history of antisocial behavior, was convicted and had long sentences for five rapes which had occurred in the space of about two months. During the course of psychotherapy it required two years for him to remember an automobile accident which occurred prior to the time of these rapes. After the accident, which was not a serious one, his general social and vocational adjustment deteriorated until the time the rapes occurred and he was caught and incarcerated.[13]

In conclusion, transient criminality appears to be associated with diffuse cognitive impairment arising from alcohol intoxication, hypoglycemia, drug ingestion, and possibly from psychosocial stress, and, as Bowerman's case report suggests, from head injury. There may be a complicated interactive effect involving: psychosocial stress, leading to cognitive impairment, leading to poor diet and/or excessive drug or alcohol intake, leading to further cognitive impairment and stress, culminating eventually in some form of deviant or criminal act (cf., Senay & Wettstein, 1983). It is to be hoped that future research will investigate and unravel these complexities.

Environmental Design, Cognitive Maps, and Crime. As proposed above, criminal activity may be associated with a deteriorating cognitive map. In addition, certain features of the manmade environment may contribute indirectly to crime on a communitywide basis, due to architectural designs and layouts which fail to provide clear boundaries between public and private property.

Ideas along these lines have been pioneered by Oscar Newman (1972, 1973, 1975), who argues that crime may be due, in part, to the loss of "defensible space" created by modern city planning and architectural designs. Newman's thesis is that people defend and keep watch over areas they perceive as their own territory. Certain manmade environments, however, discourage residents from feeling that the immediate areas around their home is their territory, and the residents therefore tend not to question strangers and are less willing to develop informal ties with neighbors. This is especially true in public housing, where the absence of territorial markers and boundaries makes it difficult to distinguish between familiar and unfamiliar people. The weak social ties so formed are responsible not only for the epidemic fear of being the victim of criminals (Newman, 1973) but tend to discourage people from "defending" their homes or home area. The net effect is that greater opportunities are provided for criminals to gain access to residential neighborhoods in order to commit crimes.

Newman recognizes that environmental design affects both victims and criminals; he believes that residential sites marked with symbols of ownership encourage homeowners to be proprietorial and deter potential criminals. However, almost all of his work to date has focused on the homeowner — the victim of crime — rather than on the psychology of the perpetrator.

A crucial aspect of the concept of territoriality is that individuals remain within their own territorial boundaries. Conflicts over territorial ownership, when they occasionally arise, are normally resolved by shouts and gestures rather than by physical violence. Perhaps this is because the intruder recognizes that he *is* intruding into another's territory, and retreats accordingly.

Territorial behavior is almost always explained functionally, that is, in terms of its adaptive consequences, and rarely in terms of proximal mechanisms. Here it is suggested that territorial behavior is a special case of congruity seeking: that is, people try to preserve the cognitive maps of their own area by seeking out and remaining in familiar territory, as well as by avoiding unfamiliar areas. Territorial behavior, then, can be considered one aspect of the process involved in maintaining a cognitive map.

If the manmade environment is so designed as to de-emphasize property ownership and territorial boundaries, it will tend to be seen as an impersonal no-man's-land by resident and stranger alike. Not only will residents not patrol and defend the area, but strangers will not avoid it. Hence, the risk of crime may be increased in such areas.[14]

Newman appears to assume that criminals and noncriminals respond alike to territorial markers and that such markers act as a general deterrent to crime. If, however, as suggested here, the response to territorial symbols is influenced by the integrity of the individual's cognitive map, the presence of territorial markers would be expected to reinforce conforming behavior. Conversely, the absence of territorial markers would be expected to facilitate various forms of crime, as Newman also proposes, and more so for those experiencing a temporary partial deterioration in their cognitive maps. Consider the example of shoplifting, which has been discussed with great insight by Walsh (1978).

In the traditional counter-service store the shopkeeper functioned as a physical barrier by standing in front of the goods, by collecting and wrapping them, and then by placing them in the shopper's basket. In the modern self-service store, however, this barrier has disappeared. Although the increased rate of shoplifting in self-service compared to counter-service stores is attributed to ease of opportunity for theft, it could also reflect the disappearance of psychological barriers between merchandise, owner, and customer. Although this hypothesis awaits investigation, some remarks by Walsh (1978) on shopping and shoplifting in England are particularly relevant.

Until the 1950s, shopping was expected to be slow and time consuming, but the loss of time was balanced by the opportunity for conversation and gossip. In such moments, we can surmise, people's cognitive maps of their neighbors, community events, shopping procedures, and norms were amplified, structured, and reinforced. Today, however, shopping is "fast and silent, rapid and rapacious, rather than slow and conversational" (p. 46). Also in the past, shopping was highly ritualized; shoppers were helped and advised on the most suitable commodity. Moreover, in the counter-service shop, it was much easier to appreciate the need to pay someone for helping to choose the goods, gather them, and bag them. All of these procedures may have helped to strengthen and structure the customer's cognitive map. However, in supermarket shopping there are few interactional confrontations and rituals, and customers are seldom recognized or even acknowledged at the check-out counter. All of this serves to emphasize the impersonality and anonymity of store, storekeeper, and shopper, and the act of shopping.

Another trend in self-service stores which illustrates the loss of territorial boundaries is the consumption of unpaid-for items of food and drink while shopping. In some places (e.g., the United States) this practice is tacitly allowed; in others it is barely tolerated (e.g., the United Kingdom). In his British study, Walsh described how self-service food stores are often "plagued by customers eating the food as they go around shopping (one shopkeeper informant said that he himself did this regularly, and would present his apple cores at the check-out counter). Especially in small self-service stores, staff complain of mothers allowing children to eat their fill of sweets while they are in the shop" (p. 70).

Finally, the owners and managers of self-service stores are usually unknown to the customer and are assumed to be plural. This, too, could explain why so little stigma attaches to shoplifters and shoplifting. Other studies suggest that the larger the organization, the more that thefts from it are tolerated by the public (Johnson, 1974, p. 43).

If shoplifting is due in part to the relative absence of clear territorial markers in the manmade environment, then measures should be adopted to increase and strengthen them — in the psychological sense, not only in the more obvious physical sense. For instance, steps might be taken to identify the owners or managers of stores visually — perhaps by installing life-size pictures of these individuals at the main entrance, and smaller pictures of them and their families at other locations in the store. Tape-recorded messages from the manager could be played at different times; signs could be put up stating the manager's name, and perhaps describing certain aspects of his personal or family life. There are undoubtedly many other ways of personalizing self-service stores and providing psychological barriers between customer and merchandise. It will be of interest to see if "territorial marking" does, in fact, reduce shoplifting.[15]

Similar measures might serve to deter potential intruders to the home, thereby reducing residential burglary (Newman, 1975). A well-kept lawn, for instance, tells intruders: "This is private property" (Zimring,

1981, p. 146). The same message might be conveyed by a low wall or fence, or distinctive paving on drives and walkways.

While certain features of the manmade physical environment may contribute to the breakdown of spatial boundaries and various forms of property crime, the same may be true of the increasingly impersonal world of work, and hence of embezzlement. Cameron (1964, p. 172) observes that:

> Increasingly people work for, buy from, and administer the affairs of impersonal corporations. People who would never consider stealing articles from a friend's home or even from the "corner" grocer may have very different feelings about stealing merchandise displayed for sale in a branch of a large retail chain store. Someone who would be scrupulous about returning borrowed money to a friend can rationalize till-tapping from an employing organization.

What applies to shoppers may also apply to shop assistants, many of whom quit their jobs before learning to identify themselves with the store, internalize its special customs and rules, or recognize frequent shoppers (i.e., before making the store a salient part of their own cognitive map). Just as geographical mobility and transience in general increase in today's world, so the proportion of strangers among our social contacts increases likewise.

Territorial markers would of course be expected to have a negligible effect on those with poorly defined cognitive maps, because such individuals would fail to respond to them (see Chapter 9). The lack of an intact cognitive map (and a correspondingly weak sense of territorial boundaries) may be a relatively enduring characteristic of persistent or habitual criminals.[16, 17] In order to deter such individuals from property crime, physical barriers ("target hardening") in the form of locks, bolts, and alarm systems, may be the first and only line of territorial defense.

The cases discussed so far have been those in which homeowners "defend" a particular residential area, and where the same area is seen as "private" or as a virtual no-man's-land by others, depending on territorial markers and individual cognitive maps. A potentially greater risk of social conflict and criminality would be expected to arise in situations where the same area is seen as the personal territory of two sets of owners. In such cases, individual X may enter a space that he thinks is his, but which individual Y also perceives as belonging to him. Y then attempts to defend his territory against X, and vice versa, and a spiraling conflict ensues. As an example, it has been suggested that conflicts between juvenile gangs and the police may have their origins in territorial disputes of this kind. Werthman and Piliavin (1967, pp.61–62) write:

> The very places that are defended like homes by gang members also constitute places of work or "beats" to the police, and the home-like uses to which gang members put the streets are often perceived as threats to the patrolman's task of maintaining the conventional rules. . . . The relationship between gang members and the policemen thus has its roots in an ecological conflict over claims to final authority in the same setting.

An actual case which seems to fit this description received widespread media coverage in 1980 and was discussed in the U.S. television news show "60 Minutes." On the surface, it was a case of an elderly man shooting a teenager who had been pelting his house with snowballs, shouting obscenities, and physically threatening him. A UPI account of the incident is reproduced below (*Times-Picayune,* June 1, 1980, Sn. 1, p. 6. Reprinted with permission).

TEEN'S DEATH STIRS TROUBLE

TOWSON, MD. (UPI) — The murder trial of an elderly man charged with killing a drunk teen-ager who was pelting his home with snowballs has stirred a rumble of discontent in this Baltimore suburb.

Roman G. Welzant, 68, is charged in Baltimore County Circuit Court with the Jan. 4 shooting of 18-year-old Albert R. Kahl, Jr. But some contend the real defendants should be the neighborhood youths who Welzant say waged a reign of terror against him and his home for more than a decade.

Welzant contends he fired in self-defense because he thought his life was in danger. Both he and his wife, Genevieve, say their home was a constant target of vandalism by rowdy toughs.

Welzant testified Thursday that he called the police "as much as 50 times" before the shooting to complain about vandalism. He bought a gun "because the neighborhood had developed over the years we had lived there and there began to be instances of breaking into houses which has continued up until recently."

Both Welzant and his wife told jurors they had been harassed by youths for 12 years. The glass in the windows of their home had been replaced with Plexiglas because more than 70 percent of the windows had been broken over the years.

Mrs. Welzant testified "they set our hedge on fire. Beer bottles on the lawn everyday. We had the car painted not so long ago. We brought it home and the next day somebody scratched it with a nail from one end to the other."

"I prayed every time Halloween came around," Mrs. Welzant said.

Welzant told jurors he fired his gun because "I was afraid they were going to smash my head open and stomp on me because that's the way it happens around our house."

Photographs taken from the front of the Welzants' home and shown on the television program indicated that the house stood on a corner lot. It was constructed on high ground and sloped down to a low brick wall which formed the L-shaped perimeter of the property. Directly across the road adjacent to the Welzants' house was an open playing field (see Figures 8.2 and 8.3).

A striking aspect of this landscape is the indistinctness of the boundary separating the Welzants' property from the surrounding area of public property. In addition, the low brick wall offers a convenient seat or grandstand, especially for the teen-agers whose playing grounds are directly across the road. Our suggestion is that this lack of clarity of

Figure 8.2
View of the Welzants' home.
Source: Baltimore News American. Reprinted with permission.

Figure 8.3
View of the Welzants' home.
Source: Baltimore News American. Reprinted with permission.

territorial boundaries may have played a role in the 12-year history of
conflict between the Welzants and the local youth, and for the spiraling
hostilities which led to the fatal shooting. The local boys appeared to have
considered the low wall surrounding the Welzants' property *their* wall —
or at least as a public wall on which they had a right to sit — while the
Welzants felt that the wall was part of *their* territory. The origin of the
fatal incident may therefore have been a conflict over territorial
ownership.

Mr. Morley Safer (of the "60 Minutes" program) talked with the boys
who had been involved in the shooting incident (and earlier incidents)
and, separately, with the Welzants. It emerged from these conversations
that a typical occasion for the start of an altercation between the boys and
Mr. Welzant was one in which the boys would be sitting on the low wall,
and Mr. Welzant (according to the boys) would come out of his house
and threaten them. Mr. Welzant, however, said that he would come out
of his house and tell the boys to leave, and their reaction would be to

shout obscenities at him. Evidently, the boys thought they had a right to sit on the wall, whereas the Welzants thought the wall was part of their property and the boys did not have a right to sit there.[18]

To summarize, it has been suggested that crime is facilitated by disturbances in the individual's cognitive map, and environments that provide insufficient data for cognitive structuring in terms of territorial ownership. Three different types of situations were discussed: (1) those in which individuals with intact or deteriorating cognitive maps enter and/or commit a crime in a location which is "owned" by other individuals but which is inadequately marked as such (e.g., shoplifting in self-service stores); (2) those in which individuals lacking a well-defined cognitive map enter private areas that are territorially marked to a greater or lesser extent (e.g., housebreaking); and (3) situations in which individuals with intact cognitive maps disagree over the ownership of a specific area or location (e.g., gang fights; altercations between individuals, and between nations).

NOTES

1. LeBon has this to say about the leaders of crowds: "As soon as a certain number of living beings are gathered together, whether they are animals or men, they place themselves instinctively under the authority of a chief. . . . In the case of human crowds the chief is often nothing more than a ringleader or agitator, but as such he plays a considerable part. His will is the nucleus around which the opinions of the crowd are grouped and attain to identity" (1895/1977, pp. 117–19). He goes on to observe that: "The leaders we speak of are more frequently men of action than thinkers. . . . They are especially recruited from the ranks of those morbidly nervous, excitable, half-deranged persons who are bordering on madness. However absurd may be the idea they uphold or the goal they pursue, their convictions are so strong that all reasoning is lost upon them" (p. 118). As for the influence of leaders on opinions, "The majority of men, especially among the masses, do not possess clear and reasoned ideas on any subject outside their own specialty. The leader serves as their guide" (p. 120). For discussions of the role of leaders in crowds, the types of individuals who become leaders of crowds, and the various means they employ to induce others to conform to their wishes, see Yablonsky (1962), Patrick (1973), and Conway and Siegelman (1979).

2. Although it would be impossible in most cases to obtain measures of physiological activity, it could be determined whether murder-suicide cases had experienced more (or more serious) setbacks in the period immediately preceding the

crime than the members of a control group (e.g., other pilots). This could be accomplished by interviewing friends, relatives, and business associates of both groups. Several studies on the biochemistry of suicide and depression have used brain tissue post mortem to determine neurotransmitter concentrations and metabolism at the time of death (e.g., Beskow et al., 1976).

3. This portion of the chapter is based on a paper presented by the author at the Annual Meeting of the American Society of Criminology, San Francisco, November 1980, entitled *Conscience, cognitive maps, and crime.*

4. Trasler (1979a) has questioned the assumption that juvenile delinquents have a global defect in conscience. For him, most delinquents do have a conscience in that they are aware of the wrongfulness of certain acts. In general, he suggests, juvenile delinquency is not a matter of a weak conscience, but a form of risk-taking behavior, carried out for excitement.

5. This distinction between rules as *defining* action versus *constraining* action is borrowed from Alisdair MacIntyre's (1967) discussion of Winch's (1958) *The Idea of a Social Science.* MacIntyre notes that the concept of "rule-governed" action can mean either that rules are contingently related to behavior and actually *constrain* it (like the governor on the steam engine), or that rules are logically related to behavior in the sense of *defining* the actions that are permissible (as in the case, described by MacIntyre, where the rules of chess define the possible moves on the chess board).

6. First, there is the widespread fear of meeting strangers face-to-face, and of entering the homes of strangers. Even if the house and its occupants are familiar, elaborate rituals must be carried out before entry. Except for close relatives and intimate acquaintances, the mode of entry is always via the front gate and walkway. Obviously, it is not acceptable to walk over flowers and shrubbery. Next, one must go to the front door, not to the rear door (unless it is used as the main entrance) nor to an open window. If one's presence has not been signaled in advance it must be audibly announced by ringing the doorbell, sounding the car horn, or by suitable cries and shouts. Once inside, one is never free to wander about the house at will. Only certain rooms are accessible to visitors; others, such as the bathroom, can be visited with permission, and still others, such as the bedroom, are typically "off limits" to most visitors. This division of a home into areas of greater or lesser "salience" is also institutionalized in that some houses are designed with a room, usually at the front of the building, where visitors are met, business is transacted, and other relatively formal social activities take place.

7. In some instances this is actually the case (see Walsh, 1980b, and Chapter 10).

8. Home, then, is the "territorial core" (Porteus, 1976), the most strongly personalized of all forms of territory, and a highly salient part of one's cognitive map. For many people it is nothing less than a part of their very being.

9. Dr. W. M. Bowerman (personal communication, September 1980) informs me that he has tried several objective methods of assessing cognitive impairment in offenders, but none is sufficiently sensitive. These methods have included the Hoffer-Osmond diagnostic test (HOD), as well as its later development, the EWI; McHugh's

mini-mental state test; the Shipley Institute of Living scale; the Hooper visual organization test; and the MMPI (Scales 4, 8, and F). Cohen and Dunner (1980) have pointed out that adequate behavioral measures of cognitive dysfunction are lacking and that "most of the existing tests for both diagnosis and assessment of change either lack reliability and validity or are conceptually limiting and misleading" (p. 125). These authors emphasize the need for tests of specific aspects of thought, memory, attention, and perception; that is, a technology for the "microanalysis" of cognitive dysfunction.

10. For data on cognitive impairments in juvenile delinquents and chronic adult offenders, see Reckless (1967), Lewis and Balla (1976), Berman and Siegel (1976), Spellacy (1977), Hirschi and Hindelang (1977), Hippchen (1978), Zinkus et al. (1979), Schauss (1980), and Bryant et al. (1984).

11. This observation seems to support the low-arousal hypothesis of SSB and contradicts the high-arousal hypothesis of Zuckerman (1979) and the present author. The following accounts also seem to support the low-arousal hypothesis: "(T)he defendant [a man on trial for murder] was observed as being asleep, lethargic, in a daze, and unable to adequately perform a job he was quite good at the day he murdered his girlfriend. . . . [In another case] the defendant . . . reported experiencing visual hallucinations as well as feeling stuporous, in a trance, and fragmented prior to the stabbing of his girlfriend 64 times (a number which further indicates a state of frenzy)" (Bell, 1980, p. 1095). An important future step in psychophysiological research on crime will be to record vital signs telemetrically in ambulant subjects so that physiological measures can be taken in a wide range of situations, perhaps while the subject is actually being violent.

12. The patient was charged primarily with "causing death by dangerous driving." The argument of the defense was that "the defendant suffered from reactive hypoglycemia and that at the time of the accident she was probably hypoglycemic to the extent that her state of consciousness was altered" (Bovill, 1973, p. 358). A nominal fine was imposed and she was disqualified from driving for seven years, on the grounds of her present ill-health.

13. Dr. Bowerman (personal communication, September 1980) informed me that the individual had abruptly left his executive position, moved to another state, and started work as a fireman. After carefully questioning the man to discover why he had changed his residence and job, it occurred to Dr. Bowerman that the man's explanations for everything that had happened were simply rationalizations and that he really did not know why he had acted as he did. It was from this that Dr. Bowerman learned that the patient had had an automobile accident immediately preceding this change in vocational interest. In his letter, Dr. Bowerman described several other cases where crimes had been committed during "transient episodes of detachment" or states of partial amnesia. In one such case: "A man was incarcerated . . . for having stolen a vehicle in Seattle, Washington, and having driven it to Portland where he was apprehended sound asleep in the back of the car. In spite of my warnings to the contrary he told me that he was a patient at the ____ Hospital in Seattle and had gone there on an evening to ask for admission. Since they had no bed space they told him that he would have to get to Portland. When I began to question him about the room in which this conversation

had taken place in Seattle, or related matters, he was unable to provide them, and when I asked him for details about his trip from Seattle to Portland (a distance of about 200 miles) he could not give me a single fact" (Letter).

14. Several "tests" of Newman's ideas have been carried out so far, mostly with negative or equivocal results (Mayhew, 1979). However, these tests have largely been indirect, and in some cases of questionable relevance to the theory. For a more recent version and discussions of the thesis, see Newman (1980), Greenberg et al. (1982), Clarke (1983), and Rutter and Giller (1983).

15. A marked decrease in shoplifting occurred in one department store following the introduction of antishoplifting signs (McNees et al., 1976).

16. Phelan (1977, cited in Carter & Hill, 1979, p. 73) recruited 23 ex-burglars to view a series of slides and to visit a number of burgled apartment buildings. Symbolic markers and real barriers were apparently not "registered" by the burglars at all. Phelan's conclusion (his p. 14) that the "capacity of the ex-burglars to perceive physical cues which manifest a territorial sentiment among residents was limited to only a very general notion," would be consistent with the model proposed here. However, since no control group of nonburglars was employed, conclusions about the differential effectiveness of territorial markers for criminals and noncriminals cannot yet be drawn.

17. The following remark, made about the "best" burglars by an American police inspector, seems especially relevant to the question of the cognitive maps of habitual criminals. "Even when they are married, you will find that they have no real life. They have a tendency to move around a lot. They stay away from their neighbors. Their driving licenses are false. They use the names of men in prison. And when they are finally caught, they are worn out inside. They are hollow" (Pillegi, 1968, cited in Walsh 1980a, p. 45).

18. A wooden fence, constructed on the Welzants' side of the low brick wall, might have provided a clear separation between the Welzants' property and public property. Whether this would have helped to end the conflict at an early stage is, of course, uncertain.

9

STIMULATION-SEEKING BEHAVIOR AND CRIME: THEORETICAL ASPECTS

It is recalled that individuals convicted of a given type of crime tend to have been involved in other forms of crime and deviant behavior; moreover, while particular stressors are associated with numerous criminal outcomes, particular types of crime may be preceded by many different kinds of stressors. The observation that "stress" is associated with numerous forms of deviant behavior suggests that stress-induced arousal is relatively nonspecific with respect to behavior. Earlier, this led to the suggestion that crime could be viewed in terms of three "levels" of criminal involvement (transient, age-specific, and chronic) rather than in terms of legal entities, each one requiring a separate explanation.

Our aim here is to set forth a model of transient criminality; that is, to explain how ordinarily law-abiding people, both old and young, can become temporarily involved in a wide variety of criminal acts, ranging from shoplifting to murder and rape.

STIMULATION-SEEKING BEHAVIOR AND CRIME

It has been suggested that incongruity leads to arousal, and arousal to criminality by way of (a) increased suggestibility, (b) a temporary, partial breakdown of the cognitive map (Chapter 8), and (c) increased stimulation-seeking behavior (SSB). Since there can be no crime without criminal behavior, it remains now to discuss the criminogenic role of SSB.

Several studies have reported a positive association between sensation seeking, as measured by Zuckerman's (1979) SSS, and criminality, whether measured by official records, self-report, or associated diagnoses such as psychopathic personality (cf., Thorne, 1971).

Farley and Farley (1972) studied delinquent girls in a correctional institution and found that escape attempts and disobedience were positively related to SSS scores. In a study of high school students, males and females with delinquent records scored significantly higher on the SSS than the nondelinquents (Farley & Sewell, 1976). In a study of self-reported school violence, high SSS scorers were found to misbehave more frequently than low scorers (Wasson, 1980). Perez and Torrubia (1985) studied 173 male and 173 female medical students in Spain and found a high correlation between the SSS and self-reported delinquency for both males and females. White and coauthors (1985) investigated the association between sensation seeking and self-reported delinquency as part of the Rutgers Health and Human Development Project, a prospective study on the development of alcohol- and drug-using behaviors. A predominantly white sample of 584 male and female adolescents, consisting of two birth cohorts, was interviewed on two occasions, three years apart, when the subjects were aged 15 and 18, and 18 and 21, respectively. Self-reported delinquency and sensation seeking were related for both males and females on both occasions. The delinquent adolescents scored significantly higher on the disinhibition scale but not on the experience-seeking scale. Males also scored higher than females both on self-reported delinquency and sensation seeking (disinhibition), as found in previous studies (Hindelang et al., 1981; Zuckerman, 1979, pp. 303–7).

Following Quay's (1965) suggestion that psychopathy represents "pathological sensation-seeking behavior," two studies reported statistically significant SSS differences between psychopathic and nonpsychopathic prisoners. Emmons and Webb (1974) used criteria from the Minnesota Multiphasic Personality Inventory (MMPI) to define psychopathy, and found that psychopathic prisoners scored significantly higher on disinhibition, experience-seeking, and boredom susceptibility. Blackburn (1978) identified psychopaths in a prison population by peak scores on the psychopathic deviate and impulsivity scales of the MMPI, and found them to score significantly higher than nonpsychopathic prisoners on the thrill-and-adventure-seeking and disinhibition subscales of the SSS.

Cox (1977) defined psychopathy in a college sample, using a combination of the Gough socialization scale (So) and the SSS. He predicted that subjects with low So scores and high SSS scores would show more psychopathic features than any of the other three combinations of the two scales. As predicted, the low-So/high-SSS group had the poorest occupational and school history, the highest use of alcohol and drugs, and the greatest number of criminal convictions. The high-So/low-SSS group scored at the other end of the scale on all of these measures.[1]

Another study of sensation seeking in college students sought to show that high sensation seekers have a tendency toward antisocial behavior (Larson et al., 1979). Male students with high and low sensation seeking scores participated in a task in which they were required to free-associate to a series of words, many of which had double entendre sexual meanings (e.g., lay, rubber, screw, mount, tool, beaver). The student sat opposite a female experimenter who read him a list of words. He was asked to respond as quickly as possible to each word. The subject's responses to the words were later scored for socially unacceptable sexual content by a judge who was unaware both of the subject's sensation-seeking score and of the hypothesis under investigation. The results indicated that high sensation seekers were significantly more likely to respond in socially unacceptable ways. As the stimulus words became increasingly sexual in meaning, and thereby more likely to elicit socially unacceptable responses, the high sensation seekers gave more socially unacceptable responses than the low sensation seekers.

In a recent study of the association between sensation seeking, criminality, and spinal cord injury among 140 spinal cord-injured patients admitted to the Louisiana Rehabilitation Institute between 1965 and 1984 (Mawson, 1986), spinal cord-injured patients who reported being arrested one or more times by the police after age 17 but before their injury, were found to have significantly higher scores on the disinhibition subscale (but not the boredom susceptibility subscale) than patients who reported never being arrested by the police.

As others have already suggested (e.g., Quay, 1965; Stott, 1966, 1982), and as the above review indicates, stimulation seeking appears to be associated with criminality. In accordance with its conventional definition, stimulation seeking is usually understood to mean thrill-seeking activities — a "search for fun and excitement" (Belson, 1975; Feldman, 1977) — and it is widely assumed that the behavior serves to *raise* the level of arousal.[2] There have, however, been few discussions in the professional literature on the *implications* of the stimulation-seeking hypothesis for understanding crime. For one thing, it remains uncertain how the stimulation-seeking *motive* relates to more traditional categories of motivation (viz., aggression and sex) which are also thought to play a role in crime, especially crimes of violence (see Chapters 6, 11–13). Second, the question has seldom been raised of how stimulation-seeking behavior relates to crime. It is to this issue which we now turn.

ON THE LINK BETWEEN SSB AND CRIME

There are three ways in which SSB might be expected to result in crime:

1. SSB may lead to actions that are publicly defined as deviant because of their intensity or persistence.
2. Actions may be carried out impulsively, which inadvertently result in crime.
3. SSB, combined with a deteriorating cognitive map, may lead to actions that are inherently criminal, regardless of their intensity.

Crime as a Consequence of Intense or Persistent SSB

Certain acts may be publicly defined as deviant or criminal when they become excessive either in intensity or persistence. Thus noisy but acceptable behavior at a football game or party may be steadily amplified to the point of "rowdyism," "causing a nuisance," or "disturbing the peace." Passers-by or neighbors begin to feel harassed and inconvenienced and come to perceive the fans or partygoers as a "rowdy mob" rather than as merely a "boisterous group of youngsters." "Reckless" driving similarly implies rates of speed, acceleration, and deceleration which are either above the speed limit, excessively rapid or sudden. An exceptionally vigorous football tackle may be judged "excessive," and the offender sent off the field. The intensity and persistence of an amorous advance also contributes to its being defined by the female as something that is "against her will" and hence as an unwanted sexual assault (Chapter 11, this volume; Brownmiller, 1975).

The evaluation of acts as criminal on the basis of their intensity probably varies considerably between cultures and between age groups within cultures. With regard to cross-cultural differences, some interesting observations have been reported on the differences between young American and French children at play (Wolfenstein, 1957); American children were found to engage in considerably more bodily movements and activities than the French children. With regard to age, there is probably a universal tendency for the old to complain about the "unruly" behavior of the young (Krebs, 1980). It is common knowledge that the young have a greater preference for sensations of high intensity than the old. Studies in England and the United States indicate a significant inverse association between sensation seeking and age for both males and females (Zuckerman et al., 1978).

Crime as an Indirect Consequence of SSB

In the cases discussed above, the acts constituting the crime are the "main focus" of the subject's on-going behavior in that he or she is presumably "concentrating" on performing them. However, the subject may be unaware that the actions in question have passed the critical level of intensity and entered the publicly defined realm of "crime."

In the cases to be discussed now, increased SSB may lead indirectly to crime or to some other antisocial act. The sort of incidents we have in mind are those in which a person with a high level of arousal engages in sudden, impulsive movements which result unwittingly in injury or death. For example, a man breaks off a heated argument with his wife and leaves the house to go to work. Slamming the front door, he gets into his car and backs rapidly and forcefully out of the driveway. At that moment, a child cycles across the driveway, is struck by the car and severely injured. To take another hypothetical example, a motorist is temporarily obliged to slow down at the height of rush-hour traffic. In a state of considerable agitation, he glances rapidly from side to side and lunges back and forth in his seat, drumming his fingers and pulling angrily on the steering wheel (increased SSB). At the moment the traffic begins to move forward, he slams his foot hard on the accelerator and the car screeches past those ahead — until the next car unaccountably stops, and he crashes into the back of it, injuring both himself and the occupants of the other car.[3]

SSB Can Lead to Actions that are Either
Inherently Criminal or Defined as Such by the Law

Increased SSB — combined with a deteriorating cognitive map and in some cases increased susceptibility to influence — can also lead to actions that are either "inherently" criminal or defined as such by the legal code. Some of these actions may require intense SSB in order for them to become crimes.[4] In other cases (shoplifting or forgery, for instance), the amount of physical effort required to carry out the act may be minimal. However, it is not the intensity of the action that defines it as criminal, but the fact that it has been performed.

It is recalled that the most important aspects of a person's environment are "attachment figures" (as shown by the intensity of emotional responses to their loss). According to the model, the sensory characteristics of attachment figures are stored in the cognitive map in the form of unique combinations of sensory stimuli (i.e., tactile, auditory, olfactory, and visual stimuli). Because human beings share many features in common, the task of distinguishing one person from another, forming a cognitive map of a particular person (and then maintaining it by remaining "in touch" with him or her), requires a high degree of discriminative ability. Thus the unique "pattern of stimuli" representing this particular person constitutes one of the more differentiated aspects of the cognitive map.

It is postulated that incongruity increases the level of S-system arousal, and stimulation is sought from the persons (and other objects) whose characteristics have been internalized. Sensory inputs are then evaluated against the cognitive map; if they are judged as being congruous with it, the P-system is activated. The P-system then inhibits the S-system, and a general state of calm ensues.

If, however, the individual experiences severe or prolonged incongruity, and is *unable to obtain congruent sensory feedback* — that is, attachment figures are either unavailable or rejecting — then the cognitive map begins to disintegrate. Initially a stage of cognitive impairment may occur in which the person mentally "oscillates" from one previously held cognitive map to another. It is recalled that the cognitive map is postulated to have a psychologically most important and sensorily qualitative "apex," and a less salient, sensorily quantitative "base." To take the case of a man who has lived in the same location for many years, the "apex" is his home, his immediate family, and self-image. If the individual is middle-aged he may well have held a number of relatively distinct cognitive maps and identities in the course of his lifetime.[5] For instance, there is the self-image he had as a teenager, as a student, and as a young adult when living in such and such a place.

At a given moment in time, earlier phases of one's life are recollections, memories; but once such memories are strongly entered into and relived, they come together to form a whole complex of associated memories, all connected with one's existence and identity at an earlier time. This complex of memories forms the individual's previous self-image and cognitive map, and it is presumed that all of the earlier cognitive maps are stored in the brain and are in varying degrees accessible to conscious recollection, along with one's *present* cognitive map.

Just before cognitive disintegration, then, mental "anchorages" (cf., Sherif & Harvey, 1952) to the present geographical and psychosocial environment become "unstable," and the individual shifts between cognitive maps held at different times in the past. In this state of nostalgia, he thinks intensely about earlier times of his life; tries to contact old friends and lovers, and visits the haunts, neighborhoods, and living quarters that were salient aspects of former cognitive maps. He literally "loses his bearings," feels disoriented, and may be temporarily unable to "center himself" in time and space. It is as if earlier cognitive maps are being "tried on" in the hope of finding a satisfactory "fit" with regard to current conditions. What the individual is experiencing, then, is a true crisis of identity.

Beyond the stage of shifting between previously held cognitive maps, the *present* cognitive map itself begins to disintegrate. It is hypothesized that the most highly differentiated aspects of the cognitive map (i.e., those that are the most important from the individual's point of view) disintegrate first, leaving intact the basic substratum of familiar kinds and amounts of stimulation.

Something like the following sequence of events may unfold. The unique features of individuals to whom one is closely attached "fade" from the cognitive map and partially disappear. This applies not only to their physical features but to everything that makes them unique, such as mannerisms, gestures, ways of talking, and communicating in general.

The same process of disintegration occurs in other qualitative aspects of the cognitive map; home, for instance, loses its special significance and becomes simply another house or apartment. Unique, taken-for-granted norms or ways of relating to home and to intimates, tend to disappear. One's personal sense of identity also begins to disintegrate. Subjectively, the individual loses his self-esteem and self-confidence and feels depersonalized. Once familiar surroundings now seem strange; he feels awkward with intimates, whom he now experiences as alien and unfamiliar.[6] Subtle, abstract features of the environment become "blurred" or fade from the cognitive map. Ideas, beliefs, values, and rules that were once respected, even revered, lose their meaning and significance. Thus *a general breakdown of internalized standards and boundaries* occurs — boundaries distinguishing self from not-self, familiar people and objects from unfamiliar ones, prescribed behavior from proscribed behavior, and personal possessions from other people's possessions. Hence, what remains of the "familiar world" embodied in the cognitive map is increasingly restricted to familiar types and quantities of immediate sensation.

The question now arises as to how this process increases the risk of involvement in crime. It is suggested that the risk of criminality is increased because the individual's SSB is now so diffusely directed at "stimulating objects" in the environment that one or more of the intricate rules of social behavior are likely to be broken in the course of seeking stimulation. Given that individuals attempt to preserve their cognitive maps by seeking the familiar, and a large segment of the cognitive map associated with familiar people, objects, places, and social norms is disintegrating, then the continuing tendency to seek congruous sensory input would be expected to take the form of a relatively indiscriminate approach to familiar basic kinds and quantities of stimulation. SSB will tend to be directed less and less at sources representing familiar *patterns* of stimulation (since these have partially disappeared from the cognitive map) and more and more at sources that are familiar only in the rudimentary sense of providing familiar kinds and amounts of stimulation.

It is postulated that the individual reverts to a state somewhat analogous to the "asocial" or "indiscriminate attachment" phase of infancy (cf., Schaffer & Emerson, 1964), where sensory input is sought from virtually any stimulating source, regardless of who or what it may be, and to whom it (if "it" is a thing) belongs. Instead of remaining closely within the territorial and normative limits stipulated by his former cognitive map, the individual now appears indifferent to the facts of differential ownership and the rules of propriety. Just as a child in the asocial phase of cognitive development approaches and touches things and people indiscriminately, so the same type of "sensorily promiscuous" behavior is exhibited by the older child or adult whose cognitive map is disintegrating. The result may be any one of a number of criminal or deviant actions.

In seeking familiar kinds and quantities of stimulation the individual may find himself breaking not only the countless subtle, taken-for-granted rules of social etiquette and interaction, but legal and moral rules as well. He or she may steal from department stores, break into other people's homes, and engage in various types of assaults and personal improprieties, all in a search for stimulation.

The inference should not be drawn that the search for familiar kinds and amounts of stimulation leads individuals to commit crimes without any conscious awareness of committing criminal acts. The model proposes that there is a *partial* rather than a total disintegration of the cognitive map. It is not that internalized rules are completely forgotten or obliterated. The offender may be *aware* of breaking rules; he may be aware that what he or she is doing is wrong, and may take active steps to avoid being detected and apprehended. The critical point is that the offender does not experience his behavior at the time of the offense as wrong. The usual sensations of awe and shock at the prospect of committing a crime are lacking; instead, he experiences himself and his actions as *alien*.

Dally (1969, p. 24) has described in very similar terms the state of mind of a patient with anorexia nervosa who engaged in shoplifting.

> Tension and overeating were associated with a compulsion to steal. Jean could resist the impulse for a time but always gave way to it in the end. She stole food and cheap trinkets. *She was aware of what she was doing, but was unconcerned at the time about possible consequences.* She had no need for most of what she stole, and in any case she could have afforded to buy them. . . . (*Later she felt prickings of conscience*) (p. 24, emphasis added).

In this peculiar, "dissociated" state of mind, a person may be aware of committing a crime and may try to conceal the fact, but he fails to experience his actions as incongruous and, at the same time, is unable to associate the crime with any emotive component such as shame or guilt. This could explain the paradoxical reaction of pilferers on being apprehended.[7] Cameron (1964) reports that apprehension and arrest come as a profound shock to the average shoplifter. At first, many shoplifters strongly resist the idea that they are thieves; they find it difficult to understand that they have been arrested and will be taken away by the police. " 'Yes. I took the dress,' one woman sobbed as she was being closely interrogated, 'but that doesn't mean I'm a thief' " (p. 161). When, as a result of being apprehended and publicly treated as a thief, offenders begin to realize that they *are* in fact thieves, this awareness seems to restore the missing emotive component in social behavior and, according to Cameron (1964, p. 162) "is often accompanied by a dramatic change in attitudes and by severe emotional disturbance. Occasionally even hysterical semi-attempts at suicide result." Women ask if their husband will have to be told of their arrest. Men are fearful that their employer will be so informed, and children are apprehensive about their parents' reaction. The universal and greatest fear, however, is that of being rejected by one's friends and family.[8]

Having sketched the theoretical background, we now consider how SSB, combined with a deteriorating cognitive map, can lead the individual to engage in a wide variety of particular criminal acts. The discussion in Chapters 10–12 is organized around the headings of crimes against property and crimes against persons.

NOTES

1. Notice the striking similarity between these findings and those of Buchsbaum et al. (1976) on the behavioral characteristics of college students with low platelet MAO levels (see Chapter 4, this volume).

2. It is recalled from Chapter 7 that the *model* of SSB proposed in this work differs from Quay's (1965) hypothesis and the popular view that sensory input always arouses or excites the individual. While Quay contends that SSB is due to low cortical reactivity and results in an increase in arousal, the suggestion here is that SSB results from high (S-system) arousal, and that the sensory input derived from SSB is fed back into the central nervous system, thereby activating the P-system, which acts as a "brake" on the S-system, producing a general state of calm.

3. The legal and philosophical aspects of cases of this sort are discussed by Duff (1980a, 1980b).

4. Certain ways of committing murder, for instance, may require considerable force or effort.

5. A common thread, stemming from childhood, runs through all of the maps held at different times and for varying periods of time, even though it may be vague and ill-defined.

6. These processes are described with great insight and vividness in Franz Kafka's (1952) famous short story "The Metamorphosis."

7. It could give meaning to the phrase, so often used by persons after being arrested or convicted of a crime, that they "didn't know what they were doing." It would not be a case of "not knowing" in the sense implied in the M'Naghten Rule — that is, "not knowing the nature and quality of the act . . . , or . . . in not knowing that the act was wrong" (Vetter & Wright, 1974, p. 490) — but of not knowing in the sense of having no *emotional appreciation* of the moral or legal wrongfulness of the act. This is not to imply that offenders are not emotionally aroused at the time of the offense; obviously, this would contradict the hypothesis of S-system arousal-induced SSB. Our suggestion is rather that the prospect or activity of committing a crime is not experienced as incongruous and therefore does not arouse in the offender the expected feelings of shame or guilt.

8. Cameron (1964, pp. 165–66) believes that the arrest procedure itself, and the accompanying emotional outpourings and threat to one's valued relationships, may be sufficient in many cases to cause the offender to "redefine his situation" (restructure his cognitive map?) and to cease offending in the future.

10

CRIMES AGAINST PROPERTY: THEFT, BURGLARY, VANDALISM

THEFT

Estimates of business losses from shoplifting in the United States range from $16 to $40 billion annually (U.S. Department of Justice, 1979). Little is known about shoplifting and shoplifters, however, since most shoplifters presumably remain uncaught, and studies of apprehended and convicted shoplifters necessarily deal with increasingly selected groups of offenders. Among apprehended offenders, those aged 15 years or under are heavily overrepresented; males and females are arrested in about equal proportions (Walsh, 1978); people in the upper socioeconomic groups are overrepresented; significant numbers are foreign-born (Gibbens & Prince, 1962; Bradford & Balmaceda, 1983); and most appear to lack any kind of wider involvement in crime, the vast majority having no previous convictions for any offense (Cameron, 1964). In different studies, so-called professionals comprise no more than 2 to 6 percent of those arrested for shoplifting (Walsh, 1978, p. 75; Bradford & Balmaceda, 1983).

It is widely assumed that most shoplifting is a rational activity carried out for gain, mainly by poor people who presumably need the stolen items or the money derived from selling them. Yet, if the hypothesis is correct that theft represents stimulation-seeking activity, individuals engaging in theft would be expected to approach, manipulate, pick up, and steal highly *stimulating types of objects,* not necessarily those of great cash value.[1] Objects with the preferred stimulating characteristics would include those that are shiny, sparkling, colorful, motile, sound-producing, attractive to the touch ("tactile"), odorous, and tasty.

Several observations on shoplifting are consistent with this hypothesis. Cameron (1964) found that the kinds of merchandise pilfered by women were chiefly luxury items. "Fancy goods," in particular, tended to be stolen from food stores, and less than 6 percent of arrested women had shoplifted anything that could be described as "equipment," or a household object. Department store data showed that the most frequent types of merchandise stolen by women were dress accessories (29.1 percent), jewelry (28.4 percent), other women's clothing (13.5 percent), and billfolds (11.1 percent) (see Table 10.1).

Gibbens (1960, cited in Mannheim, 1965) described a type of shoplifter (the so-called kleptomaniac) who steals for the sake of stealing and does so "in a clumsy way, sometimes without any attempt at concealment; *shining, glittering things are preferred,* and they are often hoarded without ever being used" (Mannheim, 1965, p. 261, emphasis added). In another British study of shoplifting, Walsh (1978) found that the type of item most frequently stolen was food (32.2 percent) (the types of food were not specified), followed by cosmetics (23.1 percent) and clothing (18.5 percent). As in Cameron's Chicago study, shopkeepers indicated that the most commonly stolen items were luxury goods rather than cheap necessities.[2]

The psychiatric condition known as anorexia nervosa provides an excellent "model" of transient criminality (Mawson, 1984). All of the elements that have been suggested as playing a role in transient criminality (increased arousal, a deteriorating cognitive map, and increased SSB) appear to be present in such patients while engaging in criminal activity.

Anorexia nervosa predominantly affects females (the male:female sex ratio ranging from about 1:10 to 1:20), usually within ten years of the onset of puberty, and especially those in higher socioeconomic groups. There are three essential diagnostic features: (1) the avoidance of fattening foods, leading to severe emaciation, (2) the cessation of menstruation, and (3) a morbid fear of becoming fat ("Anorexia Nervosa", 1971; Dally, 1969; Mawson, 1974; Vigersky, 1977). A subgroup of anorexia nervosa patients engages in occasional bouts of overeating ("bulimic episodes"), which are often followed by self-induced vomiting. It is during the episodes of overeating that stealing and other forms of antisocial activity tend to occur (Dally, 1969; Russell, 1970).

Crisp and his associates (1980) described 102 patients meeting the criteria of anorexia nervosa. By their own admission, 14 patients had engaged in stealing, and in 13 the stealing occurred during a phase of overeating. Based on a standardized measure of nervousness and personality (Crowne & Crisp, 1979), the "stealers" were found to be

TABLE 10.1
Kinds of Merchandise Stolen by Adult Women
(Women's Court and Lakeside Co. Data)

"Kind" of Merchandise	Court		Lakeside Co.	
	Number	Percent*	Number	Percent*
Jewelry	72	8.1	201	28.4
Billfolds	9	1.0	88	11.1
Toys	6	.7	11	1.6
Bric-a-brac	8	.9	45	6.4
Books, records	6	.7	48	6.8
Stationery	3	.2	43	6.1
Shoes	17	1.9	10	1.4
Umbrellas	9	1.0	13	1.8
Food	21	2.4	21	2.9
Gadgets	19	2.1	46	6.4
Equipment	11	1.2	6	.8
Household	38	4.3	33	4.7
Remnants	8	.9	11	1.5
Notions	8	.9	30	4.5
Cosmetics	36	4.0	41	5.8
W. coats and suits	106	11.8	35	4.9
W. dresses	235	26.4	62	8.8
W. clothing (other)	217	24.4	96	13.5
Dress accessories	156	17.5	206	29.1
Purses	153	17.2	75	5.1
M. suits	10	1.1	2	.3
M. clothing (other)	21	2.4	7	1.0
Hats	26	2.9	41	5.8
Other	38	4.3	52	7.3
Not ascertained	14	1.6	11	1.5
Total women	873		709	

*Refers to percent of all women stealing these items. Since one woman often steals more than one item, the totals do not add to 100 percent.

Source: Cameron (1964, p. 86). Reprinted with permission.

significantly more anxious than the nonstealers (t = 4.89, p = .001). The stealers also reported significantly more bodily complaints, being more depressed, and more sociable than the nonstealers. At the time of stealing, most of the patients were described as being in a highly unstable metabolic state characterized by rapid growth, overwhelming impulsivity, and a body weight in the range of active puberty (Crisp et al., 1980). Other evidence indicates that the bulimic state is characterized by a greatly increased subjective hunger, breathlessness, sweating, racing pulse, and an inflated metabolic rate, all of which suggest an increase in S-system (adrenergic/dopaminergic) arousal (Mawson, 1974).

Evidence of disturbed cognitive functioning among anorectics is found in the frequent observation of a distorted self-image; patients tend to see themselves as fat when, in reality, they are seriously emaciated (Dally, 1969). According to Crisp et al. (1980), the approach of puberty and the normal increase in sexual interest is perceived as highly threatening for some women, who respond by regressing psychologically to their "childhood selves," becoming anorexic and ceasing to menstruate. Alternatively, the illness serves the function of "relocking the parental relationship which is potentially fragile and explosive without the presence of a child" (p. 229). In both scenarios however:

> The average anorectic has never had the opportunity to come to terms with and define herself and has foundered on the brink of adolescence. Now, within her anorexia nervosa, she sees herself as nothing but her weight and shape — these alone are her destiny. Stealing, defined as appropriating *someone else's property,* is hardly a relevant concept under such circumstances (Crisp et al., 1980, p. 236).

With regard to the hypothesis that stealing represents SSB, it should be noted that stealing is only one of several behavioral correlates of bulimia; others include excessive alcohol consumption, promiscuous and often exotic forms of sexual activity, and various forms of oral behavior (Crisp, 1970; Crisp et al., 1980), all of which represent different manifestations of SSB. Patients describe their stealing as impulsive; they will say that they "found" themselves in a store and "found" themselves with goods in their possession (Crisp et al., 1980, p. 227).

Dally and Gomez (1979) described binge eating among 400 patients with anorexia nervosa. The preferred foods were sweet and highly palatable, and the urge to consume them was "irresistible." Binge eating can also occur in obese patients, particularly during times of stress, and large quantities of very sweet things tend to be consumed (Hamburger, 1951; Stunkard, 1959; Wardle & Beinart, 1981). A popular theory until recently was that eating behavior among the obese is regulated more by "external cues"; that is, by sensory factors such as the sight, smell, and taste of food, whereas in normals it is regulated primarily by internal cues presumably related to calories (Schachter & Rodin, 1974). However, research has shown that sensory factors play an important role in eating behavior regardless of the individual's weight (see Chapter 6; Wooley & Wooley, 1975; Leon & Roth, 1977). Thus binge eating perhaps represents an *exaggeration* of normal feeding, that is, more intense SSB than occurs during the SSB associated with "normal" eating.

Although stealing *food* is linked to extreme hunger (e.g., Sorokin, 1975), and hunger is experienced by anorectics during bulimic episodes, hunger does not adequately explain the phenomenon of stealing in this condition. Crisp et al. (1980) found that those who admitted stealing were older and had been ill longer than the nonstealers and, more to the point, were heavier at the time of their first clinic visit and had never lost as much weight as the nonstealers. Furthermore, food is not the only type of item stolen. Among Crisp et al.'s 14 "stealers," ten had stolen food (the kinds of food were not described), four had stolen money, four stole clothing and makeup, and one mentioned stealing alcohol. Of the 14 patients, only four had been apprehended and prosecuted. Among the sample of anorexia nervosa patients studied by Dally (1969), 11 percent were known to have stolen. Most of the thefts involved food (such as sweets) and cheap trinkets, from large stores (pp. 24, 39), and over half of the patients had been caught in the act. Dally describes such stealing as compulsive, and unrelated to the stealing of food by starving people. He writes:

> Material gain plays little or no part in it; many of the objects taken are useless. Food is frequently stolen, but most girls could easily afford to buy legitimately. None of them showed any tendency to dishonesty before the onset of anorexia nervosa. Nor did these patients behave dishonestly after recovery. . . . Theft tended to occur in a setting of tension and depression, usually in association with overeating. The compulsion to steal increased until eventually the patient was unable to resist. She stole at first in a semi-somnambulistic state; later stealing became almost habitual (p. 39).

To summarize, the hypothesis that stealing in anorexia nervosa patients represents intense SSB is supported by: the close association between stealing and binge eating, the latter of which is motivated largely by a search for highly sweet, tasty food; the association between stealing, binge eating and other activities described as constituting SSB, for example, alcohol intake and sexual activity; the impulsive nature of the behavior; and the fact that the types of items stolen tend to consist of "stimulating objects" such as sweets and cheap trinkets, many of which are not used but simply hoarded.

It will be of interest in future studies to investigate the stimulation-seeking hypothesis of theft directly. The theory would predict that if a sample of apprehended pilferers were compared with matching groups of ordinary (nonpilfering) shoppers, the pilferers would have higher scores on Zuckerman's Sensation-Seeking Scale and be found to have engaged in greater SSB shortly before their arrest, in the form of increased motor activity, cigarette smoking, drug taking, eating, and alcohol consumption.

BURGLARY

Generalizations about burglary (as with all forms of crime) must be made cautiously, since about two-thirds of all burglaries are undetected, and the offender's identity is generally unknown in such cases (Walsh, 1980a, p. 128). The conception of burglary usually portrayed in the media and espoused in the professional literature is that of a highly rational form of activity. Theft is believed to be motivated by, and oriented toward, material or financial gain, and is, in fact, profitable. Related assumptions are that burglars tend to be poor or unemployed, the rewards from burglary are sufficient to outweigh the potential cost of apprehension and imprisonment, and the victims' residences are carefully selected for their apparent wealth as well as for ease of entry. Feldman (1977), for instance, sees burglary as highly rational and calculative. The activity may be motivated initially by a search for fun; but, with pecuniary or material success on the first occasion, theft tends to be maintained and gain becomes the major motive. Based on a study of burglars' police records, Sutherland (1937, cited in Walsh 1980a, p. 187) also believed that there was a gradual progression in motivation "from a sport to a business." On the other hand, there is evidence to support a "nonrational" interpretation of burglary, especially among younger burglars; namely, that burglary is an expression of intense SSB associated with a deteriorating cognitive map and a high level of S-system arousal.

The typical apprehended burglar is a young male. In Walsh's (1980a) British study of burglary, 52 percent of offenders were 20 years of age or less, and 81 percent were 30 years or under. In Chappell's (1965) study, also carried out in Britain, over 60 percent of the juvenile offenders under 14 years of age were first offenders.

Walsh (1980a) studied all 357 recorded cases of residential burglary in 1976 in Exeter, England, interviewing a sample of 67 victims and 30 imprisoned burglars. Discussing previous studies in addition to his own, Walsh states that "it would be incorrect to assume that the act of burglary is necessarily highly rational and organized (although this is certainly the way the media attempt to portray it)" (pp. 47–48). First, although the majority of burglars were manual laborers, most were employed at the time of their last offense. Second, most burglaries yielded relatively small sums of money compared to the risk involved. In 22 percent of the cases of residential burglary the amount stolen was valued at less than £10 ($16). In 73 percent of the cases the value of the goods stolen was £50 ($80) or less, yet the potential cost of such an evening's "haul" was several years of imprisonment (p. 130). Third, in many residential burglaries nothing is stolen. Stealing is thought to be the single major motive in burglary, and most households presumably contain *something* that a burglar would find worth stealing. Yet, different studies indicate that in a surprisingly high proportion of cases, nothing is reportedly stolen (e.g., 33 percent: Sparks, 1976; 40 percent: Waller & Okihiro, 1978; and 21 percent: Walsh, 1980a). Fourth, burglaries tend to be unplanned, speculative in nature, and carried out on the spur of the moment, triggered by "obvious opportunity" (Walsh, 1980a, p. 130). Fifth, burglary victims are not usually wealthy people. Walsh found no association between the wealth of the victim and burglary victimization. More commonly, "burglars seem to be big spenders, stealing from the poor and spending the money on themselves" (p. 126).

These observations suggest that most burglars are not "in it for the money," even though the older ones in particular may make such claims.

As Walsh astutely points out (p. 130), older burglars would be expected to cite financial gain as the main motive for theft, simply to make sense of their own behavior. Adding to the seeming lack of rationality, a small proportion of burglaries involved considerable "pointless" damage and destruction, such as defecating in beds, tying the sheets in knots, slashing furniture, and defacing pictures.

Consistent with the stimulation-seeking hypothesis, Walsh contends that "burglars burgle for psychological reasons, possibly to do with the sport of hunting fixed prey or excitement" (p. 130). Many burglars in fact give thrills, fun, or excitement as their main reason for burglary, 44 percent stating that this was their reason in Waller and Okihiro's (1978, p. 75) Canadian study. One young burglar in Walsh's (1980a, p. 89) study described the anxiety he experienced during burglary as being almost "sexual, pleasurable," in intensity. Reppetto (1974), in an important study of burglary in Boston, involving interviews with 97 burglars, found that a need for money was the main reported motive for most burglaries, although interviewees admitted to additional motives such as excitement, revenge, and curiosity. Chappell (1965) studied police files on 395 English burglary cases, interviewing insurers, police, and security officers, and concluded that although the excitement of breaking into houses was part of the motivation for burglary, the major motive was the desire for cash. Yet in most instances less than £25 ($40) was taken per burglary.

Walsh notes (1980a, pp. 53–54) that burglary involves extreme risk taking and audacity, considering the low material reward and the high risk in any given instance. He suggests that the thrill and tension of getting ready to commit a burglary are crucial ingredients in the crime; that there is a very close parallel with the tension arising in the context of high-risk sport; and that burglary may be engaged in purely for excitement and the sense of doing something forbidden that involves danger.

Comment. In this vague and largely uncharted world of what might be called the psychophysiology of criminal acts, it is very difficult to distinguish between the physiological and the behavioral components of crime. Walsh, for instance, suggests that the thrill and tension of getting ready to commit a burglary play an important causal role in burglary, yet he also suggests that burglary is carried out *for* excitement. The idea that burglary is carried out *for* excitement implies that a state of low arousal leads to acts of burglary, and these acts in turn increase the level of arousal, producing "excitement" (i.e., the low-arousal hypothesis). The alternative hypothesis suggested here is that burglary is carried out *in* a state of high arousal, with a deteriorating cognitive map, and that as a result of engaging in burglary the level of arousal is reduced.

Leaving aside for a moment the question of burglary-induced arousal reduction (see Chapter 14), our thesis is that burglary is not so much carried out *for* excitement (i.e., *to increase arousal*), but is carried out *in* a state of excitement or arousal; high arousal accompanies and is believed to be part of the cause of burglary rather than its biological effect or function. On this view, burglary represents stimulation-seeking behavior; moreover, among transient offenders and more youthful burglars (many of whom turn out to be transient offenders), burglary is committed in a state of high arousal and with a deteriorating cognitive map. It is the deteriorating cognitive map which makes burglary — and hence entry into a stranger's private territory — possible, as distinct from noncriminal or legitimate expressions of SSB.

With regard to the question of a deteriorating cognitive map, it is important to note, first, that burglary is profoundly disturbing for most *victims.* For both men and women in Walsh's (1980a) study, disgust was frequently voiced about objects in the house being touched and handled by the intruder, as if they were now polluted. "Some of the smaller and less valuable of these objects were in fact thrown away or burnt afterwards as a result of this feeling, as part of the process of 'cleaning the house'" (p. 118). Individuals commonly regard their personal possessions as virtually *sacred,* and an awareness of this feeling tends to be strongly manifested by guests and strangers making house calls. The visitor's children are loudly warned by their parents not to touch this or that household article belonging to the hosts. The feeling of reverence for one's own and other people's territory, property, and possessions is probably universal. By implication, then, individuals who enter other people's homes illegally and steal their property must to some extent lack this sense of reverence. This suggests that many burglars have a deteriorating cognitive map.

One would expect this lack of a sense of personal territory to be associated with an itinerant life-style and a diminished sense of one's "own" place or territory. A suggestion that this might be the case comes from another observation by Walsh. Many of the convicted adult burglars in his sample "were people engaged in itinerant, semi-legal, semi-illegal activities, part-time crime in fact, whereby they would, for example, re-turf lawns . . . or . . . clean windows, but if the opportunity arose for a break-in, . . . they would . . . do that too" (p. 65). Pillegi (1968) quotes a well-informed American police officer as saying about the "best quality" burglars, that, "even when they are married you will find that they have no real life. They have a tendency to move around a lot. They stay away from their neighbors, their driving licenses are false, they use the names of men in prison. And when they are finally caught they are worn out inside. They are hollow inside" (cited in Walsh, 1980a, p. 45).[3] Walsh's statement that "burglaries involve territorial invasion and only rarely economic gain" (p. 148) seems particularly relevant to the hypothesis of a deteriorating cognitive map.

With regard to the hypothesis that burglary represents stimulation-seeking behavior rather than a rational form of behavior carried out for economic gain, it has already been noted that burglars are not markedly disadvantaged socioeconomically; most burglaries yield small sums of money in relation to the potential costs of apprehension; in about a third of burglaries nothing is stolen; and most burglaries are carried out on impulse. Furthermore, to quote Walsh (1980a, p. 63):

> Young burglars tend to steal less of value per burglary, and to steal odder and more unusual things, often items of low cash value which happen to catch their fancy — more of a form of looting than systematic theft. The lack of rationality is perhaps also reflected in the amount of pointless destructive damage that they frequently commit in a house, such as defecating in beds, tying the sheets in knots, slashing furniture, splashing fluids over materials and defacing pictures.

Walsh further observed that "(v)ery often too, a special signature may be left, such as a threat, slogan or initials written up prominently on a wall or mirror . . ." (p. 63). This suggests that certain aspects of burglary represent "territorial marking." Thus, being in an environment which, because of a deteriorating cognitive map, is not perceived as belonging to anyone, writing slogans or carving initials may be an attempt to identify the territory as one's own.

VANDALISM

With progressive increases in arousal and corresponding increases in the intensity of SSB, it is not enough for the individual simply to touch or pick up objects, however "stimulating" they may be. Greater amounts of sensory input must be obtained to activate the inhibitory P-system. SSB thus begins to take the form of increasingly rapid and more vigorous movement and contact with external objects and the environment in general. Objects may now be strongly manipulated, pulled, punched, kicked, beaten, thrown, or stamped upon. This will tend to result in the objects being smashed or destroyed, causing the acts to be defined as "vandalism."[4]

Regardless of whether the acts in question result in property destruction or defacement, the underlying motive for stimulation is postulated to be the same. Thus, sensations can be obtained from the stimulation-seeking movements themselves, as well as from the destructive consequences of such movements. For instance, considerable stimulation can be obtained by witnessing and hearing objects being destroyed. Glass windows may be broken to hear the sound of breaking glass and to see the fragments cascading to the ground. In general, children are known to derive great pleasure from building and then destroying sand castles, and knocking over structures made of blocks or bricks; adults are similarly fascinated by the sight and sound of buildings being demolished.

To consider the hypothetical case of a teenager returning home from a soccer match, and in a state of tremendous excitement (induced by the game, by the proximity of other fans, the visible presence of rival fans, and by the comparative novelty of the situation), his "hunger" for stimulation would be expected to be exceptionally intense. His search for stimulation would be expected to take a variety of forms, depending on the stimulus objects available in the immediate environment and the integrity of his cognitive map, for example, cheering, shouting, gesticulating, running, consuming alcohol, cigarettes, or other drugs; breaking the antennas off parked cars; jumping on to and running over the hoods of cars, and pushing over motorcycles. Knives may be flourished and muscle power put to use by slashing tires or defacing the exterior of automobiles or buildings. Hearing the rush of escaping air and watching the car abruptly slump over sideways would provide yet further stimulation for the teenager.

The thesis, then, is that many acts of property destruction of the type referred to as vandalism result from intense SSB combined with a deteriorating cognitive map. The biological goal of the behavior, it is claimed, is not to effect destruction per se but to obtain sensory stimulation.[5]

NOTES

1. Objects of high stimulus value and cash value overlap to a large extent. It is surely no accident that many objects of considerable cash value, such as gold, silver, diamonds, emeralds, rubies, and other precious metals and stones, also shine and sparkle. It may be that these types of objects have historically been considered valuable partly because of their striking stimulus characteristics.

2. Walsh (1978) states that, "Shopkeepers are agreed that professionals *take high-value goods only and in large quantities,* and rely heavily on having a group of accomplices who can distract the attention of shop assistants" (p. 75, emphasis added).

3. I am informed by Captain Kilbride, Records Division, New Orleans Police Department (November 1983), that it is common for individuals with police records to have a great many addresses — sometimes as many as 40 — but to have one address where they can be contacted, for example, that of their mother, sister, or other relative.

4. For discussions of vandalism and its wider ideological ramifications, see Ward (1973), Ravetz (1973), and Clarke (1980b).

5. This is not to deny that destruction can sometimes be deliberate, as in the case of shredding documents to ensure secrecy. However, this would not necessarily be considered vandalism. On the other hand, other types of explicit property destruction may be regarded as "vandalism." For instance, in January 1983, it was reported in the press that hundreds of thousands of dollars worth of antique objects were destroyed by their owner, when he suddenly became convinced that they were creations of the devil. The demolition of historic buildings to make way for newer construction is likewise often seen as destructive vandalism by preservationists. However, the present theory does not apply to such cases.

11

CRIMES AGAINST THE PERSON, I: A CRITIQUE OF THE CONCEPT OF AGGRESSION

THE CONCEPT OF AGGRESSION

As discussed in Chapter 6, many of the categories currently used for describing behavior have been part of the English language for centuries, for example, feeding, drinking, sex, and aggression. These categories tend to be regarded as "given"; their usefulness or validity is rarely challenged, and they provide the starting point for lay discussions as well as scientific investigations of behavior. The categories at once describe an action and, in part, explain it by reference to an assumed motive. Thus "feeding" describes the action of orally ingesting certain substances, yet at the same time implicitly explains the action by reference to an assumed urge for food or calories ("hunger").

The term aggression has several different meanings (Kaufman, 1970; Johnson, 1972). At times it is used in an adjectival sense, to describe persons or actions as dynamic, vigorous, or assertive. More commonly, it refers to actions undertaken with the intention of injuring or killing another individual. Critical to the definition of aggression is the idea that the perpetrator intended to injure or kill, even though the action may not have had this result (Dollard & Miller, 1939; Moyer, 1975).[1] There is also a tendency in the popular literature to speak of individuals of many species as possessing a biological "urge to kill or destroy," or as having a "killer instinct."

There are believed to be several distinct types of aggression (Feshbach, 1964), each with its own neurochemical substrate (for example, Moyer, 1975, 1976). One suggestion is that deliberately inflicted injury may at times be the sole intent of the agent; this is referred to as "hostile" or "irritable" aggression. At other times, aggression may be a means of obtaining some other end, such as peer approval; this is described as "instrumental" aggression (Feshbach, 1964; Moyer, 1975, 1976). Nevertheless, common to all types of aggression is the

178

concept of action carried out with intent to injure, regardless of subsidiary goals.

Based on this definition, a vast literature has accumulated dealing with sociological, criminological, political, cultural, psychological, psychiatric, neurochemical, pharmacological, ethological, sociobiological, and neurophysiological determinants and aspects of "aggression."[2]

The concept of aggression is so ingrained in the lay and scientific vocabulary that the question is seldom raised of whether apparently deliberate actions that result in injury or death are most usefully described in terms of an *intention to produce this result*. The problem for the scientist is assumed to be that of explaining *how* such actions are initiated and performed, that is, attempting to elucidate the factors and combinations of factors uniquely responsible for intentional injury (that is, aggression) as opposed, say, to feeding, sexual activity, or drinking. This search for the specific cause of aggression is analogous to the ancient Aristotelian quest to discover the unique essence of phenomena (Lewin, 1935). However, just as advances in physics depended, not on identifying "essences," but on identifying features common to several apparently unrelated phenomenon (and explaining them in terms of a unifying hypothesis, for example, gravitation as an explanation both of falling apples and the movement of the tides), so immutable categories of behavior must be avoided if advances are to be made in understanding the phenomena currently described as aggression.

To describe an action as "aggressive" is to assume that the agent sought *to do something to* an object in the environment, that is, to hurt, injure, or kill it. Moreover, according to certain ethological views (for example, Lorenz, 1966), injuring the object entails the release of aggressive "energy." Thus the conventional view of aggression is that of a *destructive force,* directed either outwardly, away from the agent and toward something else, or directed inwardly, toward the self.

According to the view proposed here and in Chapter 6, however, so-called aggressive behavior represents an attempt on the part of the agent *to obtain something from* the environment: namely, intense sensory stimulation. Thus the relevant flow of force is, on this view, in precisely the reverse direction: from the environment to the agent.

In developing this thesis, the problem is first considered of identifying instances of aggression in practice. Second, the hypothesis is discussed that many so-called aggressive acts represent intense attachment behavior; third, that both aggression and attachment behavior are intense stimulation-seeking behaviors aimed at familiar stimulus sources in the environment; and fourth, that while many domestic assaults result from individuals trying to maintain a threatened cognitive map (by seeking intense stimulation from attachment objects), attacks on strangers are associated with a pervasive breakdown of the cognitive map.[3]

One can distinguish between (a) observed acts, (b) the descriptive labels applied to such acts, and (c) the varying definitions of these labels. In the case of the *observed action* of someone being punched in the face, the *descriptive label* applied to this act is "aggression," and the *definition of the label* is "acting with injurious intent." There are at least two sorts of problems with this definition. First, it does not adequately encompass the kinds of actions that are considered "aggressive." In so-called attacks of rage, for instance, involving stamping on the ground, kicking walls or other objects, or banging one's fists on a table, it is not obvious that the individual is trying to harm or injure the ground, the wall, or the table. It might be suggested that the action of stamping represents a form of defensive signaling. However, stamping or kicking movements often follow sudden pain with great rapidity, and not necessarily in sight of other individuals, suggesting that this description is also incorrect.

The second problem is that it is usually very difficult, and often impossible, to apply the definition in practice (Tedeschi et al., 1974). Consider the following points:

1. In order to validate the concept of aggression as "acting with injurious intent," one must ascertain the agent's intentions. Since this is impossible in the case of animals and preverbal children, the label of aggression cannot, strictly speaking, be applied to animals or preverbal children, yet most experimental research on "aggression" involves animals.

2. Even when people can be questioned about their intentions after having injured or killed someone in an apparently deliberate way, injurious intent is often absent or strongly denied. According to Wolfgang and Ferracuti (1967), less than 5 percent of all known homicides are both premeditated and intentional; the vast majority are

unplanned and are associated with momentary states of intense emotion.

3. Individuals may genuinely recall never having had *any* clear or specific intention after attacking themselves or someone else in an apparently deliberate way (Johnson, 1972; Briscoe, 1975).

4. Individuals may be unable to remember their intention at the time of inflicting death or injury, while admitting that they did have some sort of intention.

5. An individual may have had several intentions in addition to that causing injury. The problem in such cases is to determine the main intention.

6. An intention *other* than injury, such as a desire to punish without causing bodily harm, may be offered following a deliberate, perhaps fatal, attack on another person. Technically, such actions would not qualify as aggression in spite of the injurious result.

There are, in fact, many instances of seemingly deliberate assault and homicide, particularly where victim and offender are closely related or well-acquainted, where injurious intent is absent and where, as a result, the concept of aggression is strictly inappropriate. In such cases, injurious intent is often vehemently denied; profuse and frequent expressions of love for the victim may be offered, and grief may be exceptionally intense. Among murderers as a whole, from 4 percent to more than 40 percent subsequently kill themselves (West, 1966; Ferracuti & Newman, 1974), indicating that grief is often genuine and intense.

All of this is not to deny that individuals do, on occasion, claim to have intended to harm, injure, or kill someone else. For instance, in a study of criminal motivation involving 65 British men convicted of assaulting another male, most said that their main intention was to injure their opponent, and very few mentioned peer approval as a motive (Berkowitz, 1978). As part of the Cambridge study in delinquent development, 389 youths aged 18 to 19 were asked to describe fights in which they had been participants (Farrington et al., 1982). Based on these reports, Berkowitz (1978, p. 332) concluded that two-person fights "are primarily examples of hostile aggression, whereas group fights primarily involve instrumental aggression." On the other hand (as the authors themselves noted) the boys were not asked about their motive during their most serious fights; very few said spontaneously that they were angry at the time of the fight; the boys were not asked directly if they had fought in order to conform to group norms; and it was impossible to tell if they had told the truth (although other evidence suggested that their accounts were not exaggerated).

Even if the boys had been closely questioned about their motives, however, and were being truthful, it is difficult to know what credence to attach to their statements. For one thing, memories of such incidents are notoriously subject to rationalization and distortion, especially under the influence of a persistent and possibly biased interviewer (Briscoe, 1975). Second, people are frequently not aware of their motive(s) for acting at any given moment, especially in the case of sudden, impulsive actions. Third, faced with the request to supply a motive, people will try to make sense of their behavior by reference to established behavioral categories. Thus, in some instances of both studies referred to above, the person's reasoning may have been: "Yes, I recall hitting and seriously hurting someone. . . . Presumably, I must have been *trying* to hurt him." But, even granting that this was the person's intention at the time, and not an after-the-fact rationalization, it does not follow that the person's own account of his behavior is the most useful way of describing it from a scientific point of view, that is, the explanation that best fits the facts. Other explanations can be invoked which transcend the motivational understanding or vocabulary of the citizen.

As noted above, the conventional definition of aggression is based on the concept of injurious intent. Given the difficulties involved in trying to prove injurious intent, an alternative approach might be to restrict the use of the term aggression to injury- or fatality-causing actions, and ignore the agent's intentions. The problem with this solution is that, by ignoring intentions, there is no separation of purely accidental injury from deliberate injury; nor is it possible, within the category of deliberate injury, to separate doctor-induced (that is, surgical) injury and malicious injury.

Despite this problem, the criterion of aggression adopted in practice in experimental studies typically involves a specific act such as biting, or a combination of acts (for example, unsheathing the claws, hissing, stalking, erections of the hair (piloerection), arching the back, biting, killing, etc.). The difficulty is that the same acts are constitutive of supposedly unrelated motivational systems, including eating, sex, flight, and play. Killing is an integral part of the feeding response in predatory species and a part of sexual activity in insects such as the praying mantis (Roeder, 1967). Biting occurs in feeding, sex, and play. Erection of the hair (for example, in cats) is seen not only in aggression but also in escape and defensive behavior; and penile erection occurs in both courtship and intermale aggressive displays in monkeys (MacLean, 1983, p. 367). The question therefore arises as to the basis on which, say, biting, is to be classified as an aggressive act rather than an expression of hunger, sex, or playfulness? This question is seldom raised in practice because the researcher defines what is to account as an aggressive response before carrying out the experiments. Recognizing this dilemma, Bandura and Walters (1963) have noted that the classification of behavior often involves making value judgments, and that the term aggression is implicitly applied when the observed behavior exceeds a certain level of vigor or intensity. Thus, biting is characterized as an aggressive response when the action is exceptionally vigorous. To illustrate their point they present the following hypothetical case.

> (A) young child kicks his mother's leg when he has failed to obtain a desired toy that is placed beyond his reach, and the mother has not attended to his verbal request for assistance. If the kick is mild, there is a good chance that the child's response will be regarded as dependent; if the kick is strongly administered, it is more likely that the response will be labeled "aggressive." The covert assumption, of course, is that a hard kick is *intended* to hurt. But in the case cited, it may be argued that the hard as well as the mild kick is intended to procure the mother's attention and so can be categorized as dependent. Indeed, negative attention-getting behavior provides a good example of a response pattern the categorization of which consistently baffles research workers . . . (Bandura and Walters, 1963, pp. 139–40).

The problem with behavioral intensity as a criterion of aggression is that the precise level of intensity at which a given act is considered aggressive is entirely subjective, particularly at the lower end of the spectrum;[4] moreover, if aggression is identified by the *intensity* of a response, the implication is that any intense activity or response can be considered aggressive regardless of motivation. Thus we would speak, for instance, of aggressive "eating" or aggressive "sex" or aggressive "play." But the question is, how are acts to be characterized that are neither instances of feeding, sexual activity, nor play, but which involve interpersonal behavior of such intensity as to cause pain, injury, or death? In other words, the problem remains unresolved of how to classify acts which have traditionally been considered instances of aggression, assault, and homicide. It is to this issue which we now turn.

AGGRESSION AS ATTACHMENT BEHAVIOR

In an earlier publication by the author (Mawson, 1980), it was proposed that many so-called aggressive acts could be reinterpreted as "attachment behaviors"; that is, as proximity- or contact-seeking behaviors of high intensity. The suggestion was that injuries inflicted in the course of the behavior were a fortuitous result of the perpetrator's attempts to achieve intense physical contact with the victim, and that individuals convicted of such crimes tended to have a strong predisposition for attachment behavior, as evidenced by a general tendency toward intense and persistent proximity-seeking behavior. To refer back to the example from Bandura and Walters (1963, pp. 139–40), I suggested that instead of there being two motivational systems — dependency and aggression — there was in fact only a single system; namely dependency or (to avoid the negative connotations of this term) *attachment behavior*. Attachment behavior can vary over a wide range of intensities and at times have injurious consequences for the recipient, consequences which are normally referred to as aggression on the assumption that the injuries were *intentionally* inflicted.

The argument began by noting that aggression and attachment behavior have long been considered closely related phenomena. Freud (1922), for instance, noted that in almost all intimate relationships feelings of love and hate are intermingled. Lorenz (1966) suggested that social bonds develop only in aggressive animal species, and Bernstein and Gordon (1974) observed that strong social bonding is particularly evident in pigtail monkeys, a species known for its aggressiveness. Simmel (1955), Bard (1971), and Goldstein (1975) have also suggested that the closer and more intimate an association between two people, the greater the likelihood of aggression. With regard to crimes of violence, homicide involves familiars more than strangers (Ferracuti & Newman, 1974; Constantino et al., 1977), and killings within the victim or offender's home tend to be more brutal than those committed against nonfamily members or committed outside the home (Wolfgang, 1958). Among violent crimes in general (homicide, assault, rape, armed robbery), the lethality or degree of violence is inversely related to the percentage of strangers involved in the offense (Lystad, 1975). It has been suggested on the basis of such evidence that the incidence of homicide is directly related to the strength of social attachments (Henry & Short, 1954; Mohr & McKnight, 1971).

Despite the apparent connection between aggression and attachment behavior, the conventional view is that they are discrete systems of behavior with unique defining features and separate, though possibly overlapping, determinants. To show that aggression is instead an extreme manifestation of attachment behavior, the two forms of behavior were compared point by point in terms of their environmental determinants, targets, functional consequences, and topography. Overall, aggression and attachment behavior are strikingly similar in each of these respects. The main points of the argument are sketched below.[5]

1. *Determinants*. Aggression and attachment behavior can both be elicited by fatigue, hunger, ill-health, pain, and cold; the absence, departure or rebuff of a mother; the occurrence of alarming events; and rebuffs by other individuals.[6]

2. *Targets*. Once a certain level of perceptual development has been achieved, attachment behavior (proximity-seeking activity) tends to be directed at familiar persons and objects. A considerable amount of mild and serious aggression is likewise directed at familiars (for example, Gelles & Straus, 1979; Straus, 1980; Pagelow, 1981; Gelles, 1982).[7] Reviewers of the animal literature, however, appear to support the opposite view; namely, that aggression is mainly directed toward "outsiders" (Scott, 1975; Marler, 1976). Marler (1976, p. 243), for instance, states that "the most bitter fighting of all is provoked by the addition of a new animal, a stranger to the group," but he goes on to note that the strange animal is likely to be attacked most vigorously and persistently if it is of the *same species,* the *same sex,* and possibly the *same strain and breed* as the attacker. Thus, "strange" animals may be "attacked" because they present a combination of familiar and unfamiliar stimulus characteristics.

3. *Functional Consequences*. Aggression and attachment behavior seem to be reciprocally related in that aggression or attachment behavior on the part of individual A toward individual B can evoke either aggressive *or* proximity-seeking responses in B toward A. These intriguing parallels suggest that there is some fundamental similarity in

the behaviors to which the different labels of "aggression" and "attachment behavior" are usually applied. This takes us to the next issue.

4. *Topography.* As noted above, aggression is difficult to identify in practice because of the elusiveness of intentions, and the label is implicitly based on the intensity of the behavior. But the question remains as to the underlying motive of the behavior. The suggestion put forward in the paper (Mawson, 1980) was that the underlying goal is intense *contact* with the object of the behavior. Since injuries can result from intense contact, the behavior has mistakenly been labeled aggression. Instead, the real goal may be physical contact.

The paper then went on to apply the same analysis to criminal violence. The determinants, targets, and topography of a large proportion of assaults and homicides were found to be very similar to those of attachment behavior; moreover, perpetrators tend to have a strong predisposition for attachment behavior. With regard to *determinants* the precipitating stimulus for most homicides and assaults can be subsumed under one or more of the three major determinants of attachment behavior, that is, (a) those involving abandonment or rejection; (b) those in which the perpetrator is the recipient of intense attachment behavior, (in the form of insults, antagonism, and threatened or actual assault); and (c) those involving other kinds of environmental stress, such as business failure, job termination or prolonged social isolation. Second, with regard to *targets,* homicide and assault tend to be intragroup phenomena (Mulvihill et al., 1969). Third, with regard to *topography,* assaults themselves can be reinterpreted as contact-seeking behaviors. In support of this point it was noted that the great majority of assaults are unplanned, unpremeditated, and unintended; intense mourning and regret often follow the act, together with professions of love for the victim; attacks often far exceed the force needed to cause injury or death; and many assaults and homicides occur either shortly before, during, or after sexual intercourse (Morris & Blom-Cooper, 1964). Fourth, with regard to *individual predisposition,* many perpetrators of assault and homicide have a strong predisposition for attachment behavior. The bond between victim and offender is often so close as to be described as "symbiotic." In the case of child abusers, the roles of parent and child are often reversed (Justice & Justice, 1976) and offenders are commonly described as unusually dependent, jealous and/or aggressive (Showalter et al., 1980).

Just as attachment behavior and aggression are said to form a single continuum of contact-seeking behavior, so the *traits* of dependency and aggression can be reinterpreted as forming a single continuum, "aggression" being a more intense expression of "dependency." Parenthetically, it may be noted that aggressive pre-adolescent boys tend to show a great deal of dependency behavior toward parents, teachers, and peers; aggressive adolescents are highly dependent during their pre-adolescent years; and maternally deprived aggressive children also tend to be intensely dependent (Bandura & Walters, 1963, pp. 147–48).

While the hypothesis sketched above (Mawson, 1980) applies to spousal homicide and domestic violence in general, its major limitations are that it only addresses interpersonal aggression *within* a social bond; it does not explain aggression directed at inanimate objects; and it does not explain aggressive behavior toward strangers, a problem of increasing magnitude in the United States (Rushforth et al., 1977). Finally, the hypothesis remains to be integrated into the broader theory of cognitive maps and stimulation-seeking behavior. To correct these deficiencies, it is first proposed that *attachment behavior is itself a form of stimulation-seeking behavior.*

ATTACHMENT (AND AGGRESSIVE) BEHAVIOR AS SSB

Having argued that much so-called aggressive behavior is intense attachment behavior, it is now suggested that both forms of behavior represent SSB. Thus attachment behavior in older children and adults is stimulation-seeking activity directed at familiar targets; that is, behavior aimed at maintaining a cognitive map.

The concept of attachment behavior is inseparably linked with the work of John Bowlby, as set forth in his three magisterial volumes (1969, 1973, and 1981). According to Bowlby (1969), attachment behavior is a distinct motivational system akin to reproductive and parental behavior. It is elicited by specific environmental conditions; namely, fatigue, hunger, ill-health, pain, and cold; mother's absence, departure or discouragement of proximity; alarming events, and rebuffs by other adults or children. The set-goal of the system is proximity and/or contact with mother or mother-figure; and achievement of proximity terminates attachment behavior. The evolutionary-adaptive function of attachment behavior is said to be protection from predators. In infants and young children, attachment behaviors include (a) signaling behavior, for example, crying, smiling, calling and (b) approach behavior, for example, actual approach and following behavior, and nonnutritional sucking. In older persons, attachment behavior takes on increasingly symbolic forms; photographs, letters, and telephone calls become important ways of keeping in touch with attachment figures.

When the activating conditions are of mild intensity, attachment behaviors in infants and toddlers include smiling, relaxed locomotion, watching, and touching; when the conditions are of high intensity, attachment behaviors include rapid following, approach, and fierce clinging. Nothing short of physical contact will terminate attachment behavior under these conditions (Bowlby, 1969, p. 258).

While Bowlby's theory has been influential not only in the study of parent-infant bonding and child development, but also in the field of psychiatric disorders, we are concerned here with the question of whether the concept of attachment behavior — defined by Bowlby (1969, pp. 198–209) as a response designed to maintain proximity to a particular individual — adequately describes the set of responses elicited by alarming stimuli. In the case of approach and following behaviors, there can be little doubt that the infant is attempting either to contact or maintain proximity with mother. But what about the case of nonnutritional sucking, which Bowlby also classifies as attachment behavior? Sucking is said to have two forms; *nutritional sucking,* which occurs in response to hunger and is directed toward food; and *nonnutritional sucking,* which is elicited by alarming stimuli, is characterized by the shallowness of sucking movements, and is directed at a "comforter." In human and primate infants nonnutritional sucking often consists of thumb sucking; in infant monkeys separated from their mother, it can also take the form of autoerotic sucking, which supposedly serves as a substitute for the mother's nipple. In nonnutritional sucking the nipple is grasped not as a source of food but as a means of holding on to the mother.[8] Nipple grasping is therefore regarded as serving the same function as clinging. Bowlby also observes that nonnutritional sucking has a quietening effect on infants; that is, it terminates attachment behavior independently of any connection with food. For instance, it is known that babies who cannot swallow food because of atresia of the esophagus (a congenital defect) nevertheless stop crying when given something to suck (Bowlby, 1969, p. 292). If an infant is greatly distressed, however, rocking movements, especially at a speed of about 60 cycles per minute, are much more effective. Bowlby explains this by suggesting that 60 cycles per minute or above is similar to the rate at which an adult primate normally walks, and that an infant carried on a mother's back or hip would be rocked at this speed.

There are problems, however, in attempting to subsume the above activities under the rubric of attachment behavior. The assumption that *alarming stimuli* give rise to nonnutritional sucking, whereas *hunger* gives rise to nutritional sucking, is invalid, since alarming stimuli can give rise both to eating and to sex. It is recalled that in their classic study of the behavior of children separated from their mothers during wartime, Burlingham and Freud (1944) observed that the children had an "insatiable greed" for food, and engaged in prolonged and intense thumb sucking, head banging, destructiveness, and masturbation. Other evidence indicates that alarming stimuli of many kinds can elicit increased eating and sexual activity in humans and in a number of animal species that have been studied (Hinde, 1966, pp. 150–63; Fentress, 1978). Such observations suggest that the rubric of attachment behavior is not sufficient to encompass all of the behaviors elicited by alarming stimuli; instead there appears to be a more fundamental common behavior. The suggestion is that attachment behavior, thumb sucking, head banging, aggression, sexual activity, feeding — indeed all behaviors that involve increased contact with environmental objects and surfaces — represent an active search for sensory stimulation.

The question now arises as to why *mother* is the focus of so-called attachment behavior. The reason may be that mother represents a composite pattern of basic stimuli — tactile, auditory, olfactory, visual, and gustatory — and is likely to be the most stimulating object to which the infant is exposed. This composite pattern is gradually incorporated, becoming the most important stimulus object within the child's cognitive map. The child's attempt to make contact with mother *and* the various correlated activities, such as eating, sexuality, and aggressiveness, represent localized and generalized forms of SSB. On the one hand, there is a general search for *familiar amounts and kinds of sensory input.* On the other hand, there is also a search for *familiar composite patterns* of sensory stimulation, viz., mother herself. Burlingham and Freud (1944) observed that young children separated from their mother have a tendency to form passionate temporary attachments to volunteers working within the institutions. This may be explained in terms of a *partial breakdown of the child's cognitive map,* and hence the tendency for SSB to be directed at environmental objects that are not only "stimulating" in basic ways, but also embody the generic patterned characteristics of the missing object.

In Chapter 7, it was proposed that the sensory input derived from SSB, after being evaluated as congruous with the individual's cognitive map, activates the P-system; this in turn inhibits the S-system, leading to a generalized state of calm. This explanation is now applied to other observations explained by Bowlby in terms of attachment behavior as a separate behavioral system. The observation that nonnutritional sucking has a calming effect (Wolff, 1969, cited in Bowlby, 1969, p. 294) may be due to the fact that the comforter provides *oral stimulation.*

Distressed infants can be calmed by other forms of vigorous stimulation such as rocking, jumping, being swung round and round, sliding, riding, etc., and these forms of stimulation have little to do with the normal walking pace of primate mothers. Infants can also be calmed and their heart rates decrease if they are rocked in specially built cribs. These observations suggest that it is sensory stimulation rather than contact with mother which is responsible for the calming effect.

Our thesis, then, is that attachment behavior is part of a broader system of stimulation seeking behavior. The greater the level of S-system arousal, the greater the intensity of sensory stimulation required to activate the inhibitory P-system and thereby damp down the S-system; hence, the greater the intensity of stimulation-seeking activity. Attachment behavior represents SSB of relatively mild intensity, whereas aggression represents SSB above an arbitrarily defined level of intensity.[9]

CONCLUSIONS

It has been suggested that the initial interactions of infants with their external environment represent stimulation-seeking behavior of a nonspecific kind. Later on, the developing organism repetitively approaches particularly stimulating objects — activities that are commonly labeled social attachments, attachment objects, or social bonds. Organisms form *cognitive maps* of the sensory characteristics of these objects. Thus, what begins as an attempt to maintain familiar kinds and amounts of sensory input develops into an attempt to maintain the *patterns* of sensory stimulation represented by the stimulus characteristics of environmental objects. This involves maintaining proximity to the objects in question, the result being that individuals tend simultaneously to avoid the unfamiliar and to seek out the familiar.

In a series of valuable papers dating from the early 1960s, Salzen (1978) has sketched a model of social attachment which has similarities to that described here. Instead of the term cognitive map, Salzen uses the concept of neuronal model. He notes that attachment behavior is initially based on "contact stimulation" and that it is part of a "sensory homeostatic system" which later matures into a more cognitively oriented system whereby the organism orients away from strangeness and toward familiar objects and places. Salzen further notes that the behavioral system is activated by discrepancy (or incongruity) and terminated by the reappearance or discovery of congruity. He also suggests that persistent incongruity eventually alters the organism's neuronal model. On the other hand, Salzen contends (with, for example, Scott [1958]) that there are three basic systems of behavior, one group centering on physiological homeostasis (for example, "ingestive" behaviors), another focusing on "sensory homeostasis" (which includes attachment behavior), and a third group collectively termed "reproductive," which includes both sex and aggression as distinct subsystems.

The alternative conception of behavioral organization proposed here is that, from the beginnings of fetal development, behavior forms a *gestalt* or global pattern of stimulation-seeking activity, reflected in the general tendency of organisms to be motile in their environment. Moreover, instead of there being several "primary drive" behaviors which lead to various "secondary drives" via the linkage between new environmental stimuli and the satisfaction of a "basic need" (Hull, 1943), the complexity of response organization emerges in a sort of "deductive process" in which certain broad parameters of SSB (for example, intensity, frequency, duration) are progressively refined through the learned discrimination of sensory inputs. In particular, "attachment behavior" in the mature organism is part of a more general system of stimulation-seeking activity in which the person approaches and maintains contact with other individuals, objects, and places whose sensory characteristics have been incorporated into his (or her) cognitive map. Furthermore, aggression is a more intense expression of this same tendency to seek the familiar and avoid the unfamiliar, a tendency which is especially likely to occur in situations of extreme incongruity and S-system arousal, and one that can bring the individual into direct contact with the criminal justice system.

NOTES

1.   Injurious intent is emphasized in order to distinguish clearly between deliberate injury (i. e., aggression) and *accidental* injury (which is usually not regarded as aggression).

2.   A few selected references must suffice: Scott, 1958; Lorenz, 1966; Wolfgang and Ferracuti, 1967/1982; Bandura, 1973; Goldstein, 1975; Field and Sweet, 1975; Moyer, 1976; Ball-Rokeach, 1980; Hamburg and Trudeau, 1981; Wolfgang and Weiner, 1982; Geen and Donnerstein, 1983.

3.   In the discussion which follows I will be arguing with myself. In an earlier paper (Mawson, 1980) the argument was presented that much interpersonal aggression represents intense proximity or contact-seeking behavior. Here I will argue that proximity-seeking behavior itself is a form of stimulation-seeking behavior, directed at familiar persons and objects in the environment.

4.   Bandura and Walters and their associates (Bandura & Walters, 1963; Walters & Parke, 1964), while noting that the label of aggression is often invoked arbitrarily according to behavioral intensity, still appear to assume that aggression is a distinct form of behavior with unique and objective identifiers, and that aggression can be distinguished from say, dependency, by the *social context* in which the acts occur. On the other hand, as they themselves noted in the quotation cited above, even trained experts are frequently unable to distinguish between aggression and dependency behavior in the context of maternal-child relationships.

5.   Attachment behavior, as defined by Bowlby (1969, pp. 198–209), refers to responses designed to maintain proximity to, or contact with, a particular individual. However, the motivation to seek contact is not necessarily conscious and the accompanying emotional state is not necessarily one of love or affection. As applied to human infants, attachment behaviors of low intensity include rapid following, approach and fierce clinging (Bowlby, 1969, p. 250). An attachment or social bond is defined in terms of attachment behavior that is preferentially directed to a specific individual over a period of time (cf., Rosenthal, 1973).

6.   The determinants of aggression and attachment behavior may also be similar at the physiological or neurochemical level. Redmond et al. (1975) have shown that low-MAO activity in rhesus monkeys is associated both with "social affiliative" *and* agnostic (i. e., aggressive) behavior in the same individuals.

7.   The National Crime Survey (U.S. Department of Justice, 1980), carried out during the 1970s on a large representative sample of the U.S. population, indicated

that 3.8 million "incidents of violence" (including only rape, robbery, and assaults among adults) occured among "intimates" (relatives and friends) during the four-year period 1973–1976. In contrast, 14.1 million violent incidents were reported as occurring among nonintimates during the same period. However, as the report notes, *attacks by strangers are far more likely to be reported to the police than are attacks by intimates;* hence the figure of 3.8 million violent crimes among intimates is undoubtedly an underestimate of the true figure. According to the survey, 55 out of every 100 violent incidents were unreported. However, in a Scottish study of violence against wives (Dobash & Dobash, 1979, p. 437) it was found that only 2 out of every 98 assaults on wives were reported to the police. When one includes serious violence against children — estimated to number 500,000 or more incidents a year (Light, 1974; Gelles, 1982) in the U.S., as well as lesser forms of violence among intimates that would be reported as crimes if committed against strangers — it is quite possible that the true incidence of serious violence among intimates exceeds that among nonintimates.

8. Hinde and his associates (1964) have noted that when a rhesus infant is clinging to its running or climbing mother, it holds on to her with both arms and legs and simultaneously grasps one or both nipples with its mouth (a "5-point hold").

9. Viewed as overlapping levels of intensity of SSB, aggression and attachment behavior share two additional features in common. First, just as attachment behavior in infants tends to be directed at highly stimulating objects and attachments tend to be formed to such objects (Schaffer & Emerson, 1964), so aggression tends to be directed toward stimulating objects. For instance, live and moving targets are attacked in preference to dead or stationary ones (Levison & Flynn, 1965); Siamese fighting fish (*Betta splendens*) fight and display more with responsive than with unresponsive opponents (Johnson & Johnson, 1973; Bols, 1977); and prey animals that "freeze" when confronted with a predator are less likely to be attacked than if they flee, attack, or engage in other kinds of vigorous movement (Hediger, 1955; Gallup, 1974). Second, sensory stimulation can offset or prevent both intense attachment behavior and so-called aggressive behavior. Mason (1967) reports that installing a swinging pendulum in the cage markedly reduced the initial arousal and agitation associated with maternal and social deprivation in young chimpanzees. Providing a rag for puppies or a pacifier for babies also dampens their immediate reaction to maternal separation (Cairns, 1977). Self-mutilation can also be suppressed or eliminated by various forms of stimulation including: electric shock (Forehand & Baumeister, 1976), spanking (Albin, 1977), sharp taps on the fingers (Singh, 1976), back or hand vibration (Nunes et al., 1977), playing with toys (Levy, 1944), gentle bouncing on the knees of an adult (Nunes et al., 1977), and touching or putting an arm around the individual just before the act of self-injury (Graff & Mallin, 1967).

12

CRIMES AGAINST THE PERSON, II: HOMICIDE AND ASSAULT

How, then, does the model explain actual criminal violence? Under what conditions is SSB likely to be intensified to the point of causing injury or death? The discussion is divided into three parts: attacks on intimates; attacks on strangers; and rape (Chapter 13).

ATTACKS ON FAMILIARS[1]

As already noted, the proportion of criminal and noncriminal attacks on familiars (that is, relatives, friends, and neighborhood acquaintances) probably far exceeds that on strangers. A clue to understanding such attacks may be found in the typical response of human beings to disasters — which is to seek the proximity of familiar persons and the familiar environment. Here it is similarly argued that much criminal violence is an intense manifestation of the tendency of people in stressful conditions to seek out other familiar people, *even though the person with whom proximity is sought is the cause of the stress*. Injuries suffered by the victim in the course of the behavior can thus be viewed as an unintended result of the perpetrator's attempt to obtain intense stimulation from a familiar object. Intense SSB toward an individual occurs because the person has acted in a way which the perpetrator interprets as incongruous. Hence, in attacking (that is, seeking stimulation from) the individual, the attacker is attempting to maintain his or her cognitive map.

The steps of the argument are presented in detail one by one:

People build, and attempt to maintain, hierarchically organized cognitive maps of their interpersonal and physical environment. Such maintenance is achieved by obtaining congruous stimuli from the objects whose characteristics have been internalized. Incongruous events result in increased S-system arousal and SSB, that is, attempts to obtain congruous stimuli. The greater the level of arousal the greater the intensity of SSB, aimed at the familiar. Attachment objects, that is, people who are preferentially sought out on an enduring basis, are the most important aspect of one's environment and cognitive map, since incongruous behavior on their part is generally more arousing than incongruities of other sorts, for example, many physical hazards. Hence, auditory, visual, and tactile stimulation is sought from the person whose behavior has been incongruous; the greater the incongruity, the greater the intensity of SSB.

Mild levels of incongruity and SSB result in what is commonly recognized as affiliative behavior; at higher levels, the intensity of SSB increases to the point where observers are likely to describe it as aggressive. If injuries are inflicted, the criminal justice system intervenes and the behavior is labeled an assault or homicide, depending partly on the severity of the injuries.

In discussing aggression and crimes of violence among intimates, we are necessarily dealing with a *relationship* between two or more individuals. A dyadic relationship (i.e., between two people) exists when each member of the dyad is internalized in the cognitive map of the other. To consider a "close" relationship between two persons, P and Q, P is a highly salient part of Q's cognitive map, and vice versa. The relationship is maintained insofar as P and Q continue to seek and obtain congruous stimulation from each other.

There are at least three scenarios in which SSB between familiars could be intensified to the point of causing injury or death, although in some instances more than one scenario might be expected to occur. Using the relationship between P and Q as an illustration, the initial steps of the three scenarios in which *P injures or kills Q* are as follows:[2]

Scenario 1. SSB toward P on the part of Q, i.e., P ← Q.
Scenario 2. Abandonment or rejection of P by Q. Thus, P Q →
Scenario 3. Incongruity in the wider environment, leading P to seek stimulation from Q. Thus, P → Q.

Each scenario is now discussed in turn.

Scenario 1. The stimulation-seeking behavior of a child is not only preferentially directed at familiar persons, but also tends to elicit reciprocal SSB. For example, the crying of an infant is a form of SSB as well as a potent stimulus for eliciting SSB, that is, approach, contact, and holding by the parent. According to Bowlby (1969, 1973), attachment behavior is normally self-terminating once the preferred "object" has been reached; for instance, a small child (let us call him Q) will usually stop crying when picked up by the parent (P) and held. In terms of the model, Q's approaches to P are terminated (i.e., Q becomes calm) when P acts in a reassuring or calming fashion. We interpret P's care-giving response as being elicited by the perception of incongruity in Q's behavior, that is, by cries or other signals of apparent distress. P's actions are in turn interpreted by Q as providing congruous stimulation, thereby reaffirming Q's cognitive map, and inducing a state of behavioral quiescence. To see Q become calm is likewise a congruous stimulus for P; this reaffirms P's cognitive map and de-arouses him or her also.

If, however, P should *overreact* to Q's approaches by, say, shouting and gesticulating angrily, (e.g., "What's the matter with you?!") this excessively intense *congruity-seeking response* on P's part is interpreted by Q as *incongruous*. It therefore arouses Q physiologically even more, resulting in still greater intensities of congruity-seeking behavior toward P. The obvious example is that of a parent who shouts ill-temperedly at his distressed child, instead of picking him up, thereby causing him to cry still more loudly and vigorously. P once more overreacts, but this time his congruity-seeking behavior reaches a level of intensity that involves physical contact in the form of slaps or squeezing. P's distress and anger communicates itself to Q as a higher degree of incongruity, and Q reciprocates with his own form of intense congruity-seeking behavior, for example, hysterical screaming. Thus a positive-feedback spiral of SSB is set in motion between P and Q with, in this case, injurious or fatal results for Q. In each phase of the encounter both individuals overreact to the other's *congruity-seeking responses* by engaging in reciprocal *congruity-seeking responses,* but of such excessive intensity and of such a quality that they are interpreted by the other as *incongruous,* and hence as a signal for increasing rather than decreasing the intensity of their own congruity-seeking behavior, thereby unwittingly increasing the probability of a violent outcome. As Steele and Pollock (1974, p. 107) observed about parent-child interactions resulting in child abuse, "(t)he crying infant who does not respond to comforting may be severely shaken or hit on the head."

It is important to emphasize the term *unwitting* with the respect to destructive consequences. Child-abusing parents often state that their violence was unintended and that they were not aware of how rapidly its intensity had escalated (Vasta & Copitch, 1981). On the basis of their study of 60 child-abusing families, Steele and Pollock (1974) reported that some abusing parents who habitually hit and pulled their children were "not aware of the extra force used at the time [they had inflicted injuries on their children]" (p. 117). In a recent study which attempted to simulate the interpersonal events leading to child abuse (using undergraduate subjects and duration of pressing a mechanical level as an indirect measure of interpersonal response and child abuse), Vasta and Copitch (1981) found that the subjects were *unaware* that the duration of their lever pressing was increasing as a function of the child's so-called inadequate performance on a series of tasks. (In fact, no children were used in the experiment, unbeknownst to the subjects, and the "child's" performance was automatically programmed to deteriorate gradually.) The authors concluded that their research demonstrates "the relative ease with which conditions can be created to produce a rapid acceleration of adult responding toward a child from a low to a comparatively high level of intensity" (p. 169).

Examples of this type of scenario might be (a) an encounter between two male acquaintances in a bar which leads to criminal violence, (b) a series of progressively intense interactions between mother and child, resulting in child abuse (cf., Parke & Collmer, 1975; Patterson, 1975; Vasta & Copitch, 1981), and (c) spousal violence in which either husband or wife is injured or killed.

Scenario 2. In the second scenario, individual Q for some reason rejects or abandons individual P — or so P interprets Q's behavior. The more Q attempts to avoid P, the more vigorously P attempts to regain proximity (i.e., seek congruity), again with possibly injurious or lethal results for Q. Situations involving perceived abandonment or rejection by an attachment figure are cited repeatedly in the literature on criminal, and especially domestic, violence, as noted in Chapter 11. Indeed, rejection or abandonment by a loved one may be more disturbing, both physiologically and psychologically, than most physical disasters, and certainly more disturbing than involuntary separation or bereavement (cf., Jacobs & Ostfeld, 1977; Bloom et al., 1978). In terms of the model, Q's rejection of P is highly incongruous for P, leading to SSB directed at Q. The more Q persists in rejecting P (usually within a limited time span of weeks or months), the more vigorously P seeks Q's sensory characteristics by way of auditory, visual, olfactory, and especially tactile contact, again with potentially fatal consequences for Q.[3]

Scenario 3. A third scenario leading P to injure or kill Q is one in which P seeks stimulation from Q in response to stress from outside the relationship. Examples of such stressors and their association with criminal violence were discussed in Chapter 2. A typical case would be that of a man who, after a hard day at work, goes to a bar, has a few drinks, comes home, and then, with little provocation, assaults his wife or children. In terms of the model, the incongruous experience of a stressful day at work leads to an increase in S-system arousal and SSB aimed at the familiar objects and persons in his environment. "Aggression" and the resulting injuries are thus viewed as a more extreme manifestation of the affiliative or proximity-seeking response toward the familiar, which occurs normally in response to environmental stress. Since incongruities originating in the familiar interpersonal environment are more disturbing than those in the external environment, the first two scenarios would be expected to be the main ones conducive to extreme SSB and serious or fatal injury, with combinations of scenarios (1) and (3), or (2) and (3), representing still more potent stimulus conditions for interpersonal violence.

To summarize the model, criminal violence between intimates results from attempts on the part of one person, the perpetrator, to obtain intense sensorial contact with another person (the victim), the goal being to reaffirm his cognitive map of that individual. In the first scenario, violence occurs as part of a positive feedback process in which the attempt to seek congruous stimulation results in mutual incongruity and further more intense, injurious, and destructive congruity seeking. In the second scenario, violence occurs as part of a negative feedback process in which incongruity generated by the victim's attempt to abandon the other causes the latter to seek proportionately intense congruous stimulation; the greater the incongruity generated by the separation, the more intense and potentially destructive are the abandoned individual's attempts to seek congruity. In the third scenario, incongruities in the wider social or physical environment cause the individual to seek congruous stimulation in the form of intense (and potentially injurious) contact with intimates.

It should be noted that in most instances of all of these scenarios, the behavior of the perpetrator begins with a so-called attachment, affiliative or dependency response. Only under exceptional circumstances is the intensity of the behavior such as to exceed the threshold for causing injury or death. This interpretation allows for a more charitable view of the typical perpetrator of violence than is found in the criminological literature or popular press; for instead of casting him or her as a malevolent individual bent on a course of harm and destructiveness, the agent can be seen as attempting to *maintain* the social bond of which he is a part (albeit with excessive intensity and with unhappy consequences for both parties), rather than attempting to destroy it. From this point of view, it is a tragic irony that the perpetrator should deprive himself of the very thing he most needs and wants to maintain: namely, an enduring relationship with another live human being (Mawson, 1980).

Predisposition for Violence

Since not all individuals react to the incongruity of, say, abandonment, with SSB of such intensity as to cause injury or death, it is necessary to postulate a strong *predisposition for stimulation-seeking behavior*. The reader will notice that this is an expansion of the more limited concept of a "strong predisposition for intense *attachment behavior*," which was discussed earlier in the chapter and in the paper referred to above (Mawson, 1980). In suggesting that attachment behavior is part of a more general stimulation-seeking response (aimed at familiar sources of stimulation), one would also expect that a strong predisposition for intense attachment behavior would be part of a more general predisposition for seeking familiar amounts and types of stimulation.

The concept of a *strong predisposition for SSB* refers to (a) a low threshold for SSB, and (b) a tendency to overreact with more intense and persistent SSB to a given stimulus than would be shown by other individuals of comparable age, sex, race, or social background. Such a tendency to overreact may result fortuitously in the injury or death of the individual toward whom the behavior is directed, and hence in criminal violence.

A strong individual predisposition for SSB would be expected to show itself in the behavioral correlates of sensation seeking, as measured by Zuckerman's (1979) Sensation-Seeking Scale; that is, heavy smoking and drinking; more frequent and more varied sexual activity and drug abuse; and gambling. Unlike Zuckerman's concept of sensation seeking, however, the present concept of stimulation seeking (tied as it is to the idea of preserving a cognitive map, and hence of seeking *familiar* amounts and types of stimulation) does not necessarily predict a tendency to become involved in activities outside familiar locations, for example, parachuting or skiing (cf., Zuckerman's thrill and adventure-seeking subscale). Rather, intense stimulation seeking would be expected to take the form of activities that enhance sensory input, that are directed at familiar persons (e.g., attachment behavior) or at the self (e.g., smoking, drinking, drug abuse) and are performed in a familiar location (e.g., the home.)[4]

The concept of *sensation seeking* emphasizes a purely quantitative search for sensations; by contrast, the present concept of *stimulation seeking* emphasizes the idea of seeking stimulation within and from the familiar interpersonal and physical environment. Hence, in addition to general stimulation-seeking activities such as those already mentioned, the predisposition for SSB would be expected to manifest itself in an interpersonal context. Thus, individuals with the predisposition would tend to have a *low threshold for approaching familiar persons* and a tendency to react with *more intense and persistent attachment behavior* than other individuals of comparable age, sex, race, or social background. Since an attachment or social bond between two individuals is only recognizable in terms of *attachment behavior,* individuals with the predisposition would be expected, first, to be exceptionally "close" to their attachment objects; and second, to be described (by friends, relatives, and close acquaintances) as extremely jealous, dependent, and aggressive (given that the trait of "aggressiveness" is an extension or extreme expression of dependency/affiliativeness). Hence, one would expect such features to be highly prevalent among individuals convicted of murder or assault, particularly those who have assaulted a family member or close associate. There is much evidence that this is the case:

1. *Intense bonding* between the parties involved in domestic criminal violence, often to the point of symbiotic attachment, has been frequently described in the literature. In his study of murder followed by suicide, West (1966) noted that among adult victims killed by "sane" murderers, "almost invariably a strong emotional tie bound victim and offender together in the fatal situation" (p. 141). In a study of men who had killed their spouses, Cormier (1962) found that the murder had

occurred in a relationship "where ties were strong and interlocking, where the murderer and victim had a great need for each other" (p. 2). Macdonald (1968) cited the case of a patient who, before killing her son, had expressed fears that someone would kidnap him. Among women who had threatened to kill their husbands or children, horrifying dreams were sometimes reported, involving the death of the individual whom they themselves later threatened to kill; in other cases, the murderer might accuse people of planning to murder, kidnap, or harm the very person who later became the object of their own death threats (Macdonald, 1968). West (1966) likewise commented on the "very close sense of identification" between mothers and the children they had murdered. In all four instances of maternal filicide described by Forrest (1974), the mother viewed the child as being her "own possession." Parents who killed their children were similarly diagnosed as having a "child-centered obsessional depression" (McDermaid & Winkler, 1955). Batt (1948) observed that depressed murderers usually pick an "overloved" individual for their victims, and Olive (1967) found a 40 percent incidence of incest among a group of 15 filicidal women. The same situation applies in reverse to matricide. Thus Wertham (1941), who appears to have been one of the first investigators to draw attention to this phenomenon, found that in most instances of matricide the sons had been excessively attached to their mothers. Situations in which "an aggressive, destructive mother encourages a symbiotic attachment" (Sendi and Blomgren, 1975) are frequently mentioned in studies of matricide (Sendi & Blomgren, 1975; Sargant, 1972; McKnight et al., 1966). In the case of child abusers, many authors have emphasized the extreme emotional overinvolvement and intense attachment which commonly exists between parent and child (Kaufman, 1962; Steele & Pollock, 1974; Smith & Hanson, 1975), and also interestingly, between the parents themselves — a relationship that Steele and Pollock (1974, p. 93) have described as "often a desperate, dependent clinging together out of a fear of loneliness and losing everything." Blair and Rita Justice (1976), who believe that the concept of symbiosis[5] is the key to understanding abusing families, have stated that the "kind of emotion and relationship that characterizes the abusing family is one of great intensity, force, and fusion (the 'stuck togetherness' that has been found in dysfunctional families). Either the spouses are tightly bound to one another, one parent is fused with the child, or the husband or wife is still intensely tied to his or her family of origin" (p. 61).[6] Battering parents are often heard to say that the battered child "meant everything to them" (Smith & Hanson, 1975, p. 522). Earlier investigators (e.g., Young, 1964; Howells, 1966) similarly noted that some types of child abuse were associated with remorseful overprotectiveness and emotional explosiveness.

2. A further aspect of intense attachment is, of course, *jealousy,* which is frequently mentioned as a characteristic of murderers and assaulters (Shepherd, 1961; West, 1966; Mowat, 1966; Swanson, 1970), and of men who have repeatedly assaulted their wives (Faulk, 1974; Gayford, 1975; Walker, 1979). In addition, murderers and assaulters are frequently described — not unexpectedly — as *extremely aggressive* (West, 1966) but also as *extremely dependent.* Concerning men who had been hospitalized for making homicidal threats, Macdonald (1968, p. 101) wrote, "it became apparent that sometimes the aggressive, outspoken, independent behavior [of the men] masked deep dependent longings and fear that emotional involvement with the [hospital] staff might be followed by the trauma of rejection." Forrest (1974) has described the intense needs for nurturance, the fear of abandonment, and the symbiotic relationship with husbands found in cases of maternal filicide. Faulk (1974) noted that the most common personality type of men who assaulted their wives was "dependent and passive." Many murderers have likewise been described as submissive and passive and desirous of avoiding conflict, especially if the result was to gain affection (Schultz, 1968; Houts, 1970).

As previously mentioned, child abusers are reported to have excessively hostile-dependent relationships not only with their spouses (Steele & Pollock, 1974; Justice & Justice, 1976), but also with their parents (Dawe, 1973) and with their children (Terr, 1970; Bishop, 1971; Kempe, 1971; Spinetta & Rigler, 1972; Steele & Pollock, 1974). So marked is the child abuser's dependence upon, or attachment to, the child that a kind of "role reversal" is said to occur, in which the parent demands from the child what the child should be receiving from the parent (Kaufman, 1962; Morris & Gould, 1963,; Melnick & Hurley, 1969). This observation forms the basis of one current theory of child abuse (Steele & Pollock, 1974); namely, that abuse occurs when the parent's unrealistic demands for love, comfort, and maternal behavior on the part of the child are frustrated. However, a controlled study of self-reported child-rearing practices among 214 parents of battered babies

(Smith & Hanson, 1975) found that battering parents were no more demanding than control parents with respect to the timing of toilet and other training, the severity of toilet training, and tolerance for screaming and aggressiveness. Thus "role reversal between battering parents and their children was . . . no greater than any normal sample" (Smith & Hanson, 1975, p. 254). On the other hand, battering parents were found to use physical punishment more frequently than expected for their age and social class, and mothers were generally more punitive, demanding of obedience, careless in supervision, unhappy with their spouse, and more emotionally involved with their child than the controls. To the extent that these findings can be replicated they would tend to support the overall explanation of criminal homicide and assault among familiars, including child abuse, offered here: namely, that child abusers (like other assaulters) are predisposed to overreact with more intense SSB toward their children and spouses than nonabusers. Thus to repeat the thesis, the injuries actually inflicted are the largely unintended consequences of the parents' effort to seek intense stimulation from their children.

One observation, however, which is difficult to reconcile with this interpretation, is that abusing mothers (in the Smith and Hanson study) were "relatively careless over the whereabouts or well-being of their child" (p. 521). The tendency of child abusers to vacillate between extreme overinvolvement with their children, and extreme rejection or neglect, has been noted by other investigators (Steele & Pollock, 1974; Baldwin & Oliver, 1975), and warrants further study. One possibility is that parental *violence* and parental *neglect* are committed by two largely distinct groups. According to the model outlined here, there should be little overlap between violent abuse and neglect since we would expect violence to be associated with an intense attachment toward the child, whereas neglect would seem to imply the absence of attachment. Another possibility is that the same parent may be involved both in violence and neglect, and that neglect occurs as a type of rebound phenomenon, associated with fatigue and exhaustion, following a prolonged period of excessive vigilance and attention directed at the child.

There appears to be some support for the first of these possibilities, that is, that physically abusive and neglectful parents represent separate but overlapping groups. It has been estimated by Gil (1970) that one-third of abusing parents also neglect their children. Justice and Justice (1976, p. 19), however, state that in their experience the percentage is smaller. Other studies support the view that abusing parents have much more of an emotional investment in their children than neglectful parents (Polansky et al., 1973, pp. 2–3). Steele and Pollock (1974, p. 99) also note that:

> Physical abuse of infants is associated more with breakdown in motherliness than with deficits in . . . mothering. The infants in our study were almost always well-fed, clean, and well-clothed, but the emotional attitudes of the one who was caring for the infant were fraught with constant tension and frequent disruptions. It is often during the mothering acts of feeding, cleaning, and comforting the infant that abuse occurs. This is because of the difficulties of maintaining an attitude of motherliness, not because of an inability or lack of desire on the part of the caretaker to perform the caretaking acts.

Steele and Pollock observe that the abusing parent and the neglectful parent have many common characteristics; both need and demand much from their infants and are distressed by inadequate responses. Hence, "it is not surprising that we occasionally see an infant or child who is both neglected and abused" (p. 95). One striking difference between them, however, is that the "neglecting parent responds to distress or disappointment by giving up and abandoning efforts to even mechanically care for the child [whereas] the abusive parent seems to have more investment in the actual life of the child and moves in to punish it for failure and make it 'shape-up' and perform better" (p. 95).[7]

The Interchangeability of Victims and Offenders

The perpetrators and victims of criminal violence are known to share many characteristics in common, including age, sex, race and a previous criminal record (Wolfgang, 1958). This could be explained, in part, on the hypothesis that an individual with a strong predisposition for SSB is not only at greater risk of committing homicidal assault, but also of being the victim of such crimes, because his behavior provides a stimulus to which other people are prone to react with reciprocally-intense SSB. As noted earlier, 26 percent of the 588[8] recorded homicides in Philadelphia between 1948 and 1952 were described as "victim-precipitated," that is, the victim was the first to use physical violence in the fatal confrontation (Wolfgang, 1958). Typically, a black male assaulted his wife and was then killed by her in the course of the ensuing struggle.[9] The victims of these homicides also tended to have a previous arrest record, especially a record of assault. According to Wolfgang (1958), some of the victims may have wanted to commit suicide and therefore presented themselves as willing targets for violence. An alternative explanation is that many of these victims of violence have a strong predisposition for SSB; in seeking intense stimulation from their wives (i.e., in the initial assault), they provide so much incongruity that their wives are provoked into seeking intense stimulation from them (see Scenario 1).

Where *both* parties in a dyadic relationship have a strong predisposition for SSB, the probability of injury occurring as a result of their interaction is increased accordingly, and chance factors may determine which of the two will play the role of victim or perpetrator. According to theories of assortative mating, persons with similar characteristics tend to seek each other out. Thus, people with a strong predisposition for SSB would be expected to form couples (cf., Dominion, 1972). Steele and Pollock (1974) noted that many abusing parents show "an uncanny ability to become involved with and marry people who tend to accentuate rather than solve their problems. The spouse is too much like the patient and too much like the patients' parents. Despite many other admirable qualities ... , the spouse is often needy, dependent, unable to express clearly his needs, and at the same time is demanding, critical, and unheeding of the patient" (p. 106). Lewis and Balla (1976), in their study of juvenile delinquents and their families of origin, similarly reported that fathers who had been treated by a psychiatrist tended to marry psychiatrically treated mothers; and fathers with criminal records appeared to gravitate toward psychiatrically treated women. The parents of delinquent children were also significantly more likely to be psychiatrically hospitalized and/or treated than a demographically comparable sample of the general population.

In the case of interspousal violence, Gayford's (1979) study of 100 battered women produced evidence of a predisposition for SSB in many women and their male partners, for example, a high frequency of suicide attempts, alcohol use, and explosive outbursts toward their children on the part of the women, and a high frequency of morbid jealousy, drunkenness and bad temper on the part of the men, together with a constant need to be placated — as reported by the wives, who alone were interviewed. Obviously, in this physically unequal situation, it is the wife who is most likely to be the victim of serious violence. Similarly, if an infant or child is one of the predisposed individuals, then he or she will almost invariably be the victim rather than the adult or adults with whom they are involved. This could explain why only certain children in a family rather than all tend to be abused. Premature, hypersensitive, colicky, and even unresponsive babies (perhaps because their behavior is interpreted as "rejection" by the parent) are especially vulnerable to abuse (Milowe & Lourie, 1964; Harrington, 1972b; Justice & Justice, 1976), as are babies born with varying degrees of congenital defect and who, as a result, are often fussy, difficult to comfort, and need much more medical and general attention than normal babies (Steele & Pollock, 1974). Whereas mild or even vigorous crying will elicit care and solicitousness of appropriate intensity in a normal mother (Bowlby, 1969, 1973), it is understandable that the combination of a child with a tendency to cry intensely and persistently (indicating a strong predisposition for SSB), and a mother whose SSB is habitually intense, persistent, and elicited at low threshold (indicating a similar predisposition) is a potentially very dangerous one indeed.

Why do They Stay?

The question is often raised of why so many women and children who are abused and battered by their husbands, fathers, or other family members, tend to remain in the abusing situation instead of leaving. The answers that have been offered are that: for those who stay, the abuse is less frequent and severe; the victim was abused as a child and is therefore habituated to it; the victim has both limited resources and power and a greater number of external constraints (Gelles, 1976); the victim faces an unhelpful attitude and lack of support from institutions or other official agencies; and the victim herself has conservative attitudes about the role of women in the family (Pagelow, 1981). Pagelow (1981) tested these hypotheses in an interview study of 350 battered women who had left their male partners and who were living in official shelters. With the partial exception of the "resources" variable, which explained 43 percent of the variance in the dependent variable, none of the factors was found to be associated with or predicted length of stay with the male partners. In the case of one factor — severity of abuse — a strong association was found, but in the opposite direction to that expected; that is, *the more severe a woman's physical injuries, the longer she tended to remain with her spouse* (Pagelow, 1981, pp. 161–63). Although this finding is counter-intuitive, it is explicable in terms of the present hypothesis.

It is suggested that the tendency of victims to remain with their abusers is one manifestation of a more general and well-documented tendency for aggression and/or punishment to elicit and promote attachment behavior in the individual toward whom the aggression is directed. As noted earlier when discussing the "functional consequences" of aggression and attachment behavior, aggression (or punitive behavior) in individual A increases attachment behavior in individual B, as well as speeding up the formation of attachments.

The suggestion that punishment-aggression speeds up the formation of attachments and strengthens attachment to the aggressor is well-documented in numerous species (e.g., Scott, 1963; Lynch, 1970). Scott (1963, 1967) has suggested that any strong emotional state, whether this be hunger, fear, pain, or loneliness has the effect of speeding up attachment formation. With regard to humans, numerous studies have indicated that aggressive or punitive parents tend to make their off-spring more "dependent" both as children and as adults (Maccoby & Masters, 1970, pp. 142–44). In their classic study, *The Authoritarian Personality,* Adorno and his associates (1950) found that individuals who had been subjected to severe physical punishment as children tended to idealize and glorify their parents — feelings that the authors themselves believed could not be genuine in view of the "exaggerated and stereotyped" superlatives used in describing the parent. Bettelheim (1960, p. 159) also described the apparently paradoxical tendency of many of the longer held prisoners in Nazi concentration camps to develop a peculiar fascination, respect, and even fondness for their captors — a phenomenon he labeled "identification with the aggressor."

More recently, the term "Stockholm syndrome" has been coined to describe the tendency of individuals who have been forcibly taken hostage to develop an intense attachment toward their captors and, at the same time, strongly negative feelings toward the authorities responsible for their rescue. Sometimes the attachment is reciprocated by the hostage-takers (Strentz, 1980; Ochberg, 1980). This term originated after a bank robbery in Sweden in 1974 in which an employee named Kristin was held hostage for several days by a robber named Olsson. The two reportedly fell in love and had sexual relations. During her captivity Kristin publicly criticized the Swedish prime minister for failing to appreciate her captor's point of view. Following her release Kristin retained a lasting affection for her captor.

There appears to be a marked similarity between the phenomena described above and the tendency of family members who are physically abused to remain with the abuser. Baldwin and Oliver (1979, p. 90) found that "(m)any ill-treated children cling to their abusive parent, show affection for them and even defend them by collusion by their deceits." Yates (1981) also described a severely abused child who, after three years of therapy and separation from her abusive mother, still displayed in her drawings "an intense exclusive investment in her mother" (p. 61). Many battered wives are similarly described as lacking in self-esteem, passive, overly dependent on their husbands, and thus placing greater value on maintaining the marriage then ensuring their own safety (Dewsbury, 1975). Other authors describe battered women as guilt-ridden, accepting responsibility for their beatings (Walker, 1979), showing a paralyzing "learned-helplessness" toward continuous abuse, and as having "distorted" views of marital roles (Rounsaville, 1978).

It must be emphasized that the concept of intense attachment, as used here, is not synonymous with love or affection; it refers to a pattern of approach behavior (i.e., stimulation-seeking behavior) that is directed to a specific individual over time, is elicited at a low threshold, and at a high level of intensity. Attachment behavior may be associated with any intense emotional state, whether this be love, anger, hate, fear or, more commonly, a varying mixture of emotions. As Scott (1963) found in his work on attachment formation in dogs, it is the intensity or degree of arousal evoked by a person or object rather than the quality of the emotional state which seems to be the critical factor determining the formation of an attachment.

Our suggestion, then, is that it is precisely the strong "bond of attachment," as manifested in various aspects of attachment behavior, which commonly exists between the parties involved in domestic violence (a bond that does not necessarily imply constant love or affection) that may account, in part, for the failure of the parties to separate before serious violence occurs. On this view it is not so much the *lack* of anything — resources, incentives, a place to go — which keeps an abused woman with her husband, but the *presence of a strong physical and emotional attachment to the batterer*. They may love, hate, or fear their husbands, yet they remain; and the stronger the intensity of the emotion — the greater the "fascination" — the more likely they are to remain.[10]

But if punishment, pain or aggression elicits and enhances attachment and causes the victim of abuse to remain with the abuser, what is it about these conditions that has this effect? In other words, how does punishment increase the strength of attachments? We would suggest most emphatically that it is not due to any masochistic interest in pain or punishment per se. Surveys of battered women provide no support for this hypothesis (Gayford, 1979; Pagelow, 1981). The tendency to approach the punisher following punishment is viewed not as a desire for more pain and punishment but as a reaction *to* pain. Recall the thesis that individuals form cognitive maps of the objects and persons in their environment; that other people in the immediate family are the psychologically most important aspect of their cognitive maps, and that individuals attempt to maintain their cognitive maps by seeking out and maintaining contact with the external objects or persons whose characteristics they have internalized. Incongruous stimuli — stimuli which are unexpected, which fail to match the cognitive map, or which are intensely painful — produce an increase in arousal and cause the individual to remain in the familiar environment and to approach the (familiar) source of the punishment. Each instance of punishment and of subsequent approach to the punisher serves to strengthen the individual's cognitive map of the punisher and ensures that the individual remains within his or her proximity.

According to this model, mild or "normal" parental punishment has the important function of keeping the family together by strengthening the cognitive map that each member of the family possesses of every other member. Severe punishment or "abuse," being more extreme, would be expected to bind the family together even more strongly. Hence it is not "ironical," to quote Schlesinger and Revitch (1980) but, on the contrary, entirely predictable that many child abusers say they love their children (Kempe et al., 1962) and that "ties" between abused women and abusing family members are "strong," albeit to a symbiotic degree, and extremely exclusive (Justice & Justice, 1976).[11]

Concluding Remarks

Two additional issues must be briefly mentioned: social supports, or the lack thereof, and the origin of the predisposition for SSB.

It is frequently mentioned in the literature that abusing families tend to be socially isolated and cutoff from their extended families (e.g., Spinetta & Rigler, 1972; Steele & Pollock, 1974; Garbarino & Crouter 1978; Berger, 1980). One study reported that 95 percent of severely abusing families had no continuing social relationships with people outside the nuclear family (Young, 1964). Social isolation could be both a consequence of the life-style of the abusing family as well as a cause of abuse. Abusing families are often found to be highly mobile (Gil, 1970) thus lacking the opportunity for establishing social ties. Steele and Pollock (1974, p. 106) reported that an unusually high percentage of their abusing families kept the blinds down in the house even on sunny days and had unlisted telephone numbers, suggesting an almost deliberate effort to avoid social contact.[12]

As noted in Chapter 1, there is much evidence to indicate that frequent and socially intimate contacts with other people have health-maintaining effects in themselves as well as a protective influence in the face of psychosocial stress. We have suggested that individuals experiencing a variety of stressful life events in a context of reduced or absent social supports are at high risk of involvement in crime. On the basis of the literature reviewed above and in Chapter 2, we suspect that this combination of circumstances is very common among child-abusing families.

To touch briefly on the *origin* of the predisposition for SSB, the predisposition may reflect constitutional factors in addition to long-term exposure to environmental stress. With regard to constitutional factors, there is growing evidence that the enzyme monoamine oxidase (MAO), which is involved in the degradation of noradrenaline and dopamine, is the underlying biological trait or counterpart of sensation-seeking behavior (as measured by Zuckerman's sensation-seeking scale). As noted in earlier chapters, significant negative correlations have been found between MAO levels and scores on the SSS; the lower the MAO level, the higher the SSS score (Zuckerman et al., 1980, for a review). Low-MAO college students of both sexes also report more criminal convictions than high-MAO subjects, more psychiatric contacts, using a greater number of drugs, smoking more cigarettes, more sociopathic traits, and more suicide attempts in their families (Buchsbaum et al., 1976). Thus, low platelet MAO appears to be a biological predictor of criminality, related forms of deviant behavior, and stimulation-seeking behavior in general. It is also noteworthy that males have lower MAO levels than females, and MAO levels increase markedly with age (Zuckerman, 1979) — observations that have a striking parallel in the epidemiology of crime.

Long-term exposure to environmental stress would also be expected to produce a strong predisposition for SSB; most notably, exposure to (a) intense SSB in the form of overprotectiveness or seductiveness, and extending to extreme punitiveness and brutality; (b) separation, rejection or abandonment; and (c) other stress, for example, job loss.

To conclude the section on violence against familiars, a study is summarized which amply illustrates the main points of the model. This was a social and psychiatric analysis of 11 persons charged with killing or seriously wounding a spouse or spouse equivalent (Showalter et al., 1980). The similarities between these 11 cases were so striking that the authors evoked the concept of a "spousal-homicide syndrome." The mean age of the subjects was 38, significantly older than the norm for persons charged with violent criminal offenses. All subjects were male, mostly with unskilled or semi-skilled jobs, but all had stable work histories. Although only six offenders had actually killed their wives, the nature of the violence in the other cases was judged to be functionally equivalent. The common features are described below; references to the proposed model are inserted in brackets.

1. In 9 of the 11 cases there was a history of significant parental rejection [cf., strong predisposition for SSB].
2. All viewed themselves as having unhappy, unfulfilled childhoods [cf., a predisposition for SSB].
3. The offenders and their parents viewed each other with considerable emotional ambivalence [cf., symbiotic attachment]. In each case the offender had been made to feel unimportant and insignificant.
4. In 8 of the 11 cases the offenders came from unusually large sibships, containing five or more siblings.

5. In most cases where parental abuse had occurred the abuse had been psychological rather than physical [cf., a strong predisposition for SSB].

6. Psychiatric evaluation revealed the presence of strong features of passivity in each of the 11 cases, "coupled with tendencies towards infantile and childish emotionality" (p. 125) [cf., strong predisposition for SSB].

7. Most of the men lacked recorded histories of assaultive or other socially disturbing behaviors [i.e., they appeared to be transient offenders].

8. In only two cases had the offender had any prior contact with the mental health system, and that was precipitated by spousal conflict.

9. In every case there was evidence of a poor self-image [cf., unstable cognitive map], of emotional isolation, and problems in forming and maintaining social relationships.

10. In every case the offender stated that his relationship with the victim was either the first or the only close relationship that he had been able to develop [see 11, below].

11. Intense emotional bonding had occurred between offender and victim; the offender had incorporated into his own self-concept the personality features of the spouse which he felt were highly desirable but lacking in himself. "One summed up his feelings, 'I didn't just love her I worshipped her . . . we were always meant to be together'" (p. 127). The mean length of the relationship between victim and offender was 11 years [cf., symbiotic attachment].

12. In nine of the cases the offender believed he had been in competition with the victim's family for the victim's loyalty and affection. Early on, this led to distrust and jealousy on the offender's part and to accusations by the victim of excessive sensitivity and possessiveness.

13. Each offender reported having been severely abused by his wife. Most frequently, the wife berated him for failing to support her in an acceptable fashion, and taunted him about his masculinity and sexual prowess [cf., Scenario 1].

14. In all 11 cases the victim was engaged in an affair with another man or had led the offender to believe that she was being unfaithful to

him. In 8 cases the victim voluntarily separated from her husband (but never vice versa), taking her children with her [cf., Scenario 2].

15. Although in some cases several separations occurred, neither the victim nor the offender was able to effect a permanent dissolution of the relationship [cf., symbiosis].

16. In ten cases, an immediate threat of leaving, which was viewed by the offender as a final separation, occurred shortly before the assault [cf., Scenario 2].

17. In ten cases there was no evidence of conscious planning or premeditation before the homicidal act.

18. In ten cases, death or serious injury resulted from a gunshot wound; in the eleventh case the wife died from multiple stab wounds.

19. In only three cases was there any evidence of a chemically altered state of consciousness at the time of the assault.

20. In nine cases there was a claim of loss of memory for a period of time surrounding the homicidal act; in five cases the loss was limited to the actual moment in which the injury was inflicted.

21. In four cases the offender attempted suicide immediately after the homicidal act (three shootings, one attempted drowning).

22. In every case the offender felt guilt and remorse for the injury or death of the victim. In no case was there any indication of "relief" that a major source of conflict and friction had been removed. Many of the offenders became seriously depressed following their acts of violence, several reporting significant weight loss, insomnia, and social withdrawal.

Showalter and associates noted that all of the violent acts directed at spouses or spouse equivalents were "unplanned and carried out in periods of intense emotional arousal" [cf., S-system arousal]. They further noted that the perpetrator's memory for the events at the time of the crime was often confused and distorted; that the violence bore no relation to any previous psychiatric history; and that it was completely untypical of the person's normal behavior. These observations suggested that the violent outbursts were associated with "some form of pathological mental functioning" (p. 132), but the impairment was not one of "dissociation"; that is, the "functional equivalent of a psychosis" or "temporary insanity" (p. 133). Instead, the offender's ambivalent relationship with his spouse represented an "attempt to reconstruct the earlier ambivalent dyad with the mother figure and also an attempt to engage a reparative process" (p. 138). When these attempts failed, and the violent act occurred, the offender's typically fragmentary recall of events was more a form of denial than of dissociation, and the offender's ego regressed to a childhood level comparable to that experienced with the mother figure. "Like the toddler, the offender is left confused and in emotional disarray" (p. 139).

The arguments of the authors against the concept of dissociation are that (a) none of the offenders had a history of hysterical neurosis which, in their view, is necessary in order to invoke the concept of dissociation; (b) the disturbances of consciousness did not involve amnesia; and (c) "the mental mechanisms were functioning to release aggression rather than to control or inhibit aggressive impulse discharge, as is normally the case in dissociative states" (p. 134).

Yet, if one sets aside the psychoanalytic assumptions underlying the concepts of dissociation, together with the (in our view) unwarranted assumption that dissociation necessarily entails complete amnesia, and simply uses the concept to describe the feelings of confused unreality that accompanied and followed the violent act, the term "dissociation" would seem to be unexceptionable. However, the term preferred here is cognitive map. This is how the sequence of events would be interpreted according to the present model:

The spouse's taunts and threats of abandonment represented extreme incongruity and led to a high level of S-system arousal. Unable to obtain congruent sensory feedback in the form of a resolution of the conflict or reassuring physical contact with the spouse, the offender continued to experience high S-system arousal which may have led to the alterations in cognitive-perceptual functioning. The violent act itself is considered an intense stimulation-seeking response, designed to "match" the offender's internal representation of the spouse with the latter's actual characteristics, thereby reaffirming the offender's cognitive map.

While the intense incongruity and high arousal level resulting from the victim's behavior may have had a temporary disorganizing effect on the offender's cognitive map, it is suggested that intrafamilial violent acts represent intense SSB designed to restore or reaffirm the offender's cognitive map. As noted in the earlier publication (Mawson, 1980), SSB directed at attachment figures normally has the effect of eliciting reciprocal SSB in the individual toward whom it is directed, thereby *strengthening* social bonds.

ATTACKS ON STRANGERS

This topic is ostensibly damaging to the model; for, if SSB tends to be directed at the familiar, the existence of attacks on strangers appears inconsistent with the model. Although knowledge on this issue is very limited compared to that on intrafamiliar violence, the model is not necessarily invalidated by the existence of attacks on strangers. While attacks on familiars can be understood in terms of SSB aimed at preserving the cognitive map of an individual, for example, spouse, the thesis of the model with respect to attacks on *strangers* is that such attacks are associated with an already much *disintegrated* cognitive map.

Earlier it was argued that much intrafamilial violence represents a highly intense expression of so-called attachment behavior, that is, seeking intense contact with familiar persons. To introduce the proposed explanation of attacks on strangers, let us briefly continue the analogy between aggression and attachment behavior. In most natural disasters and personal crises, individuals seek the company of familiars (e.g., Hill & Hansen, 1962). However, in many natural and manmade disasters, individuals occasionally seek identical forms of help from many different sources (Tyhurst 1951; Kinston & Rosser, 1974); they become highly "dependent" or "childlike" and readily approach strangers. Our suggestion is that violence toward strangers is one manifestation of this apparently promiscuous attachment behavior in disaster or crisis situations, except that it is performed at a much higher level of intensity; hence, it is characterized as aggression rather than attachment behavior, affiliativeness or dependency.

What is the underlying mechanism? What causes an individual's proximity-seeking behavior to be directed toward strangers rather than, as is more usual, familiar persons? The explanation is the same as that given earlier for theft and burglary; it involves (a) a deteriorating cognitive map, (b) a high level of S-system arousal, and (c) SSB that is consequently no longer adequately constrained within familiar directions.

To summarize, prolonged or severe incongruity and S-system arousal, combined with an inability to obtain congruous sensory feedback (i.e., attachment figures are either unavailable or rejecting) leads to a progressive disintegration of the individual's cognitive map; that is, a gradual fading from memory of the unique stimulus characteristics of familiar persons and things. Hence, there is an increasing tendency to classify persons and objects in terms of their *generic* characteristics rather than in terms of their *unique* attributes. The process of cognitive disintegration is associated with relatively "indiscriminate" SSB, aimed increasingly at familiar generic patterns of stimulation and, at a still more rudimentary level, at familiar basic types and quantities of stimulation. The individual in such a predicament reverts to a state somewhat analogous to that of the "asocial" or "indiscriminate attachment" phase of infancy (Schaffer & Emerson, 1964), in which sensory input is sought from virtually any stimulating source, regardless of whether it lies outside or within the individual's previously held territorial boundaries.

Thus, attacks on a stranger or group of strangers ("amok murder") can be explained in terms of arousal-induced cognitive disintegration and intense SSB that is now directed at familiar types and quantities of stimulation.[13] In many instances of amok murder, "familiarity" with respect to the targets of aggression may nevertheless show itself in certain ways. As Palmer (1974) has noted about many so-called stranger murders, the offender is usually acquainted with *some* of the victim's characteristics or with the characteristics of individuals like the victim. For instance, "A college student who feels out of place and snubbed by his peers climbs to the top of a campus tower. He shoots to death a number of students crossing the yard below. While they may have been individually unknown to him, the victims represent or personify those who he sees as his frustrators" (Palmer, 1974, p. 92).

Of course, unfamiliarity is rarely, if ever, total. It is recalled that when a strange animal (mouse or rat) is deliberately placed in the cage of another, the strange animal is likely to be attacked most vigorously and persistently if it is of the same species, same sex, and same strain or breed of the attacker (Marler, 1976). Similarly, when humans in disaster situations approach strangers for help or assistance, these strangers are usually in the same predicament.

On other occasions of "stranger murder," it emerges that although victim and perpetrator have never previously met, and the perpetrator is indeed a total stranger to the victim, the perpetrator appears to have developed a peculiar fascination, respect, and even love for his actual or intended victim. Thus, rather than being apparent exceptions to the intense-attachment model of violence, such homicides provide unexpected support for the model.

The prevalence of this phenomenon in relation to homicide as a whole is uncertain. However, there have been a number of striking and well-publicized instances of it in recent years. To mention the first of three examples, Sirhan Sirhan, Robert Kennedy's assassin, reportedly said of his victim, "I loved that man" (Kaplan, 1978, p. 249).[14]

Arthur Bremer, who shot and paralyzed Governor George Wallace of Alabama, also stalked and intended to kill President Richard Nixon. In his introduction to Bremer's diary, Lemay (1973, p. 16) comments: "As he [Bremer] assumes his role [of assassin], he evolves an almost intimate relationship with the man he hopes to kill. His references shift from 'the President,' to 'he,' to 'Nixon,' to 'Nixy,' and finally, to 'Nixy-boy.'" Giving up hope of killing President Nixon, Bremer decides to hunt and kill Governor Wallace instead. The latter is scheduled to give a speech a short distance away. As Bremer follows Wallace to his various speaking engagements, he again identifies with his victim. Governor Wallace becomes "Wally," and "Wallyboy" (Lemay,1973, p. 111). Lemay (pp. 23–24) writes:

> Watching him closely at the rallies, Bremer sympathizes because the audience is not sufficiently responsive: *"I did the most hand-clapping, all the shouting, was going to start three different standing ovations, but felt the crowd wouldn't follow me. . . .* A great disappointment for him I bet. Poor guy . . . what would he have done without *me?"*

Mark Chapman, currently serving 20 years to life in prison for the murder of singer-musician and former Beatles member, John Lennon, claimed to idolize Lennon and went to considerable lengths to emulate him and the Beatles. Like Lennon, he had a Japanese wife as well as an avid interest in modern music and humane causes.

Many intriguing questions remain unanswered, of course. As already noted, we need to know the prevalence of this "attachment phenomenon" in apparent stranger-murders and assassinations. Are there any common elements or antecedents in these seemingly dissimilar occurrences? How do these intense attachments develop? Our suspicion is that homicides of this sort will be found to involve the following factors and processes: prolonged isolation or alienation from familiar social and physical surroundings; a disintegrated cognitive map; high (or highly variable) levels of S-system arousal; and a resulting tendency to develop passionate attachments to strangers which — thankfully in relatively few cases — is intensified to the point of causing someone to be injured or killed. As noted above, such processes may be identical to those observed among adults and children in disaster situations (Tyhurst, 1951). Similarly, children who have been separated from their parents and placed in institutions reportedly develop passionate though temporary attachments to strangers (Burlingham & Freud, 1944). The thesis is that, under conditions of prolonged stress and a deteriorating cognitive map, the desire to "reach out and touch someone" can become so exaggeratedly intense that it results in injury or death.

NOTES

1.   For an excellent review of definitions, sources of data, theories, and methods of preventing interpersonal violence and spouse abuse see Rosenberg et al. (1985).

2.   The arrows indicate the direction of SSB.

3.   Bischof (1975) has noted that patterns of attachment between people can be considered homeostatic (i.e., self-equilibrating) systems involving negative feedback (equilibrating) and positive feedback (disequilibrating) processes. He offers the interesting suggestion that negative feedback processes are analogous to the properties of an *elastic band,* while positive feedback processes are analogous to those of a *magnet.* The two scenarios discussed so far can be similarly described. In the first, where proximity seeking (SSB) between P and Q increases in a positive-feedback spiral, the process is somewhat analogous to magnetic forces, in which "attraction" between two magnets increases as they (i.e., people) are brought closer together. In the second scenario, where Q rejects P, a negative feedback process occurs in which P responds by attempting to reduce the distance between himself and Q. Here, the more Q attempts to withdraw, the more intensely P seeks proximity, a process somewhat analogous to an elastic band "that exerts more force the greater it is expanded" (Bischof, 1975, p. 805).

4.   Since this book deals with *transient offenders* rather than chronic or habitual offenders, no attempt will be made to review the literature on the behavioral correlates of offending by habitual offenders. Suffice it to say that suicidal and self-injurious behavior can be considered SSBs; in fact, there is much evidence that self-injury is common among habitual offenders (e.g., Rada & James, 1982) and serious juvenile delinquents (Lewis et al., 1983). The same is also true of gambling (Gayford, 1979), arson, and many of the behavioral correlates of sensation seeking described by Zuckerman (1979).

5.   Symbiosis is "the attachment that one individual establishes with another in an effort to be taken care of. The symbiotic relationship that exists between mother and child is healthy and necessary, but symbiosis between adults, or when a parent tries to make his child take care of him, is destructive" (Justice & Justice, 1976, pp. 31, 70).

6. In a study of ten abusive mothers and ten carefully selected controls, Melnick and Hurley (1969) found that the abusive mothers had severely frustrated dependency needs. Kertzman (1978) compared 40 abusers and 40 matched nonabusers and found evidence of greater dependency among the abusers.

7. Sourkes (1976) attempted to differentiate the correlates of abuse and neglect in a sample of 30 mothers whose infants were enrolled in a primary prevention mental health program. There was some overlap between the correlates, but generally they seemed distinct. Abuse and neglect emerged as "complex, psychosocial phenomena, with potentially different etiologies" (Friedrich and Wheeler, 1982, p. 583).

8. In my original article describing these issues the erroneous figure of 158 criminal homicides was printed (Mawson, 1980, p. 108). The statement should have read: such victim-precipitated crimes accounted for 26 percent (153) of the 588 criminal homicides. . . .

9. Voss and Hepburn (1968), using the same definition of victim precipitation as Wolfgang, found that 38 percent of the homicides they studied in Chicago were victim-precipitated.

10. A. Symonds (1979) similarly argues that a pathological form of bonding often characterizes the relationship between abused and abuser. She suggests that the victim of spouse abuse enters a state of traumatic "psychological infantilism" in which she clings to the abuser and cooperates with him in a desperate attempt to save her life. M. Symonds (cited in Symonds, 1979) noted that victims of violent crimes (such as rape), and of natural disasters often show "infantile" reactions of extreme dependency and irrational guilt. A. Symonds (1979) similarly notes that abused children also tend to cling to their parents and beg for forgiveness, no matter how badly they are treated. "At Bellevue Hospital, on the children's ward, we saw many youngsters who had been removed from homes where they had been seriously mistreated and abused and placed in a foster home, only to run away repeatedly from the foster home and try to get back to the parents" (p. 170). Thus Symonds (1979) also suggests that victims of abuse tend to remain with abusers because of a pathological form of bonding; however, she explains this reaction psychoanalytically, in terms of a reversion to infancy.

11. Many battered women and children do, of course, succeed in breaking away from their families, some women after a quarter of a century or more of intermittent abuse. Considering that the model predicts a strong attachment to the abuser, how is it possible for the victim of abuse to leave? Presumably, it involves a breakdown and transformation of the victim's cognitive map of the abuser and the familiar environment. It will be of interest in future research to determine the initiating conditions and processes by which this hypothetical transformation occurs.

12. Of course, this could be a way of avoiding unwanted callers such as debt collectors.

13. People in general, as well as pets and other animals, are more stimulating than inanimate objects.

14. Kaplan (1978) also states, "like imitation, violence, too, may be a form of flattery. That each person kills the thing he or she loves is romanticist moonshine, but psychopathology gives it substance" (p. 249).

CRIMES AGAINST THE PERSON, III: RAPE

CRITIQUE OF THE CONCEPT OF SEXUAL ACTIVITY

Forcible rape is defined as "carnal knowledge of a female through the use of force or the threat of force" (U.S. Department of Justice, 1982). On the basis of communitywide interviews it is estimated that 40–50 percent of forcible rapes are not reported to the police (Law Enforcement Assistance Administration, 1975). The likelihood of reporting seems to be proportional to the differences between victim and offender, for example, age and racial differences, the severity of injury inflicted on the victim, and lack of acquaintanceship between victim and offender. Although the true incidence of rape and the characteristics of rapists as a group are uncertain, much is known about rape and identified rapists. Rabkin (1979) summarizes the epidemiology of rape as follows:

1. In 1977 the United States had an incidence rate of reported rape of 29.1 per 100,000 population.
2. Between 1960 and 1977 the incidence rate more than tripled, a pattern also observed for other violent crimes.
3. The incidence of rape in urban areas is about twice that of rural areas.
4. In the United States in 1977 only 51 percent of forcible rapes were cleared by arrest; of these, only 31 percent of individuals arrested were convicted of this crime.
5. Most offenders are young men between the ages of 16 and 25, the peak age group being 16 to 20.

This chapter is based on a paper presented at the Annual Meeting of the American Society of Criminology, San Diego, California, November 1985.

6. Arrest rates for blacks are about 11 times higher than those for whites.
7. Rape is largely intraracial, that is, black men usually rape black women, white men usually rape white women.
8. The highest rates of rape occur in poor, run-down urban areas, as do the highest rates of robbery and homicide. The strongest population predictors of all three crimes are: percent black, percent aged 14–21, and low median family income.
9. Although the proportion of offenders reported to be complete strangers to the victims varies considerably across studies, the typical estimate is about 50 percent. However, it appears that the more familiar the offender is to the victim, the less likely she is to report the incident to the police. Thus in most forcible rapes, victim and offender are probably acquainted with each other.
10. Most rapists are not multiple sex offenders and are more likely than other sex offenders to have a criminal record for nonsexual offenses.
11. In 70–75 percent of reported forcible rapes, the act is said to be premeditated (Amir, 1971).

Rape has conventionally been viewed as a "sexual" crime (e.g., Guttmacher & Weihofen, 1952). Offenders were thought to be sexually frustrated, oversexed, or lacking appropriate controls over their sexual impulses. One difficulty with this thesis is described by West and his associates (1978, p. 144);

> It fails to explain why some men, at great risk to themselves and notwithstanding the availability of wives, girlfriends and prostitutes, should go out of their way to seek out strange and unwilling women, all for the sake of brief release under condition of struggle and considerable discomfort. They may afterwards display anxiety and remorse about their conduct with an intensity of guilt unusual in a simple sociopath. Such offenders appear to be driven by strong impulses that are not just urges for straightforward sexual gratification.

Such doubts about a purely sexual motivation have led to the suggestion that rape is an *aggressive* act, or more generally, "an act of violence expressing power, aggression, conquest, degradation, anger, hatred, and contempt [12 references cited]" (Holdstrom & Burgess, 1980, p. 427). A related view is that rape is *primarily* motivated by anger or power but involves sexuality as a "component" (e.g., Gies, 1977,

p. 30; Groth & Burgess, 1977; Groth et al., 1977; Henn, 1978, pp. 301–2).

To what extent is it useful to interpret rape as an expression of aggression *or* of sex, or even as a mixture of the two? Several groups of researchers have challenged such views, including the suggestion that most rapes are premeditated (Amir, 1971). Gibbens and associates (1977) have noted that, "It is very difficult to say, even with the most detailed information what constitutes a 'sexual offense'. The most obvious example is the case of rape-murder which will be recorded as murder and not rape" (p. 41). Moreover, "in very serious crimes it may be very difficult and possibly artificial to decide whether aggression dragged in a sexual component or a sexual act led to aggression" (p. 37). Gibbens et al. further suggest that arousal is relatively nonspecific with regard to behavioral outcome, and that whether rape or some other crime is committed depends partly on situational opportunity. Thus, "a man in the midst of a series of successful housebreakings may pick up and rape a girl, as a sort of excited bonus to celebrate his success. In [other] cases the property offender, on breaking into an empty house or stealing a car or motorcycle is aware of sexual arousal" (p. 37, cf. Chapter 4, this volume, pp. 106–7). Regarding the nonspecific character of arousal, Gibbens et al. observed that "there are a few in whom the excitement/anxiety of the moment flows into sexual excitement and converts a burglary almost instantaneously into a rape of the householder" (p. 40).

West and his associates (1978), in a detailed study of 12 convicted rapists, note that "legal labels like rape and indecent assault are unhelpful because they cover such a wide range of circumstances and take no account of the motives or characteristics of the participants" (p. 143). Concerning men convicted of very violent rapes, typically against complete strangers, West and his associates found that many of the offenders had police records for repeated nonsexual as well as sexual crimes. The problem shared by these men seemed to be a general "lack of control over impulsive, unsocialized behavior rather than any obvious peculiarity of sexual appetite" (p. 143). Moreover, "sex crimes and property crimes are inextricably mingled in those cases in which offenders have taken advantage of female victims encountered in the course of robbery and burglary" (p. 143). Of the 12 rapists studied in detail, two admitted that their "sexual" and "thieving" motives were "all mixed up" (p. 121). Break-ins often began by peeping through windows in the hope of catching women undressing, and then led, or progressed, to thefts, rape, or attempted rape, depending on opportunity (West et al., 1978, p. 122, Crime No. 21).

Lewis and her associates (1979) have also questioned the concept of the "sexual assaulter" as a distinct type of offender. They compared the psychiatric, neurological, and psychoeducational status of 17 sexually assaultive male juveniles and 61 controls who had committed violent acts other than sexual assault. No outstanding differences were found between the two groups on any of the measured factors (see Table 13.1). Moreover, all but one of the juvenile sexual assaulters had committed numerous offenses other than sexual offenses, and all had extensive histories of threatening family, friends, and teachers, and of engaging in frequent fights with peers and adults. The fact that the juvenile *sexual* assaulters had also committed extraordinarily violent but *nonsexual* acts led the authors "to question the psychoanalytic distinction between the sexual and aggressive drives" (p. 1196). In view of other similarities between the two groups of offenders the authors concluded that "violence of any kind and sexual violence per se may reflect similar underlying etiologic vulnerabilities" (p. 1196). Adler (1984), in a study of over 900 incarcerated sex offenders, also found that rapists tended to be similar to both serious property and violent offenders.

TABLE 13.1
Comparisons between Juvenile Male Sexual Assaulters and Violent Controls

	Sexual Assaulters (N = 17; %)	Others Assaulters (N = 61; %)
Depressive symptoms	75.0	63.0
Auditory hallucinations	46.7	41.2
Olfactory and/or gustatory hallucinations	18.8	13.8
Paranoid symptoms	73.3	82.7
Loose, rambling, illogical thought processes	70.0	57.9
Grossly abnormal EEGs or grand mal seizures	23.5	31.3
History of physical abuse	76.5	75.5
Abused by mothers	46.2	42.9
Abused by fathers	58.3	54.3
Witnessed extreme violence	78.6	78.6

Source: Based on data reported by Lewis et al. (1979). Reprinted with permission.

As noted in Chapter 2, there is considerable evidence that offense specialization is the exception rather than the rule (Farrington, 1979a; Klein, 1984). Very few rapists (Soothill et al., 1976) or other types of serious sex offenders (Soothill & Gibbens, 1978) have previous convictions for the same type of criminal activity in the past; most of their previous convictions are for property offenses.

The observations of Gibbens, Lewis, and West and their associates suggest that the concepts of aggression and sex are of limited value for describing or explaining crimes of rape. To summarize the foregoing points: (1) Rapes are difficult to classify as "pure expressions" of either sex or aggression, or even as predominantly sexual or aggressive acts. (2) Rape is associated with a relatively nonspecific increase in arousal, and whether rape or some other crime is committed depends partly on situational opportunity (Gibbens, West). (3) The underlying motivation for rape is unclear and appears to be closely related to the motivation underlying crimes against property (West) and crimes of violence in general (Lewis).

Thus, the need arises for an alternative mode of classifying rape. Here it is proposed that sexual activity and rape represent stimulation-seeking behavior (SSB) of high intensity.

The problem of understanding rape is closely related to the traditional view of motivation (discussed in Chapter 6), which contends that there are a number of discrete motivational behaviors, each regulated by mechanisms which for the most part are specific to each activity (Hinde, 1966, for a review). Thus, according to Freud (1922/1961, cited in Bancroft, 1978), aggression and sex are two distinct forms of behavior, biological forces or drives. Fentress (1978, p. 579) has similarly noted that the concept of sexual behavior implies "a distinction between this one class of activities and all others."

Sexual activity is commonly defined in terms of its presumed biological purpose or function; that is, in terms of fertilization and/or reproduction. Thus sexual activity is equated with reproductive activity, the most obvious manifestation of which is copulation. As a result, the scientific study of sex principally concerns the factors that influence copulation.

A major difficulty with this definition is that much human and animal behavior that is broadly considered "sexual" is *unrelated to reproduction*. Wundram (1979, p. 100) defines nonreproductive sexual activity as "all sexual activity wherein the probability of a sperm reaching an egg approaches zero." Included in this category are masturbation, homosexuality, voyeurism, pedophilia, fetishisms, and necrophilia, among others. Wundram points out that in a wide variety of species many heterosexual couplings occur, such as anal and oral intercourse, which also serve no reproductive function. Activities such as stroking the genitalia of infants in situations of alarm (stump-tailed macaques), forced copulation ("rape") when the female is not in estrus (orangutans), and penile erections in situations of fear or danger (squirrel monkeys, chimpanzees) (MacLean, 1983), likewise appear to be unrelated to reproduction. Wundram further notes that although all mammalian females have clitorises, this organ serves no reproductive purpose. Thus the question remains unresolved of the biological function served by these activities, and by the clitoris.

Recent sociobiological views of rape as a behavioral strategy for achieving reproductive success (e.g., Shields & Shields, 1983; Thornhill & Thornhill, 1983) can likewise be criticized on the grounds that: (1) rape often involves oral and/or anal intercourse, or penetration with foreign objects; (2) rape sometimes ends in the murder of the victim; (3) assailants are sometimes unable to achieve an erection; (4) a proportion of rapes involve male victims; and (5) some female victims are not of reproductive age. Thus, in many instances rape has either nothing or very little to do with increasing the rapist's reproductive success (Baron, 1985).

The second problem with equating sexual activity and reproductive activity, is: What constitutes reproductive activity? Reproductive activity is commonly defined operationally in terms of specific behavioral acts, for example, copulation or mounting. However, many behaviors that occur in close temporal contiguity with copulation are not readily classifiable in terms of the traditional functional categories. Is the "love bite," for instance, an example of sex, of aggression, or even feeding? Many carnivorous species employ neckbites during copulation. These bites are similar to the movements used in the capture of prey. Hence, as noted by Fentress (1978), the functional classification of such acts remains uncertain. A related difficulty is that reproductive types of behavior, including copulatory movements, often occur in animals and humans that are not of reproductive age and in contexts that are unrelated to reproduction (Feder, 1984). In primates, for instance, mounting, thrusting movements, embracing, and presenting all occur frequently during play among juveniles (Hanby, 1976, p. 29), and penile erection occurs not only in courtship but also in intermale aggressive displays (MacLean, 1983, p. 367).

A third difficulty with the concept of sexual activity as a distinct form of behavior is that the environmental and neuroendocrinological factors that elicit it are by no means specific to it; nor is there any evidence that sexual activity is uniquely elicited by a specific pattern of factors or activating conditions. The male hormone testosterone, for instance, influences a wide variety of behaviors (Andrew, 1978; Sheard, 1979; Feder, 1984); moreover, there is no clear correlation between plasma testosterone levels and male sexual activity (Feder, 1984). Similarly, although the brain neurotransmitter dopamine facilitates sexual activity whereas serotonin inhibits it (Gessa & Tagliamonte, 1974; Meyerson & Malmnas, 1978), dopamine is involved in many different types of motor-motivational behavior, while serotonin has a generalized inhibitory effect on motor behavior.

Finally, it should be noted that many environmental stimuli which are ostensibly unrelated to reproduction can elicit copulatory activity and sexual arousal. In rats, such stimuli include handling, tail pinch, electric shock, and general disturbances in the environment (Fentress, 1978). A study of prepubertal boys indicated that many had penile erections in response to a variety of nonspecific but arousing stimuli ranging from pleasant to frightening (Ramsey, 1943, cited in Bancroft, 1978, p. 99).

In summary, (a) much so-called sexual behavior has little or nothing to do with reproduction; (b) it is difficult to determine what constitutes reproductive behavior; (c) so-called sexual stimuli have a wide range of behavioral outcomes; and (d) many supposedly nonsexual stimuli can elicit sexual behavior.

SEXUAL ACTIVITY AS STIMULATION-SEEKING BEHAVIOR

The notion that a given behavior serves a specific biological function or purpose does not necessarily mean that organisms are motivated to act in such a way as to fulfill this function. Indeed, it is argued here that the biological function of reproduction has been mistakenly wedded to the idea of a specific *motivational system* for achieving this end — namely "sexual behavior" — implying that there is a specific hormone, neurotransmitter, brain center, or pattern of neurochemical and environmental factors which uniquely leads to or elicits this behavior. It is argued, in short, that "sexual behavior" is a false reification. Instead, it is proposed that so-called sexual activity represents an arbitrarily defined band on a spectrum of increasingly intense stimulation-seeking behavior, that is, what is sought are varying intensities of bodily stimulation. Reproduction may, or may not, result from such activity. This is not to deny that animals and humans show temporal variation in their receptivity to genital activity; nor is it to deny that, with practice or experience, animals and humans acquire specific desires for orgasm, as well as varying and sometimes exotic forms of genital stimulation. On the other hand, the learned desire for having eggs cooked in a certain way, and the choice of a particular ice cream flavor or a particular item on a restaurant menu, does not necessarily mean that a specific motivational system or neural substrate exists for eliciting such preferences and choices.

Similarly, while it is acknowledged that humans can be highly selective with regard to modes of genital stimulation, it is argued that classifying such activities as "sexual activity" falsely groups certain acts together and excludes other acts on the assumption that the animal or human is "motivated," at some level of awareness, to engage in "sex." The suggestion is that active manipulation of the genitalia and, by extension, rape behavior, is part of a broader system of stimulation-seeking behavior. Thus it is proposed that the hormones, neurochemicals, and brain pathways that have been implicated in sexual behavior are more appropriately reinterpreted as serving to increase or decrease the level or intensity of sensory stimulation. It is argued that behavior is organized not in terms of a number of discrete biological drives (i.e., feeding, drinking, sex, aggression), each with a specific neural substrate but in terms of stimulation-seeking behavior which can be progressively "tuned" to make finer and finer discriminations in sensory input. It is further suggested that the intensity of stimulation-seeking behavior is a function of the level of S-system arousal, and that the type of stimulation actually sought within a given level of S-system arousal depends on many factors, as outlined in Chapter 7, situational opportunity being one of them. The suggestion that sexual behavior and rape represent intense stimulation-seeking behavior (SSB) can account for a number of observations and resolve certain conceptual issues.

1. The close connection between sexual and aggressive behavior in humans and other species has long been a subject of debate and research (see, e.g., Zillman, 1984). According to the present hypothesis, sex and aggression are connected in that both represent stimulation-seeking behavior, so-called aggressive behavior being more intense SSB than sexual behavior. As argued in Chapter 11, "aggressive" acts are very difficult if not impossible to identify in practice, and therefore distinguish from other behaviors, because *injurious intent,* which defines acts as "aggressive," is inherently elusive. Insofar as these acts involve vigorous contact with other species members, or with inanimate objects (e.g., banging the table, kicking the door, stamping the foot), and result in injury or death to the recipient, they can be reinterpreted as intense stimulation-seeking behaviors. The relevant "flow of force", so to speak, is not from the agent to the environment — the agent setting out deliberately to kill or injure, to act *on* the environment, as the traditional view of the concept of aggression would have it — but from the environment to the agent, in the form of intense sensory feedback.

2. Both "reproductive" and "nonreproductive" sexual activity (Wundram, 1979) can be incorporated within the concept of SSB. The suggestion is that there is no inherent distinction between the two and that sensory stimulation is the underlying motivation for both "types" of behavior.

3. The proposal that "sex" is part of a continuum of SSB rather than a separately identifiable class of behavior, can explain the numerous failures to discover a unique set or pattern of activating conditions. According to the present hypothesis, the reason is that such conditions do not exist.

4. Reinterpreting sexual activity as SSB serves to draw attention to the fact that "sexual activity" in humans and other species involves numerous forms of bodily contact. Examples include kissing, licking, touching, stroking, fondling, biting, smelling, and actual rubbing. Hanby (1976), observing that numerous "sociosexual gestures" occur among primates in situations of excitement and tension, notes that these gestures involve "a conspicuous component of tactile and bodily contact, especially in sensitive areas such as the mouth, rump, and genitals" (p. 39).

5. The reason that "mouth, rump, and genitals" are among the main foci of "sexual" behavior may be precisely because of their being richly supplied with nerve endings, thus affording opportunities for heightened sensory stimulation.

6. Supporting the view that sensory stimulation in general is sought rather than genital stimulation alone, is the observation that genital satisfaction can be enhanced or facilitated by additional nongenital stimulation, for example, changing bodily positions, kissing, tickling, slapping, biting, scratching, visual stimulation, etc.

7. "Sexual" activity is not only enhanced by additional stimulation, but almost always *involves* a search for stimulation, for example, by changes in body position and touch of varying intensities, odors, visual displays, bodily coloration, tastes, etc. Komisaruk (1978, p. 377), describing the copulatory behavior of porcupines, notes that during copulation the female pushes actively against the thrust of the male. He writes: "it seems likely that the female porcupine organizes her own bodily movements to increase the intensity of genital stimulation, rather than simply reacting to stimulation by the male."

8. Certain kinds of stimulation, for example, cigarette smoking, drug ingestion, eating, drinking, touching, and exercise, are known to influence sexual arousal and may be capable of substituting for directly genital types of stimulation (cf., the Freudian concept of "sublimation"). Such anecdotal observations support the hypothesis that the underlying motivation in "sexual" activity is for bodily stimulation.

9. One of the problems of tying genital activity to the function of reproduction is that it obliges one to distinguish between genital activity and contact-seeking activity. As Hanby (1976, p. 51) observes, some of the sociosexual gestures of primates, such as male-male mounting and females presenting or touching each other in situations of alarm, are often interpreted as being sexually motivated. She suggests, however, that these behaviors are related more to contact seeking and a desire for reassurance than they are to dominance or copulation. She notes that the difficulty we have in interpreting these behaviors shows the extent to which "copulatory and contacting systems are confused in human behavior" (Hanby, 1976, p. 52). It is of interest to note that males in this culture are often accused by their partners of "just wanting sex," and several studies have shown that males are more preoccupied with sex than females (e.g., Abbey, 1982; Shotland, 1985). Yet, if the present

thesis is correct, this belief stems from the mistaken notion that copulation and contact seeking are motivationally distinct. However, if both activities are viewed as stimulation-seeking behaviors, then the more intense and supposedly more genitally focused SSB of males may be due to (a) a higher background level of physiological arousal, and (b) a consequent tendency to optimize sensory stimulation on those areas of the body that are most highly enervated with sensory receptors, that is, mouth, rump, and genitals.

It is also of interest that, as in the case of rape, excessive sexual desire was once thought to be a major etiological factor in casual sexual liaisons. However, a heightened need for bodily contact or stimulation may be a more fundamental determinant of the behavior. Malmquist and his associates (1966) described 20 women who had had three or more illegitimate pregnancies. Eight of the 20 stated that sexual activity was a price they had to pay for being cuddled and held and that pregenital activity was more pleasurable for them than intercourse. Hollender (1970) studied the need for body contact in 39 women with acute psychiatric disorders, most commonly depression, and suggested that the need for body contact may intensify during periods of stress ("incongruity"). Slightly more than 50 percent of the women reported using sex to entice a male to hold them. Hollender also suggested that the need to be held or cuddled is a major underlying cause of promiscuity in some women. A former call girl was quoted as saying, "In a way, I used sex to be held." Montagu (1972), commenting on the above studies, speculates that "in the Western world it is highly probable that sexual activity, indeed the frenetic preoccupation with sex that characterizes Western culture, is in many cases not the expression of a sexual interest at all, but rather a search for the satisfaction of the need for contact" (p. 192).

In conclusion, the suggestion is that rape is an expression of a desire for intense sensory stimulation, for bodily contact. Whether rape or some other criminal or noncriminal act occurs at times of intense stimulation-seeking behavior may partly depend on the situational opportunities that are immediately available for obtaining stimulation.

To test the stimulation-seeking hypothesis of rape, the stimulus needs and preferences of convicted rapists and matched controls could be compared using Zuckerman's (1979) sensation-seeking scale as well as new measures of SSB, to assess such tendencies at particular times, either retrospectively (e.g., at the time of the rape) or concurrently. It will also be of interest to explore the implications of the hypothesis with regard to (a) the treatment of rapists and (b) the prevention of both homosexual and heterosexual rape behavior. With regard to (a), the implication is that rape is associated with a generalized increase in S-system arousal rather than with endocrine dysfunction per se. With regard to (b), one implication is that the incidence of rape behavior in prisons could be reduced by providing appropriate outlets for intense SSB, for example, vigorous physical exercise (see Chapter 15; Vest, 1985).

14

THE SPECIFICITY OF CRIME, FUNCTIONAL CONSEQUENCES, AND VARIETIES OF SUBJECTIVE EXPERIENCE

It has been proposed that the underlying basis of transient criminality is an arousal-induced increase in stimulation-seeking behavior coupled with a deteriorating cognitive map. Crimes are committed as a result of these processes either because the intensity of SSB exceeds the threshold of social acceptability, because injuries are inflicted fortuitously, or because the breakdown of the cognitive map allows SSB to be directed, with varying intensities, at strangers or at objects that do not belong to the perpetrator.

To complete the discussion of the relationship between SSB, cognitive maps, and crime, we now consider: (a) SSB and the specificity of crime; (b) the emotional aftermath ("functional consequences") of crime; and (c) the relationship between cognitive dysfunction and variations in offenders' subjective states.

SSB AND THE SPECIFICITY OF CRIME

In the preceding four chapters an attempt was made to explain how individuals with convictions for one type of crime tend to have convictions for other types, and how a given factor appears to be related to a wide variety of criminal acts; it was an attempt to explain the considerable *nonspecificity* with regard both to the deviant behavior of criminals and the criminogenic effects of particular stressors. A further implication of the construct of SSB is that it explains other types of deviant activity that are frequently engaged in by offenders, such as excessive smoking, alcohol intake, and the use of illicit drugs.

What, then, determines the type or form of stimulation sought by offenders? What determines the type of criminal outcome to be expected of a one-time offender? It is suggested that the specificity of SSB with respect to crime depends largely on two conditions:

1. *The degree of incongruity and S-system arousal, and hence the intensity of SSB*. The more intense the behavior, the greater the likelihood that a violent crime will be committed rather than, say, shoplifting or indecent exposure. The degree of incongruity and S-system arousal depends in turn on the *source* of incongruity (interpersonal sources being more salient and hence more arousing than impersonal ones) and on the *nature* of the incongruity (threats of, or actual, abandonment being especially incongruous and arousing).

2. *The availability and stimulus value of particular stimulus objects*. SSB is aimed at whatever stimulus objects are available in the situation. Other people — especially familiar people — and objects that can be picked up, manipulated, easily broken, that are valuable, shine, move, make noises, or are in other ways stimulating, are the ones most likely to be selected.[1] In the absence of readily available sources of stimulation, SSB may be directed at the self, possibly resulting in self-mutilation or self-inflicted death ("suicide").

THE EMOTIONAL AFTERMATH

As pointed out in Chapter 9, the suggestion that transient crime is associated with intense SSB does not necessarily mean that individuals are consciously aware of seeking stimulation, that is, that the tendency to seek stimulation is recognizable at the level of subjective reasons and motives. Offenders may, at different times, have various reasons, excuses, and motives for their behavior, while at other times may be unable to offer any explanation for their conduct. Statements to the effect that the offender engaged in a criminal action for "excitement," "fun," or because he enjoyed taking a risk (cf., Miller, 1958), would only be roughly compatible with the explanation proposed here in terms of a biological motive for stimulation and its relationship to the S- and P-systems; that is, while the layman's view is that the individual seeks stimulation to arouse himself, the view here is that the individual is already in a state of S-system arousal and seeks stimulation as a means of *reducing* it by way of activating the inhibitory P-system.

Many instances can be cited in which individuals have reported feeling immensely relieved and calm after committing a crime. To mention some examples, West and Farrington (1977, p. 104) write:

". . . Case 490 reported his reasons for smashing windows on trains: 'Somebody starts it and you all follow. It's something inside you and when you do it, you feel much better . . . it's like getting something out of your system.'"

Similarly, according to Dally (1969, p. 24, 40), patients with anorexia nervosa frequently engage in shoplifting in a state of extreme tension and feel an immediate sense of relief after committing the crime. Schlesinger and Revitch (1980) note that crime may be a result of stress, and cite numerous examples of offenders who felt calm after the commission of a crime. Their Case No. 5, a 46-year-old man who fatally shot and killed his wife and three children, felt relieved after the murders. He had been unemployed for two years and the murders occurred after a series of violent arguments with his wife, who had belittled and cursed him, and told him to leave the house. Werthman (cited in Schlesinger & Revitch, 1980, p. 184) proposed the concept of "catathymic crisis" to explain cases of explosive violence. Such acts tended to be preceded by an obsessional period associated with a buildup of tension, and the violent deed served to "release" the tension. Schlesinger and Revitch (1980) suggest that the prodromal (i.e., immediately preceding) phase often involves a depressed mood, and loose, schizophreniclike thinking, and that relief follows the performance of the violent act. As another example of extreme tension before the crime, they mentioned the case of William Heirens (known for saying "catch me before I kill again — I can't help myself"), who reported having headaches and sweating profusely when trying to resist the compulsion to burgle homes and kill women. A 53-year-old married man, who became depressed after a period of unemployment, exposed himself on several occasions to his teenage daughter's girlfriends. He stated that he couldn't control himself, yet, despite feeling ashamed of himself, felt relief following the act.

In some situations, of course, crimes have profoundly distressing consequences for the offender and hence would be expected to increase rather than decrease the level of S-system arousal. For instance, the acts in question may have led to the death or injury of an attachment figure or some innocent person. In such cases the experience of incongruity would be expected to lead to guilt and agitation (Matza, 1964; Dally, 1969, p. 40; Schlesinger & Revitch, 1980, p. 186); indeed, it is recalled that from 4 to over 40 percent of intrafamilial murders are followed by self-inflicted injury or suicide (West, 1966).

VARIETIES OF SUBJECTIVE EXPERIENCE

In Chapters 2 and 8, reference was made to the fact that many offenders express remorse and guilt for their crimes and are often at a loss to explain their behavior (e.g., Case Studies, No. 1 and No. 6). However, in other places in Chapter 2, examples of transient criminality were cited where apparently well worked-out and even rational reasons were given by offenders to account for their behavior. Yet another "point of view" (Chapter 2) was that despite feeings of guilt and remorse *after* committing crimes, the acts themselves were justified by the use of "techniques of neutralization" (Matza, 1964) or other rationalizations (Janis, 1963) which, at the moment of infraction (but not necessarily afterwards), made the crimes seem reasonable or sensible to those carrying them out.

Although we have argued that transient criminality is associated with a temporary partial breakdown of the offender's cognitive map, the question arises as to whether such a breakdown is compatible with a state of mental confusion as well as the presence of conscious and clearly worked-out reasons for crime.

It is suggested that both situations are compatible with the model, and that whether "confusion" or apparent "rationality" is expressed by the offender depends on: the cognitive cues available to him or her at the time of the act; the duration of the prodromal phase of the crime; and perhaps on the length of time the offender has had to think about the crime. Reflection suggests that there are at least three possible scenarios of cognitive dysfunction and/or transformation associated with transient criminality.

Cognitive Confusion

In this, as in all of the three scenarios, the cognitive map breaks down, a crime is committed, and the offender reports that he was confused and cannot now explain how or why he acted as he did. Considerable guilt is subsequently experienced. An example of this scenario is the "attempted rape" of a stranger (by the unemployed truck driver reported in Chapter 2 (Case Study No. 6). Milgram's (1963, 1968) experimental work on "obedience to authority" provides a further illustration. While not engaging in crime as such, Milgram's subjects performed actions which, had they been real and led to genuine electric shocks, would have been immoral if not frankly criminal. It is recalled that in these experiments (e.g., Milgram, 1963) subjects were asked to administer progressively higher levels of electric shock to volunteer "learners" (seated out of sight in an adjacent room) when they failed to remember a list of words. The real object of the experiment was to see what proportion of subjects would willingly administer the maximum shock level of 450 volts.

The procedure and outcome of Milgram's experiment aptly illustrates the processes outlined in the model of transient criminality. The lone subject faced an experimenter who was calmly ordering him to perform apparently antisocial actions. This was clearly a highly incongruous situation which led to an increase in S-system arousal and SSB, as indicated by the subjects' agitated movements, uncontrollable fits of laughter, and profuse sweating. The finding that 65 percent of subjects administered the maximum level of shock may be explicable in terms of the postulated effects of arousal. The tendency to obey the experimenter can be interpreted as an arousal-induced increase in susceptibility to influence. Furthermore, since the subject was alone with the experimenter, he had no means of obtaining sensory feedback congruent with his cognitive map, that is, his own ideas of acceptable conduct and the rules of psychological experiments. The subject's own perceptions of the situation and his awareness of the victim's suffering were also systematically ignored or denied. For instance, when one subject expressed concern for the victim, saying "He's banging for help. He's evidently in trouble or he wouldn't bang . . . I don't see any sense to this — to knock him out or something" (Milgram 1968, p. 268), the experimenter's reply was: "The experiment requires you to go on" (p. 269). It is postulated that the subject's inability to confirm his own perceptions of the nature of the experiment, combined with the "stress" of being in an unfamiliar environment and hearing the victim's cries in the next room, led to an arousal-induced temporary, partial breakdown of the subject's cognitive map, with a deterioration in cognitive functioning and an increase in agitated movement. All of these processes, then, may have contributed to the tendency to continue pulling the lever of the shock machine.

Although many subjects claimed to have been confused by the situation and found their behavior inexplicable, they were, of course, acting on the commands of the experimenter. To this extent the obedience paradigm is similar to Scenario No. 2, to be discussed below.

Rationalization

In this scenario, as before, the cognitive map starts to break down. Being highly susceptible to influence, the individual uncritically takes in, accepts, or believes a criminal suggestion, and then acts upon it thereby committing a crime. It is important to emphasize that the motive or reason for committing the crime is uncritically accepted, not clearly worked-out beforehand in the perpetrator's mind, and falls apart rapidly on close questioning after the event.

The suggestion or motive for committing the crime may come from (a) the *environment* (that is, some other person or persons) or (b) the perpetrator's *own mind*.

As an example of (a), and bearing in mind that historical accuracy is less important for our purposes than finding a good illustration of the hypothetical processes involved, we refer again to LeBon's (1895/1977) discussion of criminal crowds (see Chapter 2). According to LeBon, "the usual motives for the crimes of crowds is a powerful suggestion, and the individuals who take part in such crimes are afterwards convinced that they have acted in obedience to duty" (LeBon, 1895/1977, p. 160). LeBon described the behavior of certain Parisiens in the French Revolution who, after spending nearly a week slaughtering over 1,200 inmates of several prisons, went to the authorities and demanded a reward, proudly convinced that they had carried out a patriotic duty. It may be that the underlying psychology of lynch mob behavior in general is similar, that is, suggestions are uncritically accepted, not clearly worked out, and prone to disintegrate on close questioning or under calmer conditions.

In (b), the criminal motive is presumed to originate internally, in the offender's own mind. The suggestion may be in the form of a delusion or hallucinatory voice, commanding the subject to do something. Here the cognitive map breaks down to the point of frank psychosis. The following is an illustrative case (*Times-Picayune/States Item,* New Orleans, Friday July 18, 1980, Sn. 1, p. 21). "A 28 year old . . . father admitted in court that while he was under the influence of narcotics he came to believe his sleeping 5-year-old daughter had become a 'space monster' and that he murdered her by stabbing her fourteen times." The man said that he was temporarily insane at the time because he had taken the drug phencyclidine (PCP). After the attack, immediately following his arrest, he claimed to have no memory of the attack but said later that the drug made him believe that he was stabbing a monster from space rather than his own daughter.

The strange case of David Berkowitz, arrested in New York City in 1977 after a year-long series of six murders and seven woundings, exemplifies a more long-lasting cognitive disintegration and associated criminality. Arrested for the crimes at age 24, Berkowitz was an apparently mild, somewhat overweight young man who, in various letters to local newsmen, had called himself the "Son of Sam." Berkowitz's brief criminal career is discussed as an instance of "snapping" by Conway and Siegelman (1979, pp. 211–17), in their book *Snapping: America's Epidemic of Sudden Personality Change.*

The concept of "snapping" is similar to that of "disintegration of the cognitive map," and the postulated chain of events leading up to snapping, involving a sequence of intense experiences, is also similar to the model of incongruity and S-system arousal proposed here. "Sam" was a black Labrador retriever that belonged to one of Berkowitz's neighbors in his apartment building. Berkowitz had been tormented by Sam's persistent barking and came to believe that the dog was ordering him to begin murdering young couples. Conway and Siegelman suggest that his was a case of "snapping in its most destructive form, outside the context of a cult or mass therapy" (p. 212). They note that although his early upbringing and youth were apparently normal and uneventful, Berkowitz underwent a drastic shift in personality while stationed in Korea with the U.S. Army. This was brought on by the "limbo existence" of U.S. troops in Korea, the extensive use of various drugs, and the experience of a court-martial for insubordination. After Korea, and stationed at Fort Knox, Berkowitz underwent a conversion from Judaism to evangelical Christianity. Following a year of fervent Evangelicalism Berkowitz appeared to lose interest in it and also learned of his parents' dismay at his conversion. Conway and Siegelman speculate that, returning to New York City in 1974, Berkowitz entered a "peculiar twilight zone of floating," drifting through community college and a series of uneventful jobs. His family relocated to Florida, his former girlfriend was now married, and his high school friendships had long been abandoned. Thus, lacking social supports,

> Berkowitz remained detached, withdrawn, lonely, and suggestible. . . . In that condition, the trivial but penetrating sound of a barking dog was the tiny measure required to send him over the edge. . . . So, burned out, drifting, and alone, he slipped all the way into the fantasy world with which his mind had long ago become acquainted. He began hearing voices, receiving messages from God and Satan, and following the commands of a black labrador retriever who ordered him to launch a reign of terror on New York as a warning to the world from the demons he perceived (Conway & Siegelman, 1979, p. 216).

Cognitive Transformations

In this, the third scenario, a still more dramatic alteration in cognitive functioning is postulated to occur. As in the previous scenarios, the individual's cognitive map begins to disintegrate as a result of incongruous life experiences and increased S-system arousal. However, in this situation a profound transformation of the cognitive map takes place. Having reached the point where the cognitive map is partially disintegrated, the individual may assimilate a new cognitive map, including a new sense of personal identity, together with major alterations in what he or she now considers "familiar" and "unfamiliar." After acquiring the new cognitive map, with the new values and beliefs that it entails, the individual may then (if his cognitive map requires it) engage in criminal actions which, from his own viewpoint, are completely rational. This third scenario, in short, represents a conversion experience for the individual.

The disintegration of an individual's cognitive map may, of course, be deliberately contrived by others in order to engineer such cognitive transformations, as well as being "accidents" of life. So-called "brainwashing" techniques are used by military organizations to indoctrinate recruits and turn them into fighters, to make captured members of the enemy release information of strategic importance, and (possibly to a lesser degree and not always deliberately) by social institutions such as prisons, asylums, boarding schools, convents, and the like, to enforce discipline and to impose their own set of rules on newcomers.

As an example, let us suppose that an individual soldier is captured by the enemy and subjected to a series of terrifying experiences while being kept in isolation. Thus unable to obtain any congruous environmental feedback to support his cognitive map and prevent the amplification of S-system arousal, the soldier's cognitive map begins to disintegrate. The soldier now seeks intense stimulation from any available source, the most likely sources being his guard and enemy officers. The sensory and other characteristics of these individuals are then incorporated into the soldier's newly developing cognitive map, so that the enemy is redefined as the familiar, while his own former membership group becomes "unfamiliar." The soldier thus develops a sense of attachment (often combined with very intense and positive feelings) toward his captors, and, at the same time, negative attitudes toward his former group. Hence, if his captors order him to engage in activities against his former group — whether they take the form of combat, espionage, subversion, or missions such as robbing banks or setting off explosions — the soldier will freely engage in them without a pang of conscience. Some degree of arousal may be involved, but this will be expected to derive not from a sense of personal wrongdoing but from the fear of the activities themselves and of being caught by the "enemy."

This description of cognitive transformation and reversal of allegiances will be recognized as the "Stockholm syndrome," which was described in Chapter 12. There the concept was applied to battered women who remain with their partners and protect them from social workers or the police. However, the concept can also be applied to individuals without a previous history of criminality who have committed apparently rational crimes under the influence of a powerful social movement or group leader. Such crimes defy explanation in terms of current criminological theories, most of which emphasize predispositional factors, whether personal or environmental, and ignore situational influences.

Several notorious incidents of this kind are described in fascinating detail under the rubric of "snapping" by Conway and Siegelman (1979, esp. Chapter 15; but see Barker, 1986, for alternative views). The thesis of these authors is that "snapping," that is, a sudden change of personality, life-style, attitudes, and behavior, is due to a series of intense emotional and physical experiences which have the effect of "destroying deep and long-lasting information-processing pathways in the brain" (p. 132). For instance, the authors describe the experience of the Gordons, a young couple who, in the course of attending a weekend retreat sponsored by the Unification Church, became new converts of the church. This example of snapping was attributed to the intense bombardment of the couple with information about the church in lectures, group discussions, and highly emotional personal confrontations. So great is the psychophysiological impact of such experiences that they may, according to Conway and Siegelman, "sever long-standing synaptic connections" (p. 132) in the brain. They write (p. 133):

> The Gordons, as well, underwent far more than a simple transformation of belief during their weekend among the Moonies. Their physical appearance changed noticeably — their eyes, their posture, their tone of voice; indeed they seemed to become totally different people. Furthermore their sweeping inner change also transformed the way the couple experienced the world around them. On their return ... the everyday world seemed strangely alien and sinister.

The last sentence of this quotation expresses very well the idea that, with fundamental alterations in a person's cognitive map, what was formerly considered familiar now appears alien and unfamiliar.

If the experience of snapping takes place in the context of a terrorist or criminal organization — which certain cults, partly in response to the public hostility they evoke, can become — the new convert is obviously at risk of engaging in crime. Conway and Siegelman (1979, pp. 206–11) present a fascinating account of the crimes of Charles Manson and his followers during the 1960s, and of the abduction and political conversion of Patty Hearst by the Symbionese Liberation Army in 1974.[2] What follows is a summary of the Hearst episode.

On February 4, 1974, 19-year-old Patricia Hearst, granddaughter of publisher William Randolph Hearst, was kidnapped at gunpoint from her California apartment by a group calling themselves the Symbionese Liberation Army. The SLA was a group of revolutionaries led by Donald DeFreeze, a charismatic figure with an extensive criminal record. For the first two months of her captivity Patty Hearst was kept blindfolded on the floor of a cramped closet, repeatedly threatened with death, intermittently physically and sexually assaulted, and informed that she had been abandoned by her parents and by society. Then, in April, Patty was photographed taking part in a bank robbery with members of the SLA. She carried a submachine gun and now called herself Tania. While her six captors later burned to death during a police raid on their hideout, Tania eluded the police with two remaining members of the group and was finally caught in September 1975. A famous trial ensued in which Hearst was charged with and found guilty of armed robbery.

While the defense seemed to vacillate between trying to prove that Patty had been converted and been coerced, the prosecution argued that she was a willing participant in the robbery, that she had the makings of a rebel before her kidnapping, and that she engaged willingly in all of the group's activities.

In trying to re-create the conditions leading up to Patty Hearst's involvement in the bank robbery, Conway and Siegelman (1979, p. 208) argued that her personality was deliberately and methodically destroyed by DeFreeze and his followers, and that her conversion was engineered by classic brainwashing techniques. DeFreeze's techniques included intimidation, isolation, the use of personal charm, and intense sexual experiences. His goal was reportedly to incite the underprivileged to revolution through a campaign of carefully selected acts of violence.

When interviewed on nationwide television a few months after her early release from jail and almost three years after her kidnapping, Patty Hearst expressed noticeable confusion about her involvement with the SLA. According to Conway and Siegelman (1979), she displayed "all the characteristics of a cult member who has not been properly deprogrammed" (p. 209). At the time of the police raid she had watched on television as DeFreeze and five other SLA members died in the fire, surrounded by police, and concluded that what her captives had told her was true: her family had abandoned her and the FBI was out to kill her and all of the other SLA members. Yet, when asked why she had not contacted her family in the months after the fire, she was unable to understand or explain it herself. According to the authors, both the question itself and her answer to it expressed not only her own confusion about the experience but the extent to which she had been misunderstood by the public. Most of those interviewed apparently thought she was a criminal, and that "brainwashing can only be done by experts, not by kooks" (p. 211). Conway and Siegelman conclude (pp. 209–10):

In our opinion, it was that profound and comprehensive assault on her body, her emotions, and her intellect which annihilated the foundations of Patty Hearst's personality, making her every subsequent action problematical from any traditional psychiatric view and unquestionably moot with regard to all charges of criminal intent.[3]

In sum, alterations in cognitive functioning and increased S-system arousal leading to transient criminality may be analyzed in terms of three relatively distinct scenarios: (a) that of *cognitive confusion* and bewilderment, in which the perpetrator is unable to provide any coherent explanation for his or her behavior; (b) that in which various *rationalizations* are given, in the form of criminal motives derived either from another person or from the mind of the perpetrator (possibly in association with drug taking or excessive alcohol consumption); and (c) more or less complete *cognitive transformations* (or "snapping" experiences) in which a phase of relative disintegration is followed by a phase of cognitive reintegration (often deliberately engineered by other individuals), in which crimes are committed deliberately and coolly. In this state, crimes may be dictated by the new cognitive map and carried out perfunctorily, as if they were simply a part of one's normal job or occupation.

NOTES

1. It is important, therefore, to emphasize the real danger of having objects such as guns and knives readily available and within reach of stimulus-hungry children or of adults made temporarily stimulus-hungry by interpersonal or other crises. The same is true of cars and motorcycles, both of which are frequently abused as a means of obtaining intense stimulation.

2. These authors also include David Berkowitz in their discussion of snapping. While we agree that Berkowitz underwent a "snapping" experience, it does not appear to have been as profound and all-embracing (in the sense of leading to a new personal identity) as that experienced by Manson's followers or by Hearst. Hence, it was decided to discuss Berkowitz's case in relation to the second scenario (Rationalization).

3. As Conway and Siegelman indicate, special techniques ("deprogramming") may be needed to help former cult members and people who have experienced "snapping" and engaged in criminal actions during the phase of integration into the cult to return to normal life in their own communities. Many examples are given in their book of people who had not succeeded in "snapping back," and who still appeared

disoriented and in limbo. The authors also note that the types of life events that led, say, David Berkowitz to experience a drastic alteration in his personality, are not unusual, and that there may be countless "sons of Sam" in the making who, after searching for meaning in life through drugs, religion, and therapy, "discover only the private horror of snapping" (p. 217). They also suggest that no one is immune to snapping; that it is "something new and threatening to our society" (p. 217), and that the need to understand more fully the mechanisms involved remains vital.

15

CONCLUSIONS

This chapter (a) summarizes the main themes of the book; (b) suggests ways in which the model may be helpful in understanding the so-called age-specific and chronic patterns of criminality; (c) offers suggestions for further research; and (d) comments on the implications of the model for preventing transient criminality.

SUMMARY

Individuals build cognitive maps of their interpersonal, physical, and normative-ideological environment, some aspects of which — especially certain individuals — are psychologically more important than others. Since legal and moral rules are part of the environment, they too are internalized in the cognitive map. People attempt to preserve their cognitive maps by actively seeking out the persons and places whose characteristics have been internalized, as well as by adhering to the major ideas, values, and norms of their abstract "ideological" environment. People generally obey rules, not out of a fear of punishment (which assumes that rules force or constrain people to act contrary to their real desires) but because rules *define* the patterns of behavior to which the individual conforms; that is, people are "programmed" to follow rules, just as they are to maintain other aspects of their cognitive map. Following rules and maintaining social ties are different aspects of a more general "affiliative" process in which individuals attempt to maintain the familiar environment. People might be said to be "attached" not only to persons, but also to their physical environment and to certain ideas and values.[1] Thus, a central assumption of the model is that individuals strive to maintain the constancy of their *external* environment, just as they do (echoing Claude Bernard's famous dictum) the constancy of their *internal* environment.

Events perceived as being incongruous with the cognitive map activate mechanisms designed to restore congruity, that is, to maintain the familiar. First, the level of *S-system arousal*[2] increases in proportion to the degree of incongruity,[3] giving rise to an increase in stimulation-seeking behavior (SSB), that is, any activity that enhances or facilitates contact between an organism's sensory receptors and environmental objects or surfaces. However, increased arousal and SSB can also be elicited by consuming drugs or alcohol, as well as by endogenous physiological states such as the premenstruum and hypoglycemia. It is argued that SSB forms a continuum of intensity and that behaviors conventionally labeled "attachment" behavior, "sexual" activity, or "aggression," rather than constituting separate drives in their own right, represent overlapping "bands" on a continuous spectrum of SSB.

In the event of incongruity and/or increased arousal, sensory stimulation is sought which matches that contained in the cognitive map, including: (a) basic sensorial experiences (manifested in "motor-motivational" behavior such as eating, drinking, and general activity); (2) familiar stimulus patterns, represented by particular persons and places; and (e) stimuli associated with various abstract ideas. When, and if, congruity is restored as a result of SSB, the P-system (i.e., parasympatheticlike) is activated, the S-system is inhibited, and a state of calm supervenes.

Since the notion of "congruous stimulation" entails an extremely wide range of sensory patterns and experiences, practically any form of stimulation would be expected to activate the P-system and inhibit the S-system; that is, have a calming effect in the event of incongruity. Indeed, there appears to be a high degree of substitutability with regard to the types of activities and stimuli which can calm people under stress (e.g., eating, smoking, drinking, many forms of intense physical activity, massage, being in the presence of familiar people, and remaining at home). However, since the cognitive map is organized hierarchically in terms of psychological salience, the threatened or actual loss of valued persons cannot be entirely "compensated for" by obtaining other forms of familiar stimuli. Under these conditions, congruity can only be achieved by renewed contact and/or reconciliation with the individual in question; or the "fading" of the valued person's image from the affected person's cognitive map.

The model proposes that individuals are at risk of engaging in transient criminality when highly aroused by incongruous events, alcohol, drugs and/or certain endogenous conditions, particularly in a context of diminished social supports. Individuals normally remain calm under stress because familiar persons or objects are readily available who provide "congruous" stimulation, thereby (according to the model) activating the P-system, which damps down or inhibits the S-system. If, however, the usual sources of congruity (i.e., "social supports") are unavailable or *constitute* the source of incongruity, for example, by threatened or actual abandonment, *and* the incongruity cannot be resolved, then the level of S-system arousal increases proportionately, giving rise to increased suggestibility, a temporary, partial deterioration of the cognitive map, and increased SSB.

It is postulated that transient criminality occurs in one or more of three ways: due to (a) the sheer intensity of SSB, (b) the suddenness of impetuosity of SSB, or (c) a deteriorating cognitive map combined with increased SSB.

In the case of (a), many behaviors are publicly defined as criminal when they exceed a certain level of intensity, not because they are wrong in themselves. An example of this category would be rowdyism ("disturbing the peace"). As the intensity of SSB increases, the acts may result unwittingly in damage to people or property, and therefore in additional crimes. For instance, vandalism may result from highly intense SSB directed unspecifically at "stimulating" physical targets such as automobile antennae, playground toys, and windows. Certain crimes of violence and actual or "attempted" rapes may similarly result from intense SSB directed at specific persons. If, for instance, a woman deserts a man, the desertion constitutes an incongruous event which increases the level of S-system arousal and elicits a high level of SSB aimed at the woman, in an effort to restore and maintain congruity (i.e., to "maintain the bond"). While threats of abandonment may elicit various manifestations of attachment behavior, actual abandonment — especially for a person lacking other sources of social support — may produce SSB of such intensity that the partner may be inadvertently injured or killed.

In the case of (b), some crimes result inadvertently from sudden and impetuous actions associated with a high level of S-system arousal and intense SSB. For instance, negligent homicide may result from sudden and intense increases in acceleration by the driver of an automobile. The distinguishing feature of (a) is that the agent *directs* his SSB specifically at the person or object that becomes injured or damaged because of the intensity of SSB, while in (b) the agent's actions are *indirect* and the injuries or damages are inadvertent.

With regard to (c), it is proposed that severe or prolonged incongruity results in a temporary, partial deterioration of the individual's cognitive map. Drugs, alcohol, the premenstruum and hypoglycemia are postulated to have a similar effect. As a result, the individual experiences feelings of confusion or unreality, and his SSB is no longer guided exclusively toward familiar persons or places. The more abstract and developed aspects of the map disintegrate first, leaving intact the basic substratum of familiar kinds and amounts of stimulation on which *patterns* of stimulation representing, say, specific individuals such as mother and father, are constructed. There occurs a cognitive-perceptual loss not only of the sense of spatial and interpersonal familiarity, but of major abstractions including legal rules and mores. Individuals in this state are highly susceptible to influence and are guided increasingly toward basic kinds and amounts of stimulation — that is, "attractive" people or "attractive" objects, regardless of whether the people in question are strangers, or the objects in question belong to someone else.

These suggestions were applied in Chapters 9 through 14 to the explanation of vandalism, theft, burglary, and crimes of violence toward both familiars and strangers. The type of crime actually committed may depend, inter alia, on the source of incongruity, on the momentary level of S-system arousal (and hence on the intensity of SSB), and on opportunities for obtaining stimulation that are immediately available in the situation.

TRANSIENT, AGE-SPECIFIC, AND CHRONIC CRIMINALITY

In the case of *transient criminality,* that is, brief episodes of major and minor crime committed by normally law-abiding individuals, the source of incongruity and the duration of both increased S-system arousal and SSB are assumed to be relatively short-lived. Here it is suggested that similar psychophysiological mechanisms may be operative in the so-called age-specific and chronic patterns of criminality. Where they differ from transient criminality is in the origin and duration of the operative factors.

With respect to *age-specific criminality*, that is, criminality limited to adolescence, it is speculated that the underlying increase in S-system arousal is mainly linked to puberty and the adolescent growth spurt (Mawson, 1978b). There is some evidence to suggest that the hormonal changes of puberty are initiated by increases in catecholaminergic (CA) activation (Swerdloff, 1978). This endogenous increase in the background level of CA (i.e., S-system) arousal may combine with concurrent environmental stress, leading to increased suggestibility, a partial deterioration of the cognitive map, and increased SSB (Mawson, 1977, 1978b).

Several observations suggest an association between puberty and juvenile delinquency (see also Ellis, 1978, 1983; Brooks-Gunn & Petersen, 1983). Studies of the age distribution of offending indicate that delinquency increases markedly in the early teens, peaks in the middle or late teens, and declines steadily thereafter (Hirschi & Gottfredson, 1983). The apparent universality of this finding suggests an underlying biological explanation. Considering that girls attain puberty approximately two years earlier than boys (Valadian & Porter, 1977), it is of interest that the peak incidence of arrests of females in the United States also occurs about two years earlier than that of males (see Figure 1.3, Chapter 1). Consistent with this hypothesis, Wadsworth (1979, p. 99), observed in his report on the British National Survey that "manual social-group boys who were fully physically mature at age 15 appeared to have a slightly younger than average age at first offense." Conversely, pubertally immature boys at age 15 had a later than average onset of delinquency, leading Wadsworth to suggest that "glandular development *per se*" may be an important factor in relation to delinquency.

Turning to the processes subsequent to increased arousal, nondelinquent teenagers show signs of increased suggestibility, alterations in cognitive functioning (e.g., self-concept), and increased SSB (e.g., drug and alcohol use, sexual activity, loud music, fast motorcycles, cars, etc.) (Simmons et al., 1973; Hamburg, 1975; Rutter et al., 1976; Hays, 1978), while adjudicated delinquents appear to show these changes to a more marked degree, as the model would predict (see, e.g., Farley, 1977; Lewis & Balla, 1976; Lewis, 1981).

In summary, the processes which have been suggested as playing an important role in transient criminality, and which occur in response to environmental stress (i.e., increased arousal, suggestibility, SSB, and cognitive-perceptual dysfunction), seem to occur as a *normal* aspect of adolescence, and could therefore explain the heavy concentration of offending in this age group.

With regard to *chronic criminality,* the suggestion is that for certain individuals, starting early in life and continuing well into adulthood, the level of S-system arousal is frequently higher than the norm, resulting in a chronically increased risk of involvement in crime. This is not to imply that arousal level in the criminal is *always* higher than that of the noncriminal, or higher in *every* situation. Rather, a characteristic feature of both age-specific and chronic criminality may be a greater degree of *variability* in arousal level, criminality being associated with phases of hyperarousal.

The postulated increased variability in arousal level and episodes of hyperarousal may reflect a number of factors, including heredity, injury involving the central nervous system, poor nutrition, and/or chronic psychosocial stress (see Lewis, 1981, for several pertinent reviews). According to the model, affected individuals would be expected to show a chronic pattern of increased suggestibility, SSB, and cognitive-perceptual dysfunction. As discussed in Chapter 9, there is much evidence that persistent adult criminality, psychopathy, and juvenile delinquency are associated with high scores on the sensation-seeking scale. There is also increasing evidence of pervasive cognitive and perceptual dysfunction among persistent juvenile and adult offenders (Lewis, 1981; Karniski et al., 1982; Brickman et al., 1984; Bryant et al., 1984).

It is of further interest that just as SSS scores decline with age both in males and females (Zuckerman et al., 1978), so too does the rate of criminality. Indeed, the decline in criminality with age appears to be as universal a finding as the peak age of criminality during adolescence, suggesting a biological basis for this interrelated set of observations. It is conjectured that the decline in SSB and criminality with age is associated with the endogenous decrease in catecholaminergic (S-system) activity which is known to occur with advancing age (Samorajski, 1977; Beck, 1978). Monoamine oxidase activity (which is thought to be inversely related to catecholaminergic activity) has also been found to increase with age in one study (Robinson et al., 1971) but not in another (Murphy et al., 1976). While SSB peaks during adolescence and early adulthood, and involves a preference for intense sensations of many different kinds, there may be a correlative increase in the tendency to *avoid* such sensations among older age groups.

SUGGESTIONS FOR FURTHER RESEARCH

Suggestions for testing the model have been made in a number of places throughout the book. Here a summary will be attempted of the main directions that research might take, organized in terms of the key concepts of the model.

Incongruity

Although an enormous literature has accumulated on the association between stressful life events and both mental and physical disorders, little research of this sort has been carried out on juvenile or adult offenders and matched samples of nonoffenders. However, it will be important in such research to take into account the extent and availability of social supports, since the model postulates that criminality is more likely to result from environmental stress *combined* with diminished or absent supports. In addition to retrospective studies, it would also be of interest to carry out prospective studies aimed at determining the relative risk of criminality and related forms of deviant behavior following the occurrence of particular stressors, for example, abandonment by a loved one, and diminished supports in general. According to the model, such stressors are linked to criminality because they are interpreted by the affected individual (at some level of awareness), as "incongruous with his or her cognitive map, and because they elicit an increase in S-system arousal.

Arousal

Increased S-system arousal may be associated with criminality by way of alterations in cognition and increased stimulation-seeking behavior. As noted in Chapter 4, there is contradictory evidence regarding both (a) arousal level at the moment of infraction, and (b) "baseline" or resting arousal levels in official delinquents and adult offenders (particularly those diagnosed as psychopaths). With regard to (a), some reports indicate that offenders are excited and highly agitated during the commission of property and violent crimes, while others suggest that perpetrators of violent crimes are often sleepy or "dazed" at the moment of the crime. With regard to (b), many reports indicate lower levels of arousal in psychopaths and delinquents compared to controls; others suggest increased arousal and arousability; and still others (the author included) suggest that psychopaths may be characterized by unusual variability in arousal levels and arousability, depending on the situational context, ranging from hypoarousal in calm situations or when asked to relax, to hyperarousal in situations which the individual himself finds "incongruous." As already noted, the model assumes that criminality is associated with phases of hyperarousal (Mawson & Mawson, 1977).

It was suggested that an adequate test of arousal hypotheses requires telemetric or automatic monitoring of physiological parameters (e.g., heart rate) in offenders and suitably matched controls over a period of hours or days. Only in this way can an adequate sampling of "arousal levels" be obtained.

The overall hypothesis could be further evaluated using Milgram's "obedience" paradigm as a model for understanding transient criminality. Subjects' heart rates could be monitored telemetrically, and repeated measures of blood catecholamines could be obtained. Those subjects initially refusing but eventually succumbing to the experimenter's demands to proceed to the maximum level of shock ("transient offenders") would be expected to have higher heart rates and catecholamine levels than those not giving in to the experimenter's demands. Measures of cognitive functioning could also be obtained during or immediately following the experiment. Behavioral agitation (i.e., stimulation-seeking behavior) could be monitored telemetrically during the experiment.

As another test of the high-arousal hypothesis, newly arrested persons could be asked to rate their own level of excitement (arousal) immediately before, during, and after committing the crime for which they were arrested.

Cognitive Maps

The concepts of cognitive map, and of intact and "deteriorating" cognitive maps, were discussed in Chapters 8 and 9. As noted, the term is not new, and the present concept incorporates many familiar but more restricted concepts such as self-esteem, self-concept, ego, roles, cognitive schemata, and models in the brain, to mention only a few such concepts. The notion of a deteriorating cognitive map was described as including (in varying degrees) the loss of a sense of familiarity, propriety, and ownership with regard to people, places, and objects; a feeling of alienation from one's surroundings; mild confusion; altered sensation and perception, sometimes with paranoia and/or hallucinations; and memory disturbances.

Neuropsychiatric tests do not appear to be available as yet for assessing the subtle, subclinical disturbances of cognition reportedly found in many offenders (Chapter 8). Hence, there is a need to develop reliable and valid tests of this sort and to assess offenders in the areas of cognitive-perceptual disturbances as soon as possible after arrest or incarceration, to try to determine the extent of the offender's cognitive disturbance at the time of the crime. An important methodological issue will be the problem of separating the effects of arrest and incarceration themselves from the effect of the stressors supposedly associated with the crime. In addition to studying perceptual and sensorimotor disturbances, the cognitive maps of offenders could also be studied and compared to those of nonoffenders in the form of a series of questions dealing with, for example, their sense of the familiar, their sense of ownership of material objects and personal property, their feelings about home, and key people in their lives, their self-concept, their "attachment behavior" in terms of family members, and the physical location of their home.

Stimulation-Seeking Behavior

Chapters 6, 11, and 13 were devoted to a critique of traditional motivational categories and to a reinterpretation of various "drives" or motor-motivational activities in terms of a continuum of stimulation-seeking behavior (SSB) aimed at familiar types, amounts, and patterns of stimulation. SSB was defined as any response that enhances or facilitates contact between an organism's sensory receptors and external objects or surfaces. It was proposed that the intensity of SSB is proportional to the level of S-system arousal, and that the sensory stimulation obtained via SSB is "fed back" into the central nervous system where it activates the P-system, which in turn inhibits the S-system, producing a general state of calm.

As applied to crime, the concept of SSB was used to account for: the high correlation between various forms of socially deviant behavior, notably drug taking, alcohol consumption, sexual promiscuity, self-injury and criminality; crimes of violence, including homicide, assault, and rape; shoplifting; burglary; vandalism; the types of objects taken (and not taken) by shoplifters and burglars; the overwhelming tendency among convicted offenders toward nonspecialization in crime; and the sense of calm that often occurs immediately after the commission of crime.

Differences between Zuckerman's (1979) concept of sensation seeking and that of stimulation seeking, as described here, were discussed. Since SSB, by definition, embraces most of the traditional categories of motivational and emotional behavior, conventional measures of such behavior (including Zuckerman's sensation-seeking scale) may provide partial or approximate measures of SSB. However, there is a need to develop explicit, behavioral measures of SSB that can be used for research purposes. There is also a need to design empirical tests of the stimulation-seeking hypothesis as it applies to crimes against persons and property.

IMPLICATIONS FOR CRIME PREVENTION

A view of crime which is currently in vogue is that it tends to be a "rational," consciously planned, or at least intentional activity, with definite goals, involving a careful weighing of potential costs and benefits. Due to various long-standing environmental and/or hereditary influences, criminals are also thought to be constantly ready to commit a crime if the opportunity arises; moreover, insofar as crime is precipitated by recent events, the event is assumed to impinge directly on the offender's welfare, thereby creating a "logical need" to commit a crime (e.g., job termination, and consequent loss of income, as a cause of theft or burglary).

Against this view, there is the observation that many crimes committed in the wake of a recent setback seem to bear no readily understandable relationship to the preceding event — for example, shoplifting as a sequel to bereavement or the breakup of a relationship (see Chapter 2). Furthermore, the relationship between financial hardship and crimes against property is more complex than would be expected if the generalization were true that "people steal when they need money" (see e.g., Carr-Hill & Stern, 1984; Parker & Horowitz, 1986). In addition, there is little evidence of careful planning or of cost-benefit analyses on the part of offenders prior to engaging in crime. Many crimes (it is difficult to make any sort of quantitative estimate) appear to be carried out in a state of considerable agitation, with little thought for the consequences of being apprehended. Subtle alterations in cognition and perception have been noted. Frequently, too, the offender later experiences considerable remorse and is unable to account for his behavior.

The model proposed in this book attempts to explain these seemingly "irrational" aspects of criminal behavior in terms of the hypothesis of a stress- and arousal-induced deterioration in the offender's cognitive map. It is suggested that an individual who loses his job and source of income normally does not resort to theft because his cognitive map differentiates between personal and other people's property; it is "programmed" to keep him within his own proprietorial and territorial boundaries and to avoid other people's property and territory. The legal rule against stealing is "concretized" in terms of a clear perception of, and continuous pursuit of, the "familiar, " and the avoidance of what is "unfamiliar." It is postulated that the cognitive map must first undergo a partial disintegration as a result of continued high arousal and an inability to achieve congruity, before the individual can violate hitherto accepted social rules.

The result of such a breakdown is thought to be relatively indiscriminate stimulation-seeking behavior (SSB). It is recalled that the cognitive map is structured in such a way that *patterns* of stimulation, representing the more differentiated aspects of the environment, develop from combinations of simple sensations of touch, vision, smell, etc. It is postulated that the more differentiated aspects disintegrate first; that is, people lose their "sense of belonging," including the sense of what belongs to them, and what belongs to other people. The SSB of such individuals is now guided more by what is immediately available and attractive to the senses than by "higher order" concepts and rules of ownership.

According to the model, the cognitive map as a whole undergoes a partial disintegration as a result of intense or unrelieved incongruity; hence, the "loss" of rules regarding territorial and proprietorial behavior is part of a more general deterioration in cognitive functioning and loss of the sense of familiarity and unfamiliarity. This implies that efforts to prevent crime should not be focused solely on learning, understanding, and respecting laws and mores as such (i.e., developing a so-called conscience), but on the maintenance and development of the individual's cognitive map as a whole. Since the cognitive map is threatened by (and may disintegrate as a result of) prolonged incongruity and increased S-system arousal, the theory suggests the following steps as a means of preventing crime on an individual basis:[4] (1) reducing or avoiding incongruity, and avoiding or minimizing other causes of S-system arousal; (2) indirectly reducing the impact of incongruity and the associated increase in S-system arousal by maintaining and strengthening the cognitive map through increased and deepened personal and community ties; and (3) utilizing nonharmful forms of SSB or other procedures as a means of reducing S-system arousal. Each is discussed in turn below.

1. With regard to *sources of incongruity in the environment,* there is probably little that can be done to avoid every one of the stressors associated with criminality that were described in Chapter 2. Everyone experiences loss or rejection at some time in their life, not to mention other common causes of unhappiness. Recalling that participation in crowd behavior appears to be associated with criminality, almost everyone forms part of a crowd at some time in his life. Many people also overindulge in alcohol or drugs from time to time, suffer from premenstrual tension, and/or become hypoglycemic. On the other hand, educational programs could be designed to inform children and adults

about the criminogenic potential of such factors in addition to their adverse effects on physical health, and methods could be suggested for reducing their impact.

2. With regard to strengthening the cognitive map, Cassel (1976) has pointed out in his valuable essay on the link between stress and disease that it is not so much exposure to a disease agent that causes disease (except in the case of the most virulent agent or organism), but the *resistance* of the person exposed to it, as influenced by his or her social supports. Similarly, it appears likely that individuals must already be vulnerable to stressful life events, due to the loss or absence of attachment objects, before stress will lead to crime.

According to the model, incongruous events have a lessened impact on arousal level if the individual has access to sources of stimulation which match his cognitive map, that is, close friends and relatives and familiar surroundings. Hence, he or she will be less likely to engage in crime or other forms of deviant behavior. From the point of view of preventing crime, therefore, it is important to develop and maintain strong "bonds" with family members and friends, and with the community as a whole. This can be facilitated by refraining from moving house or excessive travel, by keeping in regular contact with the people, places, or objects that are part of one's cognitive map, as well as by establishing a variety of new social relations by participating in voluntary organizations such as churches and social clubs. Evidence is increasing that strong social and community ties play a vital role in the maintenance of health in general (Lindheim & Syme, 1983; Kessler et al., 1985; cf., Alloway & Bebbington, 1987). Although there are a number of unresolved issues regarding the definition and measurement of "social supports," and the way in which they affect the risk of disease or ill-health (Henderson, 1984; Berkman, 1984; Alloway & Bebbington, 1987), the weight of evidence suggests that, in the absence of social supports, people are more vulnerable to the effects of stressful life events and have an increased risk of psychiatric and physical illness.[5]

This is not, of course, to imply that people should never separate, obtain divorces, live alone, move house, or accept job offers in unfamiliar locations. However, such events should be recognized for what they are; namely, risk factors for mental and physical disease and probably for criminality. As far as possible, their effects should be reduced or minimized by developing new relationships and meaningful forms of social interaction rather than solitary pursuits.

Some observers believe that, particularly since the industrial revolution, social trends and technologies have consistently tended to weaken human social relations and communities, thereby increasing people's vulnerability to disease.[6] With regard to social trends, the view is widely held that contemporary social relations tend to be superficial and transitory. According to Pilisuk (1982, p. 27), "The very social currents of careerism, autonomy, mobility, privacy and achievement that tend to disrupt our traditional roots and ties also make difficult the continuity of new bonds." Additionally, the automobile, the air conditioner, the clothes dryer, the television set, the lack of sidewalks, the loss of small intimate shops and stores, and the growth of huge impersonal supermarkets and shopping centers, have further isolated neighbors, friends, and families from one another, inhibiting spontaneous interaction and the development of social relations. As suggested in Chapter 8, these changes have made it increasingly difficult for people to acquire a consistent picture of themselves and of their social and geographical world. At the same time, architectural and landscaping changes have led to the erection of fewer physical and psychological boundaries separating different people's territory and property, which may also have contributed to the growth of shoplifting and burglary. Such trends could perhaps be slowed or halted by altering the design of buildings, shops, and living structures so as to emphasize territorial and proprietorial boundaries (Newman, 1973; Stokols, 1983).

A sense of self-worth or self-esteem is also a part of the cognitive map, and low self-esteem is, according to the model, associated with weakened internalized rules and values. Programs for building self-esteem (see, e.g., Furth, 1983), particularly among the chronically lonely (Rook, 1984), would therefore be expected to strengthen the cognitive map as a whole thereby reducing the risk of criminality. As suggested earlier, social rules may be most effectively learned and internalized within a context that reinforces the individual's cognitive map by providing an overall framework of consistent and stable social support.

3. Finally, nonharmful forms of stimulation and of SSB could be utilized as a crime-preventive measure. According to the model, such stimulation serves to activate the inhibitory P-system and dampen the S-system, thereby reducing the arousability of the latter in the face of

environmental stress. Stimulation could be obtained passively, for example, by massage, or actively, for example, by physical exercise. There is now considerable evidence that regular physical exercise is beneficial for cardiovascular health, weight control, and mental health (see, e.g., Boone, 1983; Mason & Powell, 1985). The type of exercise most likely to be beneficial, for example, walking, jogging, swimming, or cycling, requires rhythmical contractions of large muscle groups for 20–30 minutes at least every other day (Haskell et al., 1985). Physical exercise reduces depression, anxiety, and anger, reduces physiological responses to stress, improves cognitive functioning and self-confidence, and leads to a general sense of well-being (Taylor et al., 1985). Highly fit individuals are less depressed, anxious, and tense than unfit individuals (Wilson et al., 1980), and display reduced catecholamine responses to exercise stress (Galbo, 1983). A recent review (Taylor et al., 1985) indicates that physical activity and exercise may also be beneficial in the treatment of alcoholism and substance abuse. Given the close association between alcohol and/or drug abuse and criminality, physical exercise may also reduce the risk of becoming involved in crime: that is, the associated reduction in S-system arousal and the intensity of SSB would make it less likely for people to commit crimes of violence, to indulge in alcohol or drugs, or to seek stimulation by shoplifting or burglary. At the same time, physical and mental disorders associated with wide fluctuations in S- and P-system arousal would be less likely to develop or would be milder than if the activity had not been performed. As a test of this hypothesis, regular joggers and matched groups of nonjoggers could be compared retrospectively and prospectively in terms of criminal arrests, traffic offenses, alcohol consumption, and depression — the expectation being that jogging would be associated with a reduced risk of criminality. Considering that nearly half of the United States population is sedentary, and that physical exercise reduces morbidity and mortality as well as being readily available and inexpensive, the adoption of a more physically active life-style can be safely recommended for society as a whole (Mason & Powell, 1985).

In addition to stimulation-induced reductions in arousal via physical activity, there are indications that S-system arousal may be lowered by several "stress management" techniques, including muscle relaxation, biofeedback, meditation, cognitive restructuring, behavioral skills training, and combinations of such methods (Schwartz, 1980; Murphy,

1984, for review). However, physical fitness training may "produce improvements in physiological responses to stress comparable to or greater than those produced by some relaxation techniques" (Taylor et al., 1985, p. 199). Dietary methods, including the consumption of tryptophan (Wurtman, 1983; Leathwood & Pollet, 1982/83; Spring, 1986), which increases brain serotonin (part of the postulated P-system), may also be used for reducing S-system arousal.

In conclusion, the adoption of a public health approach toward crime can be strongly recommended. First, the risk factors for criminality appear to overlap closely with those associated with numerous mental and physical diseases. Second, the proposals for preventing crime offered above are identical to those that have been suggested for preventing a wide range of chronic diseases. Third, it might be useful to regard criminal behavior, like disease, as the outcome of risk factors and causal processes that are, nonetheless, subject to personal as well as societal intervention. Diseases such as heart disease and cancer are increasingly seen, not as inevitable, but as potentially preventable as a result of *individual* as well as societal measures, for example, proper nutrition and exercise, adequate sleep, stress management techniques, and other health-maintaining habits (Boone, 1983). Similarly, much crime could perhaps be prevented if we as a society, and those at high risk of committing it (either transiently or chronically), were better educated about the known risk factors for crime and would take active steps to minimize or eliminate them, for example, by drastically reducing opportunities to buy or sell handguns, which are so often used impulsively and accidentally by *non*criminals to kill or injure themselves or others; by selling alcohol within restricted hours, by refraining from excessive alcohol consumption and the use of other criminogenic or crime-related substances; and by a variety of other, relatively novel steps in relation to crime, as outlined above, including exercise, diet, and the maintenance or development of social supports. Such proposals, though speculative and piecemeal compared to the sweeping economic, political, and educational changes often proposed as solutions to the crime problem, may nevertheless provide a sound, practical, and realistic framework for primary and secondary prevention and possibly the rehabilitation of some offenders.

NOTES

1. The term *attachment* is not to be confused with its customary meaning of feelings of love or affection; it refers to consistent patterns of proximity seeking directed by one individual toward another, or toward an object, as well as thinking intensely about people, objects, and one's beliefs or values. Attachment behavior as defined here may be associated with any intense emotion.

2. Broadly defined as the sympathetic branch of the autonomic nervous system.

3. Beyond a certain degree of incongruity the P-system (broadly defined as the parasympathetic system) is activated.

4. Steps that might be taken by communities, store owners, or homeowners, to prevent residential crime and shoplifting, were proposed in Chapter 8.

5. Social ties (or supports) not only protect against the effects of concurrent stress, but seem to have a health maintaining effect in their own right, judging by the strong association between social isolation and both morbidity and mortality (e.g., Lynch, 1977).

6. Fortunately, other social changes, notably improved sanitation and nutrition, have had the opposite effect of substantially reducing the incidence of many infectious diseases, in some instances virtually eliminating them.

BIBLIOGRAPHY

Abbey, A. (1982). Sex differences in attributions for friendly behavior: Do males misperceive females' friendliness? *J. Pers. Soc. Psychol., 42,* 830–838.

Adesso, V. J. (1979). Some correlates between cigarette smoking and alcohol use. *Addict. Behav., 4,* 269-273.

Adler, M. W. (1980). Opioid peptides. *Life Sci., 26,* 497–510.

Adler, C. (1984). The convicted rapist: A sexual or a violent offender? *Crim. Just. Behav., 11,* 157–177.

Adorno, T. W., Frankel-Brunswick, E., Levinson, D. J., & Sanford, N. (1950). *The authoritarian personality.* New York: Harper and Row.

Ahlenius, S., Engel, J., Svensson, T. H., & Sodersten, P. (1973). Antagonism by alpha-methyltyrosine of ethanol-induced stimulation and euphoria in man. *Clin. Pharmacol. Ther., 14,* 568–591.

Aiello, J. R., Epstein, Y. M., & Karlin, R. A. (1975). Effects of crowding on electrodermal activity. *Soc. Symposium, 14,* 42–57.

Aiello, J. R., Nicosia, G., & Thompson, D. C. (1979). Physiological, social, and behavioral consequences of crowding on children and adolescents. *Child Dev., 50,* 195–202.

Albin, J. B. (1977). The treatment of a self-injurious and aggressive 2-year-old. *Clin. Pediat., 16,* 920–922.

Alexander, F., & Staub, H. (1931). *The criminal, the judge, and the police: A psychological analysis.* New York: Macmillan.

Allman, L. R., Taylor, H. A., & Nathan, R. (1972). Group drinking during stress: Effects on drinking behavior, affects and psychopathology. *Am J. Psychiat., 129,* 669–678.

Alloway, R., & Bebbington, P. (1987). The buffer theory of social support — a review of the literature. *Psychol. Med., 17,* 91–108.

Amir, M. (1971). *Patterns in forcible rape.* Chicago: University of Chicago Press.

Andrew, R. J. (1978). Increased persistence of attention produced by testosterone, and its implications for the study of sexual behavior. In J. B. Hutchinson (Ed.), *Biological determinants of sexual behavior.* Somerset, NJ: Wiley.

Andrews, G., Tennant, C., Hewson, D., & Schonell, M. (1978). The relation of social factors to physical and psychiatric illness. *Am. J. Epidemiol., 108,* 27–35.

Anisman, H. (1975). Time-dependent variations in aversively-motivated behavior: Nonassociative effects of cholinergic and catecholaminergic activity. *Psychol. Rev., 82,* 359–385.

Anorexia nervosa. (1971). *British Med. J., 4,* 183–184.

Antelman, S. M., & Caggiula, A. R. (1977). Norepinephrine-dopamine interactions and behavior. *Science, 224,* 646–653.

Antelman, S. M., Rowland, N., & Fisher, A. (1976). Stimulation-bound ingestive behavior: A view from the tail. *Physiol. Behav., 17,* 743–748.

Antelman, S. M., & Szechtman, H. (1975). Tail pinch induces eating in sated rats which appears to depend on nigrostriatal dopamine. *Science, 189,* 731–733.

Archer, J. (1976). The organization of aggression and fear in vertebrates. In P. P. G. Bateson & P. H. Klopfer (Eds.), *Perspectives in ethology: Vol. 2* (pp. 231–289). New York: Plenum Press.

Aronfreed, J. (1968). *Conduct and conscience.* New York: Academic Press.

Asch, S. (1956). Studies of independence and conformity. A minority of one against a unanimous majority. *Psychol. Monog., 70,* No. 9.

Asso, D. (1978). Levels of arousal in the menstrual phase. *Br. J. Soc. Clin. Psychol., 17,* 47–55.

Back, K. W., & Bogdonoff, M. D. (1964). Plasma responses to leadership, conformity and deviation. In P. H. Leiderman & D. Shapiro (Eds.). *Psychobiological approaches to social behavior.* Stanford, CA: Stanford University Press.

Backstrom, T., & Carstensen, H. (1974). Estrogen and progesterone in plasma in relation to premenstrual tension. *J. Steroid Biochem., 5,* 257–260.

Baker, G. W., & Chapman, D. W. (Eds.). (1962). *Man and society in disaster*. New York: Basic Books.

Baldwin, J. A., & Oliver, J. E. (1975). Epidemiology and family characteristics of severely-abused children. *Br. J. Prev. Soc. Med., 29*, 205–221.

Baldwin, J. A., & Oliver, J. E. (1979). Severe child abuse: Implications of the epidemiology. *Int. J. Ment. Health, 7*, 78–95.

Baldwin, J., Bottoms, A. E., & Walker, M. (1976). *The urban criminal: A study in Sheffield*. London: Tavistock.

Ball, R. A. (1983). Development of basic norm violation. *Criminology 21*(1), 75–94.

Ball-Rokeach, S. J. (1973). Values and violence: A test of the subculture of violence thesis. *Am. Soc. Rev., 38,* 736–749.

Ball-Rokeach, S. J. (1980). Normative and deviant violence from a conflict perspective. *Soc. Prob., 28,* 45–62.

Bancroft, J. H. (1978). The prevention of sexual offenses. In C. B. Qualls, J. P. Winze, & D. H. Barlow (Eds.), *The prevention of sexual disorders: Issues and approaches*. New York: Plenum Press.

Bandura, A. J. (1973). *Aggression : A social learning analysis*. Englewood Cliffs, NJ: Prentice-Hall.

Bandura, A., & Walters, R. H. (1963). *Social learning and personality development*. New York: Holt, Rinehart and Winston.

Bannister, R. (1971). Degeneration of the autonomic nervous system. *Lancet, 2,* 175–179.

Barchas, P. R. (1976). Physiological sociology: Interface of sociological and biological processes. In A. Inkeles, J. Coleman, & N. Smelser (Eds.), *Ann. Rev. Soc., 2,* 299–333. Palo Alto, CA: Annual Reviews.

Barchas, P. R., & Barchas, J. D. (1977). Social behavior and adrenal function in relation to psychiatric disorders. In E. Usdin, D. A. Hamburg, & J. D. Barchas (Eds.), *Neuroregulators and psychiatric disorder*. New York: Oxford University Press.

Bard, M. (1971). The study and modification of intra-familial violence. In J. L. Singer (Ed.), *The control of aggression*. New York: Academic Press.

Barker, E. (1986). Religious movements: Cult and anticult since Jonestown. *Ann. Rev. Soc., 12,* 329–346.

Baron, L. (1985). Does rape contribute to reproductive success? Evaluation of sociobiological views of rape. *International Journal of Women's Studies, 8*(3), 266–277.

Batt, J. C. (1948). Homicidal incidence in depressive psychosis. *J. Ment. Sci., 96,* 782–792.

Beaumont, P. J. V., Richards, D. H., & Gelder, M. G. (1975). A study of minor psychiatric and physical symptoms during the menstrual cycle. *Br. J. Psychiat., 126,* 431–434.

Beck, C. H. M. (1978). Functional implications of changes in the senescent brain: A review. *Can. J. Neurol. Sci., 5,* 417–424.

Becker, H. (1963). *Outsiders: Studies in the sociology of deviance.* New York: The Free Press.

Bell, C. C. (1980). Interface between psychiatry and the law on the issue of murder. *J. Nat. Med. Assoc., 72,* 1093–1097.

Bell, R. (1978). Hormone influences on human aggression. *Irish J. Med. Sci., 147*(Suppl. 1), 5–9.

Belmaker, R. H., Murphy, D. L., Wyatt, R. J., & Loriaux, L. (1974). Human platelet monoamine oxidase changes during the menstrual cycle. *Arch. Gen. Psychiat., 31,* 553–556.

Belson, W. A. (1975). *Juvenile theft: The causal factors.* New York: Harper and Row.

Bennett, A. M. H. (1961). Sensory deprivation in aviation. In P. Solomon, P. Kubzansky, P. H. Leiderman, et al. (Eds.), *Sensory deprivation.* Cambridge: Harvard University Press.

Berger, A. M. (1980). The child abusing family: II, Child and child-rearing variables environmental factors and typologies of abusing families. *Am. J. Fam. Ther., 8*(4), 52–68.

Berger, L. R. (1981). Childhood injuries: Recognition and prevention. *Curr. Prob. Pediat., 14,* No. 1 (Entire issue).

Berger, P. A., Akil, H., Watson, S. J., et al. (1982). Behavioral pharmacology of the endorphins. *Ann. Rev. Med., 33,* 397–415.

Berkman, L. F. (1984). Assessing the physical health effects of social networks and social supports. *Ann. Rev. Public Health, 5,* 413–432.

Berkman, L. F., & Syme, S. L. (1979). Social networks, host resistance, and mortality: A nine-year follow-up study of Alameda County residents. *Am. J. Epidemiol., 109,* 186–204.

Berkowitz, L. (1974). Some determinants of compulsive aggression: Role of mediated associations with reinforcements for aggression. *Psychol. Rev., 81,* 165–176.

Berkowitz, L. (1978). Is criminal violence normative behavior? *J. Res. Crime Delinq., 15,* 148–161.

Berkowitz, L., & Geen, R. (1966). Film violence and the cue properties of available targets. *J. Pers. Soc. Psychol., 3,* 525–530.

Berkowitz, L., & Macaulay, J. (1971). The contagion of criminal violence. *Sociometry, 34,* 238–260.

Berlin, I. (1973). *The hedgehog and the fox.* New York: Simon and Schuster.

Berlyne, D. E. (1960). *Conflict, arousal, and curiosity.* New York: McGraw-Hill.

Berman, A., & Siegel, A. (1976). A neuropsychological approach to the etiology of juvenile delinquency. In A. Davids (Ed.), *Child personality and psychopathology: Current topics: Vol. 3.* New York: Wiley.

Bernstein, I. S., & Gordon, T. B. (1974). The function of aggression in primate societies. *Am. Sci., 62,* 304–311.

Berscheid, E., & Walster, E. (1969). *Interpersonal attraction.* New York: Addison-Wesley.

Beskow, J., Gottfries, C. G., Ross, B. E., & Winblad, B. (1976). Determination of monoamines and monoamine metabolites in the human brain: Post mortem studies in a group of suicides. *Acta Psychiat. Scand., 53,* 7–20.

Bettelheim, B. (1970). *The informed heart.* Glencoe, IL: The Free Press.

Bexton, W. A., Heron, W., & Scott, T. H. (1954). Effects of decreased variation in the sensory environment. *Can. J. Psychol., 8,* 70–76.

Bieliauskas, L. A. (1980). Life events, 17-OHCS measures and psychological defensiveness in relation to aid-seeking. *J. Human Stress, 6,* 28–36.

Bindra, D. (1974). A motivational view of learning, performance, and behavior modification. *Psychol. Rev., 81*, 199–213.

Bischof, N. (1975). A systems approach toward the functional connections of attachment and fear. *Child Devel., 48*, 801–817.

Bishop, F. I. (1971). Children at risk. *Med. J. Aust., 1*, 623–628.

Blackburn, R. (1978). Psychopathy, arousal, and the need for stimulation. In R. D. Hare & D. Schalling (Eds.), *Psychopathic behavior: Approaches to research* (pp. 157–164). New York: Wiley.

Blasi, A. (1980). Bridging moral cognition and moral action: A critical review of the literature. *Psychol. Bull., 88*, 1–45.

Bloom, B. L. (1979). Prevention of mental disorders: Recent advances in theory and practice. *Commun. Mental Hlth. J., 15*, 179–191.

Bloom, B. L., Asher, S. J., & White, S. W. (1978). Marital disruption as a stressor: A review and analysis. *Psychol. Bull., 85*, 867–894.

Blumenthal, J. A., Williams, R. S., Williams, R. B., & Wallace, A. G. (1980). Effects of exercise on the Type A (coronary prone) behavior pattern. *Psychosom. Med., 42*, 289–296.

Bolles, R. C. (1979). Drive. In H. J. Eysenck, W. Arnold, & R. Meili (Eds.), *Encyclopedia of psychology*. New York: Seabury Press.

Bols, R. J. (1977). Display reinforcement in the Siamese fighting fish, Betta splendens: Aggressive motivation or curiosity? *J. Comp. Physiol. Psychol., 91*, 233–244.

Bolton, R. (1973). Aggression and hypoglycemia among the Qolla: A study in psychobiological anthropology. *Ethnology, 12*, 227–274.

Bonnett, P. L., & Pfeiffer, C. C. (1978). Biochemical diagnosis for delinquent behavior. In L. J. Hippchen (Ed.), *Ecologic-biochemical approaches to treatment of delinquents and criminals*. New York: Van Nostrand, Reinhold.

Boone, J. L. (1983). A new curriculum for fitness education. *Public Health Rep., 98*(5), 507.

Bourne, P. G. (1970). Military psychiatry and the Vietnam experience. *Am. J. Psychiat., 127*, 481–488.

Bovard, E. (1959). The effects of social stimuli on the response to stress. *Psychol. Rev., 66,* 267–277.

Bovill, D. (1973). A case of functional hypoglycemia — a medico-legal problem. *Br. J. Psychiat., 123,* 353–358.

Bowerman, W. M. (1979). Impaired cognition — a ubiquitous finding in psychiatric disorders. *Orthomol. Psychiat., 8,* 227–234.

Bowlby, J. (1960). Grief and mourning in infancy and early childhood. *Psychoanal. Study Child, 15,* 9–52.

Bowlby, J. (1969). *Attachment and loss: Vol. 1. Attachment.* London: Hogarth.

Bowlby, J. (1973). *Attachment and loss: Vol. 2. Separation, anxiety and anger.* London: Hogarth.

Bowlby, J. (1981). *Attachment and loss: Vol. 3. Loss.* London: Hogarth.

Bradford, J., & Balmaceda, R. (1983). Shoplifting: Is there a specific psychiatric syndrome? *Can J. Psychiat., 28,* 248–254.

Brickman, A. S., McManus, H., Grapentine, W. L., & Alessi, N. (1984). Neuropsychological assessment of seriously delinquent adolescents. *J. Am. Acad. Child Psychiat., 23*(4), 453–457.

Briscoe, O. V. (1975). Intention at the moment of crime . . . beyond reasonable doubt. *Med. Sci. Law, 15,* 42–46.

Brill, N. Q., & Beebe, G. W. (1955). *A follow-up study of war neuroses.* Washington, DC: Veterans Administration Medical Monograph.

Brody, S. R. (1976). *The effectiveness of sentencing* (Home Office Research Study No. 35). London: Her Majesty's Stationery Office.

Brooks-Gunn, J., & Petersen, A. C. (Eds.). (1983). *Girls at puberty: Biological and social perspectives.* New York: Plenum.

Broverman, D. M., Klaiber, E. L., Kobayashi, Y., & Vogel, W. (1968). Roles of activation and inhibition in sex differences in cognitive abilities. *Psychol. Rev., 45,* 23–50.

Brown, G. L., Ebert, M. H., Goyer, P. F., et al. (1982). Aggression, suicide, and serotonin: Relationships to CSF amine metabolites. *Am. J. Psychiat., 139,* 741–746.

Brown, G. L., Goodwin, F. K., Ballenger, J. C., et al. (1979). Aggression in humans correlates with cerebrospinal fluid amino acid metabolites. *Psychiat. Res., 1,* 131–39.

Brown, G. W., & Harris, T. (1978). *Social origins of depression: A study of psychiatric disorder in women.* London: Tavistock.

Brownfield, C. (1965). *Isolation: Clinical and experimental approaches.* New York: Random House.

Brownmiller, S. (1975). *Against our will: Men, women, and rape.* New York: Simon and Schuster.

Bryant, E. T., Scott, M. L., Golden, C. J., & Tori, C. D. (1984). Neuropsychological deficits, learning disability, and violent behavior. *J. Consult. Clin. Psychol., 52*(2), 323–324.

Buchsbaum, M. S., Coursey, R. D., & Murphy, D. L. (1976). The biochemical high-risk paradigm: Behavioral and familial correlates of low platelet monoamine oxidase activity. *Science, 194,* 339–341.

Burgess, R. L., & Conger, R. D. (1977). Family interaction patterns related to child abuse and neglect: Some preliminary findings. *Child Abuse and Neglect, 1,* 269–277.

Burlingham, D., & Freud, A. (1944). *Infants without families.* London: Allen and Unwin.

Burney, C. (1952). *Solitary confinement.* New York: Coward-McCann.

Butterfield, W. J., Sells, R. A., Abrams, M. E., Sterky, G., & Whichelow, M. J. (1966). Insulin sensitivity of the human brain. *Lancet, 1,* 557–560.

Byrd, R. E. (1938). *Alone.* New York: G. P. Putnam's Sons.

Cairns, R. B. (1977). Beyond social attachment: The dynamics of interactional development. In T. Alloway, P. Pliner, & L. Krames (Eds.), *Advances in the study of communication and affect: Vol. 3. Attachment behavior* (pp. 1–24). New York: Plenum Press.

Caldwell, J. M., Ranson, S. W., & Sacks, J. E. (1951). Group panic and other mass disruptive reactions. *U.S. Armed Forces. Med. J., 2,* 541–567.

Calne, D. B. (1970). *Parkinsonism: Physiology, pharmacology and treatment.* London: Edward Arnold.

Cameron, M. (1964). *The booster and the snitch: Department store shoplifting.* New York: The Free Press.

Camp, G. M. (1967). *Nothing to lose: A study of bank robbery in America.* Unpublished doctoral dissertation Yale University, New Haven, Conn.

Cannon, W. B. (1929). *Bodily changes in pain, hunger, fear and rage* (2d ed.). New York: Appleton-Century-Crofts.

Cannon, W. B., McIver, M. A., & Bliss, S. W. (1924). Studies on the conditions of activity in endocrine glands, 13. A sympathetic and adrenal mechanism for mobilizing sugar in hypoglycemia. *Am. J. Physiol., 69,* 46-60.

Caplan, G. (1974). *Support systems and community mental health: Lectures on concept development.* New York: Behavioral Publications.

Cappell, H. (1975). An evaluation of tension models of alcohol consumption. In R. J. Gibbens, Y. Israel, H. Kalant, et al., (Eds.), *Research advances in alcohol and drug problems* (Vol. 2, pp. 177–209). New York: Wiley.

Carlsson, A. (1978). Does dopamine have a role in schizophrenia? *Biol. Psychiat., 13,* 23–21.

Carlsson, A., Engel, J., & Svensson, T. H. (1972). Inhibition of ethanol-induced excitation in mice and rats by a-methyl-p-tyrosine. *Psychopharmacologia (Berl.), 26,* 307–312.

Carlsson, A., & Lindquist, M. (1973). Effect of ethanol on the hydroxylation of tyrosine and tryptophan in rat brain in vivo. *J. Pharm. Pharmacol., 25,* 437–440.

Carr-Hill, R. A., & Stern, N. H. (1984). Unemployment and crime: A comment. *J. Soc. Policy, 12*(3), 387–94.

Carter, R. L., & Hill, K. Q. (1979). *The criminal's image of the city.* New York: Pergamon.

Cassel, J. (1976). The contribution of the social environment to host resistance. *Am. J. Epidemiol., 104,* 107–123.

Chambliss, W. J. (1976). Functional and conflict theories of crime: The heritage of Emile Durkheim and Karl Marx. In W. J. Chambliss & M. Mankoff (Eds.), *Whose law? What order?* New York: Wiley.

Chappell, D. (1965). *The development and administration of the English law relating to breaking and entering.* Unpublished doctoral dissertation, University of Cambridge.

Clarke, R. V. G. (1977). Psychology and crime. *Bull. Br. Psychol. Soc., 30,* 280–283.

Clarke, R. V. G. (1980a). 'Situational' crime prevention: Theory and practice. *Br. J. Crim., 20,* 136–147.

Clarke, R. V. G. (1980b). *Tackling vandalism.* London: Her Majesty's Stationery Office; New York: Science Editions, Wiley.

Clarke, R. V. G. (1983). Situational crime prevention: Its theoretical basis and practical scope. In M. Tonry & N. Morris (Eds.), *Crime and justice: An annual review of research* (Vol. 4, pp. 225–256). Chicago: University of Chicago Press.

Clausen, J. P. (1979). Effect of physical training on cardiovascular adjustments to exercise in man. *Physiol. Rev., 57,* 779–816.

Clinard, M. B., & Quinney, R. (1973). *Criminal behavior systems: A typology* (2d ed.). New York: Holt, Rinehart and Winston.

Cloward, R. A., & Ohlin, L. (1960). *Delinquency and opportunity.* New York: The Free Press.

Cobb, S. (1976). Social support as a moderator of life stress. *Psychosom. Med., 38,* 300–314.

Cobb, S., & Jones, J. M. (1984). Social support, support groups, and marital relationships. In S. Duck (Ed.), *Personal relationships: 5. Repairing personal relationships* (pp. 47–66). London: Academic Press.

Cofer, A. N., & Appley, R. H. (1964). *Motivation: Theory and research.* New York: Appleton-Century-Crofts.

Cohen, A. K. (1955). *Delinquent boys: The culture of the gang.* New York: The Free Press.

Cohen, A. K. (1965). The sociology of the deviant act: Anomie theory and beyond. *Am. Soc. Rev., 30,* 9–14.

Cohen, A. K., & Short, J. F., Jr. (1971). Crime and juvenile delinquency. In R. K. Merton & R. Nisbet (Eds.), *Contemporary social problems* (3rd ed.). New York: Harcourt, Brace, Jovanovich.

Cohen, D., & Dunner, D. (1980). The assessment of cognitive dysfunction in dementing illness. In J. O. Cole & J. E. Barrett (Eds.), *Psychopathology in the aged.* New York: Raven Press.

Cohen, S. (1971). Directions for research on adolescent group violence and vandalism. *Br. J. Crim., 11,* 319–340.

Cohen, S., & Syme, S. L. (Eds.). (1985). *Social Support and health.* New York: Academic Press.

Constantino, J. P., Kuller, L. H., Perper, J. A., & Cypress, R. H. (1977). An epidemiologic study of homicides in Allegheny County, Pennsylvania. *Am. J. Epidemiol., 106,* 314–324.

Conway, F., & Siegelman, J. (1979). *Snapping: America's epidemic of sudden personality change.* New York: Dell.

Cooley, C. H. (1909). *Social organization: A study of the larger mind.* New York: Charles Scribner's Sons.

Cormier, B. M. (1962). Psychodynamics of homicide committed in a marital relationship. *Corr. Psychiat. J. Soc. Ther., 8,* 187–196.

Coursey, R. D., Buchsbaum, M. S., and Murphy, D. L. (1979). Platelet MAO activity and evoked potentials in the identification of subjects biologically at risk for psychiatric disorder. *Br. J. Psychiat., 134,* 372–381.

Cox, D. N. (1977). *Psychophysiological correlates of sensation seeking and socialization during reduced stimulation.* Unpublished doctoral dissertation, University of British Columbia.

Cox, T. (1979). *Stress.* London: Macmillan.

Craik, K. J. W. (1943). *The nature of explanation.* Cambridge: Cambridge University Press.

Cressey, D. R. (1953). *Other people's money: A study in the social psychology of embezzlement.* Belmont, CA: Wadsworth.

Crisp, A. H. (1970). Psychological aspects of some disorders of weight. In O. W. Hill (Ed.), *Modern trends in psychosomatic medicine* (Vol. 2, pp. 124–146). London: Butterworths.

Crisp, A. H. (1979). Some psychobiological aspects of adolescent growth and their relevance for the fat/thin syndrome (anorexia nervosa). *J. Clin. Psychiat., 40,* 332–335.

Crisp, A. H., Hsu, L. K. G., & Harding, B. (1980). The starving hoarder and voracious spender: Stealing in anorexia nervosa. *J. Psychosom. Res., 24,* 225–231.

274 *Bibliography*

Crowne, S., & Crisp, A. H. (1979). *Manual of the Crowne Crisp experiential index.* London: Hoder and Stoughton.

Curtis, L. A. (1978). Violence, personality, deterrence and culture. *J. Res. Crime Delinq., 15,* 166–171.

Daitzman, R. J., Zuckerman, M., Sammelwitz, P. H., & Ganjam, V. (1978). Sensation-seeking and gonadal hormones. *J. Biosoc. Sci., 10,* 401–408.

Dally, P. J. (1969). *Anorexia nervosa.* London: Heinemann.

Dally, P. J., & Gomez, J. (1979). *Anorexia nervosa.* London: Heinemann.

Dalton, K. (1960). Menstruation and accidents. *Br. Med. J., 2,* 1425–1426.

Dalton, K. (1961). Menstruation and crime. *Br. Med. J., 2,* 1752–1753.

Dalton, K. (1964). *The premenstrual syndrome.* Springfield, IL: C. C. Thomas.

D'Asaro, B., Groesbeck, C., & Nigro, C. (1975). Diet-vitamin program for jail inmates. *J. Orthomol. Psychiat., 4,* 212–222.

D'Atri, D. A., & Ostfeld, A. (1975). Crowding: Its effects on the elevation of blood pressure in a prison setting. *Prev. Med., 4,* 550–566.

Davidson, S. (1979). Massive psychic traumatization and social support. *J. Psychosom. Res., 23,* 395–402.

Davis, J. M., & Janowsky, D. (1974). Cholinergic and adrenergic balance in mania and schizophrenia. In E. F. Domino & J. M. Davis (Eds.), *Neurotransmitter balances regulating behavior.* Ann Arbor, MI: Edwards Bros.

Davis, K. L., & Berger, P. A. (1978). Pharmacological investigations of the cholinergic imbalance hypothesis of movement disorders and psychosis. *Biol. Psychiat., 13,* 23–49.

Dawe, K. E. (1973). Maltreated children at home and overseas. *Aust. Paediat. J., 9,* 177–184.

Dean, A., & Lin, N. (1977). The stress-buffering role of social support. *J. Nerv. Ment. Dis., 165,* 403–417.

DeCharms, R., & Rosenbaum, M. E. (1960). Status variables and matching. *J. Pers., 28,* 492–502.

Dement, W. C. (1960). The effects of dream deprivation. *Science, 131,* 1705–1707.

Dewsbury, A. R. (1975). Battered wives: Family violence seen in general practice. *Roy. Soc. Health J., 95,* 254–290.

Dienstbier, R. A. (1972). The role of anxiety and arousal attribution in cheating. *J. Exp. Soc. Psychol., 8,* 168–179.

Diethelm, O. (1932). Panic. *Arch. Neurol. Psychiat., 28,* 1153–1168.

Diethelm, O. (1934). The nosological position of panic reactions. *Am. J. Psychiat., 13,* 1299–1316.

Dietz, P. E. (1978). Social factors in rapist behavior. In R. T. Rada (Ed.), *Clinical aspects of the rapist.* New York: Grune and Stratton.

Dimsdale, J. E., & Moss, J. (1980). Plasma catecholamines in stress and exercise. *J. Am. Med. Assoc., 243,* 340–342.

Dixon, B. (1978). *Beyond the magic bullet: The real story of medicine.* New York: Harper and Row.

Dmitruk, V. M. (1973). Intangible motivation and resistance to temptation. *J. Genet. Psychol., 123,* 47–53.

Dobash, R. E., & Dobash, R. P. (1979). *Violence against wives: Case against the patriarchy.* New York: The Free Press.

Doctor, R., Naitoh, R., & Smith, J. (1966). Electroencephalographic changes and vigilance behavior during experimentally induced intoxication with alcoholic subjects. *Psychosom. Med., 28,* 605–615.

Dohrenwend, B. R., & Dohrenwend, B. S. (Eds.). (1974). *Stressful life events: Their nature and effects.* New York: Wiley.

Dohrenwend, B. S., & Dohrenwend, B. P. (1978). Some issues in research on stressful life events. *J. Nerv. Ment. Dis., 166,* 7–15.

Dohrenwend, B. S., & Dohrenwend, B. P. (Eds.). (1980). *Life stress and illness.* New York: John Wiley.

Doleschal, E. (1979). Crime — some popular beliefs. *Crime and Delinquency, 25,* 1–8.

Dollard, J., & Miller, N. E. (1939). *Frustration and aggression*. New Haven: Yale University Press.

Dominion, J. (1972). Marital pathology: A review. *Postgrad. Med. J., 48*, 717–725.

Domino, E. F., & Davis, J. M. (Eds.). (1975). *Neurotransmitter balances regulating behavior*. Ann Arbor: Edwards Brothers.

d'Orban, P. T., & Dalton, J. (1980). Violent crime and the menstrual cycle. *Psychol. Med., 10*, 353–359.

Dostoyevsky, F. (1951). *Crime and punishment*. Harmondsworth: Penguin.

Downes, D. (1966). *The delinquent solution*. London: Routledge and Kegan Paul.

Duff, R. A. (1980a). Recklessness. *Crim. Law Rev.*, pp. 282–292.

Duff, R. A. (1980b). Intention, reckless, and probable consequences. *Crim. Law Rev.*, pp. 404–412.

Dunn, W. L. (1978). Smoking as a possible inhibitor of arousal. In K. Battig (Ed.), *Behavioral effects of nicotine*. Basel: S. Karger.

Easterbrook, J. A. (1959). The effect of emotion on cue utilization and the organization of behavior. *Psychol. Rev., 66*, 183–201.

Eliasson, K. (1984). Stress and catecholamines. *Acta Med. Scand., 215*, 197–204.

Eliot, T. D. (1955). Bereavement: Inevitable but not insurmountable. In H. Becker & R. Hill (Eds.), *Family, marriage, and parenthood*. Boston, MA: Heath.

Elliott, F. A. (1978). Neurological aspects of antisocial behavior. In W. H. Reid (Ed.), *The psychopath*. New York: Brunner/Mazel.

Ellis, L. (1978). *Androgens and criminality: Recent research and theoretical implications*. Paper presented at the Annual Meeting of the American Society of Criminology, Dallas, TX.

Ellis, L. (1983). *Androgens, the nervous system and criminal behavior*. Unpublished doctoral dissertation, Florida State University, Tallahassee, FL.

Ellison, G. D. (1975). Behavior and the balance between norepinephrine and serotonin. *Acta Neurobiol. Exp., 35*, 499–515.

Emmons, T. D., & Webb, W. W. (1974). Subjective correlates of emotional responsivity and stimulation-seeking in psychopaths, normals and acting-out neurotics. *J. Consult. Psychol., 42*, 620–625.

Empey, L. T. (1978). *American delinquency: Its meaning and construction.* Homewood, IL: The Dorsey Press.

England, R. W., Jr. (1955). A study of postprobation recidivism among five hundred federal offenders. *Fed. Prob., 19*, 10–16.

Epley, S. (1974). Reduction of the behavioral effects of aversive stimulation by the presence of a companion. *Psychol. Bull., 81*, 271–283.

Erickson, M. L., & Empey, L. T. (1963). Court records, undetected delinquency, and decision-making. *J. Crim. Law Crim. Pol. Sci., 54*, 456–469.

Erickson, M. L., & Jensen, G. F. (1977). Delinquency is still group behavior: Toward revitalizing the group premise in the sociology of deviance. *J. Crim. Law Criminol., 68*, 262–273.

Erlanger, A. S. (1974). The empirical status of the subculture of violence thesis. *Soc. Prob., 22*, 280–292.

Evans, G. W. (1979). Behavioral and physiological consequences of crowding in humans. *J. Appl. Soc. Psychol., 9*, 27–46.

Eysenck, H. J. (1978). *Crime and personality* (3rd ed.). London: Routledge and Kegan Paul.

Eysenck, H. J. (1979). The origins of violence. *J. Med. Ethics, 5*, 105–107.

Falk, J. L. (1983). Drug dependence: Myth or motive? *Pharmacol. Biochem. Behav., 19*, 385–391.

Farley, F. (1977). The stimulation-seeking motive and extraversion in adolescents and adults. *Adolescence, 12*, 65–71.

Farley, F. H., & Farley, S. V. (1972). Stimulus-seeking motivation and delinquent behavior among institutionalized delinquent girls. *J. Consult. Clin. Psychol., 39*, 140–147.

Farley, F. H., & Sewell, T. (1976). Test of an arousal hypothesis of delinquency: Sensation-seeking in delinquent and non-delinquent black adolescents. *Crim. Just. Behav., 3*, 315–320.

Farrington, D. P. (1973). Self-reports of deviant behavior: Predictive and stable? *J. Crim. Law Criminol., 64,* 99–110.

Farrington, D. P. (1979a). Longitudinal research on crime and delinquency. In N. Morris & M. Tonry (Eds.), *Crime and justice: An annual review of research* (Vol. 1, pp. 289–348). Chicago: Univerity of Chicago Press.

Farrington, D. P. (1979b). Experiments on deviance with special reference to dishonesty. *Adv. Exp. Soc. Psychol., 10,* 207–252.

Farrington, D. P. (1982). Longitudinal analyses of criminal violence. In M. E. Wolfgang & N. A. Weiner (Eds.), *Criminal violence* (pp. 171–200). Beverly Hills: Sage.

Farrington, D. P., Berkowitz, L., & West, D. J. (1982). Differences between individual and group fights. *Br. J. Soc. Psychol., 21,* 323–333.

Farrington, D. P., & West, D. J. (1979). The Cambridge study in delinquent development. In S. A. Mednick & A. E. Baert (Eds.), *An empirical basis for primary prevention: Prospective longitudinal research in Europe.* New York: Oxford University Press.

Faulk, M. (1974). Men who assault their wives. *Med. Sci. Law, 14,* 180–183.

Fauman, M. A., & Fauman, B. J. (1979). Violence associated with phencyclidine abuse. *Am. J. Psychiat., 136,* 1584–1586.

Feder, H. H. (1984). Hormones and sexual behavior. *Annual Review of Psychology, 35,* 165–200.

Feine, R., Belmaker, R. H., Rimon, R., & Ebstein, R. P. (1977). Platelet monoamine oxidase in women with premenstrual syndrome. *Neuropsychobiology, 3,* 105–110.

Feldman, M. P. (1977). *Criminal behavior: A psychological analysis.* London: Wiley.

Fentress, J. C. (1973). Specific and nonspecific factors in the causation of behavior. In P. P. G. Bateson & P. H. Klopfer (Eds.), *Perspectives in ethology.* New York: Plenum.

Fentress, J. C. (1978). Conflict and context in sexual behavior. In J. B. Hutchinson (Ed.), *Biological determinants of sexual behavior.* Somerset, NJ: Wiley.

Fernstrom, J. D., & Wurtman, R. J. (1971). Brain serotonin content: Increase following ingestion of carbohydrate diet. *Science, 174,* 1023–1025.

Ferracuti, F., & Newman, G. (1974). Assaultive offenses. In D. Glaser (Ed.), *Handbook of criminology*. Chicago: Rand-McNally.

Feshbach, S. (1964). The function of aggression and the regulation of aggressive drive. *Psychol. Rev., 71*, 257–272.

Festinger, L., Riecken, H. W., & Schachter, S. (1956). *When prophesy fails*. Minneapolis: University of Minnesota Press.

Field, W. S., & Sweet, W. A. (Eds.). (1975). *Neural bases of violence and aggression*. St. Louis: W. H. Green

Flanders, J. P. (1968). A review of research on imitative behavior. *Psychol. Bull., 69*, 316–337.

Fleming, D. (Ed.). (1964). The mechanistic conception of life, by Jacques Loeb (original ed., 1912). Cambridge, MA: Harvard University Press.

Fogel, D. (1975). *We the living proof*. Cincinnati, OH: Anderson.

Forehand, K., & Baumeister, A. A. (1976). Deceleration of aberrant behavior among retarded individuals. In M. Hersen, R. M. Eisler, & P. M. Miller (Eds.), *Progress in behavior modification* (Vol. 2). New York: Academic Press.

Forrest, T. (1974). The family dynamics of maternal violence. *J. Am. Acad. Psychoanal., 2*, 215–230.

Fowler, H. (Ed.). (1962). *Curiosity and exploratory behavior*. New York: Macmillan.

Frankenhaeuser, M. (1975a). Experimental approach to the study of catecholamines and emotion. In L. Levi (Ed.), *Emotions: Their parameters and measurement* (pp. 209–234). New York: Raven.

Frankenhaeuser, M. (1975b). Sympathetic adrenomedullary activity, behavior and the psychosocial environment. In P. H. Venables & M. J. Christie (Eds.), *Research in psychophysiology* (pp. 71–94). New York: Wiley.

Frankenhaeuser, M. (1976). The role of peripheral catecholamines in adaptation to understimulation and overstimulation. In G. Serban (Ed.), *Psychopathology of human adaptation*. New York: Plenum.

Frankenhaeuser, M. (1979). Psychoneuroendocrine approaches to the study of emotion as related to stress and coping. In H. E. Howe & R. A. Dienstbier (Eds.), *Nebraska Symposium on Motivation, 1978* (pp. 123–161). Lincoln: University of Nebraska Press.

Frankenhaeuser, M., & Johansson, G. (1975). Behavior and catecholamines in children. In L. Levi (Ed.), *Society, stress, and disease: Vol. 2. Childhood and adolescence* (pp. 118–126). New York: Oxford University Press.

Frankenhaeuser, M., Mellis, I., Rissler, A., Björkvall, C., & Pátkai, P. (1968). Catecholamine excretion as related to cognitive and emotional reaction patterns. *Psychosom. Med., 30,* 109–120.

Frazier, S. H. (1974). Murder — simple and multiple. *Res. Pub. Assoc. Res. Nerv. Ment. Dis., 52,* 304–312.

Frederickson, P., & Richelson, E. (1979). Mayo seminars in psychiatry: Dopamine and schizophrenia — a review. *J. Clin. Psychiat., 40,* 399–405.

Freud, S. (1922). *Group psychology and the analysis of the ego.* London: Hogarth.

Freud, S. (1962). *The ego and the id.* New York: The Norton Library.

Fried, M. (1963). Grieving for a lost home. In L. Duhl (Ed.), *The urban condition.* New York: Basic Books.

Friedman, M. I., & Stricker, E. M. (1976). A physiological psychology of hunger: A physiological perspective. *Psychol. Rev., 83,* 409–431.

Friedrich, W. N., & Einbender, A. J. (1983). The abused child: A psychological review. *J. Clin. Child Psychol., 12,* 244–256.

Friedrich, W. N., & Wheeler, K. K. (1982). The abusing parent revisited: A decade of psychological research. *J. Nerv. Ment. Dis., 170,* 577–587.

Funkenstein, D. (1956). Norepinephrine-like and epinephrine-like substances in relation to human behavior. *J. Nerv. Ment. Dis., 124,* 58–60.

Furth, M. (1983). Building self-esteem. *Acad. Ther., 19,* 11–15.

Gal, R., & Lazarus, R. S. (1975). The role of activity in anticipating and confronting stressful situations. *J. Human Stress, 1,* 4–20.

Galbo, H. (1983). *Hormonal and metabolic adaptation to exercise.* New York: Thieme-Stratton.

Gallup, G. G., Jr. (1974). Animal hypnosis: Factual status of a fictional concept. *Psychol. Bull., 81,* 836–853.

Galvin, J. A. V., & Macdonald, J. M. (1959). Psychiatric study of a mass murderer. *Am. J. Psychiat., 115,* 1057–1061.

Ganong, W. F. (1979). *Review of medical physiology* (9th ed.). Los Altos, CA: Lange Medical Publications.

Garbarino, J., & Crouter, A. (1978). Defining the community context for parent-child relations: The correlates of child maltreatment. *Child Devel., 49,* 604–616.

Garfinkel, H. (1967). *Studies in ethnomethodology.* Englewood Cliffs, NJ: Prentice-Hall.

Gatewood, J. W., Organ, C. H., & Mead, B. T. (1975). Mental changes associated with hyperparathyroidism. *Am. J. Psychiat., 132,* 129–132.

Gayford, J. J. (1975). Battered wives. *Med. Sci. Law, 15,* 237–265.

Gayford, J. J. (1979). The aetiology of repeated physical assaults by husbands on wives (wife battering). *Med. Sci. Law, 19,* 19–24.

Geen, R. G., & Donnerstein, E. L. (Eds.). (1983). *Aggression: Theoretical and empirical reviews* (Vols. 1–2). New York: Academic Press.

Geis, G. (1977). Forcible rape: An introduction. In D. Chappell, R. Geis, & G. Geis (Eds.), *Forcible rape: The crime, the victim, and the offender.* New York: Columbia University Press.

Gelfand, D. M. (1962). The influence of self-esteem on rate of verbal conditioning and social matching behavior. *J. Abnorm. Soc. Psychol., 65,* 259–265.

Gelles, R. J. (1976). Abused wives: Why do they stay? *J. Marr. Fam., 38,* 659–668.

Gelles, R. J. (1982). Domestic criminal violence. In M. E. Wolfgang & N. A. Weiner (Eds.), *Criminal violence* (pp. 203–235). Beverly Hills: Sage.

Gelles, R., & Straus, M. (1979). Violence in the American family. *J. Soc. Issues, 35,* 15–39.

Gellhorn, E. (1967). *The principles of autonomic-somatic integrations.* Minneapolis: University of Minnesota Press.

Gessa, G. L., & Tagliamonte, A. (1974). Role of brain monoamines in male sexual behavior. *Life Sci., 14,* 425–436.

Gibbens, T. C. N. (1960). Theft from department stores. General Report to the Fourth International Criminological Congress, The Hague.

Gibbens, T. C. N. (1970). Hooliganism and vandalism. *Medico Legal J., 38,* 122–134.

Gibbens, T. C. N., Palmer, C., & Prince, J. (1971). Mental health aspects of shoplifting. *Br. Med. J., 3,* 612–615.

Gibbens, T. C. N., & Prince J. (1962). *Shoplifting.* London: Institute for the Study and Treatment of Delinquency.

Gibbens, T. C. N., Way, C., & Soothill, K. L. (1977). Behavioral types of rape. *Br. J. Psychiat., 130,* 32–42.

Gibbons, D. C. (1975). Offender typologies — two decades later. *Br. J. Crim., 15,* 140–156.

Gibbons, D. C. (1977). *Society, crime and criminal careers* (3rd ed.). Englewood Cliffs, NJ: Prentice-Hall.

Gil, D. G. (1970). *Violence against children.* Cambridge, MA: Harvard University Press.

Gilmore, N. J., Robinson, D. S., Nies, A., Sylvester, D., & Ravaris, C. L. (1971). Blood monoamine oxidase levels in pregnancy and during the menstrual cycle. *J. Psychosom. Res., 15,* 215–220.

Glaser, D. (1974). The classification of offenses and offenders. In D. Glaser (Ed.), *Handbook of criminology.* Chicago: Rand-McNally.

Glaser, D. (1979). A review of crime-causation theory and its application. In N. Morris & M. Tonry (Eds.), *Crime and justice: An annual review of research* (Vol. 1, pp. 203–237). Chicago: University of Chicago Press.

Glass, D. C. (1977). Stress, behavior patterns, and coronary disease. *Am. Sci., 65,* 177–187.

Goldman, H. (1977). The limits of clockwork: The neurobiology of violent behavior. In J. P. Conrad & S. Dinitz (Eds.), *In fear of each other: Studies of dangerousness in America.* Lexington, MA: Lexington Books.

Goldstein, J. H. (1975). *Aggression and crimes of violence.* New York: Oxford University Press.

Goodwin, D. W. (1973). Alcohol in suicide and homicide. *Quart. J. Stud. Alcohol.,* *34,* 144–156.

Goodwin, D. W., & Guze, S. B. (1979). *Psychiatric diagnosis* (2d ed.). New York: Oxford University Press.

Goodwin, D. W., Othmer, E., Halikas, J. A., & Freeman, F. (1970). Loss of short-term memory as a predictor of the alcoholic "blackout." *Nature, 227,* 201–202.

Gould, L. (1969). The changing structure of property crime in an affluent society. *Soc. Forces, 48,* 50–59.

Gould, P., & White, R. (1974). *Mental maps.* Harmondsworth: Penguin.

Gottlieb, B. H. (Ed.). (1981). *Social networks and social support. Studies in community mental health No. 4.* Beverly Hills, CA: Sage Publications.

Graff, H., & Mallin, R. (1967). The syndrome of the wrist-cutter. *Am. J. Psychiat., 124,* 35–62.

Graham, K. (1980). Theories of intoxicated aggression. *Can. J. Behav. Sci., 12,* 141–158.

Grassian, S. (1983). Psychopathic effects of solitary confinement. *Am. J. Psychiat., 140,* 1450–1454.

Greenberg, S. W., Rohe, W. M., & Williams, J. R. (1982). Safe and secure neighborhoods: Physical characteristics and informal territorial control in high and low crime neighborhoods. Washington, D.C.: National Institute of Justice, U.S. Government Printing Office.

Grossman, S. P. (1967). *A textbook of physiological psychology.* New York: Wiley.

Groth, A. N., & Burgess, A. W. (1977). Rape: A sexual deviation. *Am. J. Orthopsychiat., 47,* 400–406.

Groth, A. N., Burgess, A. W., & Holdstrom, L. L. (1977). Rape, power, anger and sexuality. *Am. J. Psychiat., 134,* 1239–1243.

Gugten, J., Van der, & Slangen, J. L. (1977). Release of endogenous catecholamines from rat hypothalamus in vivo related to feeding and other behaviors. *Pharmacol. Biochem. Behav., 7,* 211–219.

Guhl, A. M. (1965). Sociobiology of man. *Bull. Atom. Sci., 21,* 22–24.

Gurr, T. (1974). *Why men rebel.* Princeton: Princeton University Press.

Guttmacher, M., &Weihofen, H. (1952). *Psychiatry and the law.* New York: Norton.

Haberman, D. W., & Baden, M. M. (1974). Alcoholism and violent death. *Q.J. Stud. Alcohol, 35,* 221–231.

Hall, E. T. (1959). *The silent language.* Garden City: Doubleday.

Hamburg, B. (1975). Early adolescence: A specific and stressful stage of the life cycle. In G. V. Coelo, D. A. Hamburg, & J. E. Adams (Eds.), *Coping and adaptation.* New York: Basic Books.

Hamburg, D. A., Moos, R. H., & Yalom, I. D. (1968). Studies of distress in the menstrual cycle and post partum period. In R. P. Micheal (Ed.), *Endocrinology and human behavior.* London: Oxford University Press.

Hamburg, D. A., & Trudeau, M. (Eds.). (1981). *Biobehavioral aspects of aggression.* New York: Allan R. Liss.

Hamburger, W. W. (1951). Emotional aspects of obesity. *Med. Clin. N. Am., 35,* 483–699.

Hamilton, V. (1979). Information processing aspects of neurotic anxiety and the schizophrenias. In V. Hamilton & D. M. Warburton (Eds.), *Human stress and cognition.* New York: Wiley.

Hammond, W. H., & Cheyen, E. (1963). *Persistent criminals.* London: Her Majesty's Stationery Office.

Hanby, J. (1976). Sociosexual development in primates. In P. P. G. Bateson & P. H. Klopfer (Eds.), *Perspectives on ethology* (Vol. 2). New York: Plenum Press.

Hare, R. D. (1970). *Psychopathy: Theory and research.* New York: Wiley.

Hare, R. D., & Schalling, D. (Eds.). (1978). *Psychopathic behavior: Approaches to research.* New York: Wiley.

Harrington, J. A. (1972a). *Soccer hooliganism: A preliminary report.* Bristol: J. Wright.

Harrington, J. A. (1972b). Violence: A clinical viewpoint. *Br. Med. J., 1,* 228–231.

Hartman, A. A., & Nicolay, R. C. (1966). Sexually deviant behavior in expectant fathers. *J. Abnorm. Psychol., 71,* 232–234.

Harvey, O. J., & Schroeder, H. (1963). Cognitive aspects of self and motivation. In O. J. Harvey (Ed.), *Motivation and social interaction: Cognitive determinants.* New York: Ronald.

Haskell, W. L., Montoye, H. J., & Orenstein, D. R. (1985). Physical activity and exercise to achieve health-related fitness components. *Public Health Rep., 100,* 202–212.

Hauty, G. T. (1978). Personal communication to Dr. M. Zuckerman, cited in M. Zuckerman (1979). *Sensation-seeking: Beyond the optimal level of arousal* (pp. 317–319). Hillsdale, NJ: L. Erlbaum.

Hays, S. E. (1978). Strategies for psychoendocrine studies of puberty. *Psychoneuroendocrinology, 3,* 1–15.

Hebb, D. O. (1955). Drives and the C.N.S. (conceptual nervous system). *Psychol. Rev., 62,* 243–254.

Hediger, H. (1955). *The psychology and behavior of animals in zoos and circuses.* New York: Dover.

Henderson, A. S. (1977). The social network, support and neurosis: The function of attachment in adult life. *Br. J. Psychiat., 131,* 185–191.

Henderson, A. S. (1980). A development in social psychiatry: The systematic study of social bonds. *J. Nerv. Ment. Dis., 168,* 63–69.

Henderson, A. S. (1984). Interpreting the evidence on social support. *Soc. Psychiat., 19,* 49–52.

Henley, F. H. (1928). Menstruation in relation to mental disorders. *J. Ment. Sci., 74,* 488–492.

Henn, F. A. (1978). The aggressive sexual offender. In I. L. Kutash, S. B. Kutash, L. B. Schlesinger, et al. (Eds.), *Violence: Perspectives on murder and aggression.* San Francisco: Jossey-Bass.

Henry, A. F., & Short, J. F. (1954). *Suicide and homicide.* New York: Free Press.

Herberg, L. J., & Stephens, D. N. (1977). Interaction of hunger and thirst in the motivational arousal underlying hoarding behavior in the rat. *J. Comp. Physiol. Psychol., 91,* 359–364.

Herjanic, M., & Meyer, D. A. (1977). Alcohol consumption and homicide. In F. A. Seixas (Ed.), *Currents in alcoholism* (Vol. 2, pp. 421–428). New York: Grune and Stratton.

Hess, W. R. (1957). *The functional organization of the diencephalon.* New York: Grune and Stratton.

Hilgard, E. R. (1980). The trilogy of mind: Cognition, affection, and conation. *J. Hist. Behav. Sci., 16,* 107–117.

Hill, R., & Hansen, D. A. (1962). Families in disaster. In G. W. Baker & D. W. Chapman (Eds.), *Man and society in disaster.* New York: Basic Books.

Hill, D., & Sargant, W. (1943). A case of matricide. *Lancet, 1,* 526–527.

Hinde, R. A. (1960). Energy models of motivation. *Symp. Soc. Exp. Biol., 14,* 199–213.

Hinde, R. A. (1966). *Animal behavior.* New York: McGraw-Hill.

Hinde, R. A., Rowell, T. E., & Spencer-Booth, Y. (1964). Behavior of socially living rhesus monkeys in their first two-and-a-half years. *Anim. Behav., 15,* 169–196.

Hindelang, M. J. (1971). Age, sex and the versatility of delinquent involvements. *Soc. Probl, 18,* 522–535.

Hindelang, M. J. (1973). "Causes of delinquency": A replication. *Soc. Prob., 21,* 471–487.

Hindelang, M. J., Hirschi, T., & Weis, J. G. (1981). *Measuring delinquency.* Beverly Hills, CA: Sage.

Hinkle, L. (1974). The effect of exposure to culture change, social change, and changes in interpersonal relationships on health. In B. S. Dohrenwend & B. P. Dohrenwend (Eds.), *Stressful life events: Their nature and effects.* New York: Wiley.

Hippchen, L. (Ed.). (1978). *Ecologic-biochemical approaches to treatment of delinquents and criminals.* New York: Van Nostrand Reinhold.

Hirsch, J. (1973). Introduction to the Dover edition. In J. Loeb, *Forced movements, tropisms, and animal conduct.* New York: Dover.

Hirschi, T. (1969). *Causes of delinquency.* Berkeley: University of California Press.

Hirschi, T., & Gottfredson, M. (1983). Age and the explanation of crime. *Am. J. Sociol., 89*(3), 552–584.

Hirschi, T., & Hindelang, M. J. (1977). Intelligence and delinquency: A revisionist review. *Am Sociol. Rev., 42,* 571–587.

Hocking, F. (1965). Human reactions to extreme environmental stress. *Med. J. Australia, 2,* 477–483.

Hodgson, R. J., Stockwell, T. R., & Rankin, H. J. (1979). Can alcohol reduce tension? *Behav. Res. Ther., 17,* 459–466.

Hokanson, J. E. (1979). *The physiological bases of motivation.* New York: Wiley.

Hokanson, J. E., & Shetler, S. (1961). The effect of real aggression on physiological arousal level. *J. Abnorm. Soc. Psychol., 63,* 446–448.

Holdstrom, L. L., & Burgess, A. W. (1980). Sexual behavior of assailants during reported rapes. *Arch. Sexual Behav., 9,* 427–439.

Hollender, M. H. (1970). The need or wish to be held. *Arch. Gen. Psychiat., 22,* 445–453.

Holmes, T. H., & Rahe, R. H. (1967a). The social readjustment rating scale. *J. Psychiat. Res., 11,* 213–218.

Holmes, T. H., & Rahe, R. H. (1967b). *Booklet for schedule of recent experience (SRE).* Seattle: University of Washington.

Home Office (1981). *Criminal statistics, 1980.* London: Her Majesty's Stationery Office.

Hood, R., & Sparks, R. (1970). *Key issues in criminology.* London: Weidenfeld and Nicholson.

Hore, B. D. (1977). An overview. In F. A. Seixas (Ed.), *Currents in alcoholism* (Vol. 2). New York: Grune and Stratton.

Houts, M. (1970). *They asked for death.* New York: Cowles.

Howells, J. G. (1966). The psychopathogenesis of hard-core families. *Am. J. Psychiat., 123,* 1159–1164.

Hull, C. L. (1943). *Principles of behavior.* New York: Appleton-Century-Crofts.

Hunt, J. McV. (1963). Motivation inherent in information-processing and action. In O. J. Harvey (Ed.), *Motivation and social Interaction.* New York: Ronald Press.

Hutt, S. J., Lenard, H. G., & Prechtl, H. F. R. (1969). Psychophysiology of the newborn. In L. P. Lippsitt & H. W. Reese (Eds.), *Advances in child development and behavior.* London: Academic Press.

Ingham, R. (1985). The psychology of the crowd — A social psychological analysis of British football "hooliganism." *Med. Sci. Law., 25*(1), 53–58.

Isaacson, R. L. (1974). *The limbic system.* New York: Plenum.

Jacobs, H. C., & Sharma, K. N. (1969). Taste versus calories: Sensory and metabolic signals in the control of food intake. *Ann. N.Y. Acad. Sci., 157,* 1084–1125.

Jacobs, S., & Ostfeld, A. (1977). An epidemiological review of the mortality of bereavement. *Psychosom. Res., 39,* 344–357.

Janis, I. (1951). *Air war and emotional distress.* New York: McGraw-Hill.

Janis, I. L. (1963). Group identification under conditions of external danger. *Br. J. Med. Psychol., 36,* 227–238.

Janis, I. L., & Leventhal, H. (1968). Human reactions to stress. In E. F. Borgatta & W. W. Lambert (Eds.), *Handbook of personality theory and research.* Chicago: Rand-McNally.

Janis, I. L., & Mann, L. (1977a). *Decision making: A psychological analysis of conflict, choice and commitment.* New York: Free Press.

Janis, I. L., & Mann, L. (1977b). Emergency decision making: A theoretical analysis of responses to disaster warnings. *J. Human Stress, 3,* 35–48.

Janowsky, D., Gorney, R., & Kelley, B. (1966). "The curse" — viscissitudes and variations of the female fertility cycle: Part I. Psychiatric aspects. *Psychosomatics, 7,* 242–247.

Jeffery, C. R. (1977). *Crime prevention through environmental design* (2d ed.). Beverly Hills, CA: Sage.

Jenkins, C. D. (1979). Psychosocial modifiers of response to stress. In J. E. Barret, et al. (Eds.), *Stress and mental disorder* (pp. 265–278). New York: Raven Press.

Jessor, R., & Jessor, S. (1977). *Problem behavior and psychosocial development: A longitudinal study of youth.* New York: Academic Press.

Johansson, E. D. B. (1969). Progesterone levels in peripheral plasma during the initial phase of the normal human menstrual cycle measured by rapid competitive binding technique. *Acta Endocrinologica, 61,* 592–606.

Johansson, G. (1972). Sex differences in the catecholamine output of children. *Acta Physiol. Scand., 85,* 569–572.

Johansson, G., Frankenhaeuser, M., & Magnusson, D. (1973). Catecholamine output in school children as related to performance and adjustment. *Scand. J. Psychol., 14,* 20–28.

Johnson, E. H. (1974). *Crime, correction and society.* Homewood, IL: Dorsey.

Johnson, J. H., & Sarason, T. G. (1979a). Recent developments in research on life stress. In V. Hamilton & D. M. Warburton (Eds.), *Human stress and cognition: An information-processing approach.* New York: Wiley.

Johnson, J. H., & Sarason, I. G. (1979b). Moderator variables in life stress research. In I. G. Sarason & C. D. Spielberger (Eds.), *Stress and anxiety* (Vol. 6). New York: Wiley.

Johnson, N. R., & Feinberg, W. E. (1977). A computer simulation of the emergence of consensus in crowds. *Am. Soc. Rev., 42,* 505–521.

Johnson, N. R., Stamler, J. G., & Hunter, D. (1977). Crowd behavior as risky shift: A laboratory experiment. *Sociometry, 40,* 183–187.

Johnson, N. R., & Glover, M. (1978). Individual and group shifts to extreme: Laboratory experiments on crowd polarization. *Sociol. Focus, 11,* 247–254.

Johnson, R. E. (1979). *Juvenile delinquency and its origins: An integrated theoretical approach.* New York: Cambridge University Press.

Johnson, R. N. (1972). *Aggression in man and animals.* Philadelphia, PA: W. B. Saunders.

Johnson, R. N., & Johnson, L. D. (1973). Intra- and interspecific social and aggressive behavior in the Siamese fighting fish, Betta splendens. *Anim. Behav., 21,* 665–671.

Justice, B., & Justice, R. (1976). *The abusing family.* New York: Human Sciences Press.

Kafka, F. (1952). The metamorphosis. In W. & E. Muir (Trans.), *Selected short stories of Franz Kafka* (pp. 19–89). New York: Modern Library.

Kalant, H. (1973). Biological models of alcohol tolerance and physical dependence. In M. M. Gross (Ed.), *Alcohol intoxication and withdrawal: Experimental studies.* New York: Plenum Press.

Kanin, E. (1971). Sexually aggressive college males. *J. Coll. Stud. Pers., 112,* 107–110.

Kanin, E., & Parcell, S. R. (1977). Sexual aggression: A second look at the offended female. *Arch. Sexual Behav., 6,* 67–76.

Kaplan, A. (1964). *The conduct of inquiry.* San Francisco: Chandler.

Kaplan, A. (1978). The psychodynamics of terrorism. *Terrorism: An International Journal, 1,* 237–254.

Kaplan, B. H., Cassel, J. C., & Gore, S. (1977). Social support and health. *Med. Care., 15,* 47–58.

Karki, N. T. (1956). The urinary excretion of noradrenaline and adrenaline in different age groups, its diurnal variation and the effect of muscular work on it. *Acta Physiol. Scand., 39,* Supp. 132.

Karniski, W. M., Levine, M. D., Clarke, S., Palfrey, J., & Meltzer, L. J. (1982). A study of neurodevelopmental findings in early adolescent delinquents. *J. Adolescent Health Care, 3,* 151–159.

Kaufman, H. (1970). *Aggression and altruism: A psychological analysis.* New York: Holt, Rinehart and Winston.

Kaufman, I. (1962). Psychiatric implications of physical abuse of children. In *Protecting the battered child.* Denver, CO: Childrens Division, American Humane Association.

Keller, M. (Ed.). (1971). *Alcohol and health.* Washington, DC: Government Printing Office.

Kempe, C. H. (1971). Psychiatric implications of the battered baby syndrome. *Arch. Dis. Child, 48,* 28–37.

Kempe, C. H., Silverman, F. N., Steele, B. F., Droegemueller, W., & Silver, H. K. (1962). The battered-child syndrome. *J. Am. Med. Assoc., 181,* 17–24.

Kertzman, D. (1978). Dependency, frustration tolerance, and impulse control in child abusers. Doctoral dissertation, State University of New York at Buffalo. (University Microfilms No. 78-17050.) *Diss. Abstr. Int., 38,* 1484-B.

Kessler, R. C., Price, R. H., & Wortman, C. B. (1985). Social factors in psychopathology: Stress, social support, and coping processes. *Ann. Rev. Psychol., 36,* 531–572.

Kiely, W. F. (1974). From the symbolic stimulus to the pathophysiological response: Neurophysiological mechanisms. *Int. J. Psychiat. Med., 5,* 517–529.

Kilduff, M., & Javers, R. (1978). *The suicide cult: The inside story of the People's Temple sect and the massacre in Guyana.* New York: Bantam Books.

Kimbrell, D., & Blake, R. (1958). Motivational factors in the isolation of a prohibition. *J. Abnorm. Soc. Psychol., 56,* 132–133.

Kinston, W., & Rosser, R. (1974). Disaster: Effects on mental and physical health. *J. Psychosom. Res., 18,* 437–456.

Kinzie, J. D., Fredrickson, R. H., Ben, R., Fleck, J., & Karls, W. (1984). Post traumatic stress disorders among survivors of Cambodian concentration camps. *Am. J. Psychiat., 141,* 645–650.

Kiritz, S., & Moos, R. H. (1974). Physiological effects of social environments. *Psychosom. Med., 36,* 96–113.

Kish, G. B. (1966). Studies of sensory reinforcement. In W. K. Honig (Ed.), *Operant behavior.* Englewood Cliffs, NJ: Prentice-Hall.

Kissin, B. (1974). The pharmacodynamics and natural history of alcoholism. In B. Kissin & H. Beglieter (Eds.), *The biology of alcoholism: Vol. 3. Clinical pathology.* New York: Plenum Press.

Kissin, B., & Platz, A. (1968). The use of drugs in the long term rehabilitation of chronic alcoholics. In D. H. Efron (Ed.), *Psychopharmacology: Review of progress, 1957–1967* (pp. 835–851). Publich Health Service Publication No. 1836.

Klein, M. (1984). Offense specialization and versatility among juveniles. *Br. J. Criminol., 24*(2), 185–194.

Klinger, E. (1967). Modeling effects on achievement imagery. *J. Pers. Soc. Psychol., 7,* 49–62.

Kohlberg, L. (1969). Stage and sequency: The cognitive-developmental approach to socialization. In D. A. Goslin (Ed.), *Handbook of socialization theory and research.* Chicago: Rand-McNally.

Komisaruk, B. R. (1978). The nature of the neural substrate of female sexual behavior in mammals and its hormonal sensitivity: A review and speculation. In J. C. Hutchinson (Ed.), *Biological determinants of sexual behavior.* Somerset, NJ: Wiley.

Koppell, B. S., Lunde, D. T., Clayton, R. B., & Moos, R. H. (1966). Variations in some measures of arousal during the menstrual cycle. *J. Nerv. Ment. Dis., 148,* 180–187.

Kramer, M. (1980). The rising pandemic of mental disorders and associated chronic diseases and disabilities. *Acta Psychiat. Scand., 62* (Suppl. 285), 382–397.

Krause, C. A. (1978). *Guyana massacre: The eyewitness account.* New York: Berkley.

Krebs, H. (1980). On the biology of juvenile delinquency: Comments on the essay by Felton Earls, "The sad reconstruction of adolescence: Toward an explanation of increasing rates of violence in youth." *Pers. Biol. Med.,* (Winter), 179–188.

Kubzansky, P. E. (1961). The effects of reduced environmental stimulation on human behavior: Review. In A. P. Biderman & H. Zimmer (Eds.), *The manipulation of human behavior.* New York: Wiley.

Lader, M. H. (1975a). The peripheral and central role of the catecholamines in the mechanisms of anxiety. *Int. Psychopharmacopsychiat, 9,* 125–137.

Lader, M. H. (1975b). The psychophysiology of anxious and depressed patients. In D. C. Fowles (Ed.), *Clinical applications of psychophysiology.* New York: Columbia University Press.

Lader, M. H., & Marks, I. (1971). *Clinical anxiety.* London: Heinemann.

Lader, M. H., & Wing, L. (1966). *Physiological measures, sedative drugs, and morbid anxiety.* London: Oxford University Press.

Laing, R. D. (1961). *The self and others.* London: Tavistock.

Lake, C. R., Ziegler, M. G., & Kopin, I. J. (1976). Use of plasma norepinephrine for evaluation of sympathetic neuronal function in man. *Life Sci., 18,* 1315–1326.

Lamm, H., & Myers, D. B. (1978). Group-induced polarization of attitudes and behavior. In L. Berkowitz (Ed.), *Advances in experimental social psychology* (Vol. 2). New York: Academic Press.

Lang, A. R., Goechner, D. J., Adesso, V. J., & Marlatt, A. G. (1975). Effects of alcohol on aggression in male social drinkers. *J. Abnorm. Psychol., 84,* 508–516.

Larson, J. R., Jr., Johnson, J. H., & Easterbrooks, M. A., (1979). Sensation-seeking and antisocial behavior: Some laboratory evidence. *Pers. Soc. Psychol. Bull., 5,* 169–172.

Laub, J. J. (1983). Trends in serious juvenile crime *Crim. Just. Behav., 10*(4), 485–506.

Law Enforcement Assistance Administration (1975). *Criminal victimization surveys in 13 American cities.* Washington, DC: U.S. Government Drug Office.

Lazarus, R. S. (1966). *Psychological stress and the coping process.* New York: McGraw-Hill.

Leathwood, P. C., & Pollet, P. (1982/1983). Diet-induced mood changes in normal populations. *J. Psychiat. Res., 17*(2), 147–154.

LeBon, G. (1895/1977). *The crowd.* London: Benn.

Lemay, L. (1974). Introduction to A. H. Bremer, *An assassin's diary.* New York: Pocket Books.

Lemert, E. B. (1953). An isolation and closure theory of naive check forgery. *J. Crim. Law Criminol. Pol. Sci., 44,* 296–307.

Lemert, E. B. (1972). *Human deviance, social problems and social control* (2d ed.). Englewood Cliffs, NJ: Prentice-Hall.

Leon, G. R., & Roth, R. (1977). Obesity: Pathological causes, correlations and speculations. *Psychol. Bull., 84,* 117–139.

Lester, D., & Lester, G. (1975). *Crime of passion: Murder and the murderer.* Chicago: Nelson-Hall.

L'Etang, H. (1966). *Some thoughts on panic in war* (pp. 278–285). Brassey's Annual: The Armed Forces Yearbook.

Levenson, R. W., Sher, K. J., Grossman, L. M., Newman, J., & Newlin, D. B. (1980). Alcohol and stress response dampening pharmacological effects, expectancy, and tension reduction. *J. Abnorm. Psychol., 89,* 528–538.

Levi, L. (1972). Stress and distress in response to psychosocial stimuli. Laboratory and real life studies on sympathoadrenomedullary and related reactions. *Acta Med. Scand.,* (Suppl. 528).

Levison, P. K., & Flynn, J. P. (1965). The subjects attacked by cats during stimulation of the hypothalamus. *Anim. Behav., 13,* 217–220.

Levy, D. M. (1944). On the problem of movement restraint: Tics, stereotyped movements, and hyperactivity. *Am. J. Orthopsychiat., 14,* 644–671.

Lewin, K. (1935). *A dynamic theory of personality: Selected papers.* New York: McGraw-Hill.

Lewis, D. O. (Ed.). (1981). *Vulnerabilities to delinquency.* New York: SP Medical and Scientific Books.

Lewis, D. O. & Balla, D. A. (1976). *Delinquency and psychopathology.* New York: Grune and Stratton.

Lewis, D. O., Shanok, S. S., & Pincus, J. H. (1979). Juvenile male sexual assaulters. *Am. J. Psychiat., 136*(9), 1194–1196.

Lewis, D. O., Shanok, S. S., Grant, M., & Ritvo, E. (1983). Homicidally aggressive young children: Neuropsychiatric and behavioral correlates. *Am. J. Psychiat., 140,* 148–153.

Lidberg, L., Levander, S., Schalling, D., & Lidberg, Y. (1978). Urinary catecholamines, stress, and psychopathy: A study of arrested men awaiting trial. *Psychosom. Med., 40,* 116–125.

Light, R. J. (1974). Abused and neglected children in America: A study of alternative policies. *Harvard Educ. Rev., 43,* 556–598.

Lindemann, E. (1944). Symptomatology and management of acute grief. *Am. J. Psychiat., 101,* 141–148.

Lindesmith, A. R., & Dunham, H. E. (1941). Some principles of criminal typology. *Soc. Forces, 198,* 307–314.

Lindheim, R., & Syme, S. L. (1983). Environments, people, and health. *Ann. Rev. Public Health, 4,* 335–359.

Linnoila, M., Virkkunen, M., Scheinim, M., et al. (1983). Low cerebrospinal fluid 5-hydroxy indoleacetic acid concentration differentiating impulsive from nonimplusive violent behavior. *Life Sci., 33,* 2609–2614.

Liskey, N. E. (1972). Accidents — rhythmic threat to females. *Accid. Anal. Prev., 4,* 1–11.

Little, B. C., Matta, R. J., & Zahn, T. P. (1974). Physiological and psychological effects of progesterone in man. *J. Nerv. Ment. Dis., 159,* 256–262.

Little, B. C., & Zahn, T. P. (1974). Changes in mood and autonomic functioning during the menstrual cycle. *Psychophysiology, 11,* 579–590.

Lloyd, C. (1980). Life events and depressive disorder reviewed, II Events as precipitating factors. *Arch. Gen. Psychiat., 37,* 541–548.

Lloyd, C. W., & Weiss, J. (1972, March 9–11). *Hormones and aggression.* Paper presented at Houston Neurological Symposium on Neural Bases of Violence and Aggression, Houston, TX.

Loeb, J. (1917/1973). *Forced movements, tropisms, and animal conduct.* New York: Dover.

Lorenz, K. (1966). *On aggression.* New York: Harcourt, Brace, Jovanovich.

Lubman, A., Eurick, C., Mosimann, W. F., & Freedman, R. (1983). Altered mood and norepinephrine metabolism following withdrawal from alcohol. *Drug and Alcohol Dependence, 12,* 3–13.

Luce, E. G. (1971). *Biological rhythms in human and animal physiology.* New York: Dover.

Ludwig, A. M., Wikler, A., Cain, R., Buchsbaum, M., Rinsky, G., & Taylor, R. (1977). Alcoholics and high-low sensory input: A pilot study. *Dis. Nerv. Sys., 38,* 681–683.

Lyman, S. M., & Scott, M. B. (1967). Territoriality: A neglected sociological dimension. *Soc. Prob., 15,* 236–249.

Lyman, S. M., & Scott, M. B. (1970). *A sociology of the absurd.* New York: Appleton-Century-Crofts.

Lynch, J. J. (1970). Psychophysiology and the development of social attachment. *J. Nerv. Ment. Dis., 152,* 231–244.

Lynch, J. J. (1977). *The broken heart: The medical consequences of loneliness.* New York: Basic Books.

Lystad, M. H. (1975). Violence at home: A review of the literature. *Am. J. Orthopsychiat., 45,* 328–345.

Maccoby, E. E., & Masters, J. C. (1970). Attachment and dependency. In P. H. Mussen (Ed.), *Carmicheal's Manual of Child Psychology* (2d ed.). New York: Wiley.

Macdonald, J. M. (1968). *Homicidal threats.* Springfield, IL: C. C. Thomas.

Macdonald, J. M. (1980). *Burglary and theft.* Springfield, IL: C. C. Thomas.

MacIntyre, A. (1967). The idea of a social science. *Proc. Arist. Soc.* (Suppl. vol.), 95–114.

MacKay, D. M. (1956). Towards an information-flow model of human behavior. *Br. J. Psychol., 47,* 30–43.

MacKay, D. M. (1966). Cerebral organization and the conscious control of action. In J. C. Eccles (Ed.) *Brain and conscious experience* (pp. 422–445). New York: Springer-Verlag.

MacKay, D. M. (1969). *Information, mechanism and meaning.* Cambridge, MA: M.I.T. Press.

Mackinnon, P. C. B., & Harrison, J. (1961). The influence of hormones associated with pituitary-adrenal and sexual cycle activity on palmar sweating. *J. Endocrinol., 23,* 217–225.

MacPherson, M. (1984). *Long-time passing: Vietnam and the haunted generation.* New York: Signet Books.

MacLean, P. D. (1983). Brain roots of the will-to-power. *Zygon, 18*(4), 359–374.

Maguire, M. (1980). The impact of burglary upon victims. *Br. J. Crim., 20,* 261–275.

Malmquist, C. P. (1971). Premonitory signs of homicidal aggression in juveniles. *Am. J. Psychiat., 128,* 461–465.

Malmquist, C. P., Kiresuk, T. J., & Spano, R. M. (1966). Personality characteristics of women with repeated illegitimate pregnancies: Descriptive aspects. *Am. J. Orthopsychiat., 36,* 476–484.

Mann, L., & Pearce, P. (1979). Social psychology of the sports spectator. In D. Glencross (Ed.), *Psychology and sport.* Sydney: McGraw-Hill.

Mannhein, H. (1965). *Comparative criminology: A textbook* (Vol. 1). London: Routledge and Kegan Paul.

Mansback, R. S., & Lorenz, D. N. (1983). Cholecystokinin (CCK-8) elicits prandial sleep in rats. *Psysiol. Behav., 30,* 179–183.

Margules, D. M., Fisher, A., Okrutny, M., & Rowland, N. (1979). Tail-pinch induced fluid ingestion: Interactions of taste and deprivation. *Physiol. Behav., 22,* 37–41.

Marler, P. (1976). On animal aggression: The roles of strangeness and familiarity. *Am. Psychol., 31,* 239–246.

Marris, P. (1974). *Loss and change.* London: Routledge and Kegan Paul.

Marsh, P., Rosser, R., & Harre, R. (1978). *The rules of disorder.* London: Routledge and Kegan Paul.

Marshall, S. L. A. (1947). *Men against fire.* New York: Morrow.

Martinson, R. (1974). What works? Questions and answers about prison reform. *The Public Interest, 35,* 22–53.

Mason, J. O., & Powell, K. E. (1985). Physical activity, behavioral epidemiology, and public health. *Public Health Rep., 100,* 113–115.

Mason, J. W. (1974). The integrative approach in medicine — implications of neuroendocrine mechanisms. *Pers. Biol. Med., 17,* 333–347.

Mason, J. W. (1975). A historical review of the stress field. *J. Human Stress, 1,* No. 1, 6–12, No. 2, 22–36.

Mason, W. A. (1967). Motivational aspects of social responsiveness in young chimpanzees. In H. W. Stevenson, E. Hess, & H. L. Rheingold (Eds.), *Early behavior: Comparative and developmental approaches.* New York: Wiley.

Masuda, M., Cutler, D. L., Hein, L., & Holmes, T. H. (1978). Life events and prisoners. *Arch. Gen. Psychiat., 35,* 197–203.

Mattes, R. D. (1987). Sensory influences on food intake and utilization in humans. *Human Nutrition: Applied nutrition, 41A,* 77–95.

Matthew, R. J. (1979). Craving for alcohol in sober alcoholics. *Am. J. Psychiat., 136,* 603–606.

Matza, D. (1964). *Delinquency and drift.* New York: Wiley.

Mawson, A. R. (1974). Anorexia nervosa and the regulation of intake: A review. *Psychol. Med., 4,* 289–308.

Mawson, A. R. (1977). Hypertension, blood pressure variability, and juvenile delinquency. *S. Med. J., 70,* 160–164.

Mawson, A. R. (1978a.) Attenuating effect of fighting on shock-induced gastric ulceration and hypertension; hypothesis of inhibition by sensory feedback. *Medical Hypotheses, 4,* 403–410.

Mawson, A. R. (1978b, November). *Stress, arousal, and juvenile delinquency: Hypothesis.* Paper presented at the Annual Meeting of the American Society of Criminology, Dallas, TX.

Mawson, A. R. (1979). Temporal aspects of the response to stress. In D. J. Oborne, M. M. Gruneberg, & J. R. Eiser (Eds.), *Research in psychology and medicine: Vol. 1. Physical aspects: Pain, stress, diagnosis and organic damage* (pp. 93–100). New York: Academic Press.

Mawson, A. R. (1980). Aggression, attachment behavior, and crimes of violence. In T. Hirschi & M. Gottfredson (Eds.), *Understanding crime: Current theory and research* (pp. 103–116). Beverly Hills, CA: Sage.

Mawson, A. R. (1984, November). Anorexia nervosa/bulimia as a model for understanding the biopsychology of theft. Paper presented at the Annual Meeting of the American Society of Criminology, Cincinnati, OH.

Mawson, A. R. (1986). *Stimulation-seeking, criminality, and traumatic spinal cord injury: A case-control study.* Unpublished doctoral dissertation, Department of Biostatistics and Epidemiology, School of Public Health and Tropical Medicine, Tulane University, New Orleans, Louisiana.

Mawson, A. R., & Mawson, C. D. (1977). Psychopathy and arousal: A new interpretation of the psychophysiological literature. *Biol. Psychiat., 12,* 49–74.

Mayer, J. (1955). Regulation of energy intake and the body weight: The glucostatic theory and the lipostatic hypothesis. *Ann. N.Y. Acad. Sci., 63,* 15–42.

Mayfield, D. (1976). Alcoholism, alcohol intoxication and assaultive behavior. *Dis. Nerv. Sys., 37,* 288–291.

Mayhew, H., & Binny, J. (1862). *The criminal prisons of London and scenes of prison life.* London: Griffin, Bohn & Co.

Mayhew, Henry. (1862). Criminal prisons.

Mayhew, P. (1979). Defensible space: The current status of a crime prevention theory. *The Howard Journal, 18,* 150–159.

Mayhew, P., Clarke, R. V. G., Sturman, A., & Hough, J. M. (1976). *Crime as opportunity. Home office research study no. 34.* London: Her Majesty's Stationery Office.

McBurney, D. H., & Collings, V. B. (1977). Introduction to *Sensation/perception.* Englewood Cliffs, NJ: Prentice-Hall.

McClintock, F. H. (1963). *Crimes of violence.* London: Macmillan.

McClintock, F. H., & Avison, N. J. (1968). *Crime in England and Wales.* London: Heinemann.

McCord, J. (1983). The psychopath and moral development. In W. S. Laufer & J. M. Day (Eds.), *Personality theory, moral development, and criminal behavior.* (pp. 357–372). Lexington, MA: Lexington Books.

McDermaid, G., & Winkler, E. G. (1955). Psychology of infanticide. *J. Clin. Exp. Psychopathol., 16,* 22–41.

McFarlane, A. H., Norman, G. R., Streiner, D. L., Roy, R., & Scott, D. J. (1980). A longitudinal study of the influence of the psychosocial environment on health status: A preliminary report. *J. Health Soc. Behav., 21,* 124–133.

McGurk, B. J., Bolton, N., & Smith, M. (1978). Some psychological, educational and criminological variables related to recidivism in delinquent boys. *Brit. J. Clin. Soc. Psychol., 17,* 251–254.

McKissack, I. J. (1973). The peak age for property crimes: Further data. *Br. J. Crim., 13,* 253–261.

McKnight, C. K., Mohr, J. W., Quinsey, R. E., & Erochki, J. (1966). Mental illness and homicide. *Canad. Psychiat. Assoc. J., 11,* 91–98; 99–106.

McNees, M. P., Egli, D. S., Marshall, R. S., Schnelle, J. F., & Risley, T. R. (1976). Shoplifting prevention: Providing information through signs. *J. Appl. Behav. Anal., 9,* 399–405.

Mead, G. H. (1934). *Mind, self, and society,* C. W. Morris (Ed.). Chicago: University of Chicago Press.

Medlicott, R. W. (1968). Fifty thieves. *N.Z. Med. J., 67,* 183–188.

Mednick, S. A. (1977). A biosocial theory of the learning of law-abiding behavior. In S. A. Mednick & K. O. Christiansen (Eds.), *Biosocial bases of criminal behavior* (pp. 1–8). New York: Gardner Press.

Mednick, S. A., & Christiansen, K. O. (Eds.). (1977). *Biosocial bases of criminal behavior.* New York: Gardner Press.

Mednick, S. A., Pollock, V., Volavka, J., & Gabrielli, W. F., Jr. (1982). Biology and violence. In M. E. Wolfgang & W. A. Weiner (Eds.), *Criminal violence* (pp. 21–80). Beverly Hills, CA: Sage.

Meerloo, J. A. M. (1950). *Patterns of panic.* New York: International Universities Press.

Megaree, E. I. (1966). Undercontrolled and overcontrolled personality types in extreme antisocial aggression. *Psychol. Monogr., 80,* Whole No. 611.

Megargee, E. I. (1971). The role of inhibition in the assessment and understanding of violence. In J. E. Singer (Ed.), *The control of aggression and violence: Cognitive and physiological factors.* New York: Academic Press.

Megargee, E. I. (1975). *Crime and delinquency.* University Programs Modular Studies. Morristown, NJ: General Learning Press.

Melnick, B., & Hurley, J. R. (1969). Destructive personality attributes of child-abusing mothers. *J. Consult. Clin. Psychol., 33,* 746–749.

Melzack, R. (1973). *The puzzle of pain.* Harmondsworth: Penguin.

Merton, R. K. (1949). *Social theory and social structure.* New York: The Free Press.

Merton, R. K. (1960). Introduction to *The Crowd.* G. LeBon. Harmondsworth: Penguin.

Meyerson, A. T. (1966). Amnesia for homicide ("pedicide"), its treatment with hypnosis. *Arch. Gen. Psychiat., 16,* 509–515.

Meyerson, B. J., & Malmnäs, G. O. (1978). Brain monoamines and sexual behavior. In J. C. Hutchinson (Ed.), *Biological determinants of sexual behavior.* Somerset, NJ: Wiley.

Michael, J., & Adler, M. J. (1933). *Crime, law, and social structure.* New York: Harcourt Brace.

Milgram, S. (1963). Behavioral study of obedience. *J. Abnorm. Soc. Psychol., 67,* 371–378.

Milgram, S. (1968). Some conditions of obedience and disobedience to authority. *Int. J. Psychiat., 6,* 259–276; (Discussion, pp. 277–295).

Milgram, S. (1974). *Obedience to authority.* New York: Harper and Row.

Miller, P. McC., & Ingham, J. G. (1979). Reflections on the life-events-to-illness link with some preliminary findings. In I. G. Sarason & C. D. Spielberger (Eds.), *Stress and anxiety* (Vol. 6). New York: Wiley.

Miller, W. B. (1958). Lower-class culture as a generating milieu of gang delinquency. *J. Soc. Issues, 14,* 5–19.

Miller. W. B. (1965). Violent crimes in city gangs. *Ann. Amer. Acad. Pol. Soc. Sci., 342,* 105–115.

Milowe, I., & Lourie, R. (1964). The child's role in the battered child syndrome. *J. Pediatr., 65,* 1079–1081.

Mills, K. C., Bean, J. W., & Hutcheson, J. S. (1977). Shock induced ethanol consumption in rats. *Pharmacol. Biochem. Behav., 6,* 107–115.

Mineka, S., & Suomi, S. J. (1978). Social separation in monkeys. *Psychol. Bull., 85,* 1376–1400.

Mogenson, G. J. (1977). *The neurobiology of behavior: An introduction.* Hillsdale, NJ: L. Erlbaum.

Mohr, J. W., & McKnight, C. K. (1971). Violence as a function of age and relationship with special references to matricide. *Canad. Psychiat. Assoc. J., 16,* 29–32.

Monahan, I., & Klassen, D. (1982). Situational approaches to understanding and predicting individual violent behavior. In M. E. Wolfgang & N.A. Weiner (Eds.), *Criminal violence* (pp. 292–319). Beverly Hills, CA: Sage.

Monge, M. C., & Monge, C. C. (1966). *High altitude diseases: Mechanism and management.* Springfield, IL: C. C. Thomas.

Monroe, R. R. (1978). *Brain dysfunction in aggressive criminals.* Lexington, MA: Lexington Books.

Montagu, A. (1972). *Touching: The human significance of the skin.* New York: Harper and Row.

Mook, D. G., Brane, J. A., Kushner, W. Z., & Whitt, J. A. (1983). Glucose solution in the rat: The specificity of post-ingestive satiety. *Appetite, 4,* 1–9.

Moran, Lord. (1945). *The anatomy of courage.* London: Constable.

Morgan, W. P. (1979). Anxiety reduction following acute physical exercise. *Psychiat. Ann., 9*(3), 36–45.

Morris, N. (1974). *The future of imprisonment.* Chicago: University of Chicago press.

Morris, R. G., & Gould, R. W. (1963). Role reversal: A necessary concept in dealing with the battered child syndrome. In *The neglected and battered child syndrome.* New York: Child Welfare League of America.

Morris, T. P., & Blom-Cooper, L. (1964). *A calender of murder: Criminal homicide in England since 1957.* London: M. Joseph.

Morton, J. H., Addison, H., Addison, G., Hunt, L., & Sullivan, J. J. (1953). A clinical study of premenstrual tension. *Amer. J. Obstet. Gynecol., 65,* 1182–1191.

Moss, G. E. (1973). *Illness, immunity, and social interaction: The dynamics of biosocial resonation.* New York: Wiley.

Mott, J. (1973). London juvenile drug offenders. *Br. J. Crim., 13,* 209–217.

Mowat, R. R. (1966). *Morbid jealousy.* London: Tavistock.

Mowrer, O. H. (1960). *Learning theory and the symbolic processes.* New York: Wiley.

Moyer, K. E. (1975). A physiological model of aggression: Does it have different implications? In W. S. Fields & W. A. Sweet (Eds.), *Neural bases of violence and aggression.* St. Louis: W. H. Green.

Moyer, K. E. (1976). *The psychobiology of aggression.* New York: Harper and Row.

Mueller, D. P. (1980). Social networks: A promising direction for research on the relationship of the social environment to psychiatric disorder. *Soc. Sci. Med., 14A,* 147–161.

Mulvihill, D. M., Tumin, M., & Curtis, L. (1969). The interpersonal relationship between victims and offenders. In M. Mulvihill et al. (Eds.), *Crimes of violence: A study report to the national commission in the causes and prevention of violence* (Vol. 2). Washington, DC: U.S. Government Printing Office.

Munson, E. L. (1921). *The management of men.* New York: Holt.

Murphy, D. L. (1973). Technical strategies for the study of catecholamines in man. In E. Usdin & S. Snyder (Eds.), *Frontiers in catecholamine research* (pp. 1077–1082). Oxford: Oxford University Press.

Murphy, D. L. (1977). The behavioral toxicity of monoamine oxidase-inhibiting antidepressants. *Pharmacol. Chemother., 14,* 71–105.

Murphy, D. L., Wright, C., Buchsbaum, M. S., et al. (1976). Platelet and plasma amine oxidase activity in 680 normals: Sex and age differences and stability over time. *Biochem. Med., 16,* 254–265.

Murphy, D. L., Belmaker, R. H., Buchsbaum, M. S., Martin, N. F., Ciarandello, R., & Wyatt, R. J. (1977a). Biogenic amine-related enzymes and personality variations in normals. *Psychol. Med., 7,* 149–157.

Murphy, D. L., Belmaker, R., Carpenter, W. T., & Wyatt, R. J. (1977b). Monoamine oxidase in chronic schizophrenia: Studies of hormonal and other factors affecting enzyme activity. *Br. J. Psychiat., 130,* 151–158.

Murphy, L. R. (1984). Occupational stress management: A review and appraisal. *J. Occup. Psychol., 57,* 1–15.

Myers, R. D. (1978). Psychopharmacology of alcohol. *Ann. Rev. Pharmacol. Toxicol., 18,* 125–144.

Newman, G. R. (1979). *Understanding violence.* New York: Lippincott.

Newman, O. (1972). *Defensible space.* New York: Macmillan.

Newman, O. (1973). *Architectural design for crime prevention.* Washington, DC: National Institute of Law Enforcement and Criminal Justice.

Newman, O. (1975). *Design guidelines for creating defensible space.* Washington, DC: Government Printing Office.

Newman, O. (1980). *Community of interest.* New York: Anchor Press/Doubleday.

Niebuhr, R. (1944). *The children of light and the children of darkness.* New York: Scribners.

Nunes, D. L., Murphy, R. J., & Ruprecht, M. L. (1977). Reducing self-injurious behavior of severely retarded individuals through withdrawal of reinforcement procedures. *Behav. Mod., 1,* 499–516.

Nye, R. (1975). *The origins of crowd psychology.* Beverly Hills, CA: Sage.

Ochberg, F. M. (1980). What is happening to the hostages in Teheran? *Psychiat. Annals, 10,* 23–29.

O'Connell, B. A. (1963). Matricide. *Lancet, i,* 1083–1084.

Office of Juvenile Justice and Delinquency Prevention (1980). *Juvenile justice: Before and after the onset of delinquency.* United States discussion paper for the Sixth United Nations Congress on the Prevention of Crime and Treatment of Offenders. Washington, DC: Government Printing Office (cited in Laub, 1983).

O'Keefe, J., & Nadel, L. (1978). *The hippocampus as a cognitive map.* New York: Oxford University Press.

O'Keefe, J., & Nadel, L. (1979). Precis of O'Keefe and Nadel's "The hippocampus as a cognitive map." *Behav. Brain Sci., 2,* 487–533 (with critical discussion and replies).

Olive, R. O. (1967). Filicide (abstract). Roche Report: *Frontiers of Hospital Psychiatry, 4,* 3.

Ortmeyer, C. F. (1974). Variations in mortality, morbidity, and health care by marital status. In C. E. Erhardt & J. E. Berlin (Eds.), *Mortality and morbidity in the United States.* Cambridge, MA: Harvard University Press.

Pagelow, M. D. (1981). *Woman battering: Victims and their experiences.* Beverly Hills, CA: Sage.

Palmer, S. (1974). Family members as murder victims. In S. K. Steinmetz & M. A. Straus (Eds.), *Violence in the family.* New York: Dodd, Mead.

Parke, R. D., & Collmer, C. W. (1975). Child abuse: An interdisciplinary analysis. In E. M. Hetherington (Ed.), *Review of child development research* (Vol. 5). Chicago: University of Chicago Press.

Parker, R. N., & Horwitz, A. V. (1986). Unemployment, crime, and imprisonment: A panel approach. *Criminology, 24,* 751–773.

Parkes, C. M. (1971). Psychosocial transitions: A field for study. *Soc. Sci. Med., 5,* 110–115.

Parlee, M. B. (1973). The premenstrual syndrome. *Psychol. Bull., 80,* 454–465.

Patterson, G. R. (1975). The aggressive child: Victim and architect of a coersive system. In L. A. Hemerlynck, L. E. Handy, & E. J. Mash (Eds.), *Behavior modification and families. I: Theory and research.* New York: Brunner/Mazell.

Patrick, J. (1973). *A Glasgow gang observed.* London: Methuen.

Paulus, P. B., Cox, V. C., McCain, G., & Chandler, J. (1975). Some effects of crowding in a prison environment. *J. Appl. Soc. Psychol., 5,* 86–91.

Paulus, P. B., McCain, G., & Cox, V. C. (1978). Death rates, psychiatric commitments, blood pressure, and perceived crowding as a function of institutional crowding. *Envir. Psychol. Nonverb. Behav., 3,* 107–116.

Payne, C., McCabe, S., & Walker, N. (1974). Predicting offender patients' recidivism. *Br. J. Psychiat., 125,* 60–64.

Pearson, G. (1983). *Hooligan: A history of respectable fears.* London: Macmillan.

Pequignot, J. M., Peyrin, L., & Peres, G. (1980). Catecholamine-fuel interrelationships during exercise in fasting men. *J. Appl. Physiol.: Respirat. Environ. Exercise Physiol., 48,* 109–113.

Perez, J., & Torrubia, R. (1985). Sensation-seeking and antisocial behavior in a student sample. *Person. Indiv. Diff., 6*(3), 401–403.

Petersilia, J., Greenwood, P., & Lavin, M. (1977). *Criminal careers of habitual felons.* Santa Monica, CA: Rand Corporation.

Phelan, G. F. (1977). Testing architectually defensible design: How burglars perceive cues of residential vulnerability. Paper presented at the American Society of Criminology Annual Meeting, Atlanta, Georgia.

Phillips, D. P. (1974). The influence of suggestion on suicide: Substantive and theoretical implications of the Werther effect. *Am. Soc. Rev., 39,* 340–354.

Phillips, D. P. (1977). Motor vehicle fatalities increase just after publicized suicide stories. *Science, 196,* 1464–1465.

Phillips, D. P. (1979). Suicide, motor vehicle fatalities, and the mass media: Evidence toward a theory of suggestion. *Amer. J. Soc., 84,* 1150–1174.

Phillips, D. P. (1980). Airplane accidents, murder, and the mass media: Towards a theory of initiation and suggestion. *Soc. Forces, 58,* 1001–1024.

Phillips, T. R. (1943). Leader and led. In J. I Greene (Ed.), *The infantry journal reader* (pp. 289–306). New York: Doubleday, Doran and Co.

Piaget, J. (1952). *The origins of intelligence in children*. New York: International Universities Press.

Picon-Reategui, E. (1966). Insulin, epinephrine, and glucagon on the metabolism of carbohydrates at high altitude. *Fed. Proc., 25,* 1233–1239.

Pilisuk, M. (1982). Delivery of social support: The social inoculation. *Am. J. Orthopsychiat., 52,* 20–31.

Pilisuk, M., & Froland, C. (1978). Kinship, networks, social support and health. *Soc. Sci. Med., 12B,* 273–280.

Pillegi, N. (1968, November 17). 1968 has been the year of the burglar. *New York Times Magazine,* p. 54.

Platt, S. (1987). The aftermath of Angie's overdose: Is soap (opera) damaging to your health? *Br. Med. J., 294,* 954–597.

Pohorecky, L. A. (1981). The interaction of alcohol and stress: A review. *Neurosci. Behav. Rev., 5,* 209–229.

Polansky, N. A., de Saix, C., & Sharin, S. A. (1973). *Child neglect: Understanding and reaching the parent.* New York: Child Welfare League of America.

Porteus, J. D. (1976). Home: The territorial core. *Geog. Rev., 4,* 383–390.

Porteus, J. D. (1977). *Environment and behavior: Planning and everyday urban life.* Reading, MA: Addison-Wesley.

Pradhan, S. N. (1974). Balances among central neurotransmitters in self-stimulation behavior. In E. F. Domino & J. M. Davis (Eds.), *Neurotransmitter balances regulating behavior.* Ann Arbor, MI: Edwards Bros.

Pramming, S., Thorsteinsson, B., Thielgaard, A., Pinner, E. M., & Binder, C. (1986). Cognitive function during hypoglycemia in type I diabetes mellitus. *Br. Med. J., 292,* 647–650.

President's Commission on Law Enforcement and Administration of Justice (1967). *The challenge of crime in a free society.* Washington, DC: U.S. Government Printing Office.

Pribram, K. H. (1967). The new neurology and biology of emotion: A structural approach. *Amer. Psychol., 22,* 830–838.

Quay, H. C. (1965). Psychopathic personality as pathological stimulation-seeking. *Am. J. Psychiat., 122,* 180–183.

Quinney, R. (1970). *The social reality of crime.* Boston: Little, Brown.

Rabkin, J. C. (1979). The epidemiology of forcible rape. *Am. J. Orthopsychiat., 49,* 634–647.

Rabkin, J. G., & Struening, E. L. (1976). Life events, stress, and illness. *Science, 194,* 1013–1020.

Rada, R. T. (1978a). Psychological factors in rapist behavior. In Rada, R. T. (Ed.), *Clinical aspects of the rapist.* New York: Grune and Stratton.

Rada, R. T. (1978b). Classifcation of the rapist. In R. T. Rada (Ed.), *Clinical aspects of the rapist* (pp. 117–132). New York: Grune and Stratton.

Rada, R. T., & James, W. (1982). Urethral insertion of foreign bodies: A report of contagious self-mutilation in a maximum security hospital. *Arch. Gen. Psychiat., 39,* 423–429.

Rahe, R. H. (1979). Life change events and mental illness: An overview. *J. Human Stress, 5,* 2–10.

Ramsey, G. V. (1943). The sexual development of boys. *Am. J. Psychol., 56,* 217–233.

Ranson, S. W. (1949). The normal battle reaction: Its relation to the pathologic battle reaction. *Bulletin of U.S. Army Med. Dept.* (Suppl.), 3–11.

Ravetz, A. (1973). What is vandalism? (Review of Colin Ward's "Vandalism"). *Roy. Inst. Architect. J., 80,* 620–628.

Ray, M. W., Brenner, R. N., & Kravitz, M. (1978). Firearm use in violent crime: A selected bibliography. National Criminal Justice Reference Service. Washington, D.C.: National Institute of Law Enforcement and Criminal Justice, Law Enforcement Assistance Administration.

Reckless, W. (1967). *The crime problem* (4th ed.). New York: Appleton-Century-Crofts.

Redl, F., & Wineman, D. (1960). *The Aggressive Child*. New York: The Free Press.

Redmond, D. E., Jr., Murphy, D. L., & Baulu, J. (1979). Platelet monoamine oxidase activity correlates with social affiliative and agonistic behaviors in normal rhesus monkeys. *Psychosom. Med., 41*, 87–100.

Redmond, D. E., Murphy, D. L., Baulu, J., Zeigler, M. G., & Lake, C. R. (1975). Menstrual cycle and ovarian hormone effects on plasma and platelet monoamine oxidase (MAO) and plasma dopamine-beta-hydroxylase (DBH) activities in the rhesus monkey. *Psychosom. Med., 37*, 417–428.

Redmond, D. E., Jr., & Murphy, D. L. (1975). Behavioral correlates of platelet monoamine oxidase (MAO) activity in monkeys. *Psychosom. Med., 37*, 80.

Reis, D. J. (1972). The relationship between brain norepinephrine and aggressive behavior. *Res. Rub. Assoc. Res. Nerv. Ment. Dis., 50*, 266–296.

Reis, D. J., & Fuxe, K. (1969). Brain norepinephrine: evidence that neuronal release is essential for sham rage behavior following brain-stem transection in cats. *Proc. Nat. Acad. Sci., 64*, 108–112.

Reis, D. J., Doba, N., & Nathan, M. A. (1973). Predatory attack, grooming, and consummatory behaviors evoked by electrical stimulation of cat cerebellar nuclei. *Science, 182*, 845–847.

Reite, M., Short, R., & Kaufman, C., et al. (1978). Heart rate and body temperature in separated monkey infants. *Biol. Psychiat., 13*, 91–105.

Reppetto, T. A. (1974). *Residential crime*. Cambridge, MA: Ballinger.

Ribeiro, A. L. (1962). Menstruation and crime. *Br. Med. J., 1*, 640.

Richter, C. P. (1943). Total self-regulatory functions in animals and human beings. *Harvey Lecture Series, 38*, 63–103.

Riesen, A. H. (Ed.). (1975). *The developmental neuropsychology of sensory deprivation*. New York: Academic Press.

Robins, L. N. (1978). Aetiological implications in studies of childhood histories relating to antisocial personality. In R. D. Hare & D. Schalling (Eds.), *Psychopathic behavior: Approaches to research*. New York: Wiley.

Robinson, D. S., Davis, J. M., Nies, A., Ravaris, C., & Sylvester, D. (1971). Relation of sex and aging to monoamine oxidase activity of human brain, plasma and platelets. *Arch. Gen. Psychiat., 24,* 536–539.

Robinson, D. S., Sourkes, T. L., Nies, A., Harris, A., Spector, S., Bartlett, D. L., & Kaye, I.S. (1977). Monoamine metabolism in human brain. *Arch. Gen. Psychiat., 34,* 89–92.

Roeder, K. D. (1967). *Nerve cells and insect behavior.* Cambridge, MA: Harvard Univ. Press.

Rook, K. S. (1984). Promoting social bonding: Strategies for helping the lonely and socially isolated. *Am. Psychol., 39,* 1389–1407.

Rounsaville, B. J. (1978). Theories in marital violence: Evidence from the study of battered women. *Victimology, 3,* 11–31.

Rosen, G. (1958). *A history of public health.* New York: MD Publications.

Rosenbaum, M. E., Horne, W. C., & Chalmers, D. K. (1960). Level of self-esteem and learning of imitation and nonimitation. *J. Pers., 30,* 147–156.

Rosenberg, M. L., Stark, E., & Zahn, M. A. (1985). Interpersonal violence: Homicide and spouse abuse. In J. M. Last (Ed.), *Maxcy-Rosenau public health and preventive medicine* (12th ed., pp. 1399–1426). Norwalk, Conn: Appleton-Century-Crofts.

Rosenthal, M. K. (1973). Attachment and mother-infant interaction: Some research impasse and a suggestive change in orientation. *J. Child Psychol., 14,* 201–207.

Rossi, A. S. (1974, May 6–10). Psychological and social rhythms: The study of human cyclicity. paper presented at the 127th Annual Meeting of the American Psychiatric Association, Detroit, MI.

Rossler, D. E. (1981). An artificial cognitive map system. *Biosystems, 13,* 203–209.

Roth, M. (1968). Cerebral disease and mental disorders of old age as causes of antisocial behavior. In A. V. C. Reuck & R. Porter (Eds.), *The mentally abnormal offender.* Boston: Little, Brown.

Roth, R. H., & Bunney, B. S. (1976). Interaction of cholinergic neurons with other chemically defined neural systems in the CNS. In A. M. Goldberg & I. Hanin (Eds.), *Biology of cholinergic function.* New York: Raven.

Ruble, D. N., Brooks-Gunn, J., & Clarke, A. (1980). Research on menstrual-related psychological changes: Alternative perspectives. In J. E. Parsons (Ed.), *The psychology of sex differences and sex roles.* New York: Hemisphere.

Rude, G. (1964). *The crowd in history.* New York: Wiley.

Rushforth, N. B., Ford, A. B., Hirsch, C., Rushforth, N. J., & Adelson, L. (1977). Violent death in a metropolitan county: Changing patterns in homicide, 1958–1974. *N. Eng. J. Med., 297,* 531–538.

Russell, G. F. M. (1970). Anorexia nervosa — its identity as an illness and its treatment. In J. H. Price (Ed.), *Modern trends in psychological medicine* (Vol. 2). London: Butterworths.

Rutter, M. (1972). *Maternal deprivation reassessed.* Harmondsworth: Penguin.

Rutter, M., & Giller, H. (1983). *Juvenile delinquency: Trends and perspectives.* Harmondsworth: Penguin.

Rutter, M., Graham, P., Chadwick, O., & Yule, W. (1976). Adolescent turmoil: Fact or fiction? *J. Child Psychol. Psychiat., 17,* 35–56.

Rutter, M., & Madge, N. (1976). *Cycles of disadvantage: A review of research.* London: Heinemann.

Salzen, E. A. (1978). Social attachment and a sense of security — A review. *Soc. Sci. Inform., 17,* 555–627.

Sarason, I. G., & Spielberger, C. D. (Eds.). (1979). *Stress and anxiety* (Vol. 6). New York: Wiley.

Samorajski, T. (1977). Central neurotransmitter substances and aging: A review. *J. Am. Geriat. Soc., 25,* 337–348.

Sargant, D. A. (1972). The lethal situation: Transmission of the urge to kill from parent to child. In J. Fawcett (Ed.), *Dynamics of violence.* Chicago: American Medical Association.

Sargant, W. (1957). *Battle for the mind.* London: Heinemann.

Sargant, W. (1973). *The mind possessed: From ecstasy to exorcism.* London: Pan.

Schachter, S. (1971). *Emotion, obesity, and crime.* New York: Academic Press.

Schachter, S., & Rodin, J. (1974). *Obese humans and rats.* Washington, D.C.: Erlbaum.

Schachter, S., & Singer, J. (1962). Cognitive, social and physiological determinants of emotional state. *Psychol Rev., 69,* 379–399.

Schaffer, H. R. (1966). The onset of fear of strangers and the incongruity hypothesis. *J. Child Psychol. Psychiat., 7,* 95–100.

Schaffer, H. R., & Emerson, P. E. (1964). The development of social attachments in infancy. *Monog. Soc. Res. Child Devel., 29,* 1–77.

Schalling, D., Edman, G., & Asberg, M. (1983). Impulsive cognitive style and inability to tolerate boredom: Psychobiological studies of temperamental vulnerability. In M. Zuckerman (Ed.), *Biological bases of sensation-seeking, impulsivity, and anxiety.* Hillsdale, NJ: Erlbaum.

Schauss, A. (1980). *Diet, crime and delinquency.* Berkeley, CA: Parker House.

Schildkraut, J. J. (1974). Biogenic amines and affective disorders. *Ann. Rev. Med., 25,* 333–348.

Schlesinger, L. B., & Revitch, E. (1980). Stress, violence, and crime. In I. L. Kutash, L. B. Schlesinger, et al., (Eds.), *Handbook on stress and anxiety* (pp. 174–188). San Francisco: Jossey-Bass.

Schofield, W. (1980). The influence of pyschological factors on susceptibility to physical illness. In M. H. Brenner, A. Mooney, & T. J. Nagy (Eds.), *Assessing the contributions of the social sciences to health* (pp. 159–167). American Association for the Advancement of Science Selected Symposium, no. 26. Boulder, CO: Westview Press.

Schooler, C., Zahn, T. P., Murphy, D. L., et al. (1978). Psychological correlates of monoamine oxidase activity in normals. *J. Nerv. Ment. Dis., 166,* 177–186.

Schultz, D. P. (1965). *Sensory restriction: Effects on behavior.* New York: Academic Press.

Schultz, L. (1968). The victim-offender relationship. *Crime Delinq., 14,* 135–141.

Schwartz, G. E. (1980). Stress management in occupational settings. *Public Health Rep., 95,* 99–108.

Scott, J. P. (1958). *Animal behavior.* Chicago, IL: University of Chicago Press.

Scott, J. P. (1963). The process of primary socialization in canine and human infants. *Monogr. Soc. Res. Child Devel., 28,* 1–47.

Scott, J. P. (1967). The development of social motivation. In D. Levine (Ed.), *Nebraska symposium on motivation.* Lincoln: University of Nebraska Press.

Scott, J. P. (1975). Violence and the disaggregated society. *Aggress. Behav., 1,* 235–260.

Scott, T. H., Bexton, W. H., Heron, W., & Doane, B. K. (1959). Cognitive effects of perceptual isolation. *Can. J. Psychol., 13,* 200–209.

Segal, S. J. (1974). The physiology of human reproduction. *Sci. Am., 231,* 52–79.

Seiden, A. M. (1976). Overview: Research on the psychology of women: 1. Gender differences and sexual and reproductive life. *Am. J. Psychiat., 133,* 995–1007.

Sellin, T. (1958). Recidivism and maturation. *NPPA J., 4,* 241–250.

Selye, H. (1956). *The stress of life.* New York: McGraw-Hill.

Selye, H. (1973). The evolution of the stress concept. *Am. Sci., 61,* 692–699.

Selye, H. (1975). Confusion and controversy in the stress field. *J. Human Stress, 1,* 37–44.

Senay, E. C., & Wettstein, R. (1983). Drugs and homicide: A theory. *Drug and Alcohol Dependence, 12,* 157–166.

Sendi, I. B., & Blomgren, P. G. (1975). A comparative study of predictive criteria in the predisposition of homicidal adolescents. *Am. J. Psychiat., 132,* 423–427.

Shah, S. A., & Roth, L. H. (1974). Biological and psychophysiological factors in criminality. In D. Glaser (Ed.), *Handbook of criminology.* Chicago: Rand-McNally.

Shalloo, J. P. (1954). Vandalism: Whose responsibility? *Fed. Prob., 18,* 6–10.

Shapland, J. M. (1978). Self-reported delinquency in boys aged 11 to 14. *Br. J. Crim., 18,* 255–266.

Sheard, M. H. (1979). Testosterone and aggression. In Sawiller, M. (Ed.), *Psychopharmacology of aggression* (pp. 111–121). New York: Raven Press.

Sheley, J. F. (1975). *An empirical assessment of neutralization in control theories of deviance.* Unpublished doctoral dissertation, University of Massachusetts.

Shepherd, M. (1961). Morbid, jealousy: Some clinical and social aspects of a psychiatric symptom. *J. Ment. Sc., 107,* 687–753.

Sherif, M. (1936). *The psychology of social norms.* New York: Harper.

Sherif, M. (1947). Group influences upon the formation of norms and attitudes. In T. M. Newcomb & E. L. Hartley (Eds.), *Readings in social psychology.* New York: Holt.

Sherif, M., & Harvey, O. J. (1952). A study in ego functioning: Elimination of stable anchorages in individual and group situations. *Sociometry, 15,* 272–305.

Shields, W. M., & Shields, L. M. (1983). Forcible rape: An evolutionary perspective. *Ethology and Sociobiology, 4,* 115–136.

Shils, E., & Janowitz, M. (1948). Cohesion and disintegration in the Wehrmacht in World War II. *Pub. Opinion Quart., 12,* 280–305.

Short, J. F., Jr. (1974). Collective behavior, crime and delinquency. In D. Glaser (Ed.), *Handbook of criminology.* Chicago: Rand-McNally.

Short, J. F., Jr., & Strodtbeck, F. L. (1965). *Group process and gang delinquency.* Chicago: University of Chicago Press.

Shotland, R. L. (1985, November). A preliminary model of the causes of date rape. Paper presented at the Annual Meeting of the American Society of Criminology, San Diego, CA. Mimeo, Department of Psychology, The Pennsylvania State University, University Park, PA.

Showalter, C. R., Bonnie, R. J., & Roddy, V. (1980). The spousal-homicide syndrome. *Int. J. Law Psychiat., 3,* 117–141.

Siddle, D. A. T., & Trasler, G. B. (1981). The psychophysiology of psychopathic behavior. In M. J. Christie & P. G. Mellett (Eds.), *Foundations of psychosomatics.* Chichester: Wiley.

Siffre, M. (1975). Six months alone in a cave. *Nat. Geog., 147,* 426–435.

Simmel, G. (1955). *Conflict and the web of group affiliations.* New York: Free Press.

Simmons, R. G., Rosenberg, E., & Rosenberg, M. (1973). Disturbances in the self-image at adolescence. *Am. Soc. Rev., 38,* 553–568.

Simpson, M. A. (1976). Self-mutilation and suicide. In E. S. Shneidman (Ed.), *Suicidology: Contemporary developments* (pp. 286–315). New York: Grune and Stratton.

Singh, N. N. (1976). Psychological treatment of self-injury. *N.Z. Med. J., 84,* 484–486.

Smith, F. V. (1969). *Imprinting in the young.* Edinburgh: Oliver and Boyd.

Smith, S., & Lewty, W. (1959). Perceptual isolation using a silent room. *Lancet, ii,* 342–345.

Smith, S. M., & Hanson, R. (1975). Interpersonal relationships and child rearing practices in 214 parents of battered children. *Br. J. Psychiat., 127,* 513–525.

Sokolov, N. (1960). *Perception and the conditioned reflex.* Oxford: Pergamon.

Sommer, B. (1972). Menstrual cycle changes and intellectual performance. *Psychosom. Med., 34,* 263–269.

Sommer, B. (1973). The effect of menstruation on cognitive and perceptual-motor behavior: A review. *Psychosom. Med., 33,* 411–428.

Soothill, K. L., & Gibbens, T. C. N. (1978). Recidivism of sexual offenders: A re-appraisal. *Br. J. Crim., 18,* 267–276.

Soothill, K. L., Jack, A., & Gibbens, T. C. N. (1976). Rape — a 22-year cohort study. *Med. Sci. Law, 16,* 62–69.

Soothill, K. L., & Pope, P. J. (1973). Arson: A twenty-year cohort study. *Med. Sci. Law, 13,* 127–38.

Sorokin, P. A. (1975). *Hunger as a factor in human affairs* (Trans. from the Russian by E. Sorokin.) Gainesville, FL: University of Florida Press.

Sourkes, B. M. (1976). *Parental neglect and lashing out: Maladaptive styles of coping.*(Doctoral dissertation, University of Pittsburgh, 1976). (University Microfilms N. 77-3040) *Diss. Abst. Int., 37,* 4170–4171B.

Sparks, R. F. (1976). Crime and victims in London. In W. G. Skogan (Ed.), *Sample surveys of the victims of crime.* Cambridge, MA: Ballinger.

Spellacy, F. (1977). Neuropsychological differences between violent and nonviolent adolescents. *J. Clin. Psychol., 33,* 966–969.

Spinetta, J. J., & Rigler, D. (1972). The child abusing parent: A psychological review. *Psychol. Bull., 77*, 296–304.

Spring, B. (1986). Effects of foods and nutrients on the behavior of normal individuals. In R. J. Wurtman & J. J. Wurtman (Eds.), *Nutrition and the brain* (Vol. 7, pp. 1–47). New York: Raven Press.

Steele, B. F., & Pollock, C. B. (1974). A speculative study of parents who abuse infants and small children. In R. E. Helfer & C. H. Kempe (Eds.), *The battered child* (2d ed., pp. 89–133). Chicago: University of Chicago Press.

Steiner, M., & Carroll, B. J. (1977). The psychobiology of premenstrual dysphoria: Review of theories and treatments. *Psychoneuroendocrinology, 2*, 321–335.

Sterling, P., & Eyer, J. (1981). Biological basis of stress-related mortality. *Soc. Sci. Med., 15E*, 3–42.

Stevens, J. R. (1973). An anatomy of schizophrenia? *Arch. Gen. Psychiat., 28*, 177–178.

Stokols, D. (1972). On the distinction between density and crowding: Some implications for future research. *Psychol. Rev., 38*, 72–83.

Stokols, D. (1979). A congruence analysis of human stress. In I. G. Sarason & C. D. Spielberger (Eds.), *Stress and anxiety* (Vol. 6). New York: Wiley.

Stokols, D. (1983). The environmental context of behavior. In D. Perlman & C. Cozby (Eds.), *Social psychology* (pp. 443–472). New York: Holt, Rinehart and Winston.

Stoner, J. A. F. (1968). Risky and cautious shifts in group decisions: The influence of widely held values. *J. Exp. Soc. Psychol., 4*, 442–459.

Stott, D. H. (1966). *Studies of troublesome children*. London: Tavistock.

Stott, D. H. (1982). *Delinquency: The problem and its prevention*. New York: SP Medical and Scientific Books.

Strasburg, P. (1978). *Violent delinquents*. New York: Monarch.

Straus, M. A. (1973). A general systems theory approach to a theory of violence between family members. *Soc. Sci. Inform., 12*, 105–125.

Straus, M. A. (1980). Social stress and marital violence in a national sample of American families. *Ann. N.Y. Acad. Sci., 347*, 229–249.

Straus, M. A., Gelles, R. J., & Steinmetz, S. K. (1980). *Behind closed doors: Violence in the American family.* New York: Anchor/Doubleday.

Strentz, T. (1980). The Stockholm syndrome: Law enforcement policy and ego defenses of the hostage. *Ann. N.Y. Acad. Sci., 347,* 137–150

Stricker, E. M., & Zigmond, M. J. (1976). Brain catecholamines and the lateral hypothalamic syndrome. In D. Novin, W. Wyrwicka, & G. Bray (Eds.), *Hunger: Basic mechanisms and clinical implications* (pp. 19–32). New York: Raven Press.

Stunkard, A. J. (1959). Eating patterns and obesity. *Psychiat. Quart., 33,* 284–292.

Suedfeld, P. (1969a). Introduction and historical background. In J. P. Zubek (Ed.), *Sensory deprivation: Fifteen years of research.* New York: Appleton-Century-Crofts.

Suedfeld, P. (1969b). Changes in intellectual performance and susceptibility to influence. In J. P. Zubek (Ed.), *Sensory deprivation: Fifteen years of research.* New York: Appleton-Century-Crofts.

Suedfeld, P., & Borrie, R. A. (1978). Sensory deprivation, attitude change and defense against persuasion. *Can. J. Behav. Sci., 10,* 16–27.

Sumner, W. G. (1908/1940). *Folkways: A study of the sociological importance of usages, manners, customs, mores and morals.* Boston: Ginn.

Susser, M. (1981). The epidemiology of life stress. *Psychol. Med., 11,* 1–8.

Sutherland, E. H. (1937). *The professional thief.* Chicago: University of Chicago Press.

Sutherland, E. H., & Cressey, D. R. (1974). *Principles of criminology* (9th ed.). Philadelphia: Lippincott.

Swank, R. L. (1949). Combat exhaustion: Descriptive and statistical analysis of causes, symptoms and signs. *J. Nerv. Ment. Dis., 109,* 475–508.

Swanson, D. W., Bohnoxt, P. J., & Smith, J. A. (1970). *The paranoid.* Boston: Little, Brown.

Swerdloff, R. S. (1978). Physiological control of puberty. *Med. Clin. North Am., 62,* 357–366.

Sykes, G. M., & Matza, D. (1957). Techniques of neutralization: A theory of delinquency. *Am. Soc. Rev., 22,* 664–670.

Syme, L. (1974). Behavioral factors associated with the etiology of physical disease: A social epidemiological approach. *Amer. J. Pub. Health, 64*, 1043–1045.

Symonds, A. (1979). Violence against women — the myth of masochism. *Am. J. Psychotherapy, 33*, 161–173.

Syndulko, K. (1978). Electrocortical investigations of sociopathy. In R. D. Hare & D. Schalling (Eds.), *Psychopathic behavior: Approaches to research* (pp. 145–156). New York: Wiley.

Tamerin, J. S., & Mendelson, J. H. (1969). The psychodynamics of chronic inebriation: Observations on alcoholics during the process of drinking in an experimental group setting. *Am. J. Psychiat., 125*, 886–889.

Tarde, G. (1912). *Penal philosophy* (Trans. by R. Howell). Boston: Little, Brown.

Taylor, C. B., Sallis, J. F., & Needle, R. (1985). The relation of physical activity and exercise to mental health. *Public Health Rep., 100*(2), 195–202.

Taylor, I., Walton, P., & Young, J. (1973). *The new criminology: For a social theory of deviance*. New York: Harper and Row.

Taylor, S. P., & Gammon, C. B. (1975). Effects of type and dose of alcohol on human physical aggression. *J. Pers. Soc. Psychol., 32*, 169–175.

Tedeschi, J. T., Smith, R. B., III, & Brown, R. C., Jr. (1974). A reinterpretation of research on aggression. *Psychol. Bull., 81*, 540–562.

Terr, L. C. (1970). A family of child abusers. *Am. J. Psychiat., 127*, 665–671.

Thoits, P. (1982). Conceptual, methodological, and theoretical problems in studying social support as a buffer against life stress. *J. Health Soc. Behav., 23*, 145–159.

Thorne, G. L. (1971). Sensation-seeking scale with deviant populations. *J. Consult. Clin. Psychol., 37*(1), 106–110.

Thornhill, R., & Thornhill, N. W. (1983). Human rape: An evolutionary analysis. *Ethology and Sociobiology, 4*, 137–173.

Tinklenberg, J. R., & Woodrow, K. M. (1974). Drug use among youthful assaultive and sexual offenders. *Res. Pub. Assoc. Res. Nerv. Ment. Dis., 52*, 209–224.

Tizard, J. (1976). Psychology and social policy. *Bull. Br. Psychol. Soc., 29*, 225–233.

Tolman, E. C. (1948). Cognitive maps in rats and men. *Psychol. Rev., 55*, 189–208.

Totman, R. G., & Kiff, J. (1979). Life stress and susceptibility to colds. In D. J. Oborne, M. M. Gruneberg, & J. R. Eiser (Eds.), *Research in psychology and medicine: Vol. 1. Physical aspects: Pain, stress, diagnosis, and organic damage* (pp. 141–148). London: Academic Press.

Trasler, G. B. (1962). *The explanation of criminality.* London: Routledge and Kegan Paul.

Trasler, G. B. (1973). Criminal behavior. In H. J. Eysenck (Ed.), *Handbook of abnormal psychology* (2nd ed., pp. 67–96). London: Pittman.

Trasler, G. B. (1978). Relation between psychopathy and persistent criminality: Methodological and theoretical issues. In R. D. Hare & D. Schalling (Eds.), *Psychopathic behavior: Approaches to research* (pp. 273–298). London: Wiley.

Trasler, G. B. (1979a). Delinquency, recidivism and desistance. *Br. J. Crim., 19*, 314–322.

Trasler, G. B. (1979b). Conscience. In H. Eysenck, W. Arnold, & R. Meili (Eds.), *Encyclopedia of psychology* (pp. 208–210). New York: Seabury Press.

Trivizas, E. (1980). Offenses and offenders in football crowd disorders. *Br. J. Crim., 20*, 276–288.

Trotter, W. R. (1978). John Brown and the nonspecific component of human sickness. *Pers. Biol. Med., 21*, 258–264.

Turk, A. T. (1969). *Criminality and legal order.* Chicago: Rand-McNally.

Tyhurst, J. S. (1951). Individual reactions to community disaster. *Am. J. Psychiat., 107*, 764–769.

Tyler, D. (1955). Psychological changes during sleep deprivation. *Dis. Nerv. Sys., 16*, 293–299.

U.S. Department of Justice. (1979). *Uniform crime reports for the United States, 1978* (pp. 27–31). Washington, DC: Government Printing Office.

U.S. Department of Justice (1980). *Intimate victims: A study of violence among friends and relatives.* Washington, DC: U.S. Government Printing Office.

U.S. Department of Justice (1982). *Uniform crime reports for the United States, 1981.* Washington, DC: Government Printing Office.

Valadian, I., & Porter, D. (1977). *Physical growth and development from conception to maturity.* Boston: Little, Brown.

Valenstein, E. S. (1967). Selection of nutritive and nonnutritive solutions under different conditions of need. *J. Comp. Physiol. Psychol., 63,* 429–433.

Valenstein, E. (1973). *Brain control.* Englewood Cliffs, NJ: Prentice-Hall.

Valenstein, E. S. (1976). Stereotyped behavior and stress. In G. Serban (Ed.), *Psychopathology of human adaptation.* New York: Plenum Press.

Valenstein, E. S., Cox, V. E., & Kakolewski, J. (1970). Reexamination of the role of the hypothalamus in motivation. *Psychol. Rev., 77,* 16–31.

Vamplew, W. (1980). Sports crowd disorders in Britain, 1870–1914: Causes and controls. *J. Sport Hist., 7,* 4–20.

Vasta, R., & Copitch, P. (1981). Simulating conditions of child abuse in the laboratory. *Child Devel., 52,* 164–170.

Van den Haag, E. (1975). *Punishing criminals.* New York: Basic Books.

Venables, P. H., & Christie, M. J. (Eds.). (1975). *Research in psychophysiology.* New York: Wiley.

Vernikos-Danellis, J. (1972). Effects of hormones on the central nervous system. In S. Levine (Ed.), *Hormones and behavior.* New York: Academic Press.

Vernon, J. (1963). *Inside the black room.* New York: Potter.

Vest, G. W. (1985). Health promotion, health fitness and stress management for prisons. *Corr. Soc. Psychiat., 31,* 135–138.

Vetter, H. S., & Wright, J. (1974). *Introduction to criminology.* Springfield, IL: C. C. Thomas.

Vigersky, R. (Ed.). (1977). *Anorexia nervosa.* New York: Raven Press.

Virkkunen, M. (1974). Alcohol as a factor precipitating aggression and conflict behavior leading to homicide. *Br. J. Addict., 69,* 149–154.

Von Hirsch, A. (1976). *Doing justice.* New York: Hill and Wang.

Voss, H. L., & Hepburn, J. R. (1968). Patterns in criminal homicide in Chicago. *J. Crim. Law Criminol. Pol. Sci., 59,* 449–508.

Wade, A. L. (1970). Social processes in the act of vandalism. In C. A. Bersani (Ed.), *Crime and delinquency: A reader*. London: Macmillan.

Wadsworth, M. E. (1976). Delinquency, pulse rates and early emotional deprivation. *Br. J. Crim., 16*, 245–256.

Wadsworth, M. (1979). *Roots of delinquency: Infancy, adolescence and crime*. London: Martin Robertson.

Walker, L. E. (1979). *Battered wives*. New York: Harper and Row.

Waller, I., & Okihiro, N. (1978). *Burglary: The victim and the public*. Toronto: University of Toronto Press.

Wallerstein, J. S., & Wyle, C. J. (1947). Our law-abiding lawbreakers. *Probation, 25* (April), 107–112.

Wallnau, L. B., & Gallup, G. G., Jr. (1977). A serotonergic, midbrain-raphe model of tonic immobility. *Biobehav. Rev., 1*, 35–43.

Walsh, D. P. (1978). *Shoplifting: Controlling a major crime*. London: Macmillan.

Walsh, D. P. (1980a). *Break-ins: Burglary from private homes*. London: Constable.

Walsh, D. P. (1980b). Why do burglars crap on the carpet? *New Society, 54*, 10–12.

Walster, E. (1965). The effect of self-esteem on romantic liking. *J. Exp. Soc. Psychol., 1*, 184–197.

Walters, R. H., & Parke, R. D. (1964). Social motivation, dependency and susceptibility to social influence. In L. Berkowitz (Ed.), *Advances in experimental social psychology* (Vol. 1). London: Academic Press.

Ward, C. (Ed.). (1973). *Vandalism*. London: Architectural Press.

Wardle, J., & Beinart, H. (1981). Binge-eating: A theoretical review. *Br. J. Clin. Psychol., 20*, 97–109.

Warren, M. Q. (1978). The impossible child, the difficult child, and other assorted delinquents: Etiology, characteristics and incidence. *Can. Psychiat. Assoc. J., 23* (special suppl.).

Wasson, A. S. (1980). Stimulation-seeking, perceived school environment and school misbehavior. *Adolescence, 15*, 603–608.

Wattenberg, W. E., & Balistrieri, J. (1952). Automobile theft: A favored group delinquency. *Am. J. Soc., 57,* 575–579.

Wayner, M. J. (1973). Effects of ethanol on lateral hypothalamic neurons. *Ann. N.Y. Acad. Sci., 215,* 13–37.

Wayner, M. J. (1974). Specificity of behavioral regulation. *Physiol. Behav., 12,* 851–869.

Weise, V. K., & Kopin, I. J. (1976). Assay of catecholamines in human plasma: Study of single isotope radioenzymatic procedure. *Life Sci., 19,* 1673–1686.

Weiss, R. S. (1976). *Marital separation.* New York: Basic Books.

Wertham, F. (1941). *Dark legend.* New York: Druell, Sloan and Pearce.

Werthman, C., & Piliavin, I. (1967). Gang members and the police. In D. Bordua (Ed.), *The police: Six sociological essays.* New York: Wiley.

West, D. J. (1963). *The habitual prisoner.* London: Macmillan.

West, D. J. (1966). *Murder followed by suicide.* Cambridge, MA: Harvard University Press.

West, D. J. (1967). *The young offender.* Harmondsworth: Penguin.

West, D. J. (1969). *Present conduct and future delinquency.* London: Heinemann.

West, D. J. (1982). *Delinquency: Its roots, careers and prospects.* London: Heinemann.

West, D. J., & Farrington, D. P. (1973). *Who becomes delinquent?* London: Heinemann.

West, D. J., & Farrington, D. P. (1977). *The delinquent way of life.* London: Heinemann.

West, D. J., Roy, C., & Nichols, F. L. (1978). *Understanding sexual attacks.* London: Heinemann.

Westermeyer, J. (1972). A comparison of amok and other homicide. *Am. J. Psychiat., 129,* 703–709.

Wetzel, R. D., McClure, J. N. L., & Reich, T. (1971). Premenstrual symptoms in self-referrals to a suicide prevention service. *Br. J. Psychiat., 119,* 525–526.

Whalen, R. E., & Simon, N. G. (1984). Biological motivation. *Ann. Rev. Psychol.,* *35,* 257–276.

White, H. R., Labouvie, E. W., & Bates, M. E. (1985). The relationship between sensation-seeking and delinquency: A longitudinal analysis. *J. Res. Crim. Delinq.,* *22*(3), 197–211.

Wickham, M. (1958). The effects of the menstrual cycle on test performance. *Br. J. Psychol., 49,* 34–41.

Wiepkema, P. R. (1961). An ethological analysis of the reproductive behavior of the Bitterling. *Arch. Neer. Zool., 14,* 103–199.

Wilder, J. (1947). Sugar metabolism and its relation to criminology. In R. M. Linder & R. V. Seliger (Eds.), *Handbook of correctional psychology.* New York: Philosophical Library.

Wilkins, L. T. (1965). *Social deviance: Social policy, action, and research.* Englewood Cliffs, NJ: Prentice-Hall.

Williams, J. R., & Gold, M. (1972). From delinquent behavior to official delinquency. *Soc. Prob., 20,* 209–229.

Williams, R. H. (1970). *Textbook of endocrinology.* Philadelphia, PA: W. B. Saunders.

Wilson, J. Q. (1975). *Thinking about crime.* New York: Basic Books.

Wilson, J. Q., & Herrnstein, R. J. (1984). *Crime and human nature.* New York: Simon and Schuster.

Wilson, V. E., Morley, N. C., & Bird, E. I. (1980). Mood profiles of marathon runners, joggers, and nonexercisers. *Percept. Mot. Skills, 50,* 117–125.

Winch, P. (1958). *The idea of a social science.* London: Routledge and Kegan Paul.

Wolf, A. S. (1980). Homicide and blackout in Alaskan natives: A report and reproduction of five cases. *J. Stud. Alcohol, 41,* 456–462.

Wolf, P. (1965). A contribution to the typology of crime in Denmark. In K. O. Christiansen (Ed.), *Scandinavian studies in criminology* (Vol. 1). London: Tavistock.

Wolfenstein, M. (1957). French parents take their children to the park. In M. Mead & M. Wolfenstein (Eds.), *Childhood in contemporary cultures* (pp. 99–117). Chicago: University of Chicago Press.

Wolff, H. S. (1970). *Biomedical engineering.* London: Weidenfeld and Nicholson.

Wolff, P. H. (1969). The natural history of crying and other vocalizations in early infancy. In B. M. Foss (Ed.), *Determinants of infant behavior* (Vol. 4). London: Methuen.

Wolfgang, M. E. (1958). *Patterns in criminal homicide.* Philadelphia, PA: University of Pennsylvania Press.

Wolfgang, M. E. (1974). Delinquency in a birth cohort. In R. Hood (Ed.), *Crime, criminology, and public policy.* London: Heinemann.

Wolfgang, M. E., & Ferracuti, F. (1967). *The subculture of violence* (rev. ed. 1982). London: Tavistock.

Wolfgang, M. E., Figlio, R. M., & Selling, T. (1972). *Delinquency in a birth cohort.* Chicago: University of Chicago Press.

Wolfgang, M. E., & Weiner, N. A. (Eds.). (1982). *Criminal violence.* Beverly Hills, CA: Sage.

Wolgin, D. L., Cytawa, J., & Teitelbaum, P. (1976). The role of activation in the regulation of food intake. In D. Novin, W. Wyrwicka, & G. Bray (Eds.), *Hunger: basic mechanisms and clinical implications.* New York: Raven Press.

Wooley, O. W., & Wooley, S. C. (1975). The experimental psychology of obesity. In T. Silverstone (Ed.), *Obesity: Pathogenesis and management.* Lancaster: Medical and Technical Publishing Co.

Worschel, S., & Teddlie, C. (1976). The experience of crowding: A two-factor theory. *J. Pers. Soc. Psychol., 34,* 30–40.

Wundram, J. (1979). Nonreproductive sexual behavior: Etiological and cultural considerations. *Am. Anthropologist, 81,* 99–103.

Wunderlich, R. C. (1978). Neuroallergy as a contributing factor to social misfits: Diagnosis and treatment. In L. J. Hippchen (Ed.), *Ecological-biochemical approaches to treatment of delinquents and criminals.* New York: Van Nostrand Reinhold.

Wurtman, J. J., & Wurtman, R. J. (1982/1983). Studies on the appetite for carbohydrates in rats and humans. *J. Psychiat. Res., 17*(2), 213–227.

Wurtman, R. J. (1983). Behavioral effects of nutrients. *Lancet, i*(May 21), 1145–1147.

Wyrwicka, W. (1976). The problem of motivation in feeding behavior. In D. Novin, W. Wyrwicka, & G. Bray (Eds.), *Hunger: Basic mechanisms and clinical implications* (pp. 203–213). New York: Raven Press.

Wyrwicka, W. (1979). Comment on "Homeostasis and drinking," by F. M. Toates. *Behav. Brain Sci., 2,* 125.

Yablonsky, L. (1962). *The violent gang.* Harmondsworth: Penguin.

Yaryura-Tobias, J. A. (1978). Biological research on violent behavior. In L. J. Hippchen (Ed.), *Ecologic-biochemical approaches to treatment of delinquents and criminals.* New York: Van Nostrand Reinhold.

Yaryura-Tobias, J. A., & Neziroglu, F. A. (1975). Violent behavior, brain dysrhythmia, and glucose dysfunction: A new syndrome. *J. Orthomol. Psychiat., 4,* 182–188.

Yates, A. (1981). Narcissistic traits in certain abused children. *Am. J. Orthopsychiat., 51,* 55–62.

Young, J. G., Cohen, D. J., Waldo, M. C., Feiz, R., & Roth, J. A. (1980) Platelet monoamine oxidase activity in children and adolescents with psychiatric disorders. *Schiz. Bull., 6,* 324–333.

Young, J. Z. (1964). *A model of the brain.* Oxford: Clarendon.

Young, L. (1964). *Wednesday's children: A study of child neglect and abuse.* New York: McGraw-Hill.

Yudkin, J. (1963). Nutrition and palatability with special reference to obesity, myocardial infarction and other diseases of civilization. *Lancet, ii,* 1135–1138.

Yudkin, J. (1978). Psychological determinants of food choice. In J. Yudkin (Ed.), *Diet of man: Needs and wants.* London: Applied Science Publishers.

Zacur, H. A., Tyson, J. E., Ziegler, M. G., & Lake, C. R. (1978). Plasma dopamine-ß-hydroxylase activity and norepinephrine levels during the human menstrual cycle. *Am. J. Obstet. Gynecol., 130,* 148–151.

Zilboorg, G. (1967). *A history of medical psychology.* New York: Norton.

Zillman, D. (1984). *Connections between sex and aggression.* Hillsdale, NJ: L. Erlbaum.

Zillman, D., Katcher, A. H., & Milarsky, B. (1972). Excitation transfer from physical exercise to subsequent aggressive behavior. *J. Exp. Soc. Psychol., 8,* 247–259.

Zimring, C. M. (1981). Stress and the designed environment. *J. Soc. Issues, 37,* 145–171.

Zinkus, P. W., Gottlieb, M. I., & Zinkus, C. B. (1979). The learning-disabled juvenile delinquent: A case for early intervention of perceptually handicapped children. *Am. J. Occup. Ther., 33,* 180–184.

Zubek, J. P. (Ed.). (1969). *Sensory deprivation: Fifteen years of research.* New York: Appleton-Century-Crofts.

Zuckerman, M., Buchsbaum, M. S., & Murphy, D. L. (1980). Sensation seeking and its biological correlates. *Psychol. Bull., 88,* 187–214.

Zuckerman, M., Eysenck, S., & Eysenck, H. J. (1978). Sensation-seeking in England and America: Cross cultural, age, and sex comparisons. *J. Consult. Clin. Psychol., 46,* 135–145.

Zuckerman, M., Levine, S., & Biase, V. (1964). Stress response in total and partial perceptual isolation. *Psychosom. Med., 26,* 250–260.

Zuckerman, M. (1978a). Sensation-seeking and psychopathy. In R. D. Hare and D. Schalling (Eds.), *Psychopathic behavior: Approaches to research* (pp. 165–185). New York: Wiley.

Zuckerman, M. (1978b). Sensation-seeking. In H. London & J. Exner (Eds.), *Dimensions of personality.* New York: Wiley.

Zuckerman, M. (1979). *Sensation-seeking: Beyond the optimal level of arousal.* Hillsdale, NJ: L. Erlbaum.

INDEX

ABOUT THE AUTHOR

ANTHONY R. MAWSON was born in Hertfordshire, England, in 1944. After attending Aldenham School, he studied at McGill University, the University of Essex, and the London School of Economics and Political Science, becoming a Lecturer in Sociology at Keele University, U.K., in 1968. Moving to the United States in the early 1970s, he taught at Loyola University, New Orleans, and earned master's and doctoral degrees in epidemiology from the School of Public Health and Tropical Medicine, Tulane University. He is now on the faculty at the Louisiana State University Medical Center, New Orleans, engaged in full-time research. He is active in the United Methodist Church, enjoys spending time outdoors at his camp in southern Mississippi, and has one son, Richie.